PENGUIN BOOKS

THE UPSIDE-DOWN WORLD

'A superb commentary – one of the best I've ever
read – on what it means to be displaced in a never
entirely whole world, and what it means to see between
the cracks. I learned so much reading this fine
book, and so will you' Hilton Als

'A museum, Benjamin Moser writes, has an aura.
It promises improvement, elevation . . . Moser's
excitement at what he's found, along with the desire
to know more, lends a particular aura to this book'
Norma Clarke, *Literary Review*

'Moser writes with insight and sympathy
about his eighteen painters and their
pictures' Michael Prodger, *The Times*

'While many an art historian has delved into
the private lives of artists for the purposes of adding
colour to the criticism, Moser's book is a treatise
on ambition . . . asking what catalyzes people to
write (or make art), and to write (or make art)
the way they do' Oliver Basciano, *ArtReview*

'The most agreeable of companions in his encompassing
yet highly personal tour of the Golden Age of Dutch painting,
Benjamin Moser delivers fresh insights that will delight
the expert and the casual museum-goer alike, in prose
as precise and intimate as a Vermeer – and as luminous'
Jim Holt, author of *Why Does the World Exist?*

'I always dreamed of living in the rooms of my favourite paintings. Finally! A book that animates these rooms, their light, the people in them – that evokes their character and emotions and places them in the context of their culture. Profound and intensely alive, Benjamin Moser's writing describes them both as living beings and as works of art, and connects his own life as a writer to these deep insights into the meaning of art' Laurie Anderson

'No country may be read through its art as clearly as the Netherlands. Benjamin Moser's enchanting survey of the Dutch Masters offers a salutary reminder that the pantheon is never locked and that neglected artists may deserve a reappraisal' Hugh Aldersey-Williams

'A delight. It is incredibly difficult to teach the act of looking and nearly impossible to describe how to find what one needs from a painting. Moser's book is a beautifully gentle guide. Both wise and charismatic, it demonstrates and questions, rather than explains. It shows us how the Dutch Masters' magic persists across time, shooting us right in the soul when we need it' Christine Coulson

ABOUT THE AUTHOR

Benjamin Moser is the author of *Why This World: A Biography of Clarice Lispector*, a finalist for the National Book Critics' Circle Award. His work bringing Clarice Lispector to international prominence was recognized with Brazil's State Prize for Cultural Diplomacy. His most recent book, *Sontag: Her Life*, won the Pulitzer Prize. He lives in Utrecht, in the central Netherlands.

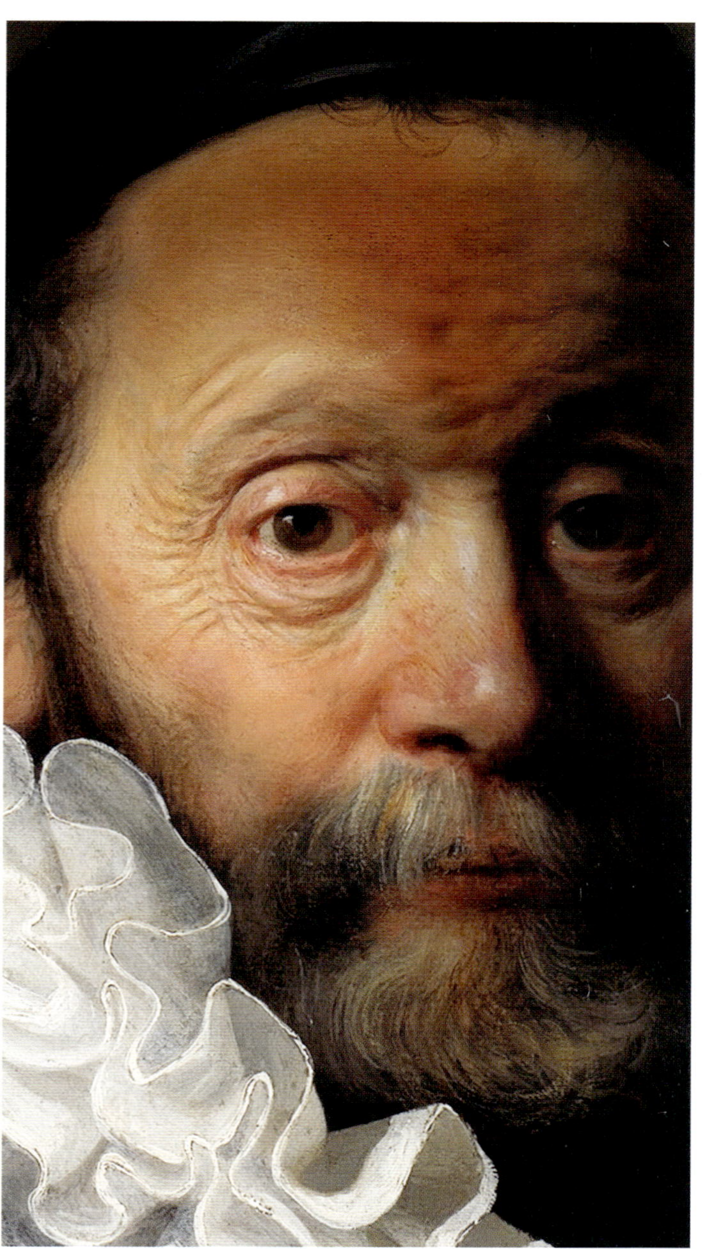

The
UPSIDE-DOWN
WORLD

Meetings

WITH THE

DUTCH

MASTERS

BENJAMIN MOSER

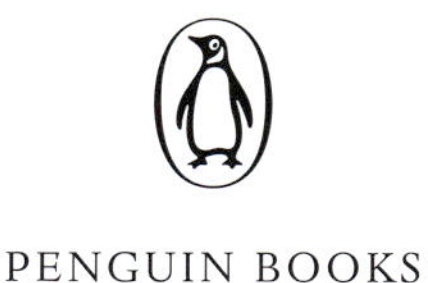

PENGUIN BOOKS

PENGUIN BOOKS

UK | USA | Canada | Ireland | Australia
India | New Zealand | South Africa

Penguin Books is part of the Penguin Random House group of companies
whose addresses can be found at global.penguinrandomhouse.com.

Penguin Random House UK
One Embassy Gardens, 8 Viaduct Gardens, London SW11 7BW

penguin.co.uk

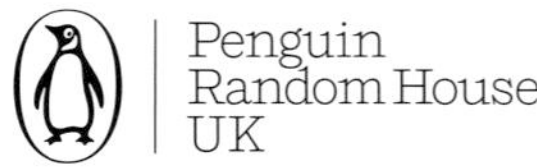

First published in the United States of America by W. W. Norton & Company, Ltd. 2023
First published in Great Britain by Allen Lane 2023
Published in paperback by Penguin Books 2025
001

Printed and bound in Latvia by Livonia Print

The authorized representative in the EEA is Penguin Random House Ireland,
Morrison Chambers, 32 Nassau Street, Dublin D02 YH68

A CIP catalogue record for this book is available from the British Library

ISBN: 978–1–802–06082–9

Penguin Random House is committed to a sustainable future
for our business, our readers and our planet. This book is made from
Forest Stewardship Council® certified paper.

For Joop and Janine van den Ende

CONTENTS

PART III
WALL POWER
177

PART IV
MAYFLOWER AND MAY FLOWERS
297

INTRODUCTION

The Way It Had to Be

WHEN I WAS TWENTY-FIVE, I moved to the Netherlands. The reason was a love affair. The place, I thought, was a detail. My interest in its culture was modest. My concerns were personal: starting life with my Dutch partner, starting life as a writer. These beginnings were so delicate, so fraught, that I hardly had time to think about anything else.

But as I started exploring this new country and tried to find a path as a writer, I stumbled upon a whole galaxy of artists who had seemed to be asking the same questions that I was. Why do we make art, and why do we need it? Who, and what, is an artist? What does it mean to have talent, and how can one develop whatever one has been given? Can an artist be a follower, or must he be original? What is the artist's duty to others, to society, to self? What is beauty, and how does it relate to taste? How can art help us see ourselves, and how can it help us see others? In a world without religion, can art provide a substitute for God? How, in a word, are we supposed to live—and must we go all the way to the end?

None of these questions had answers, or at least none that were satisfactory—and that was how I sensed that I had found a great subject. I didn't know that it would end up consuming me for twenty years, the time it has taken me to write this book. But I did not begin with these questions, or with the intention of writing a book. I began with the same excitement that I felt when, as a child, I stood in front of the skeleton of a dinosaur, or when I first saw the Rosetta Stone: that thrill of finding oneself in a room packed with old and mysterious things.

The room, or rooms, was the Dutch museums. One unfolded into the next: gallery after gallery, wing upon wing. My discovery of these rooms was one of the revelations of my life. It had a strange effect on me. I discovered that I could walk through these rooms the way I might walk through a cathedral or a forest, and that I would emerge from them the way I emerged from a good night's sleep or a long jog: calmer, happier, more focused. And I felt that there was something here I needed to know.

I didn't know what. I did know that there are places you visit and are happy to have seen—but never need to see again. I did know that there are people you enjoy meeting, enjoy spending an evening with—and whom, with no hard feelings, you never need to see again. And I knew that there are places and people that get under your skin. You want to know everything about them. They make you fall in love.

That is how I felt about Dutch art. At first, I felt the pleasure, the beauty, of this art. I felt its effect on me. It calmed me; it excited me; somehow, it calmed and excited me, simultaneously. But I didn't know anything about what I was seeing. I started jotting down notes, trying to keep track of it all. You know you are in the presence of a great subject when it raises more questions than answers: and when you realize that the subject gets bigger the more you learn about it—that the more you learn, the more ignorant you start to feel.

At first, I was embarrassed by my ignorance. I considered myself a reasonably well-educated person. But I had no idea what I was seeing. I had a quick suburban acquaintance with Rembrandt and Vermeer, and might not have gone much further if they had been the only great artists that Holland produced. But the astonishing thing about Dutch art was just how much of it there was. Every time I walked into a museum, I was sure to discover some spectacular something, by some unknown someone.

I wanted to know more. I started reading. I visited as many exhibitions as I could. Slowly, I got to know these artists—and as I did something happened. The process reminded me of the Scooby-Doo cartoons I had watched as a child. In a haunted house beehived with secret passageways, the culprit had cut out the eyes of old portraits. As the group wandered down the spooky hallways, the eyes in the pictures started to move.

I read more; I saw more; and as I did, the old pictures started to come alive.

I WAS EAGER to share the pleasure I had in this learning. I liked nothing more than taking a visitor around a Dutch museum, though I worried that I could come across with the zeal of a convert; I was a foreigner, after all, and part of my enthusiasm for Dutch art was the desire, sometimes touching, sometimes embarrassing, of a person trying to find his footing in a new country: that is how this book began.

The country became more familiar. The years passed. All that reading, all that exhibition-going, and then the beginnings of this book made me a more knowledgeable guide. I was not, in fact, especially knowledgeable, not at first, and not in the technical sense: I was helped to appear so by the general ignorance of the subject, even among the Dutch. Over time, I did grow less ignorant about the facts, which were available to anyone who bothered to look them up. More eyes started to move—and as they did, I discovered that my ignorance was of another nature. I thought I was learning, and then writing, about the history of art; I didn't know, until I was deep into writing this book, what I was actually doing, which was recording an education that went far beyond the pictures on the walls, recording my responses to people who had been asking the same kinds of questions that I was asking. Their answers were inconclusive and contradictory and often terrifying—but I didn't need their answers. I needed their questions. I needed to see how they had asked them, since they were the questions I had to formulate before I could offer any answers of my own.

For twenty years, half my life so far, I felt that these artists were guiding me, carrying me, through their world. But though their country grew more familiar, it was never my country, and I remained a foreigner, one who had traded the world from which I came for an uncertain life in a new land. It was a baffling experience. Becoming a foreigner could sometimes feel like experiencing dementia. You are you—same name, address, date of birth—but your past is wiped away. You don't know what anyone is talking about or who anyone is, and you start to wonder who you are yourself. I walked down the brick streets like the legal alien that I was, and often thought of a metaphor dear to

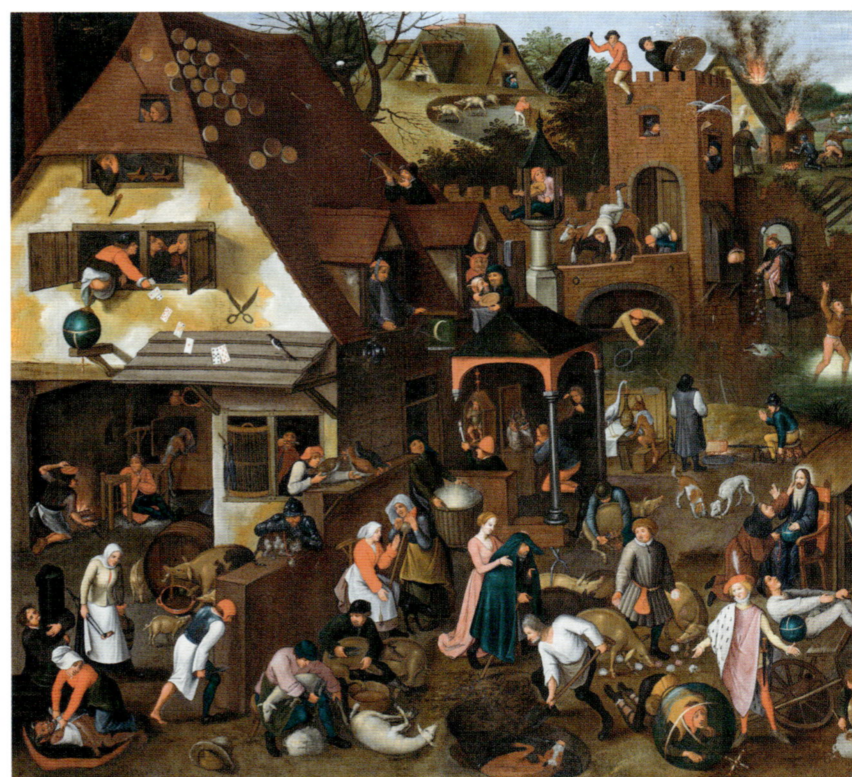

the old painters. A little globe, wrong side up, alludes to an expression still used in Dutch, *de omgekeerde wereld* or *de wereld op zijn kop*—the upside-down world or the world stood on its head. This is what you say when something unexpected happens, when the normal order of things is reversed: when a queen holds the door open for a commoner, or when it's warm and sunny in the middle of December. The theme recurs at carnival. It was popular among the comic painters, and the painters of daily life.

It is also a concise symbol for what happens when you become a foreigner. You stand on some other portion of the globe. What was up is suddenly down. If it is a great enrichment to be able to see the world from a different standpoint, it is also a great risk. It takes a while to learn that the questions are more important than the answers. At first, you don't know where to look. You don't know where you are, or what you're looking at. You don't even know where to start.

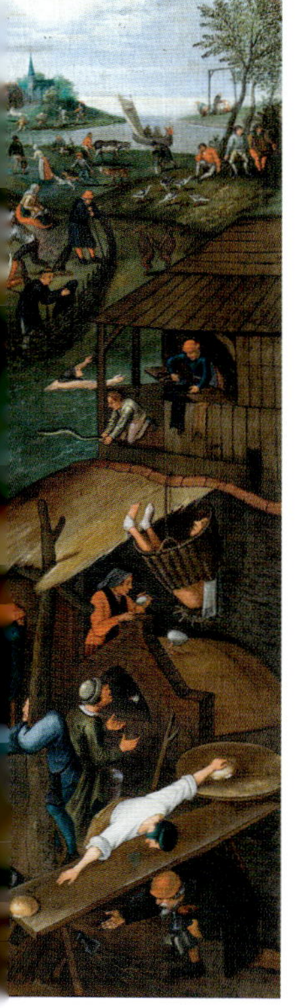

Pieter Bruegel illustrated eighty Netherlands Proverbs, *including, at left, an upside-down globe (the reversal of the normal order). The man shitting on the world (he doesn't care) is getting the best cards (fortune favors the stupid).*

WHERE TO START

SHORTLY AFTER I got to the Netherlands, I bought a book, or rather a series of books, by the American historian John Lothrop Motley. It was a nineteenth-century edition, printed on thick rag paper that was still bright and unspotted after 150 years, but these books were not collectibles: they were ratty when I bought them, and falling apart by the time I reached the end. I was surprised, in fact, that I reached the end—but the books were so momentous, so resonant, so full of incident and color, that I read them with as much pleasure as I have read anything in my life.

Born in 1814, a Bostonian of a generation that produced so many fascinating eccentrics, Motley—among whose interesting attainments was having been Otto von Bismarck's college roommate—published the three volumes of *The Rise of the Dutch Republic*, followed by the four volumes of *The History of the United Netherlands*, before and during the Civil War. They told the story of the Dutch Revolt, which began in 1566 as a local rebellion—really no more than a riot—in terms designed to appeal to Americans. He called William of Orange, who reluctantly led the Revolt, "the Washington of the sixteenth century." He described the story of Dutch independence as "a portion of the records of the Anglo-Saxon race—essentially the same, whether in Friesland, England, or Massachusetts."

> The maintenance of the right by the little provinces of Holland and Zeeland in the sixteenth, by Holland and England united in the seventeenth, and by the United States of America in the eighteenth centuries, forms but a single chapter in the great volume of human fate; for the so-called revolutions of Holland, England, and America, are all links of one chain.

Motley emphasized Dutch characteristics that Americans saw as their own. The Dutch wanted to be independent politically, to practice their own religion, to shake off tyrannical kings. They were a nation of traders and shopkeepers who rose to unprecedented power; and through their revolt, they had stubbornly refused to be enslaved: no American reading this amid their own Civil War would have failed to note the resonance. The books, and the heroic story they told, were popular for decades. The story was couched in a style as majestic as nineteenth-century writing can be, and that style, the prose equivalent of the grand operas that were its contemporaries, propelled me through volume after thrilling volume.

And they had another use. They gave me a place to start getting to know the history of the country where I had ended up.

In the fifteenth century, the Netherlands—what we now know as the Netherlands, alongside Belgium, Luxembourg, and chunks of Germany and France—were attached, by a series of inheritances, to the Habsburg rulers of Spain. It was an immensely unwieldy construction, and it was not yet cemented when, in 1517, Martin Luther nailed his Ninety-Five Theses to the door of Wittenberg church. Protestantism spread. In the Netherlands, for two generations, an edgy peace alternated with heightened enforcement of Spanish authority, which implied the suppression of religious dissent. This suppression was sharpened with the arrival of Philip II on the Spanish throne. In Motley's telling, Philip was a dumb and genocidal psychotic, and he cracked down on the Netherlanders. Among other things, this was self-defeating, since these provinces, which had long enjoyed a great deal of local autonomy, were far richer than threadbare Spain. Their response to the repression was ferocious, and resulted in a war that began in 1568 and concluded only with the Peace of Westphalia, signed eighty years later, in 1648.

By the end of the Eighty Years' War, the Dutch Republic, a small country of hardly more than a million inhabitants, was one of the leading powers in the world. Militarily, for a time, the Dutch were invincible. Economically, they were rich, the inventors of the multinational corporation and the stock exchange. Scientifically, inside drops of rainwater and sperm, deep into the night sky, and far into the unvisited regions of the world, they made one startling discovery after the next. They founded colonies from Brazil to South Africa, and from Java to Manhattan. Their radical philosophers made tyrants tremble, and the books that they printed in dozens of languages were read across the world. Their religious tolerance attracted large communities of dissenters; their women were freer than any other in Europe; their artists created a breathtaking collection of masterpieces.

The more I read Motley, the more invigorating, the more exhilarating, I found the Golden Age. I wanted to know more. But if all those achievements in all those fields gave me a sense of excitement about the place I had ended up, they were daunting, too. There was so much that it was hard to know where to begin.

My natural tendency was to start with their art—and within that art, among their thousands of accomplished artists, I knew that there could only be one place to begin. And so I began with the greatest artist of the Golden Age—and followed his genealogy, as through the generations of a royal house, down to his greatest successor.

1

REMBRANDT

The Shadow Master

ON JULY 15, 1945, Rembrandt's 339th birthday, the Rijksmuseum in Amsterdam reopened with the most emotionally charged exhibition in its history. Called "Reunion of the Masters," the show gathered 175 paintings that had spent the five years of the occupation hidden in bunkers. During those five years, private collections were looted, and museums were emptied of their greatest works. For all the average person knew, these treasures, like so many others, had been stolen or destroyed in the Nazi terror.

Now they were making a triumphant return to the center of Amsterdam. From The Hague came Fabritius's goldfinch, Potter's bull, Vermeer's pearl earring. From Haarlem came the great Hals group portraits, which were displayed alongside the Rijksmuseum's own collection—including, of course, the nation's famous Rembrandts.

In 1939, with war looming, the huge *Night Watch*, eleven by fourteen feet, had been taken to a vault made of reinforced concrete in a castle in North Holland. The location proved too dangerous. In 1940, when the Germans invaded, it was hastily removed to a bunker in Castricum, closer to Amsterdam. The painting was covered with a canvas borrowed from a local farmer. The journey of fifty kilometers took twelve hours. At one point, when an enemy plane appeared overhead, its escorts

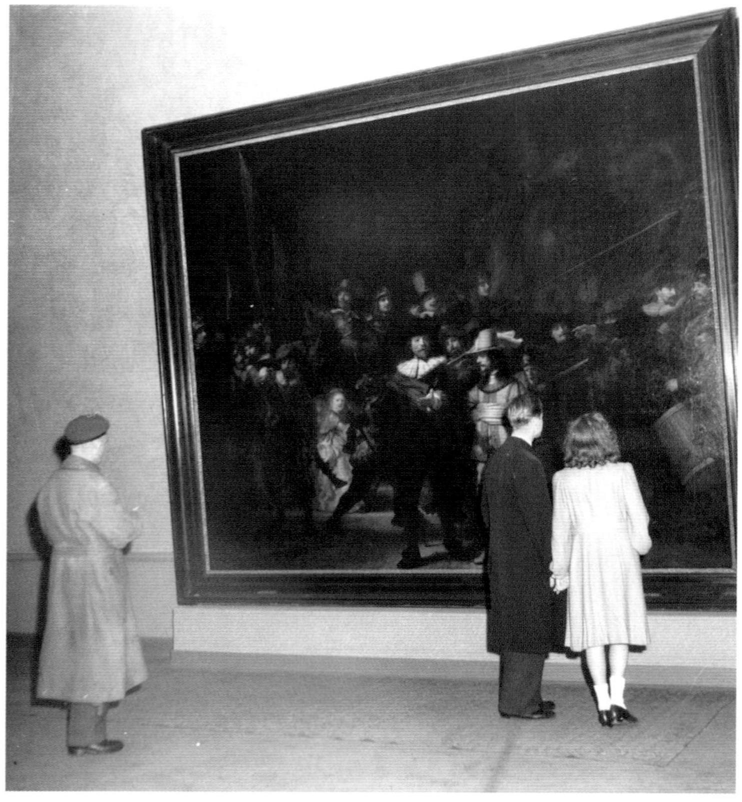

Just after the liberation of the Netherlands, the national art treasures, invisible since the Nazi invasion, returned to the Rijksmuseum.

took refuge in neighboring fields, leaving the masterpiece alone and unguarded in the middle of the road.

When it finally reached its destination, its caretakers discovered that it was too large for the entrance, and it had to be rolled up. Finally, in 1942, it was taken to a special storage site near Maastricht, where it was kept in a limestone quarry thirty-three meters underground. The director of the Frans Hals Museum, Henk Baard, recalled the scene:

"Through the slow progress of the silent bearers the remarkable spectacle, under its ghostly lighting, recalled a princely funeral."

Now it was back. One hundred and sixty-five thousand people eventually visited the show. In a country that still lacked basic provisions, many of these visitors came on an empty stomach. All understood its promise: that past glory would bring future resurrection. "A people that can display such a parade of greatness shall reclaim its special place," a journalist wrote. At the opening, a minister declared that the Canadians who liberated Holland "have also liberated Rembrandt and Frans Hals."

More than Hals, Rembrandt needed that liberation. He needed it more, in fact, than any other Dutch artist. Hitler had declared him "a true Aryan and German," and under the quisling regime he had become the focus of a bizarre cult, his birthday even replacing the exiled Queen Wilhelmina's as the national holiday. Now this unwitting German hero could become, once again, the symbol of the dignity of a free people.

Light had chased out darkness. It was precisely the kind of cosmic struggle that Rembrandt had illustrated in his works, though that struggle rarely had such a clean outcome. History was recapitulating the trajectory of Rembrandt's own evolution. If Vermeer was a painter of light, Rembrandt was a painter of dark, of dark commingled with light; and in his work the question of evil recurs more than in any other Dutch artist's—so insistently that looking at his pictures is sometimes unbearable. There are more scenes of murder, cruelty, torture, rape, betrayal, malediction, and death in Rembrandt than in any other Dutch painter's work—by far.

Vermeer painted no such scenes. Neither did Hals. Neither did any of the blither spirits, Hendrick Avercamp or Pieter de Hooch or Jan Steen. At the very most, the landscapists and the still-life painters will allude, with some graceful symbol, to mortality, to the passing of time. Most Dutch paintings were made for the wealthy middle classes, and show things those people liked to see. Who among them would have wanted a picture like *The Blinding of Samson*, in which a silver dagger is plunged into the hero's eye? The painting is so gigantic, two by three

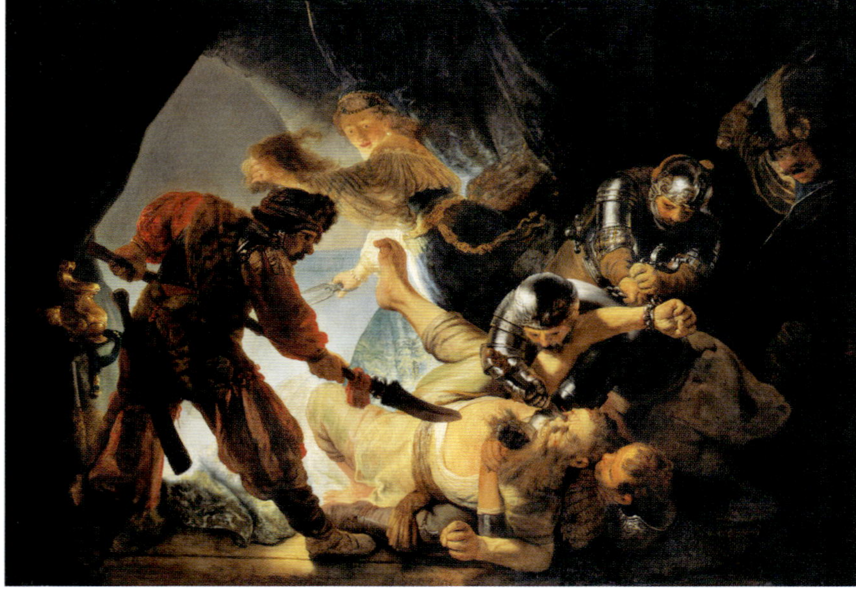

Delilah snatches Samson's magical hair as his eyes are gouged out by soldiers.

meters, that it is hard to look away from it. It is just as hard to look at it. Even Delilah can hardly contemplate her victim without a shiver.

REMBRANDT WAS so prolific that even the most ambitious museum survey will never capture more than a slice of his work. Books aren't much use, either: the images end up crammed onto the page, and that monumental quality of Rembrandt's paintings—their patina, their glow, the sense that they give of something physical, like an extraordinary geological phenomenon—goes missing too, flattened onto smooth paper.

The etchings and drawings, originally made on paper, fare better in reproduction. But there are hundreds of them, and even the most avid eye can absorb only so much. To try to see more than a few at a time is to get a reminder that, as with Dante and Shakespeare and Bach, you cannot rush an acquaintance with Rembrandt. His work took a long time to make, after all: nearly half a century between his earliest productions and the works he made in the days before his death at sixty-three.

Add, to the quantity of works and media, the quantity of genres. In England, writers were comedians or tragedians or poets, but only Shakespeare was the greatest in every field. In Holland, Rembrandt, who was nine when Shakespeare died, worked in nearly every specialty known to Dutch art, each of which absorbed the energies—the entire lives—of his most talented contemporaries. And then there is the profusion of his styles.

These make it even harder to form a coherent image of Rembrandt. Many Rembrandts do not look anything like the popular idea of a Rembrandt. His early work looks so different from his later work that the early works were not even recognized as such until deep into the nineteenth century. Over the years, all sorts of ghastly paintings have been attached to his name—including some that he actually painted.

There are still occasional rediscoveries today, though these are nearly always of lesser works that seldom add more than a footnote to the image that has emerged from two hundred years of dogged scholarship. The lacunae of that scholarship only seem to yawn in comparison to a demand for completeness. We now know as much about Rembrandt as we know about almost any figure, artistic or otherwise, of his century.

We have a large group of works. We know what they show. We know when they were painted—and, often, why and for whom. We can see that some themes interested the master only for a short period. We can see that others were there from the beginning and stayed with him until the end. Some come back in every medium, in every style, at every point in his career. And one such recurring theme is violence—evil—darkness.

THE SPECTACLE OF cruelty is there in his earliest signed painting, *The Stoning of St. Stephen*. He painted it in 1625, when he was nineteen. It shows a crowd surrounding the first Christian martyr, stones held high, ready to smash him to pieces. Unlike the *Samson*, it is not hard to look at—it is too much of an apprentice piece to feel real—but though he is not visibly joining in, it is a bit disturbing to find a chubby teenage Rembrandt among the crowd.

A few years later, the novice has matured into a master. Rembrandt was twenty-six when he painted *The Anatomy Lesson of Dr. Nicolaes Tulp*. This is a portrait of eight men around the corpse of Aris Kindt, who had been convicted for armed robbery and executed earlier that morning. The men are wearing neat clothing, and their expressions range from technical curiosity to a keen realization—or do we just imagine it?— that they themselves will soon be just as dead as Aris Kindt. Despite the decorous scientific proceedings and the sober expressions on the doctors' faces, the smell of rot tickles your nostrils.

You could derive a positive message from this painting. You were, in

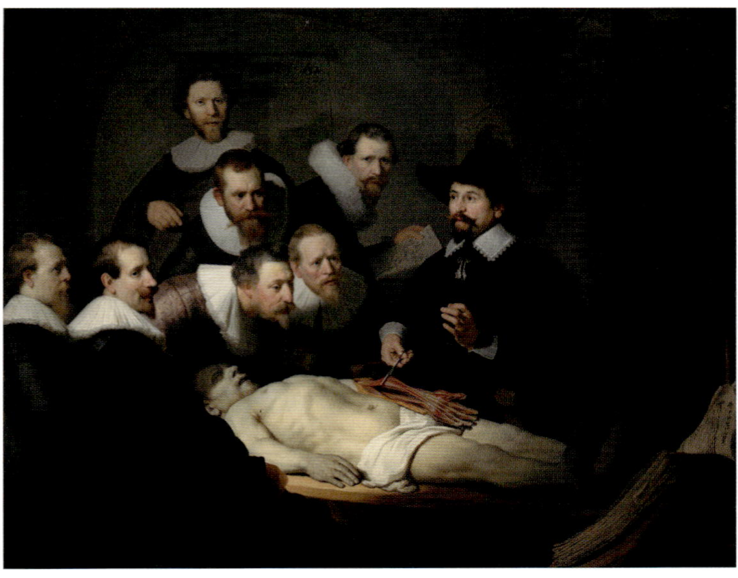

The executed criminal's right hand had previously been hacked off;
Rembrandt restored it.

fact, intended to by those who commissioned it, if not necessarily by the artist. The doctor is instructing the public with lessons that demonstrate the Dutch commitment to progressive education, lessons that were commemorated with such paintings because the medical societies were prestigious and famed; Rembrandt was one of many artists invited to paint them.

When, twenty-four years later, he returned to the theme, he showed Dr. Jan Deyman dissecting Johan Fonteyn, who broke into a draper's shop and pulled a knife. The anatomy lesson took place on the day after his execution. Of this painting, damaged in a fire in the eighteenth century, only two central figures, a spectator and the criminal, survive. All we see of Dr. Deyman are the hands peeling back Fonteyn's bright red brains.

Rembrandt's criminals have a presence that bodies in other portrayals of anatomy lessons do not. Sometimes, in these, the doctor is showing a skeleton. Frederik Ruysch, father of the still-life painter Rachel

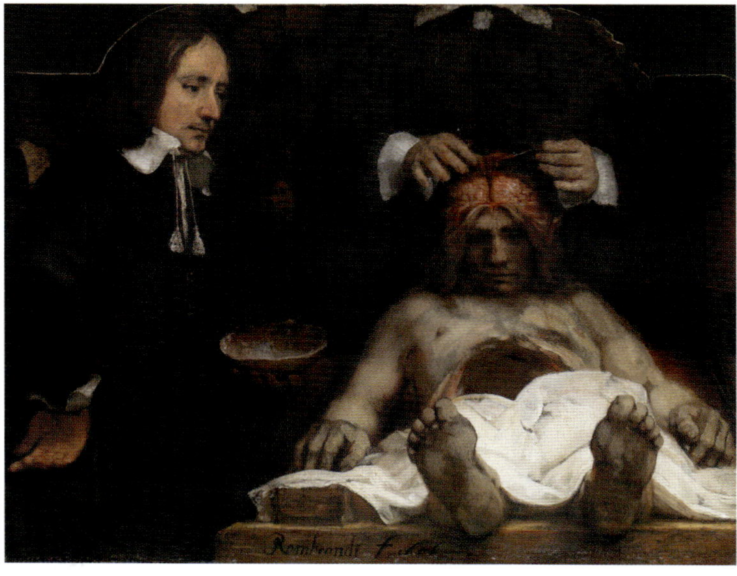

The blackened feet of an executed Flemish tailor seem to stick
out of the frame.

Ruysch, who succeeded Dr. Deyman as Amsterdam's city anatomist, was painted with rosily blooming cadavers, sleek as Greek nudes, on the dissecting table. Ruysch was famed for making dead bodies look alive. Rembrandt's bodies are unequivocally dead—and he arranges us, like the doctors, around them.

We have to look at these cadavers, just as we have to look at poor Elsje Christiaens, a teenage girl who was strangled in 1664 for killing her landlady, apparently in self-defense. She was executed on the Dam, the central square from which the city takes its name ("the dam on the Amstel"). Her body was hung on a gibbet in Volewijk, across the River IJ, where it was to remain "until the winds and birds devour her." It was there that Rembrandt saw her, strung up like a doll. He drew her twice.

Did any other Dutch artist show a body this way? A well-known image of the disemboweled De Witt brothers, murdered by a mob in 1672, comes to mind; but the painter, Jan de Baen, was undistinguished, and the picture is remembered mainly because the De Witts were among the most powerful politicians in the Netherlands. The shocking and grotesque painting shows a historical event—not the death of an obscure eighteen-year-old girl.

So it goes with many other themes. Often enough, you can find something comparable, somewhere. There are plenty of dead animals in Dutch painting. But there is no picture quite like

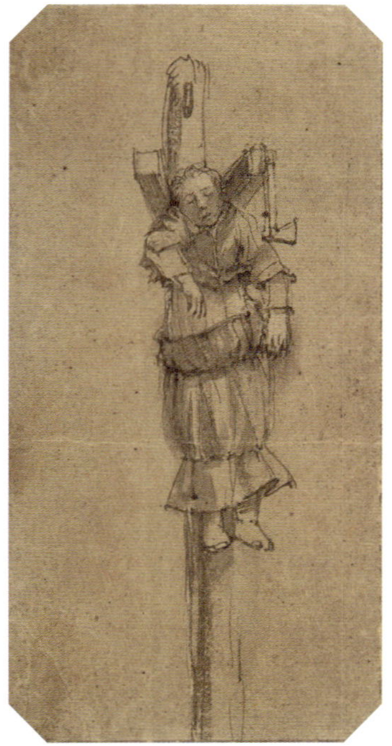

The weapon with which Elsje killed her landlord was strung up next to her dead body.

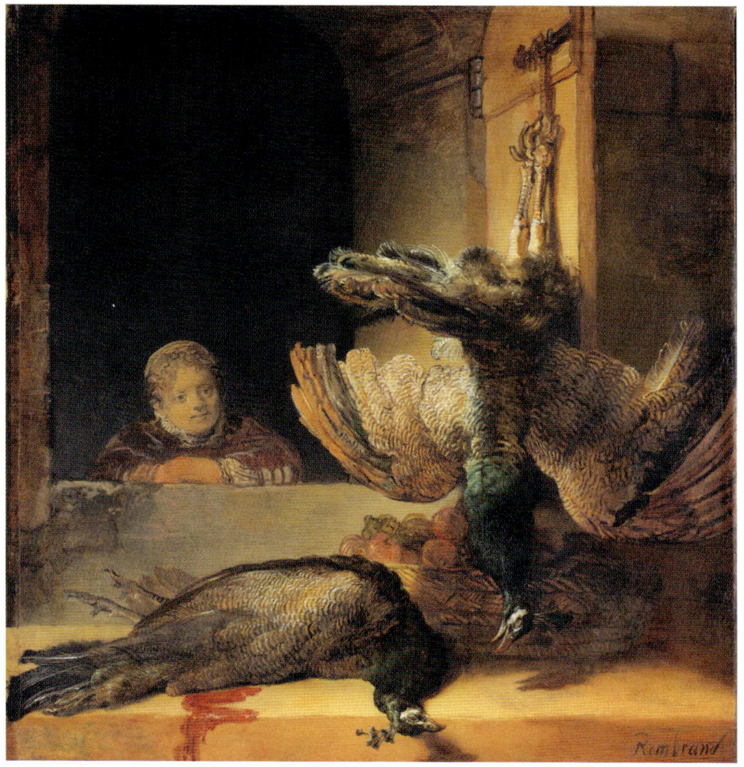

A child seems to contemplate the destiny of the murdered birds.

the *Still Life with Peacocks* in the Rijksmuseum. Here, one bird lies in a pool of its own blood. Another is hung by its feet, its mouth still agape, as if to protest its murder. It is beautiful and it is also excruciating: the hallmark of Rembrandt.

Look, too, at *The Slaughtered Ox*. Red as the brains of Johan Fonteyn, the dead animal hangs from a wooden beam. "Slaughtered" is not quite the right word. The French title uses *écorché*—mangled, flayed—and no Christ in the whole Louvre captures the pathos of sacrifice like this carcass. The painting contains no religious references. But it stirs the same spectral feeling that the most sacred mysteries evoke.

Do we identify with the ox? Or with the servant girl, barely visible, looking at it? If the anatomy lessons invite us into the circle of the learned doctors, our eyes go nonetheless directly to the dead men at their center. The light is on them; they radiate sanctity. Not martyrs,

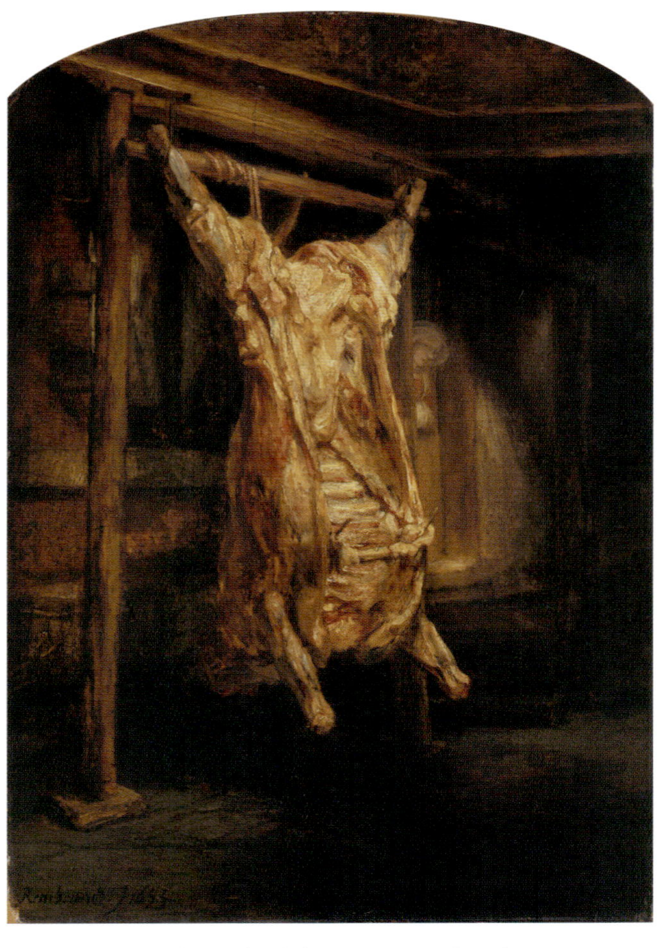

No Christ in the whole Louvre captures the pathos
of sacrifice like Rembrandt's ox.

they are still somehow numinous. It is not an accident that Rembrandt placed the criminals in the position where the dead Christ was placed in earlier paintings—or that he crucified the ox, and Elsje Christiaens.

———

THESE WORKS ARE NOT overtly religious. But Rembrandt painted plenty of religious works, too. If their contents reflect the mood of the man who created them, so does their very existence, since there was little commercial incentive to create them. In post-Reformation Holland, to the contrary, they were unfashionable to the point of career suicide. The German art historian Max Friedländer could credit an entire tradition to a single artist:

> A view of the whole of Dutch production in the seventeenth century tells us that, where it was animated by any receptive interest in the religious picture, this was Rembrandt's personal achievement or was at least set in motion by him. It was Rembrandt who, from spiritual predilection, bequeathed the non-ecclesiastical religious picture to the reformed North, which was ready to only a very limited extent to accept this present with gratitude.

Rembrandt's "spiritual predilection" sought extremes, and ways to portray them. The rough clash of light and dark could be rendered graphically, in paint, as in *The Supper at Emmaus*, painted when he was twenty-two, when the resurrected Christ reveals himself to a disciple. The dark Savior is surrounded by a halo of blazing light whose hidden source lends him the majesty of a mountain. Light triumphs over darkness.

But not always. Often, light does not have the last word. He shows the damned as well as the saved. In *Belshazzar's Feast*, the impious Babylonian king gazes in terror at the ominous writing on the wall. In *Uzziah Struck with Leprosy*, a Judean king is punished for profaning the temple. There is nothing picturesque about these scenes of hubris humbled. They fulminate, they rage, they denounce; and if their warnings are warnings to others, they are also, one feels, warnings to the artist himself.

We are in the presence of an Old Testament prophet—he painted many—who was well acquainted with the extremes that he depicted. The biographical evidence bears this feeling out. Though sainted in the nineteenth century, twentieth-century researchers discovered that Rembrandt was, in Gary Schwartz's words, a "cocktail of litigiousness, untrustworthiness, recalcitrance, mendacity, arrogance, and vindictiveness."

It turned out that Rembrandt's contemporaries had almost nothing nice to say about him, and no artist of his time could boast the number of disagreeable incidents that peppered his life. He didn't pay his bills; he was tactless and rude and prickish; he was cruel to his mistress. "To sum it up bluntly," Schwartz writes, not uncontroversially, "Rembrandt had a nasty disposition and an untrustworthy character."

In this list of incidents, Rembrandt's treatment of Geertge Dircx stands out. When his wife, Saskia, died at the age of twenty-nine in 1642, she left him a nine-month-old son, Titus. Rembrandt hired Geertge to take care of Titus. He and Geertge became lovers and were together for six years. Geertge intended to marry the widower, and, she claimed, he had promised to do so—until he began a relationship with his housekeeper, Hendrickje Stoffels.

Lawsuits ensued. Rembrandt promised Geertge alimony. In the meantime he collected unflattering testimony about her, which he used to have her committed to the Gouda *spinhuis*, an atrocious institution for women who had "fallen" for a long list of reasons, from prostitution to insanity. She was desperate to get out. Rembrandt was desperate to keep her there. After five years, she was released, and died soon thereafter.

A long-ago dispute between embittered former lovers can be read in any number of ways. In books and films, Geertge has been portrayed as a conniving, gold-digging temptress—and, more recently, as a victim of a man's determination to get her out of the way. If it weren't for all the rest of the abundant evidence of his rebarbative personality, we might, in this case, be more inclined to give Rembrandt the benefit of the doubt.

Why, in any case, should we care? Surely other painters could have been obnoxious in ways that passing time has hidden. For all we know, Adriaen Coorte liked little girls, and Jacob van Ruisdael cheated on his taxes: when names fade and personalities fall away, only an artist's work—and then usually only a portion of it—remains for us. We do not wonder whether the painter of an Egyptian fresco was likable.

Four hundred years later, we wouldn't wonder about Rembrandt, either. Yet the conflicting accounts bother us—because we love him. We know him so well, after all. We can see him: his work, and also *him*, since no artist ever exposed himself as nakedly. From the adolescent among St. Stephen's tormentors to the valediction that Jean Genet described as "a sun-dried placenta," around eighty of his self-portraits survive.

The number is astronomical. We have no idea what most painters look like. But, except for childhood, we can see Rembrandt at every phase. From the proud young man to the imperious genius to the wrecked patriarch, we can watch his life pass before us; and when, in a museum, we come across him in a new guise, we greet him as an old friend. We know him so well. Is this despite his darkness, or because of it?

The darkness is not, in any case, a secret. Even today, when confession has become a genre of its own, it is hard to think of an artist who revealed himself so remorselessly. We see him as we see Aris Kindt or Johan Fonteyn or Elsje Christiaens. The difference is that, if the ox was flayed and Aris Kindt was dissected—Rembrandt did this to himself. In the light of this destiny, do earthly transgressions matter?

———

"THE WEST TOO has known a time when there was no electricity, gas, or petroleum, and yet so far as I know the West has never been disposed to delight in shadows," the Japanese novelist Junichirō Tanizaki wrote in 1933. He described traditional lacquerware that "was finished in black, brown, or red colors built up of countless layers of darkness, the inevitable product of the darkness in which life was lived."

I wonder if Tanizaki was familiar with Caravaggio, whose *tenebroso* style used darkness to make light shine all the more radiantly, or with Rembrandt, who perfected a style that is the opposite of much Japanese painting, which dispenses entirely with light and shade. Perhaps this was an expression of nostalgia for the time without electric light, when the world would have looked unimaginably different from the way it does now.

It is surprising to realize that even in the West we do not have to look very far back to discover that time. It stretches, still today, into living memory. The Mauritshuis, the royal collection in The Hague where *The Anatomy Lesson of Dr. Nicolaes Tulp* hangs, did not acquire electric light until 1950. How did these paintings look when our grandparents saw them in "the darkness in which life was lived"—and how did they change when first seen under artificial light?

Perhaps Tanizaki was a romantic. Perhaps the Japanese really did assign a different value to darkness. But at the very least—as you feel that Vermeer's light has a meaning that exceeds the requirement to illuminate—it is possible that Rembrandt's darkness has a role akin to the one Tanizaki describes: "Our ancestors presently came to discover beauty in shadows," he wrote, "ultimately to guide shadows towards beauty's ends."

Yet Rembrandt's contemporaries did not always consider his shadows beautiful. In his lifetime and beyond, they were often criticized as no more than a murky waste of space. Many great Rembrandt portraits are indeed little more than heads, and sometimes hands, peering out of the gloom, and if we imagine them in pre-electric rooms under the moody skies of Holland, we have to imagine them even darker.

Look at the late portrait of Margaretha de Geer, from 1661. In the alert and penetrating eyes, in the right hand that grips a handkerchief, and in the left hand that resolutely holds on to the arm of her chair, as if to launch her at the viewer, you can see her great power. She is one of the richest women in Europe—yet she is very old, and her face, served

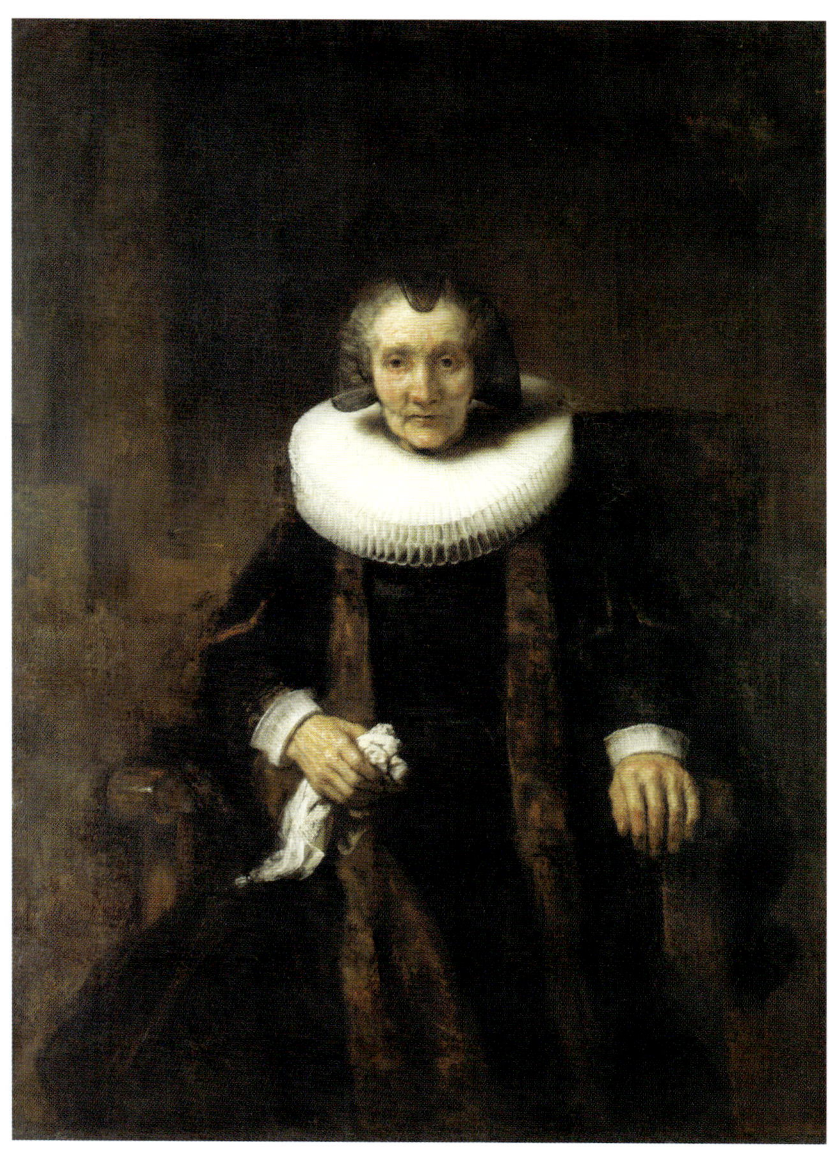

The rich and powerful Margaretha de Geer, at the threshold
between light and darkness.

on a bright millstone collar as on a platter, seems about to dissolve into the darkness that surrounds her.

There is a ghostliness to these portraits, including to those that Rembrandt made of himself, that makes them more haunting than any other art of their time. If *The Blinding of Samson* is awful to look at, it is so theatrical that it troubles us less than Margaretha. The picture was designed to hang in her children's house. One shudders to imagine them walking past it at night, the matriarch illuminated by flickering candles.

EVENTUALLY, the critical tide turned. Rembrandt's darkness acquired a positive value, ultimately coming to form a crucial part of his myth: a forerunner of the nineteenth-century Parisian bohemian. Especially the tenebrous late works—those final utterances of the discarded old genius, scorned by those who once had courted him, rotting in his cheap lodgings in the Rozengracht—were equated with spiritual profundity.

Rembrandt's darkness came to be viewed so positively that his works were even darkened artificially. The varnish that protects paintings needs to be replaced every fifty or so years, before it decays; but sometimes, at the insistence of curators, it was deliberately left on, so as not to lighten the work. Deep into the twentieth century, some restorers added pigments to new varnish in order to darken the pictures.

The practice was not restricted to Rembrandt. "A good painting, like a good fiddle, should be brown," wrote the painter and patron Sir George Beaumont in the nineteenth century. This brownness, known as "gallery tone," may have seemed appropriate to objects prized, among other qualities, for their antiquity. Perhaps here is an echo of the "beauty in shadows" that Tanizaki did not believe existed in the West.

In unlit galleries, covered with decaying varnish, how shadowy these paintings must have been! Did the darkness deepen Rembrandt—or did it make him illegible? If darkening seems inappropriate from a scientific perspective, it doesn't strike us as inappropriate for Rembrandt as it would for another painter. You wouldn't darken an Avercamp or a

Metsu—much less a Vermeer, whose genius lies in the uncanny suffusion of light in space.

Rembrandt *is*, after all, dark. But his darkness does not always have a negative implication. In his several renderings of the apocryphal story of Tobit, for example, he shows the old man whom God has blinded in order to test his faith. While their son Tobias seeks a cure—this turns out to be the entrails of a monstrous fish—Tobit and his wife, Anna, stay home, patient and impoverished: resigned to their lot, firm in their faith.

In *Anna and the Blind Tobit*, the old man sits in a ramshackle room, his face turned from a light he cannot see. Anna uses a ray from the window to wind wool on a frame; but most of the room, and most of the painting, is dark. The mood is of humility, not of expectation. We know that Tobit will be cured, but he himself has no such knowledge. His reward is unseen, and unforeseen. Faith—darkness—faith in darkness—is all he has.

YET EVEN his bleakest paintings always contain an admixture of light. The master was a moralist. He was a sensualist, too. The early works reveal a love of splendor—ostentation, even—and the paintings often contain a glint of gold. This was more than a color, or a taste. In the dark rooms where these paintings hung, it had a practical purpose ("the extravagant use of gold," Tanizaki wrote, "gleams forth from out of the darkness and reflects the lamplight") and a representational one.

In the self-portraits, as life takes its toll on the cocky young man, the light that had illuminated his figures from the outside moves inside. The background darkens, the atmosphere turns into mist—and the figures glow, like the fierce eyes of Margaretha de Geer, with something otherworldly. The artist becomes sadder and older—and grander, more imposing, the inner light shining all the more intensely—because of the approaching dark.

As Rembrandt ages, the light in his paintings takes on an added luster. It reveals a view of the world as a struggle between light and dark that is, at heart, religious: of the world as a theater in which good and evil are intertwined, and in which good only occasionally triumphs.

Sometimes, as for Belshazzar, crime meets its just punishment. Often, as for Samson, it does not. Does Rembrandt think it matters?

"He didn't care about being nice or mean, surly or patient, grasping or generous," Genet wrote of the late Rembrandt: "He didn't have to be anything more than an eye and a hand." Now life has taken everything from him. All that matters was his art—and so, "with dirty fingernails," the erstwhile lover of gold is now shuffling "from the bed to the easel, from the easel to the shitter." He is beyond good and evil, or trapped in their mixture.

A conflicted personality has been reconciled. The artistic and the spiritual are no longer in conflict; and in his last months, Rembrandt returned, after thirty years, to the parable of the prodigal son. This is the story, from the Gospel of Luke, of two brothers. One, faithful, stays home with his father. The other squanders his fortune carousing with whores. Eventually, forced to work as a swineherd, he envies the pigs.

The theme had occupied Rembrandt since his youth. In the mid-1630s, he painted himself and his wife, Saskia, in a tavern scene, *The Prodigal Son in the Brothel*. There is a peacock pie on the table, and Rembrandt's golden sword pokes out at the viewer. It is not conventional for a painter to portray himself as a wastrel, or his wife as a hooker; but this, the painting declares, is not a man interested in convention.

Thirty years later, Saskia was dead. Titus was dead. Geertge and Hendrickje were dead. He himself would follow soon; but before he went, he painted the story one more time. This time he chose another moment: the return of the prodigal son, when he comes back, humbled and repentant, causing his father to rejoice. His father dresses him richly, "putting a ring on his hand, and shoes on his feet," and orders the fatted calf killed.

"Lo, these many years do I serve thee, neither transgressed I at any time thy commandment: and yet thou never gavest me a kid," the virtuous son grumbles. "But as soon as this thy son was come, which hath devoured thy living with harlots, thou hast killed for him the fatted calf." But as Christ explains, one repentant sinner causes more joy in heaven than "ninety and nine just persons, which need no repentance."

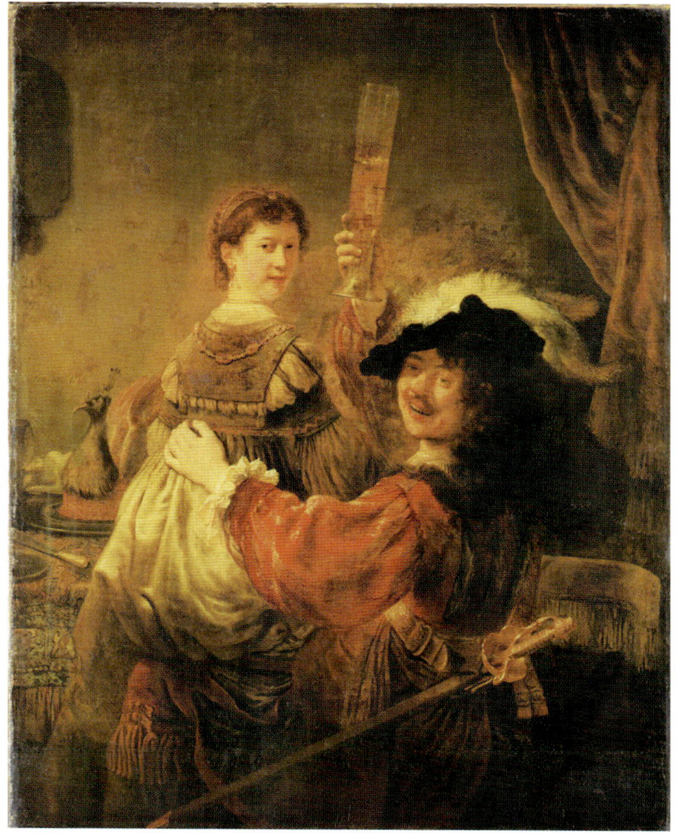

*At the peak of his success, the artist shows himself and his wife as reveler
and whore.*

Rembrandt, who painted so many Old Testament scenes of vengeance and sacrilege, now paints this epitome of the New Testament,
a scene of forgiveness and redemption and love that, even by the master's own standards, is stately and symphonic: the ragged, pathetic son
kneeling before his old father, who gazes at him through half-open eyes.
Though they are surrounded by darkness, the light is upon them.

Without passing through darkness—through the opposite of what

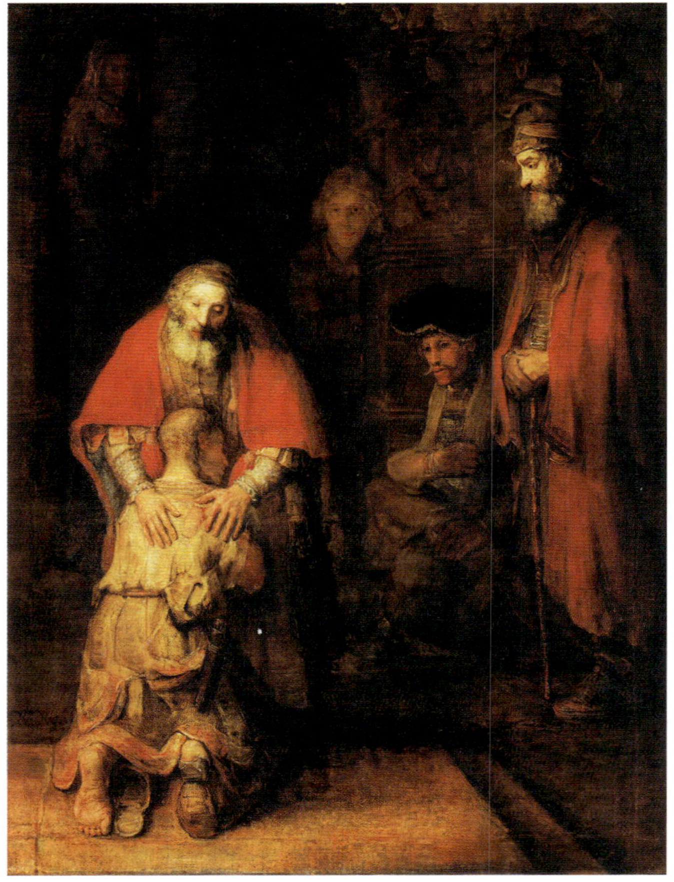

*Just before his death, Rembrandt revisits the theme
of the prodigal son.*

he meant to approach—the son could never come into the light of the father. Light cannot exist without darkness, nor virtue without sin. They are intertwined in every life. The electricity coursing between these magnetic poles—between Dr. Tulp and Aris Kindt, between Delilah and Samson, between the butcher and the ox—was the subject of Rembrandt's art.

2

JAN LIEVENS

Not Rembrandt

TWO LARGE Rembrandt reproductions hung on the wall of my grandmother's guest room. Pains had been taken to make them look authentic. They were elaborately framed and printed on an expensive polymer that had been scuffed to suggest craquelure. The figure on the left, robed and beturbanned, looked so much like my grandmother that I must have been in my teens before I realized it wasn't. On the right was a melancholic old man who looked a bit crushed by his splendid golden helmet. These pictures were familiar guardians watching over me as I slept—until I learned more about them, at which point they became something else. The figure who looked like my grandmother became far grander: he was the famous painter himself, dressed as St. Paul.

I don't remember when I learned that the man in the golden helmet was not Rembrandt: he wasn't even *by* Rembrandt. I do remember my vague disappointment, though it is hard to describe what there was to be disappointed about. It was exactly the same painting. Why did the knowledge that it was painted by someone other than Rembrandt take away the shine in the old man's helmet?

There were lots of reasons that this mattered. Scholarship, for example, needs an accurate catalog of an artist's work. If, three hundred years from now, Henrik Ibsen is believed to have written *Fifty Shades of Grey*, it will be hard to form an accurate assessment of his œuvre. (Considering some of the carbuncles that have passed for Rembrandts through the years, this scenario is not as far-fetched as it sounds.)

The name mattered for financial reasons, too. Even if the picture were considered to be of the highest quality—and nobody ever questioned the quality of *Man in a Golden Helmet*, nor convincingly attributed it to anyone else—the demotion put the old man on the wrong side of the monetary gulf that divides a Giorgione from a "School of Titian," or a Van Eyck from a "Netherlandish Master ca. 1430."

But these were learned reactions. My reaction was instinctual, and I remembered that long-ago disappointment when I read an article by

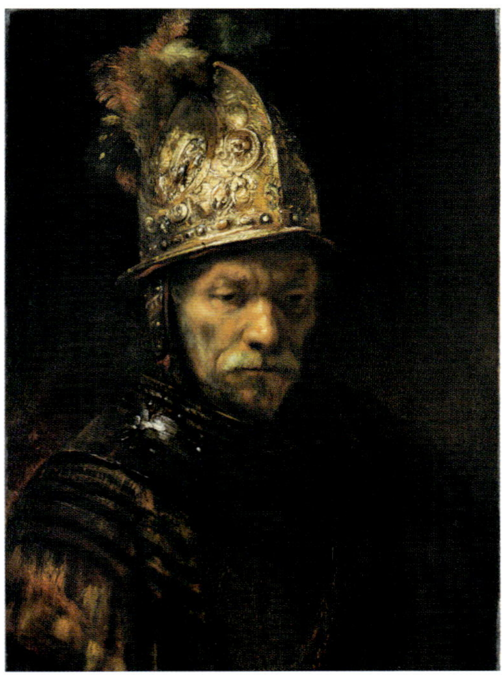

Not a Rembrandt but not quite not a Rembrandt, this picture makes us wonder what we see when we see art: a name or a work?

Erin Thompson, a professor of art crime, that explained that I was not the only one to feel that way. She wrote that

> subjects in a 2011 study showed markedly different neurological activation in response to images they were told were painted by Rembrandt compared with images they were told were copies of his work. This occurred whether or not the paintings were genuine (the investigators randomized the descriptions), suggesting that our conscious beliefs about an image can shape our biological response to it.

We have a biological response. And then, perhaps to rationalize it, we have an intellectual response. Part of the latter might come from another idea we have learned: that great art is, by definition, original. And to be "school of" is—by definition—to be a follower. In 1996, the Metropolitan Museum investigated this dilemma with a show whose title pithily, and bleakly, summed up the conundrum: "Rembrandt/Not Rembrandt."

NO ARTIST SEEMS a better candidate for Not Rembrandt than Jan Lievens. And the question of how to look at a painting by Lievens presents an aesthetic challenge. How can you look at his work without thinking of Rembrandt, and finding him wanting?

The comparison has been unavoidable since 1891, when a Dutch translation appeared of a recently discovered autobiography, in Latin, by Constantijn Huygens. Besides being one of the most influential writers in the early Dutch Republic, Huygens was a renowned musician, an accomplished poet in both Dutch and Latin, and secretary and intimate to the princes of Orange. Among its revelations, the document included a surprising glimpse of Huygens's visit, around 1629, to two young painters in Leiden:

> The first, whom I have described as an embroiderer's son, is called Jan Lievens; the other, whose cradle stood in a mill, Rembrandt. Both are

> still beardless and, going by their faces, more boys than men. . . . I venture to suggest offhand that Rembrandt is superior to Lievens in his sure touch and liveliness of emotions. Conversely, Lievens is the greater in inventiveness and audacious themes and forms. Everything his young spirit endeavors to capture must be magnificent and lofty.

The several hundred words of this description—the earliest written glimpse of Rembrandt—have been as extensively parsed as any ever written on Dutch art. Huygens was hard to impress. But he was impressed by Rembrandt and Lievens: by their seriousness, which he suspected excessive ("They regard even the most innocent diversions of youth as a waste of time, as if they were already old men burdened with age and long past such follies"), and by their dazzling promise: Lievens was "a young man of great spirit, and great things may be expected of him if he is granted a long enough life."

In their late teens and early twenties, the two friends worked together closely in the booming city of Leiden. Its heroism in the Revolt—when it was besieged, its burgomaster offered his own body as food to the starving citizens; the offer was declined—was rewarded with the right to establish a university, which turned it into a scientific and intellectual capital. In this prosperous but relatively small city, Lievens painted a portrait of Rembrandt and used him as a model; Lievens features in Rembrandt's paintings from this time, too. Both, in those years, depicted the raising of Lazarus, Christ on the Cross, Samson and Delilah, and—a theme so typical of the later Rembrandt—an elderly biblical prophet tested by hardship: *Jeremiah Lamenting the Destruction of Jerusalem* by Rembrandt, and *Job in His Misery* by Lievens.

Huygens saw different strengths without preferring one to the other. These differences would become more pronounced with time, though their early works are so similar that for generations attributions of many unsigned works have gone back and forth. In 1933, a monograph dedicated to Rembrandt's early work assigned several of Lievens's works to Rembrandt purely on the basis of their superior quality. If it was good, it was Rembrandt's.

Fate had more indignities in store for Lievens. Huygens wrote that his only objection to Lievens was "his stubbornness, which derives from an excess of self-confidence. He either roundly rejects all criticism or, if he acknowledges its validity, takes it in bad spirit." An English ambassador said that Lievens "thinks there is none to be compared with him in all Germany, Holland, nor the rest of the seventeen provinces."

These quotes make Lievens seem like a braggart—a little pathetic, even. But Lievens was a celebrity by the age of twelve. His works were commissioned or purchased by the princes of Orange and the king of England. He was invited to participate in every major Dutch decorative project of his day, and to portray such figures as Rembrandt, Descartes, Huygens, Vondel, Adriaen Brouwer, and the Prince of Wales (the future Charles II).

It is a rare artist—indeed, a rare human—who is lucky enough to live out his life without eliciting at least a handful of unflattering remarks. But Jan Lievens's undeniable failure to become the greatest painter of his century, combined with those old hints of pomposity, has been enough to suggest a whole pathology. "Maybe he had a personality disorder," mused Ken Johnson, a critic for *The New York Times*, in 2008.

UNLIKE REMBRANDT, who never left his native country, Lievens was drawn to travel. When he was twenty-four, he left for London, where he stayed three years and where, a neighbor records, "his fine works gained him immediate acclaim," including rich rewards from the king. Thereafter, he spent nine years in Antwerp before returning to Holland, where he remained until his death—like Rembrandt's, in poverty—in 1674.

In his account of "these celebrated young men, from whom I can scarcely tear myself away," Huygens wrote that their gravest fault was that "hitherto, neither has found it necessary to spend a few months traveling through Italy." They explained this "touch of folly in figures otherwise so brilliant" by telling Huygens that they were "in the bloom of youth and wish to profit from it; they have no time to waste on foreign travel."

Lievens never reached Italy, but the most advanced ideas in Italian art were in the air, and a journey he may have made during his early teens may account for some of the most striking Italianate characteristics of his, and Rembrandt's, art. He seems to have visited Utrecht around 1620. It was an obvious destination for a young painter—not Italy but the closest thing to it, and he reached the city when Caravaggism was at is peak.

Michelangelo Merisi da Caravaggio had died on a Tuscan beach, apparently murdered, ten years before, at the age of thirty-eight. In his short life, he had created a new style of painting that would echo through the rest of the seventeenth century, raising the subdued elegance and aristocratic refinement of the Italian Renaissance to a new pitch of emotional fervor, and finding enthusiastic followers in the Netherlands.

The artist Hendrick ter Brugghen returned to Utrecht in 1615,

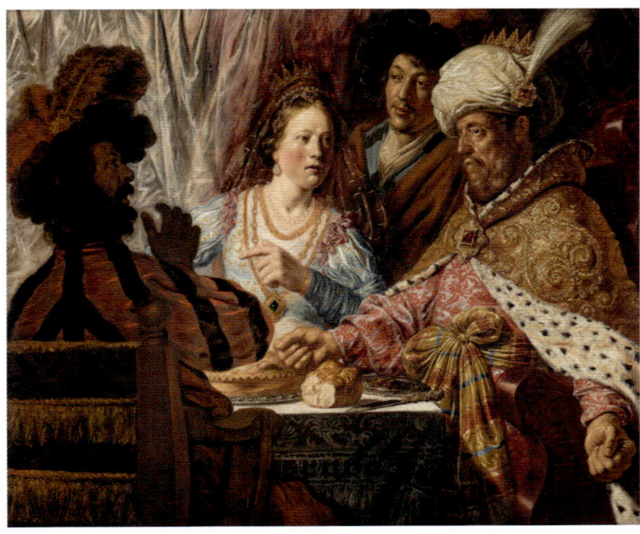

Lievens's Feast of Esther *shows the lessons the young painter might have learned during a theoretical journey to Utrecht.*

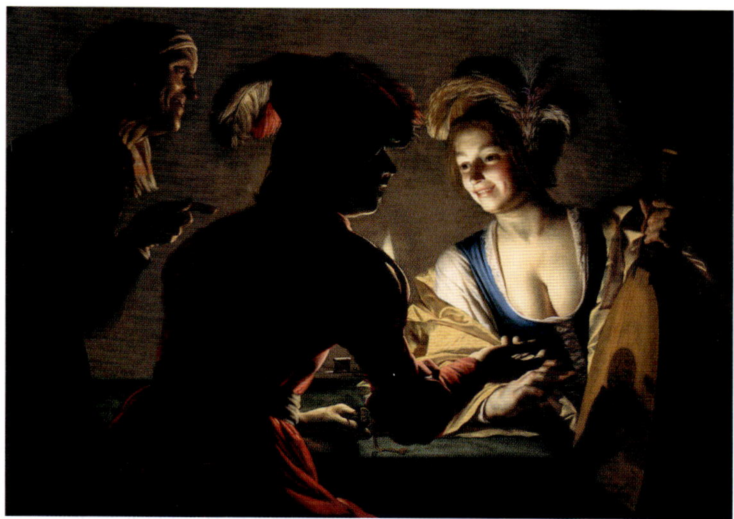

Utrecht painters like Gerrit van Honthorst borrowed the lighting techniques of Caravaggio—
which the Italians had borrowed from earlier Netherlandish artists.

the only Dutch painter in Rome during Caravaggio's lifetime. In 1620, Gerrit van Honthorst—known in Italy as Gherardo delle Notti, Gerard of the Nights—returned from Rome. The next year Dirck van Baburen arrived. They all brought back Caravaggio's ideas, painting works that often take place in a dark space, lit by a candle or torch.

Like photographs taken with powerful flash in a nightclub, the Caravaggists' paintings often focus intensely on one central figure, one dramatic gesture, favoring epiphanies, moments when everything changes, from religious conversions to secular revolutions: the delivery of a fateful letter, for example, or the swearing of an oath from which there is no turning back. Caravaggism is an art of the cliffhanger. It is all climax.

Many of Lievens's early paintings bear the distinctive mark of Caravaggio. His *Feast of Esther*, for example, employs Caravaggio's lighting effects. Wicked Haman, in the foreground, is clothed in shadow. His body blocks a light that shines all the more brightly on

Queen Esther, and underlines the finger she is dramatically pointing at Haman. The composition is lifted almost verbatim from Caravaggio, via Honthorst.

Lievens soon discarded Caravaggio's "natural"—in fact highly contrived—effects. But another form of Caravaggio's influence is visible in Lievens's *Job in His Misery*. This is a kind of naturalism that would have been considered indecorous and almost unthinkable in the smooth, idealized art of the Renaissance. The tortured old man's sagging skin—the distended veins in his arm almost visibly pulsing—looks like a wound.

The painting is enormous; the man is nearly life-size. Its scale speaks to the scale of Lievens's ambition. And it lets us take a good close look at the sometimes grotesque details of the old man's battered body, recalling, in this sense, another large painting, Rembrandt's closely contemporary *The Anatomy Lesson of Dr. Nicolaes Tulp*, in which an executed criminal is exposed to the solemn gaze of a scholarly committee.

CARAVAGGIO'S ART, controversial and scandalous in his homeland, was almost immediately comprehended, and then extensively imitated, in the Netherlands. This is because the novelty that excited and offended the Italians—his "naturalism"—had also been, since the end of the Middle Ages, the most outstanding characteristic of Netherlandish art. The Dutch were reimporting something that their ancestors had exported generations before.

Caravaggio considered that all art ought to be painted from life, from "nature," rather than from the idealized example of antique sculpture. His idea of nature, however, was not always appreciated. An Italian accused him of using a "filthy whore" as a model for the Virgin, and similar accusations were leveled at Caravaggio's Dutch successors: in 1681, only twelve years after Rembrandt's death, the poet Andries Pels wrote that "he chose no Greek Venus as his model, but rather a washerwoman, or a peat-trader from a barn, calling this aberration the imitation of nature. . . . Flabby breasts, misshapen hands, aye the welts of the stay-laces on the belly, of the garters on the legs, must be visible, otherwise nature was not satisfied."

One can almost hear the air quotes—the sneer—with which Pels would have spoken the word "nature." And if following nature alone might suggest a snapshot shorn of intermediate artifice, it also meant, in Rembrandt's or Caravaggio's time, the interposition—particularly into scenes that, because of their holiness or antiquity, were traditionally shown above and outside the regular world—of the dirt of daily life.

Taking a "filthy whore" as a model for the Virgin was a belligerent reaction to earlier painters whose sense of propriety depended on an idea of art as something above and outside of daily life. Rembrandt's detractors always accused him of a lack of decorum. His student Samuel van Hoogstraten reproached him for including, in a scene of John the Baptist, "a dog that in a most scandalous manner was mounting a bitch."

Yet this kind of grunge could show how unexpectedly the divine could burst into ordinary life. The dirty feet on the worshipper of Caravaggio's *Madonna of the Rosary*—in Vienna today but in Amsterdam in Lievens's and Rembrandt's time—stress the proximity of the heavenly. These details heighten the drama of images that, in the Mannerist works of the sixteenth century, often spun off into extremes of otherworldliness.

Certain critics wondered how a work's spiritual quality could be enhanced by the least divine, least spiritual elements of a painting, but they recognized that they were. Of Hendrick ter Brugghen, one contemporary wrote that "it remains inexplicable how paintings with so many irregularities and 'ugly' details can nonetheless possess such grandeur." That grandeur was present in paintings by Caravaggio, too.

Like Caravaggio, Ter Brugghen, and Rembrandt, Lievens had a marked taste for "aberrations." As in his painting of Job, he savored, from the beginning of his career, the drooping skin and watery eyes of old people—though it was not a fascination for the elderly, or for the ugly, per se. Throughout his life, whatever his subject, his main interest was in texture, hair, clothes, skin: in the feel of the physical world.

Some of his paintings suffer, as a result, from a kind of *horror vacui*. He is too determined to render every hair, every fold of cloth. Perhaps

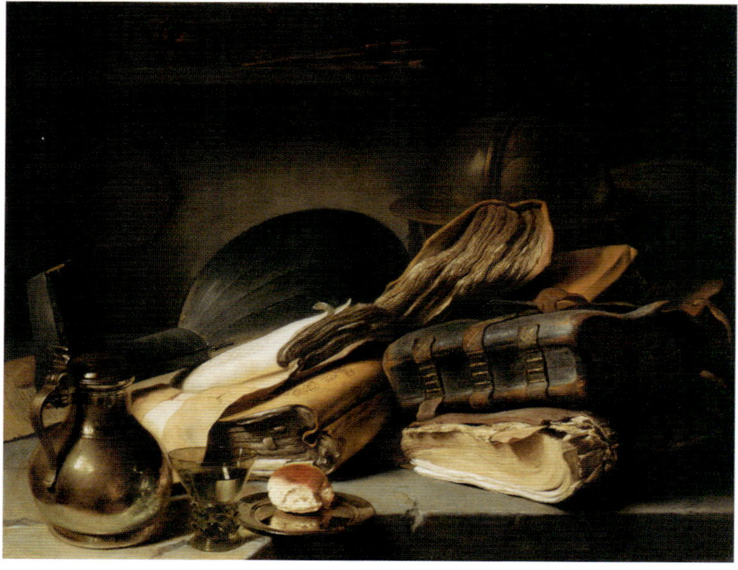

Lievens's Still-Life with Books *was once attributed to Rembrandt
purely on the basis of its excellent quality.*

from a pileup of obsessive pentimenti, the paint can be laid on so thickly
that the canvases acquire an ungainly cakiness. His *Esther*, for example,
seems to miss the point of its Caravaggesque lighting—meant to focus
on a few essential passages—by cramming every inch.

Because he often focuses on details at the expense of the whole,
Lievens's history paintings are inferior to Rembrandt's or Caravaggio's.
But when he takes direct inspiration from "nature," the results can
be magical. Look at his *Still Life with Books* in the Rijksmuseum. Long
attributed to Rembrandt, it shows Lievens as a pure painter: without
psychology, without the pressure to create a complex historical or
religious drama.

Like *Job in His Misery*, the painting is big—monumental by the standards of Dutch still-life. It bristles with energy: you can almost feel a
gust of wind blowing over the books that lie open on the table. The

painting shows books, tableware, a musical instrument, and a globe. It also shows the young painter's great ambition—and hints at how that ambition would lead a wunderkind away from the lowly genre of still-life.

———

REMBRANDT'S EARLY WORK—created when he was in closest communion with Lievens and with Utrecht—was his most highly valued in his own time. His later work was considered as vulgar as the unlettered boor who created it. In 1707, Gerard de Lairesse, an artist who was himself portrayed by Rembrandt, warned beginners against painting "like *Rembrand* or *Lievensz*, whose colors ooze down the picture like crap."

At the beginning of the nineteenth century, a revolution in taste caused Rembrandt's early oeuvre to be rejected as "baroque" and superficial, while the later work came to be valued for its spiritual depth. By the end of the century, he himself would be elevated to sainthood, and in 1885, when the new Rijksmuseum was opened, *The Night Watch* stood, in place of the altar, at the end of a cathedral-like Gallery of Honor.

If "spirituality" is the criterion, Lievens will always lose out. He is not at his best with religious or historical subjects. His early *Raising of Lazarus*, which Rembrandt owned, shows Lazarus as a pair of ghostly hands sticking out from the tomb. The atmosphere has the stormy portent of a Rembrandt, but it is hard to figure out what is going on— and when you do, the work reminds you a bit too much of a Victorian ghost story.

The contrast may best be shown in another work Lievens created during the years he was in close contact—and in close competition—with Rembrandt. In two paintings, one by Rembrandt and one by Lievens, Christ hangs crucified, entirely alone, against a dark background. The images are so close to identical that when you look at them you understand why the Rembrandt/Not Rembrandt question has been so thorny.

But there is a difference—one so slight that, at first, you hardly notice. It turns out to be instructive. Each artist portrayed a slightly different moment of the same scene. Though the bodies are in almost

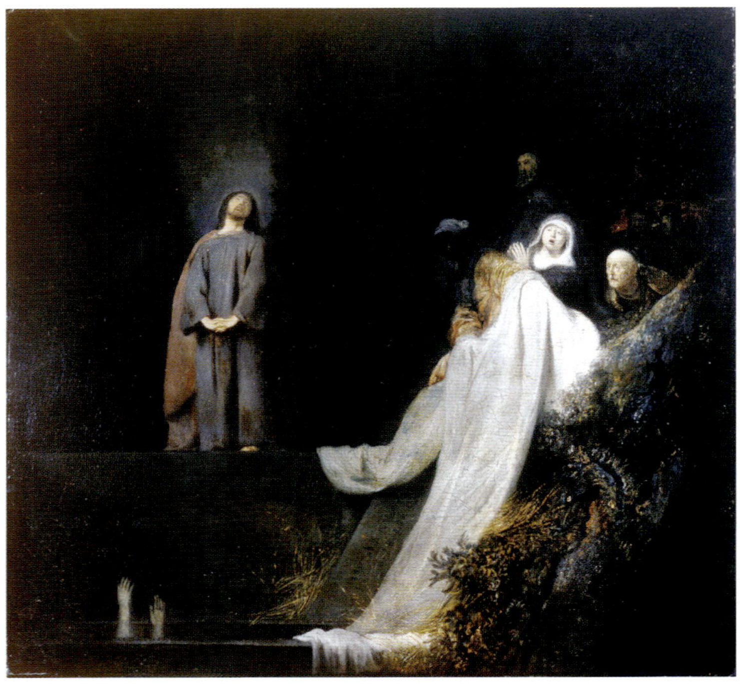

Christ summons two ghostly arms out of a black tomb in The Raising of Lazarus.

the same position in both paintings, the distinction is immense: Rembrandt's Christ is dying; Lievens's Christ has already died. Placed side by side, the paintings look like snapshots taken by the same camera, seconds apart.

The mouth of Rembrandt's Christ is open, in protest or pain; Lievens's is quiet. Rembrandt shows a man struggling, tortured; Lievens shows a corpse and a consummated crime. Rembrandt knew that a breathing, suffering man is more affecting than a cadaver; and the choice shows why Lievens rarely evokes the emotional response that Rembrandt does. But emotional response is not the only criterion for art.

Then what is the right criterion for looking at Lievens? The comparison with Rembrandt, however irresistible, helps us see what is great about Rembrandt, but not what is great about Lievens; and though it is true that the comparison of almost any artist with Rembrandt would be unfair, there is something about Lievens that makes us look for a narrative backbone to help us understand him—and Rembrandt gives us that.

This is because Lievens didn't find a theme early—as Potter did with animals or Avercamp did with winter scenes—and develop it. Such artists tinker, experiment, evolve; but their personality and interests manifest themselves early. Others, like Lievens, are restless. They accept challenges, take risks, and sometimes fail. The failures often build to success, and this succession of successes and failures gives the artist's life a narrative.

Lievens is never one thing. Even his face looks different from one self-portrait to the next. The earliest shows a young man: his flashing eyes, his floating hair. The next is done in the courtly manner of Van Dyck. Then he is surrounded by darkness, bathed in golden light. I love this painting; I hate the last, in which he is dressed to advertise his success. He looks like a lounge lizard: decadent, hard, and—to me—repellent. Which, in life or in art, was the real Lievens? His art mirrors so many trends that one can nearly always locate the source of his inspiration. If his early work could look like Rembrandt's, and vice versa, his later works could look like practically everybody else's. He borrows from everywhere and everyone. I can follow his eye, his mind, as he wanders from one experiment to the next—and as I do, I grow increasingly depressed.

There is something unnerving about Lievens. "A precocious writer doesn't have much experience to work on; his talent isn't challenged," wrote V. S. Naipaul. "The quickness of such a writer lies in assuming the manner and sensibility of his elders." Naipaul speaks of that writer's "essential mimicry," which makes it hard for him to discover a core of identity. The talent that made him so promising turns against him.

Like so many artists, Lievens died forgotten and poor. Yet it is one thing to contemplate the last years of Rembrandt, who at least— can there be any doubt?—knew who he had been. It is something else to think of the old Lievens, who died five years after Rembrandt, his childhood neighbor from Leiden, on the same canal in Amsterdam, the Rozengracht. He must have known that though he had made some great paintings, he had not lived up to his promise.

Those great paintings complicate Lievens's tragedy. Of nearly any artist, including Rembrandt and Vermeer, one can say that some works are better than others. In their case, this does not matter, because the greatness of the great works makes the ugly works trivial. In Lievens's case, the reverse is true. The ugly works reproach the great works, admonish them, and make one wonder whether one was right to admire them.

Some of Lievens's most beautiful paintings are of solitary old people. The subject seems to have been dear to him. It gave him an opportunity to show how he could paint the kinds of textures that Caravaggio and

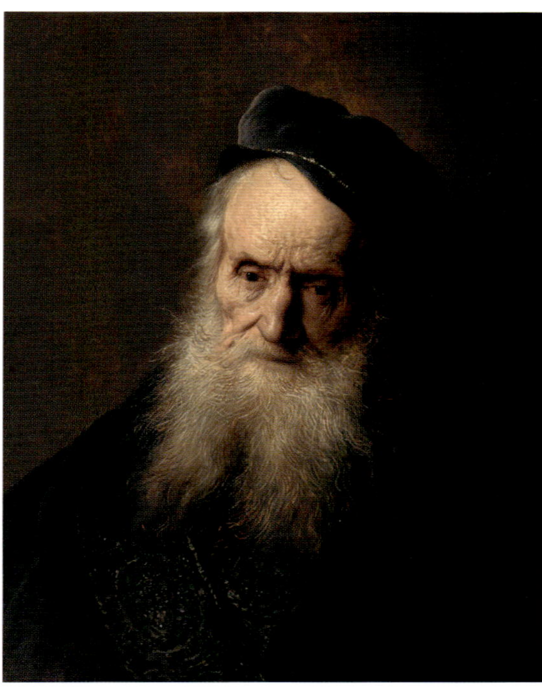

Lievens's love of painting old people could sometimes produce masterpieces, like this old man, and sometimes verge on the grotesque, like this old woman.

then Rembrandt painted, focusing on those physical aspects without shoehorning them into a narrative. The successful works keep on the right side of the line that divides the poignant from the pathetic.

Other pictures of similar subjects, however, cross another line. This is the line that divides a frank description from a repellent one. Lievens sometimes paints old people who look merely disgusting, such as a *Penitent Magdalene* whose hands seem to be made entirely of varicose veins. This is the line that Caravaggio's critics warned, decades before, was being crossed: the colors do indeed "ooze down the picture like crap."

Place a beautiful picture of an old man beside this painting of an old woman and the question arises: Is the ugly painting the exception and the beautiful painting the rule, or is it the other way around? With

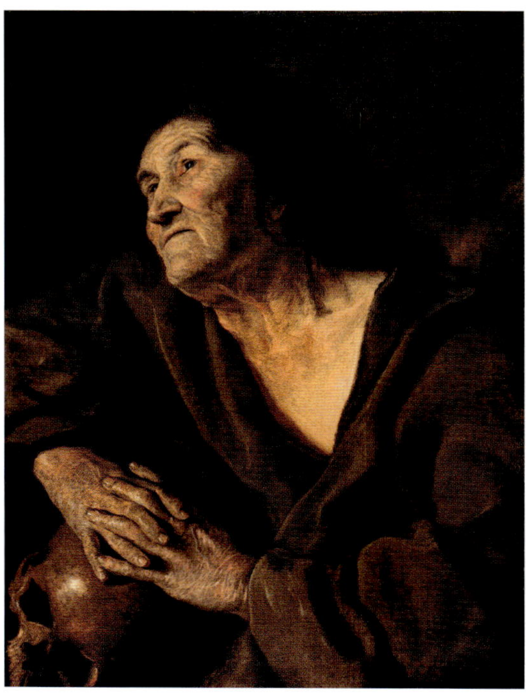

Rembrandt or Vermeer, the question is easy to answer. With Lievens it is not. There are great paintings. But there are also quite a few paintings that even the most sympathetic scholar, the most generously inclined viewer, is at pains to explain away.

Especially for an artist as naturally talented, it is one thing to follow new styles. But the danger of mimicry looms when he follows them without a core of identity. Without that core, the artist floats. For a long time, this doesn't seem to matter. The man is charming and attractive. He becomes famous, and knows that if one thing doesn't work out, something else will. For a long time, there is always a new client.

That luck runs out. Does it matter? In his last years, Lievens could look back on an illustrious career. Despite the usual reversals, he had a good run. He lived sixty-six years, longer than nearly any of the major artists of the Golden Age. But he must have known that he had not lived up to his potential. It was no tragedy not to be Rembrandt. The tragedy was not to have become himself—not to have been Lievens, either.

———

YET UNDERNEATH THE changing forms there is always a recognizable hand. You find the hand in the drawings, which have a uniformly high quality that his paintings do not. They have a freedom, too—the feeling of things made for himself, and not in order to impress someone else. Here, you feel, Lievens is Lievens, doing what he dreamed of doing when he was young, before his great promise turned against him.

His most revealing "self-portrait" might be a sketch of a forest. It is dominated by a tree whose giant branches twist in every direction. The tree's execution betrays a flawless, and seemingly effortless, mastery of perspective; and behind it, in the midst of the forest, a tiny man sits drawing. The scene reminds one of another description of Jan Lievens, recorded by a neighbor, when he was not quite ten years old:

> He applied himself with such industry and diligence to improving his
> skills that he was oblivious to anything else. Even the riots . . . during

which all the doors and windows were closed and the magistrates were forced to call in the militia to quell the uprising, failed to distract him from drawing prints. . . , for he regarded the love of art as more important than all the upheaval in the world.

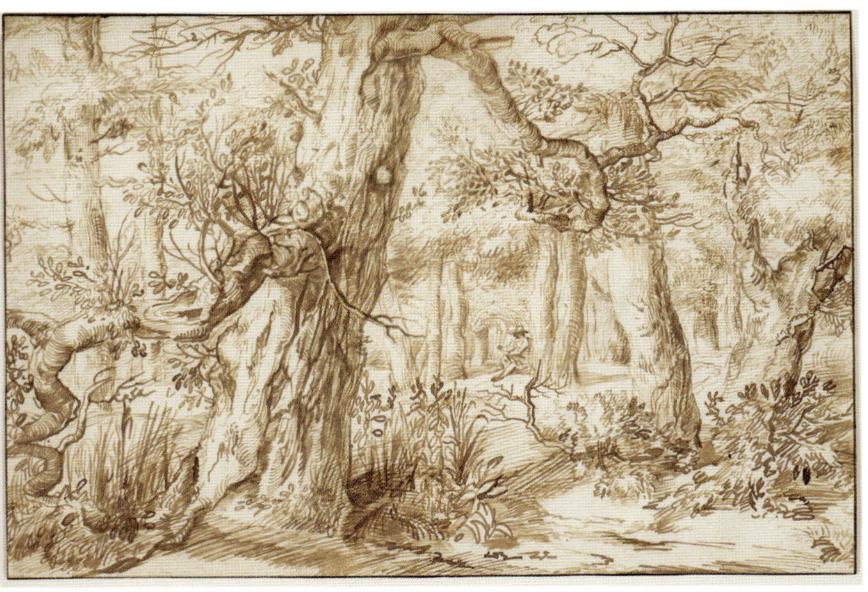

A solitary man drawing, undistracted by the world.

3

FERDINAND BOL AND GOVERT FLINCK

Who Is an Artist?

A NEARLY NAKED BOY, arms bound, chin shoved back, bare neck exposed to a dagger: Rembrandt's *Sacrifice of Isaac* is a reminder that no amount of age or official veneration can allay the shock of the dissected brains and disemboweled criminals and stripped carcasses and wounds that seem to be caked with real blood scattered throughout the painter's work.

To place the picture alongside another, painted eleven years later, is to see just how ferocious Rembrandt could be. His student Ferdinand Bol deployed the same characters in roughly the same arrangement. In Bol's version, though, the light is less bluntly surgical, and the neck is not exposed, and the boy has been allowed the dignity of a face. The two pictures, and their creators' fates, remind us that there is more to art than *terribilità*. An entire history of ideas unfolds in the gulf between Rembrandt and Bol, who was just ten years younger, and shows that art history, so often a matter of paint chips and auction records, can be as emotionally charged as the works it studies.

What should art be?

And who should get to call himself an artist?

For more than a hundred years, starting in the mid-nineteenth century, most of the academic study of Dutch art centered on determining what Rembrandt had actually painted. He had lots of students, many of whom were great talents in their own right. He ran, for many years, a large studio. It is not always easy to know what is what, and this research, still ongoing, reattributed hundreds of paintings, dispatching dozens of once famed paintings into the oblivion of the storerooms. And by establishing Rembrandt's œuvre, it also stimulated research into those works lumped into "School of," "Not Rembrandt." Though ongoing, this process has not shaken a canon that has been mostly fixed since the rediscovery of Vermeer in 1866. And it has allowed a continuing reevaluation of painters once forgotten, or even banished.

Banishment was the fate of Bol and his contemporary Govert Flinck, whose reputations once surpassed their teacher's. To read the bad reviews to which they have been subjected since the dawn of scientific art history is to see vitriol so vehement that it raises questions. What happened? In 1910, the scholar Abraham Bredius complained that Bol annoys the viewer with "superficial and minimal facial expressions." Five years later, another expert called Bol "one of the dullest of Dutch painters." In an essay in the catalog of a Bol and Flinck exhibition I visited at Rembrandt's house in 2018, I read, with a pang, that "even those who extensively studied the two artists . . . obviously had little sympathy for the painters they chose to write about."

By 1939, Flinck's reputation had sunk so low that the forger Han van Meegeren stripped one of his largest canvases to use as a support for one of his fake Vermeers. In 1983, a scholar described Flinck thus:

> A talent without creativity, he is characterized by a useless technical ability and a skill for imitation. Without existential depth and formal scruples, he was unsurpassed in satisfying social needs. His success was paradoxical, as with all other opportunistic nobodies and narrow-minded characters who have been advanced to represent the Zeitgeist.

In 2013, a Dutch graphic novel depicted him as "ugly, skinny, snobbish, and [with] a thin, villainous moustache."

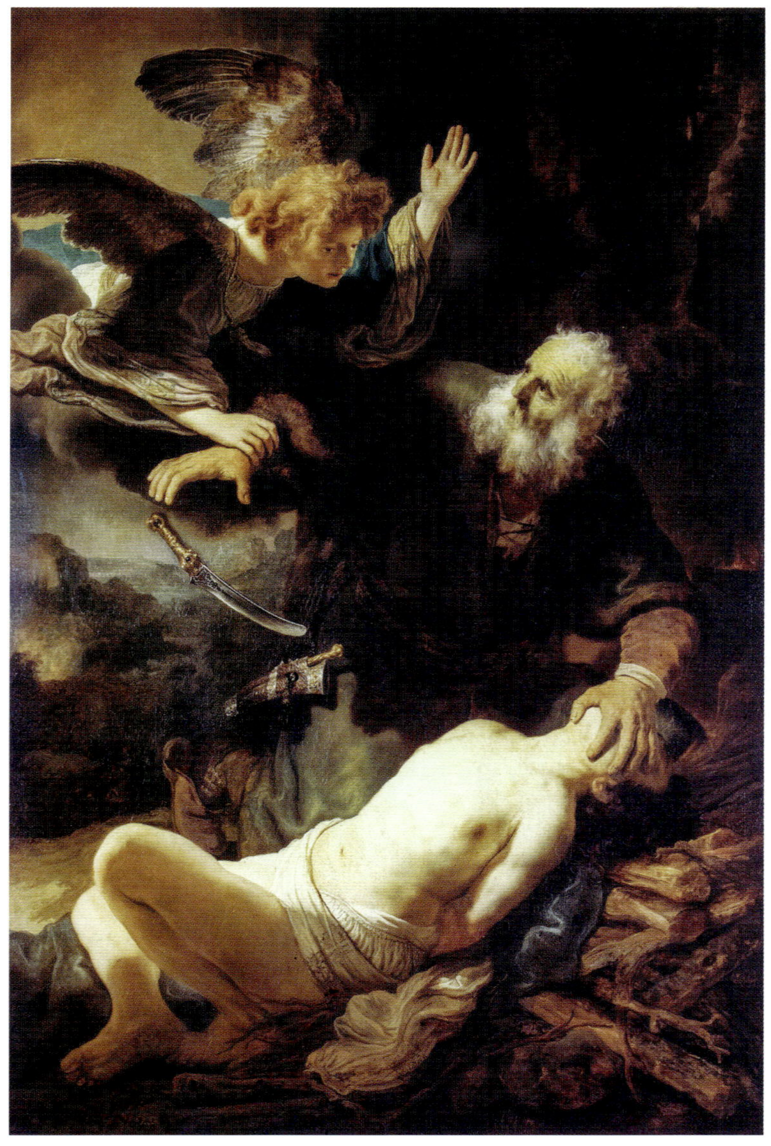

The same scene, The Sacrifice of Isaac, *by Rembrandt and by his pupil Ferdinand Bol. Which would you rather look at every day?*

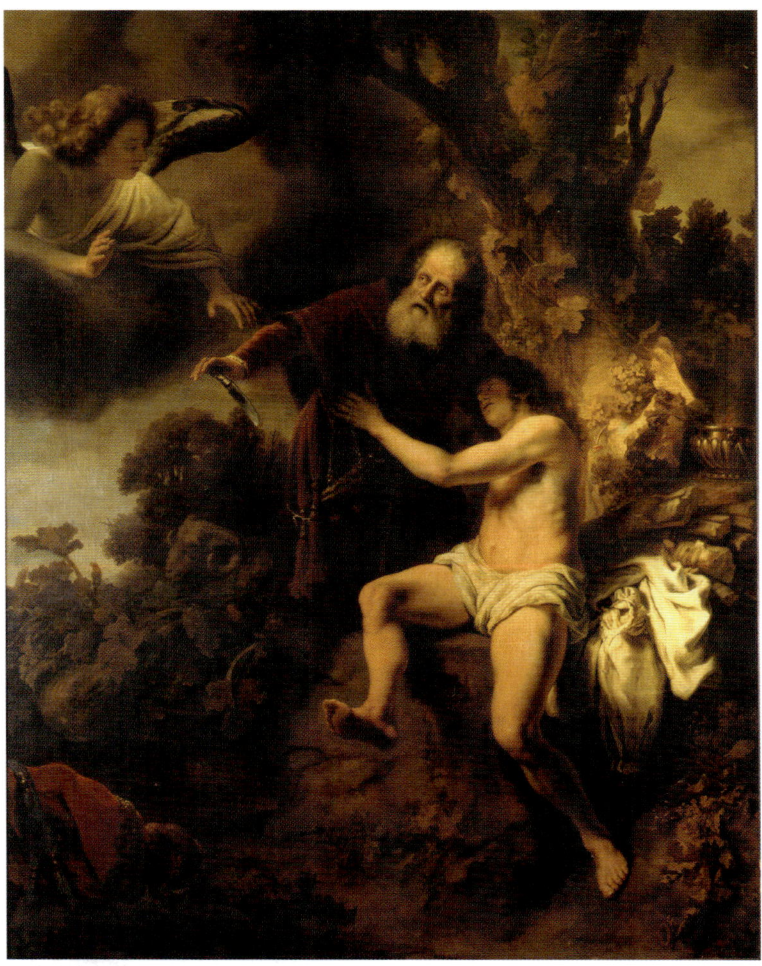

Flinck, like Bol, was around a decade younger than Rembrandt. He
was born on January 25, 1615, in Cleves, in the Dutch-German bor-
derlands. His father, a wealthy textile merchant, set his son to work
in a silk shop, but the boy spent too much time doodling and was dismissed. Then, according to the eighteenth-century chronicler Arnold

Houbraken, who wrote a massive biographical compendium of the Dutch school, a Mennonite teacher appeared in Cleves:

> To him, famous for his eloquence and modest life, Govert Flinck's parents went to listen. And they were extremely edified by his preaching. And hearing that he was also a prestigious painter, they changed their minds altogether, and decided right then and there to talk to this Lambert Jacobsz. And they instantly agreed that he would take their son to Leeuwarden, in his house and under his tutelage, and that he would teach him the Art. Since then this Flinck has often said that he has never in his life received such joyful news as when they told him this.

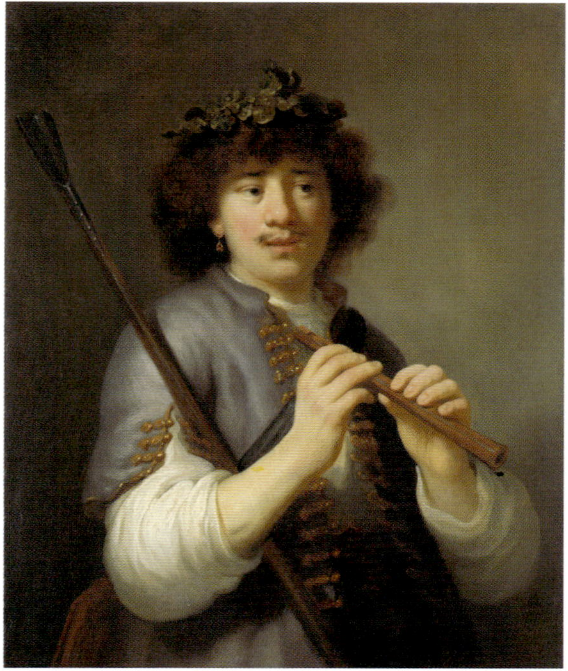

Govert Flinck's gracious portrait of the young Rembrandt elides the heavier emotions.

Flinck studied for a time in Leeuwarden, and once he and a companion "were so advanced that they could spread their wings," they went to Amsterdam.

"Here is the stock exchange and the money and the love of art," wrote the poet Thomas Asselijn. By the early seventeenth century, the once unprepossessing town of Amsterdam had expanded into perhaps the greatest trading center in the world, with a shipping network ranging from Japan to the Cape of Good Hope and from the Baltic to the Caribbean, a large industrial base, and a banking sector that had profited mightily from the Spanish destruction of Antwerp. Its inhabitants were rich and sophisticated, and the city had become an irresistible attraction for young artists from across northern Europe. One was already the most successful of all: "Rembrandt's art was generally appreciated as something wholly new, so artists had to master his manner of painting," Houbraken wrote.

After arriving in 1633, Flinck easily mastered his teacher's manner. A year after Rembrandt's *Sacrifice of Isaac*, a copy appeared with an enigmatic inscription: "Rembrandt. verandert. En overgeschildert. 1636." Rembrandt had "changed" and "painted over"—but the phrase does not say what he changed, or whose work he amended. Flinck's, we assume: the two worked in such proximity that his work was confused with Rembrandt's.

Flinck remained in Rembrandt's orbit until the end of the decade, when he went to work for the art dealer Hendrik van Uylenburgh. He did not go far: Uylenburgh's cousin, Saskia, was Rembrandt's wife. In 1636, the same year as the *Sacrifice of Isaac* upon which Rembrandt and Flinck collaborated, Flinck painted portraits of Rembrandt and Saskia in Arcadian garb, as shepherd and shepherdess. The portrait of Saskia was Flinck's earliest signed and dated work, and shows he had come into his own. This is less evident in the style, still basically Rembrandt's, than in the nature of the two pictures, which are companionable and decorative, rather than the kind of psychological portraiture in which Rembrandt specialized.

Perhaps the subject—happy young people at the height of their success—imposes this perspective. But another comparison suggests that something in Flinck's nature preferred to skirt the darkness of Rembrandt's emotions, even when painting unrelievedly dark scenes. Rembrandt's *Lamentation* of 1634 shows the dead Christ, removed from the Cross, mourned by his despondent mother. When Flinck painted it three years later, he modeled his version closely on Rembrandt's; but, in the words of the catalog of the 2018 show, "ecstasy and chaos were replaced with idealized calm and harmony."

Beginning in 1640, Flinck moved away from Rembrandt's style. In 1642, Rembrandt painted his *Night Watch* for the great hall of the harquebusiers, a building packed with monumental paintings exalting

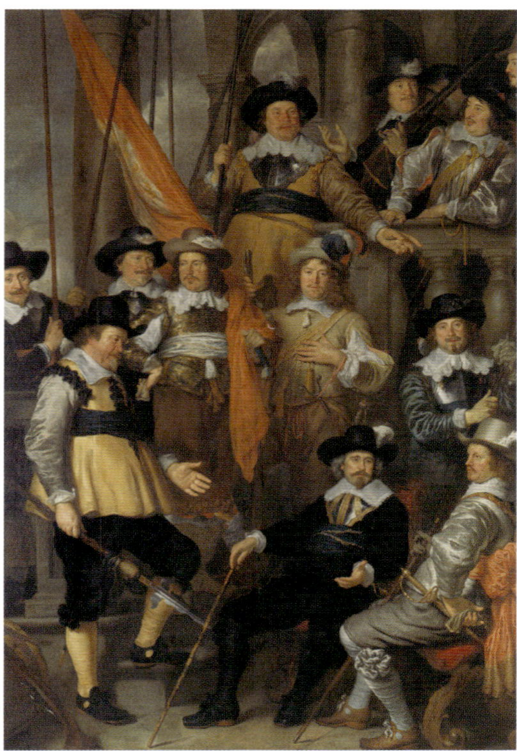

Flinck's large militia portrait was designed to be hung next to The Night Watch, *an intimidating challenge for any artist. It still stands nearby in the Rijksmuseum today.*

Amsterdam's virility and valor. Three years later, another company commissioned a similar work from Flinck: one that would hang directly beside *The Night Watch*. This would be an unnerving challenge for any artist. Rather than imitate Rembrandt's lighting, which pushes some figures forward and others back and gives the painting its churning dynamism, its appearance of movement and three dimensionality, Flinck lit his figures uniformly and posed them serenely. It was an attempt to stand in a light of his own.

Yet Flinck has always been forced to stand beside Rembrandt—and beside Ferdinand Bol. Born eighteen months after Flinck, the son of a surgeon-barber from Dordrecht, he, too, began training with Rembrandt around the age of twenty. He stayed in Rembrandt's studio twice as long as Flinck did—at least four years—and absorbed the master's style so much that his earliest-known portrait, of a tavern owner's widow named Elisabeth Bas, was long taken for a Rembrandt. Still today, staring out from above her formidable ruff at visitors to the Rijksmuseum, the shrewd dowager holds her own.

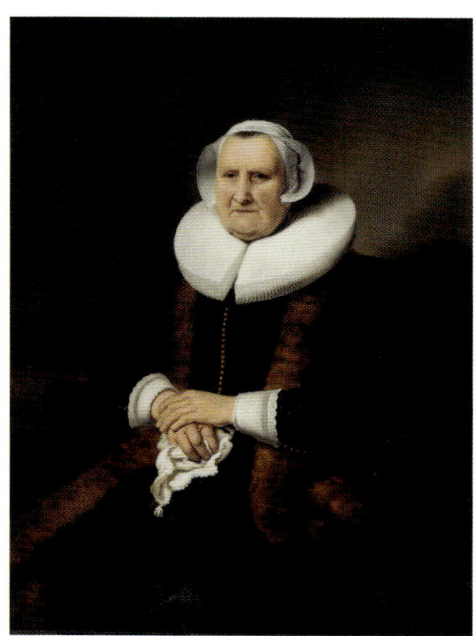

Bol's Elisabeth Bas *was long taken for a work by his teacher.*

The picture dates to 1642, only two years after Bol's first signed and dated painting, which shows Gideon saved by a provident angel. Like *Elisabeth Bas*, it could be easily mistaken for a Rembrandt. It combines the portentousness appropriate to a divine eruption with the calm of a painting designed to stimulate private piety. Like Rembrandt's *Sacrifice of Isaac*, it shows a man surprised by an angel, but it is as quiet and understated as that work is dramatic. Both *Elisabeth Bas* and *Gideon* show how well, and how quickly, Bol absorbed his teacher's lessons.

In 1641, when his father died, Bol seems to have inherited enough money to set out on his own. Yet even though he was no longer in the Rembrandt studio, Bol still found in Rembrandt a model for his art,

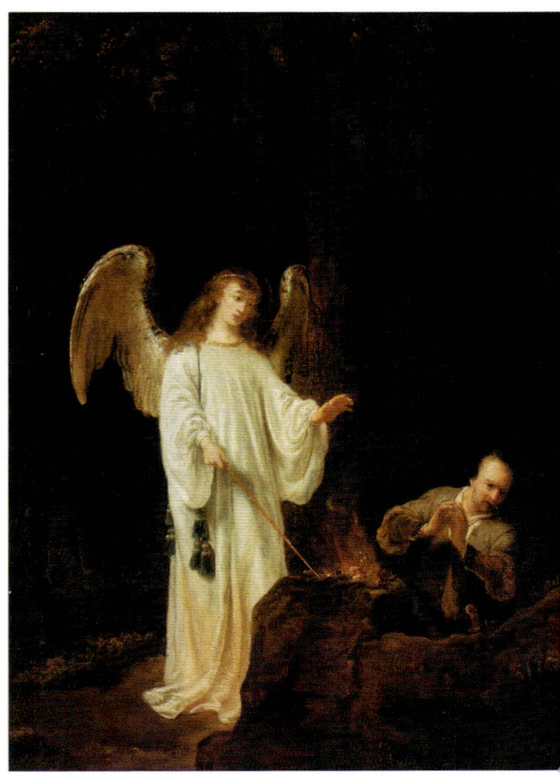

Bol's early Gideon *could easily be confused with a Rembrandt.*

and for his self-presentation as an artist. His earliest self-portrait, from 1646, is directly based on a work of Rembrandt's, itself based on Italian models that show the artist as a gentleman. It was a foretaste of Bol's stunning rise. In an era of fast fortunes, few would rise as far as Ferdinand Bol.

He came of age as the Dutch Republic was reaching the height of its opulence. In 1619, Batavia, today Jakarta, was founded; in 1624, New Amsterdam, later New York; in 1652, Kaapstad, now Cape Town. In 1648, a new City Hall was begun in Amsterdam. The greatest building constructed in Europe between the completion of St. Peter's in 1626 and the rebuilding of the Château de Versailles, from 1661—but neither royal nor ecclesiastical—it proclaimed the ambition of a city that, a century before, had been a middling town of thirty thousand. On its roof was a colossal Atlas.

And around this spectacular palace, the Dutch were settling down to enjoy their wealth. In 1648, the Eighty Years' War, the bloody global conflict by which the Dutch won their independence from Spain, ended at last. An unprecedented building boom followed, from the new canal belt in Amsterdam to the riverside mansions outside it. For artists who had previously only portrayed themselves as lords, here was a chance to behave as one, and Flinck and Bol seized it. By the mid-1640s—the decade of *The Night Watch*—both were creating large paintings for the new mansions and public buildings.

To succeed, an artist needed to please: by becoming personally palatable, and by producing work that prized elegance—brightened colors, muted emotions—over the assertion of individual expression. Bol and Flinck had an innate liking for the gracious and the decorative rather than for the dark and portentous: this is the distance between Bol's *Isaac* or Flinck's *Lamentation* and Rembrandt's versions of the same.

As Holland left the raw vigor of its war of resistance behind, Flinck and Bol moved with it. They excelled at filling estates and public spaces with the naked nymphs, virtuous rulers, and mythic warriors that the new times demanded, and these lavish pictures brought them wealth and fame. In 1669—the year Rembrandt died in a working-class quarter of Amsterdam—Bol married a great heiress and retired from art once and for all.

In November 1659, Flinck received a contract for the new City Hall. He would provide paintings to show Amsterdam as the new Rome, the enlightened ruler and greatest emporium of the world. By evoking illustrious episodes of national and classical history in twelve enormous works, he would exhort officials to incorruptibility. It was a marvelous triumph, the largest public commission ever awarded a Dutch painter. But it was not destined to be carried out. Two months later, Govert Flinck was dead, aged forty-five.

The historian Hilbert Lootsma has noted that Bol and Flinck have been "praised and scorned at practically the same moments and for practically the same reasons." Until around 1850, both ranked among the greatest Golden Age artists. By 1868, the critic Louis Viardot relegated them to "simple satellites, lost in the rays of the central luminary." This consensus took two hundred years to emerge. Shortly after Rembrandt's death, two chroniclers reproached him, as they had reproached Caravaggio, for "following nature too literally rather than seeking the idea of beauty behind appearance." Gerard de Lairesse, of whom Rembrandt painted one of his last portraits, preferred the polished finish that accorded with the courtly aspiration to good taste, *buon gusto*. In 1707—that damning quote again—he described a common objection to Rembrandt: that his clotted paint slithered down the canvas "like crap" (*gelyk drek*). It was an objection Lairesse shared with those critics.

Like the artists of the Italian Renaissance, Lairesse and his contemporaries believed that art should not reflect the gritty everyday world. It should resist it—elevate it. The quest for the beautiful ideal animated many of Rembrandt's contemporaries, who found him too determined to emphasize realities best softened. Samuel van Hoogstraten, another student, complained that he had not been taught to place models in graceful poses, but in "unpleasant and repulsive" ones. This critique found favor deep into the nineteenth century, when Rembrandt was definitely established as the greatest of Dutch masters. Jean Duchesne, in his *Musée de peinture et de sculpture* (1828–1834), preferred Flinck to Rembrandt precisely because his work was more finished, less "offensive," his figures "full of nature, and their features have a species of grandeur that Rembrandt reached when he wished to, but which he seldom sought."

A refined art required a refined artist—one who (come to think of it) looked a lot like Rembrandt in his self-portrait of 1640. Based on Raphael's portrait of Baldassare Castiglione, who a century before had codified the rules of genteel behavior in *The Book of the Courtier*, this portrait of the artist at the summit of his prosperity and fame served as a model for Flinck and Bol's own later self-portraits. Not a hint of crap sticks to its polished surface. Castiglione and Raphael would have appreciated this portrayal of an artist as fully equal to the princes of whom he was previously a servant, as Renaissance *gentiluomo*, as poised master.

Bol and Flinck attained this ideal, and sustained it until the end of their lives. Bol died in a grand canal-side mansion; Flinck was praised for behaving "the way an artist should: as a true gentleman with a cheerful demeanor." Rembrandt, in contrast, died in a rough neighborhood, the Jordaan, to which he fled after a series of heartbreaks. He would be accused of being a spendthrift and a know-it-all, of missing deadlines and consorting with whores; "ruled by avarice and pride," Houbraken wrote, "associating primarily with the lower classes." This was the note that was sounded throughout the eighteenth century.

The reversal of Rembrandt's critical fortune can be attributed to the French Revolution. Seeking an art that embraced the average man, the revolutionaries found it in another republic that had likewise overthrown a tyrannical monarch. Dutch art—and the French paid it the compliment of stealing a great deal of it—was not concerned merely with grace and beauty but democratically embraced the average citizen. Of course, to promote the idea that the Dutch painters hewed closely to the life of the man in the street, one had to hustle huge numbers of paintings into the attic.

The most energetic propagator of the view that Dutch art reflected everyday life was Théophile Thoré, mainly remembered today as the rediscoverer of Vermeer. He wrote under the pseudonym William Bürger—a choice of name that reveals much about his republican affiliations and his attachment to an idealized Holland—and turned the old reproach of Rembrandt on its head. Thoré-Bürger, as he came to be known, found the refinement prized by the classicists to be mincing and academic. As museums spread in the mid-nineteenth century, following the example of the Louvre, his formidable polemics triumphed. His work of 1858–1860, *Musées de la Hollande*, determined almost everything presented in the museums of his time, and his writings on Dutch art offered the theoretical underpinnings for many of the artistic insurgencies of the late nineteenth century in France.

The origins of this critical volte-face are contemporary with the Revolution in France. But they come from England, and show a radical change in the idea of what an artist is. The Romantics rebuked the idea of the artist as a gracious man who produced gracious art. Now what counted was fervor and truth. In 1800, Wordsworth defined poetry as "the spontaneous overflow of powerful emotions." Byron, whose own personality was in many ways similar to Rembrandt's, echoed him: "Poetry is the expression of *excited passion*." This passion, which Rembrandt and Byron shared, fit uneasily into drawing rooms, and could be expressed by the unlettered as well as by the courtly. The words

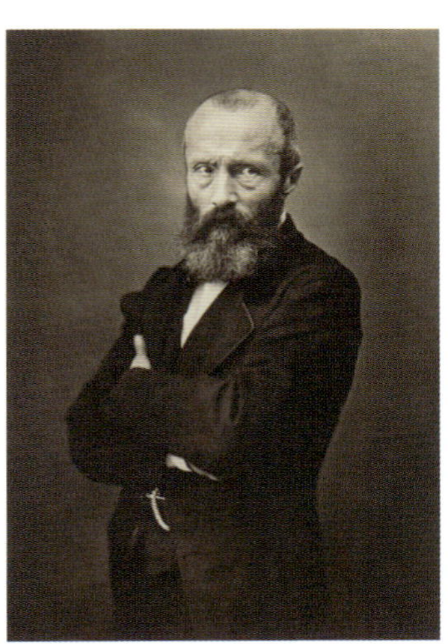

Famous as the rediscoverer of Vermeer, Théophile Thoré, who wrote under the pseudonym Willem Bürger, impressed a strong Romantic bias onto views of Dutch painting.

that described those who possessed it remitted to the supernatural—
genius, a tutelary deity; *duende*, a goblin; *diva*, a goddess—and if expression thus inspired could be imitated by academic devices, it was nothing
more than ornament without excited passion. One who followed fashion
rather than the divine afflatus—no matter how mechanically skilled—
was hardly worthy of the name of artist.

Since Aristotle, most writers on art had agreed that a balance must
be struck between natural forms and the ideal beauty behind them. This
was true of language; it was true of bodies, behavior, and emotions. But
the Romantics denounced fealty to an ideal that stifled genuine expression. Wordsworth strove to remain close to the tillers of the soil: "I have
chosen subjects from common life, and endeavored to bring my language
near to the real language of men." This language was sought as far from
the drawing rooms as possible: Lönnrot found it in the inaccessible forests of northern Finland; the Grimm Brothers in the byways of rural
Germany; the devotees of *fado* in the dockside taverns of Lisbon, and of
the flamenco among the gypsies of Seville.

This was a new idea, and one that contrasted with the neoclassical aesthetics that reigned through the first decades of the nineteenth
century. "The one way for us to become great," the eighteenth-century
German art historian Johann Winckelmann wrote, as if trying to turn
the clock back to the time before Caravaggio, "is to imitate the ancients."
This was as true for morals as it was for forms, as Bol and Flinck showed
in the City Hall. There, on opposite sides of a single room, they painted
Roman political paragons. Bol chose a symbol of austerity who spurned
wealth in favor of honorable poverty; Flinck, a consul "happy with a simple meal of turnips." Once the artist was no longer expected to educate
and elevate the common people with such allusions, these works came
to seem dated and pretentious.

But what was the point of art if self-expression were the only goal,
if the artist no longer needed the example of the classical canon, and
did not intend to instruct the public? If art, in Novalis's words, was
the "*visible* product of an ego," then anything that obscured that ego—
anything too conventional, too smooth and mannered, too calculated to

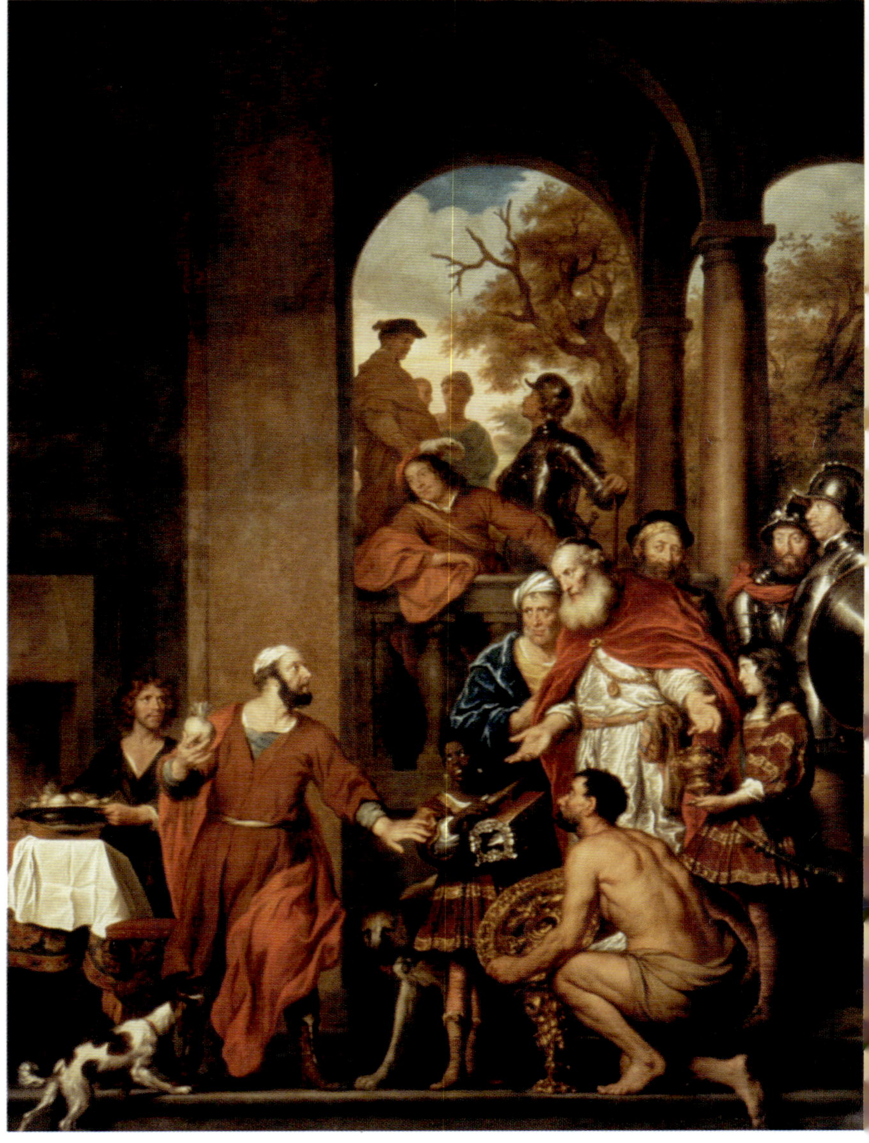

At the end of his life, Flinck was painting incorruptible antique heroes for Amsterdam's palatial city hall.

flatter a patron or uplift a gaping horde—was less even than craftsman-
ship. It was a tacky simulacrum. It affronted the imperative of authentic
individual expression.

Rembrandt seemed to be the exemplar of the Romantic artist. Unlike
Flinck and Bol, he had shown himself wrinkled, decaying, in an artist's
smock. The ego was titanic, but it was wholly visible: his works were
rough and bore all the vehement spontaneity of passion. If his difficult
personality, financial reversals, and amorous turbulence were once held
against him, they could now be interpreted as the signs of authenticity—
the opposite of the climbing courtiers that Flinck and Bol seemed to
be in contrast. As the cult of Rembrandt picked up steam, they were
attacked as worse, even, than mediocre. They became anti-artists.

This reading, of all three, was highly selective. In his self-portrait as
Castiglione—the very symbol of wily dissimulation, of muffling one's
personality in the service of personal advancement—Rembrandt showed
no excited passion, no spontaneous overflow: and here, too, is a reminder
that to underscore only the dark or earthy side of Rembrandt is to forget the man who, from early in his career, sought—and obtained—
stupendous worldly success. To recall only the shabbiness of his later
dwellings is to forget the man who was unanimously considered the
greatest master of Amsterdam almost from the moment he set foot
in the city.

As life's disappointments took their relentless toll, his art changed,
too; but his stubborn determination to maintain his individuality became
a reason to embrace him—almost, by the end of the nineteenth century,
to worship him. His canonization in the new Rijksmuseum in 1885 had
consequences for students who were now repackaged as acolytes and
judged according to their "fidelity."

Bol remained "faithful" longer, sparing himself some posthumous
spleen; Flinck, who departed from Rembrandt's style when he painted
the group portrait intended to hang beside *The Night Watch*, became
the creep with the thin, villainous moustache. By 1983, a prominent
art historian could call Flinck, the recipient of the largest public commission in the history of the Dutch Republic, "hardly a painter at all."

Both were reproached for the same talents that had earned them admiration. Their ability to adapt to changing fashions—fruit of a training that emphasized versatility—became "chameleon-like." What in their age had been refinement—decorative work that avoided the more disturbing, Rembrandtesque emotions—was now seen as an invertebrate lack of spirituality. What had been seen as success—the ability to attract a wide clientele—came to be sneered at as social climbing.

It is true that their work can get repetitive, especially when gathered in a huge exhibition like the one I saw in 2018. Walking into a new room, I played a game with myself, trying to guess which work was by which artist. I was usually wrong. Maybe I had unconsciously absorbed ideas about an assertive personal style—in my time, one was supposed to be constantly emphasizing one's own uniqueness—without realizing that there was another way. As a young writer, I was attracted to writers with unmistakable styles before realizing how dangerous such writers can be to someone starting out. The temptation to imitate them is so strong that a young person can reproduce the style without understanding what substance underlies that style, and makes it necessary. I remember how relieved I was to discover the studiously unadorned writings of V. S. Naipaul, and how long it took me to understand that in writing a lack of adornment is—as in painting or architecture—another form of adornment. It is often easier to reveal than to conceal.

And so, if Bol and Flinck do not always convey a powerful sense of their own personalities, they are highly adept at conveying those of others. Bol's portrait of an eight-year-old boy, Frederick Sluijsken, shows him in a heroic—larger than life-size—format. He grasps a wineglass as big as his head. Its unwieldiness symbolizes the weighty responsibilities he would inherit from his father, a wine merchant. Flinck's portrait of another eight-year-old, David Leeuw, is less monumental, but the contrast between the boy's shy face and his formal attire and pose shows that he, too, would be expected to grow up fast.

The Romantic definition of an artist as one able to render powerful emotions, express personal authenticity, and scorn worldly success was profoundly internalized by subsequent generations. But to seek in art "the shock of the new," especially at a remove of four centuries, is to forget that those values were utterly foreign to painters like Bol and Flinck. There is nothing wrong with preferring calm and harmony to ecstasy and chaos. When looking at Bol's *Sacrifice of Isaac* beside Rembrandt's, it is easy to see which is the greater painting. But—as we might not always want to watch King Lear on television every night, or hear Brünnhilde on the radio every morning—it is just as easy to imagine that the greater painting might also be the one we would rather not see every day.

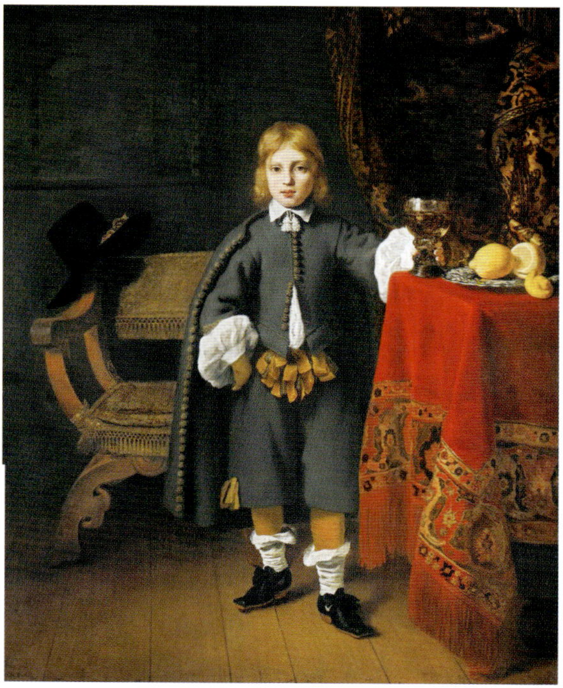

Bol's portrait of Frederick Sluijsken shows a boy on the verge of inheriting the responsibilities symbolized by the heavy wine glass.

4

CAREL FABRITIUS

The Thunderclap

WE KNOW NOTHING about the deaths of many great artists. We know that Rembrandt, for example, died on October 4, 1669, in a small rented house. We know something about the possessions of that house, since they were described by the notary who came the next day, but there is no deathbed scene, no recording of last words, no journal describing his adieux. We know much about his life, but nothing of his death.

And then there are the artists whose deaths we know better than their lives. Of the great Dutch painters, the most famous death is that of Carel Fabritius, who was traditionally seen as the link between Rembrandt, who taught him, and Vermeer, whom he taught. We have only glimpses of the life of Fabritius, "the greatest artist that Delft or Holland ever had." But we know exactly how he died, on October 12, 1654.

On that morning, eighty thousand pounds of gunpowder exploded in the middle of Delft. The "thunderclap," which destroyed a third of the city, could be heard as far away as the island of Texel, 150 kilometers away. Decades later, in his *Great Theater of Netherlands Painters and Paintresses* (1718–1721), the indefatigable artists' biographer and sometime painter Arnold Houbraken recalled the scene:

KAREL FABRITIUS, an excellent painter of perspectives, famous as the best of his day, was also a good portrait painter. Where he was born, and when, remain unclear, but it is known that he lived for many years at Delft, and also that his name is mentioned in the municipal records for the year 1654, the 12th of October, when the powder magazine exploded, along with his mother-in-law and brother and Simon Decker, sexton of the Oude Kerk, whose portrait he was painting at the time, as well as his disciple Matthias Spoors, all of whom were very pitifully crushed to death under the rubble after the collapse of the house. Fabritius alone still had some life in him when he and the others were pulled from the rubble under which they had lain for six or seven hours, and because the physicians' houses had mostly collapsed as well, he was taken to the hospital, where after a quarter of an hour his woeful soul departed from his horribly bruised body. And thus (he was only thirty years old), in the bright sun which was just rising, he unexpectedly succumbed.

WHEN AN ARTIST HAS a long life and a full career, the early works come to seem like an interesting prelude that builds to the mature masterpieces: this is the case of Rembrandt. More unusual are artists who die young—Raphael and Mozart come to mind—leaving such a large and complete body of work that it is hard to imagine what they could have left undone. We can enjoy their work without grieving their early deaths.

Such is not the case with Carel Fabritius. So few of Fabritius's works have survived that when we look at his paintings we cannot help wondering what has gone missing, and what was still to come. He is the unanswered question of Dutch art, the tie between Rembrandt, who was sixteen years older, and Vermeer, ten years Fabritius's junior. But the association with those two giants does not diminish him.

Artists like Lievens, Flinck, and Bol forever stand in the shadow of a greater name. In Fabritius's case, the name of the masters with which he

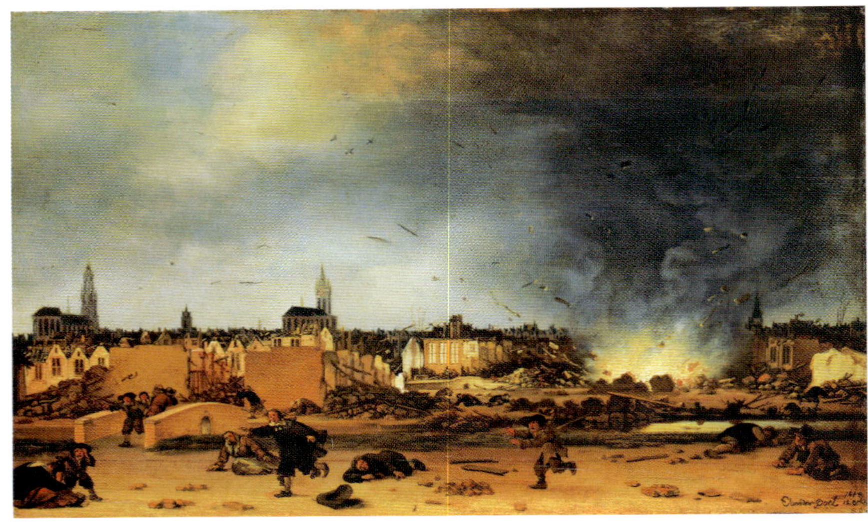

*The explosion that killed Fabritius was commemorated by the painter
Egbert van der Poel, who lost his own daughter in the disaster.*

was associated enhance his own. Historians are intrigued by Fabritius's
known works, which are vanishingly scarce and of the highest possible
quality. His unknown life and tragic death threw down a challenge to
the archaeologists who strove to excavate the Dutch masters.

He almost disappeared completely. There were scattered references
to him in the seventeenth and eighteenth centuries, and those were
vague ("Where he was born, and when, remain unclear") even in the
best-informed accounts, like Houbraken's. The suggestion of the link
between Rembrandt and Vermeer, who lived close by in Delft, was titil-
lating, but, in the absence of the work, it was mainly speculation.

Some of what we now recognize as Fabritius's paintings had been
given fake Rembrandt signatures. Others were confused with the work
of other masters. A few had slipped anonymously into private collections. In the nineteenth century, an important group portrait went up in
flames. When the British scholar Christopher Brown published a monograph on Fabritius in 1981, he could identify only eight paintings.

Some of those eight have since been demoted. Others have since been added. After more than a century and a half of looking, art historians today agree on about a dozen, give or take, with a handful of others considered strong possible contenders. Even if we take the most generous view possible, we would still have only half as many paintings by Fabritius as we do by Vermeer, whose works are a byword for rarity.

———

CAREL FABRITIUS WAS born in 1622 in a land nearing the height of its glory, renowned for its innovations in every field of science, religion, politics, art, and war. Freshly independent, it had the energy of a new country—it was often called the "New World of the Dutch Republic"—and Fabritius was born in its newest part, the Beemster Polder, north of Amsterdam.

In Dutch today, the word "polder"—a tract of reclaimed lowlands—connotes everything flat, small, and square about the Netherlands. In political parlance, "to polder" means to cobble together an unsatisfactory compromise. But in the seventeenth century, the polders were glamorous new frontiers. From 1606 to 1612, the Beemster was drained in an epic struggle that the poet Joost van den Vondel later celebrated in ringing verses:

Cream and butter came springing from her breast.
The fishy body became untainted, virginal flesh.

When Fabritius was born in the Beemster in 1622, a scant ten years after its creation, that idyll lay somewhere in the future. At that time, the Beemster was a muddy wilderness. Fabritius's parents had moved there six years earlier, at a time when pioneers were still laboring to bring the new land under cultivation. The church in Middenbeemster, one of the earliest purely Protestant churches built in the Netherlands, was not dedicated until a year and a half after Fabritius was born.

Carel Fabritius's father was the polder's first schoolmaster, and an amateur painter. Only one painting attributed to him survives, a large panel showing the Middenbeemster church. It is a bit more sophisticated than folk art, but a bit less sophisticated than something a man with professional training would have produced. Still, his interest in art must have been serious, since three of his sons became painters.

In 1641, at the age of nineteen, Carel married the sister of Middenbeemster's minister and decamped to Amsterdam. There, he became a pupil of Rembrandt, at the height of his reputation and grandeur, at the moment when he was creating *The Night Watch*. If that enormous painting is impressive now, we can only imagine the impact it must have made on a talented young man freshly arrived from a half-built provincial town.

The handful of pictures that survive from this period show the older master's influence. They have Rembrandt's shadowy colors, his love of costume and jewels, and—less visibly but more effectively—his attempt to locate the emotional center in biblical or classical stories. Rembrandt strove to banish the fussy allusions that restricted these pictures' appeal to the learned, and to create an image that would resonate with even an unlettered viewer.

Technical research shows that when Fabritius's "successor," Vermeer, revised his own works, it was often to remove exactly such allusions. Fabritius's early works show that this was not always easy. Look at one work from his training with Rembrandt, *Hera*. The subject, supposedly Homeric, has been identified as Hera's flight to the house of Oceanus and Thetis during the battle of the gods and giants.

It's a good guess—I guess. (I admit that I don't know this story.) What I see is a blond woman reclining by a waterside, stalked by some off-screen pursuer. In her fright, she has dropped a comb. The lady seems a bit too expensive to convey real terror: with the fine jars and elaborate parasol beside her, with the peacocks on the rock behind her, she could be any posh woman startled during an afternoon at the lakeside.

Is she Hera? She is tending to her hair, and drops her comb into the water—and this, to me, only enhances the improbability of the identification. Why is a woman fleeing a battle between the gods and the giants combing her golden locks by the waterside? The painting's most surprising element is the reflection in the water, which transforms a lovely young woman into a skeletal grotesque out of Munch or Ensor.

In *Hagar and the Angel*, a large, glowing canvas that Fabritius painted around the same time as the *Hera*, Hagar, Sarah's Egyptian slave, has fled into the desert. The elderly Sarah is angry that Hagar has become pregnant by her husband, Abraham. But when the angel of the lord orders her to return to her mistress, she obeys.

Hagar's trials were not over. She would have to flee a second time. When Sarah, ninety years old, finally becomes pregnant, she asks Abraham to banish Hagar and her son, Ishmael, named as the angel commanded: "God has hearkened." The poor woman and her son head back into the wilderness. There, the providential angel appears once more, saving her and Ishmael from death by thirst by pointing out a well.

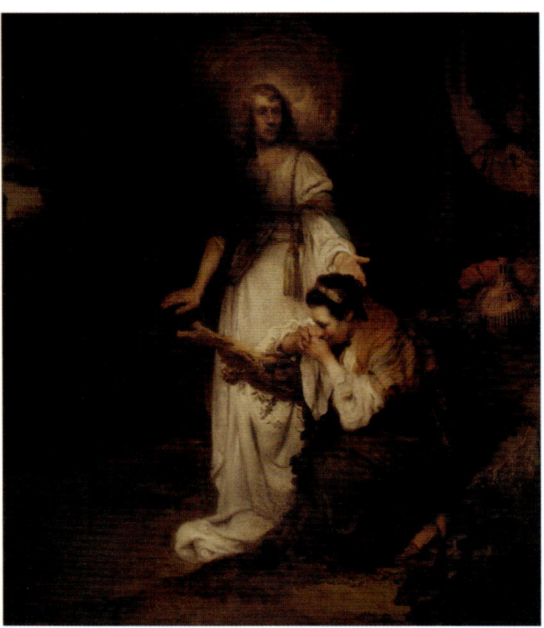

Hagar *reflects a lesson of Rembrandt's:*
in any story, find the most dramatic moment.

In a book on Fabritius published in 2005, a German curator named Gero Seelig writes that though Hagar's second flight is more commonly depicted, Fabritius seems to have portrayed Hagar's first flight, when she is pregnant. But, Seelig claims, Fabritius deliberately conflated the scenes by including an empty flask, alluding to the thirst that threatened her on the second flight, before the rescuing angel reappeared.

In an age when people knew biblical stories better—and stood in front of paintings longer—than most of us do now, this sleight of hand, if deliberate, may have struck some as clever or confounding. Nowadays, it seems wearying. And I admit that I would be crestfallen if I learned that this extremely arcane inside joke—a flask in a depiction of Hagar's first flight!—was really the artist's intention.

What makes this picture so memorable is the way the young Fabritius has followed his master's example of locating, in an old story, its most emotionally charged moment. These are the moments, which need no textual underpinning, that make these paintings resonate now. A desperate woman kneels in prayer, unaware of the angel behind her: Fabritius has stopped his hand an instant before it touches her hair.

FABRITIUS DID NOT linger in Amsterdam, or in Rembrandt's studio. By August 1643, when he was twenty-one, his life was already marked by tragedy: he had buried his wife and three children. For this reason or for some other, he was back in the Beemster a little more than a year after he left. For someone who had so recently breathed the air around the greatest artist of the day, it must have been a devastating reverse.

A few paintings can be dated to his return to the Beemster, where he remained for seven more years. We have a few portraits from this time, including the self-portrait that is now in Rotterdam. It is hard to know how he would have looked to people four hundred years ago, but when I look at this young man with curly hair falling to his shoulders and his shirt open to show his chest, I see a strength and sexuality at odds with his melancholy expression. Or am I reading Fabritius's expression

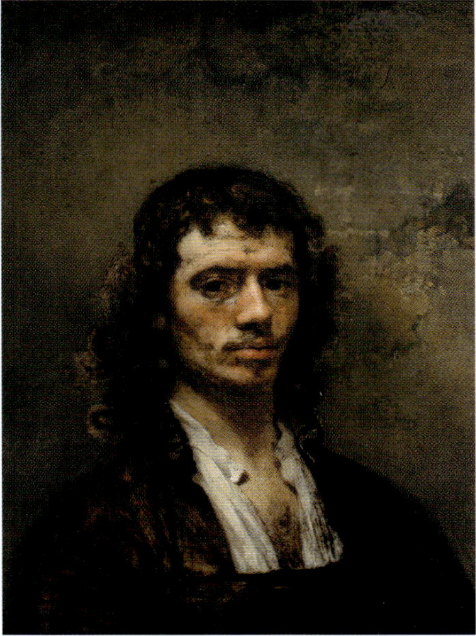

The handsome Fabritius, around twenty-three years old,
his life already touched by tragedy.

as melancholy because of what I know about his life? Maybe. But if you hang this work beside Rembrandt's self-portraits at the same age, you'll see a pride, verging on cockiness, that is missing here. Rembrandt was much older before he would show himself this vulnerable.

But because we know so little about Fabritius, we comb his works for clues to help us form a narrative. Some are quite arcane, like a little nail in a portrait painted during Fabritius's Beemster period. It shows the Amsterdam silk merchant Abraham de Potter, an investor in Beemster lands. Though De Potter, fifty-six-years old, seems to be hale, he would die not long after the portrait was completed.

The nail in question sticks out of the wall behind De Potter, between the name of the sitter and the signature of the artist, and is painted in the form of illusionism known as trompe l'œil. This means that the artist is

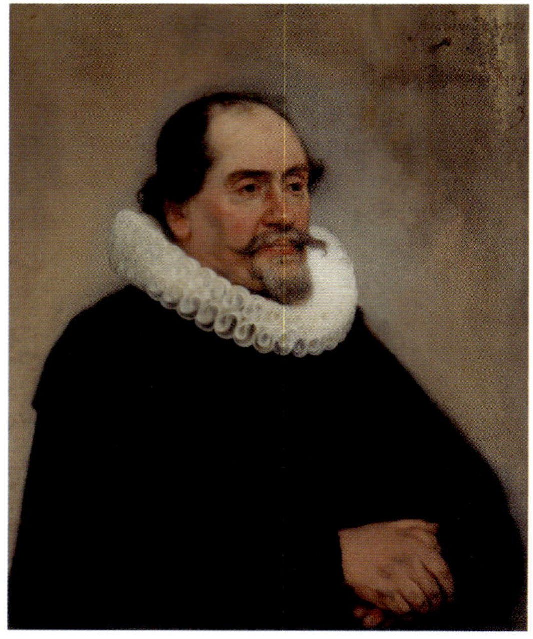

In the background of this portrait, a tiny nail in
trompe l'œil sticks out of the wall.

trying to trick you into thinking it's a real nail. The technique remits to
the original wonder of painting: the illusionist's ability to conjure three-
dimensional worlds onto two-dimensional scraps of cloth or wood.

THERE'S NO REASON trompe l'œil couldn't be used in a biblical or
historical subject. But such paintings are rare. This may be because the
virtuosity of the technique calls so much attention to itself that it can
overshadow any religious or moral message, making it more appropriate
to secular or nonliterary paintings. Instead, it placed the emphasis on
the painter, on his talent and technique, and as such could offer a way
forward for an artist wrestling with the problems we see Fabritius con-

fronting in the *Hera* or *Hagar*. History painters needed the traditional subjects furnished by religion and mythology; the genre painters were inventing new subjects. But a painter who focused only on illusion—only on the eye—could get rid of subjects entirely: a step Rembrandt never took. This would require a new kind of painter, and a new kind of eye.

When Fabritius was twenty-eight and newly remarried, he left the Beemster and moved to his new wife's hometown, Delft, a smallish city between Rotterdam and The Hague that, for a time, enjoyed a blossoming scientific and artistic reputation. In Delft, Fabritius began to produce the visual experiments, nearly all of which have disappeared, that gave him the reputation as "the greatest artist that Delft or Holland ever had."

This reputation seems largely to be founded on his mastery of "perspectives," elaborate constructions that depended on a skillful manipulation of the rules of perspective. Because so much of his work was destroyed, we can only guess what, exactly, he made. He is known to have painted perspective boxes and trompe l'œil wall paintings, which made a room look much larger than it was. He may also have created anamorphoses, illegible blobs that, when seen from a particular viewpoint, magically resolve into images.

Wooden perspective boxes became a Dutch specialty. These contained a distorted image that is spread over the four walls of the box, as well as its floor and ceiling. Viewed through a peephole placed at a strategic point, the bizarre pattern of rhomboids and freaky furniture comes together into a three-dimensional space, usually a room. These boxes are still as fun—not to mention as impressive—as they must have been when they were made.

Like so much modern art, perspective boxes change the focus from *what* we see to *how* we see it, and emphasize that the how is often more interesting than the what. It doesn't really matter what these perspective boxes show, since their purpose is to call attention to how an artist can slice up a view into unrecognizable pieces and shapes—and then leave it to our own eyes and brains to puzzle that view back together.

Only six survive. None are by Fabritius. The only perspective we have by him, *A View of Delft*, is no longer in its original box. It is a rectangular canvas no bigger than two postcards placed end to end, showing a townscape with a man seated at a table. On the table are a lute and a viola da gamba. The distorted perspective and the man's inscrutable expression give the painting an unsettling and enigmatic quality.

For years, art historians clipped out reproductions of this painting and pasted it onto different supports, trying to figure out how it was originally meant to be viewed. The answer seems to be that it was attached to a semicircular support at the back of a small triangular box. A peephole placed at the point of the triangle—opposite the center of the curved picture—would correct the distortions in the perspective.

Fabritius's *View of Delft* is not to be confused with Vermeer's *View of Delft*. But nowhere is the connection with Fabritius's younger neighbor clearer than here. The colors remind us of Vermeer, and so do the musical instruments—and so does the question of what the man is doing. As

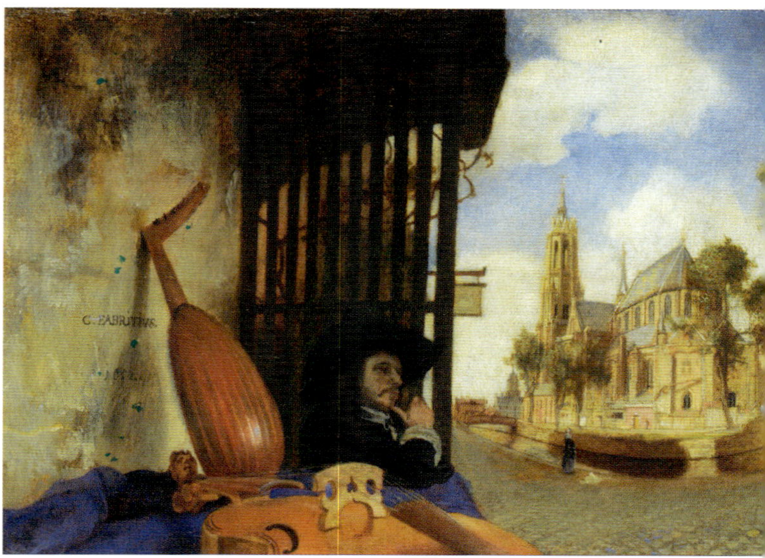

in many of Vermeer's works, the mood is enigmatic. When this painting was hidden at the back of a box, it would have been even more so.

Two years later, Fabritius conjured a more subtly mysterious world. At first glance, *The Sentry* seems straightforward. A soldier snoozes in front of a city gate, his dog more vigilant than he. ("In genre scenes there is always just enough activity to distract us from noticing how little is really going on."—Alois Riegl) But the peacefulness of *The Sentry* serves to distract us from a scene heaving with activity.

The longer you look at the picture, the fewer of its elements make sense. Everything in the painting is blocked, cut off, impossible. The staircase leads from nowhere to nowhere; the large central column supports nothing. As Gero Seelig points out, that means that the column is the remnant of some older building: but if the column were already there, why build a gateway that would be blocked?

Look at the wall on the far side of the gateway arch. It has been

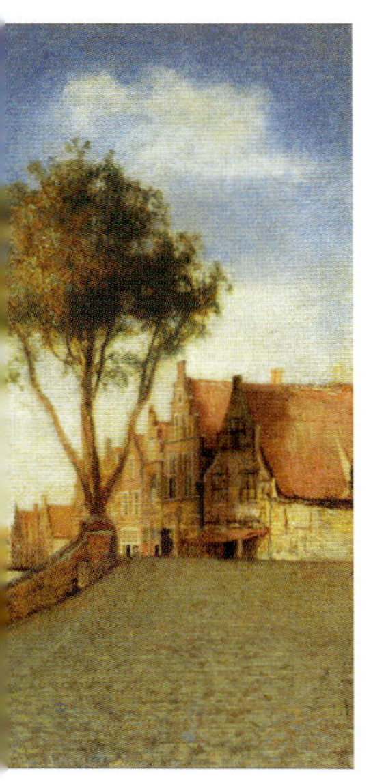

Nowhere in Fabritius's work do we feel the proximity of Vermeer as much as in this small and mysterious painting.

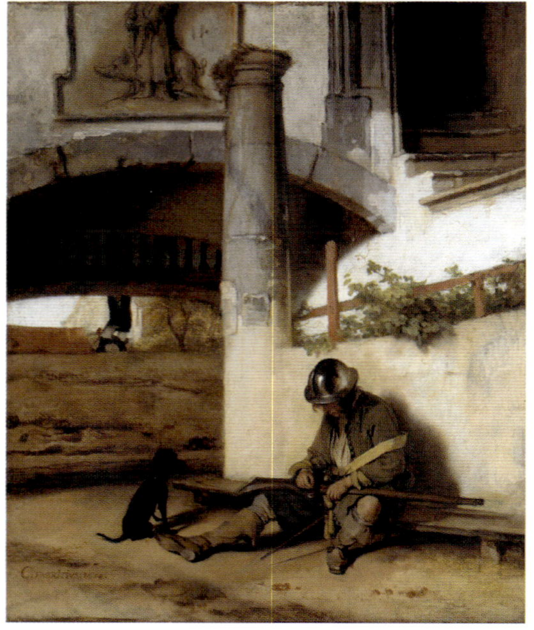

A quiet afternoon—or a world about to collapse?

built almost directly behind the gateway—far too close to allow room for a street. The sentry is sleeping on a bench that has a different spatial orientation on either side of the figure, Selig writes, and "the shadows of the dog and the man seem to be cast in different directions, while the powerful column casts no shadow at all on either the wall or the archway."

The picture seems almost like a cubist collage, made of glimpses of different objects. Or like one wall of a perspective box whose peephole is missing: you can't quite figure out how or where you're supposed to stand, or what you're supposed to be looking at. Most Dutch visual experiments have an answer, a correct viewpoint. This one doesn't. One feels that there's a kind of perversity to the way Fabritius has proffered a mystery—only to withhold the key.

The more you look at this picture, the more unsettling it becomes. The gateway is supported by two arches, one on either side. You get a little queasy when you realize that the front arch, the one closer to us and to the sleeping sentry, is skewed, and that its two halves have different radii. Such an arch would be dangerously unstable. Rather than a restful afternoon, *The Sentry* shows a world that is just about to collapse.

CREATED IN 1654, the last year of Fabritius's life, *The Goldfinch* has spawned obsessions. It was one of the two paintings from which one former owner, Théophile Thoré-Bürger, who rediscovered Fabritius as well as Vermeer, would never be parted. He died in 1869, and when his collection was sold in 1892, the catalog noted: "The charming bird sang for him; but one knows the sad path of life; one knows how everything comes to an end."

There is something fated about *The Goldfinch*, something that makes it like a votive offering, and that is perhaps connected to its creator's early death. In 2013, Donna Tartt published a novel, *The Goldfinch*, about a boy who makes off with the painting after his mother is killed in a terrorist attack on a museum. Maybe, for Tartt's purposes, any famous painting would have done; but the picture she chose to suggest the workings of fate was spookily apt.

A description of it will always fall short. It is a small, quickly painted panel. It shows a brown and yellow bird, roughly life-size, perched atop his feeding box. Nothing about it should make it unforgettable—but it is unforgettable. And when you see *The Goldfinch* you are immediately aware of being in the presence of that ineffable quality that the Greeks called *charisma*, from whose root we derive our word "grace."

This quality is different from beauty. We have all known beautiful people—great hair, symmetrical faces, worked-out bodies—who have no charisma. Maybe they're mean; maybe they're dumb; maybe they're boring. Whatever the reason, a brief conversation is enough to make any interest wilt. And we have known people whose appeal will never come through in a photograph but who are irresistible in real life.

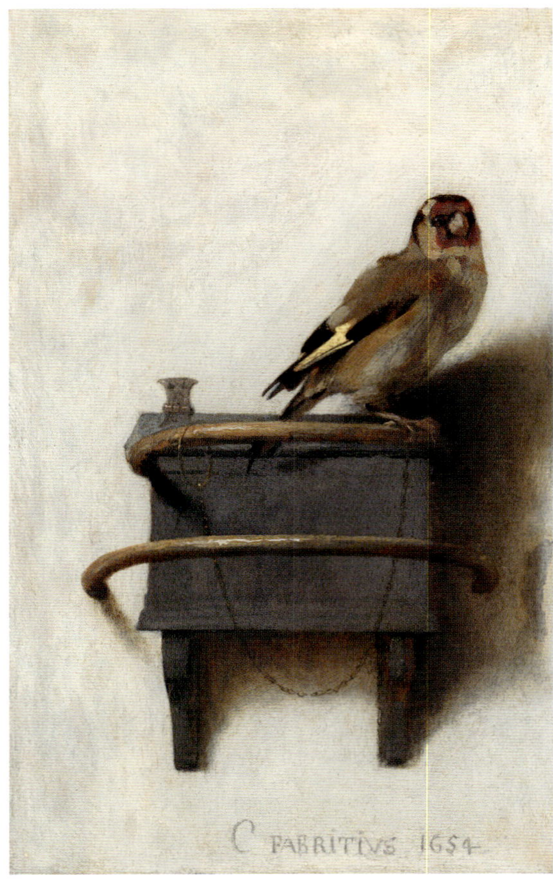

I have written two biographies of famously beautiful women, Clarice Lispector and Susan Sontag, and was always fascinated by the ways their beauty was written about, and spoken of by the people I interviewed. Maybe it's the word, "beautiful," that has been worn down by overuse, but when I looked at them—and when you write a biography you look at them for years on end—I saw something that wasn't quite beauty.

Both were intensely aware of what it meant to be a beautiful woman, or a woman perceived as beautiful. Both wrote about how beauty could make or break—make *and* break—a woman's life. Both knew that, no matter how much we might pretend it doesn't matter what we look like, there was nothing superficial about hair and clothes and makeup—the whole delicate edifice of personal appearance.

Yet in the supposedly serious world I inhabited, there was a reluctance to talk about beauty. It was fine for materialistic women—or maybe your gay hairdresser—to care about what they looked like. But I often met the suggestion that it was not quite appropriate to discuss it in connection with towering minds like those of my subjects: never mind that they themselves, and indeed nearly all great women writers, knew how profound the question was.

I knew that it was a lie that beauty was superficial. And just as I had learned, in biographical research, to pay careful attention to lies—because everybody lies about something different, and because lies always point to some deeper truth—I began to scrutinize my subjects, and realized that neither was conventionally beautiful: often enough, in pictures, they both looked awkward and uncomfortable. Yet people perceived them as beautiful.

In reading about Sontag, I came across an old question. Was the mind produced by the body, or was the body (as Freud came to believe) produced by the mind? To ask the question in another way: When we see a beautiful body, do we see a certain arrangement of features, or do we see the mind, the soul, that animates those features? Beauty was what people noticed in the women I wrote about. But were they just using an overused word and noticing some mental or spiritual quality instead?

This was the quality of charisma. A great actress or model—and many of the greatest have not quite been beautiful—could infuse this soul-power into her photographs, or onto the screen. And a great artist could infuse it into his works: technical accomplishment, no matter how refined, pales beside this quality. We have all come across works that, despite their stupendous sophistication, leave us cold.

Charisma—I didn't yet give it that name—was something I first started observing at the Mauritshuis, when I noticed how people reacted to *The Goldfinch*. Tourists on a tight schedule, who would glance distractedly at a Potter or a Steen and size up a Rembrandt with a quick flick of the eyes, would grind to a halt before Fabritius's bird—as if this little animal were reaching out of his frame and grabbing them. It emitted a force that was as real as the net of gravity, but I couldn't say what it was. When you stopped and looked at it, all you saw was a small painting of a small bird—skillfully painted, of course, but so is every other picture in the Mauritshuis. Study it, read about it, and it will inevitably be diminished.

And then sit on the bench in the gallery. Spend a few minutes watching the visitors filing past. See if a single one fails to halt in front of *The Goldfinch*. They are all feeling something, sensing something, that they wouldn't be able to define. What else could it be but the artist's charisma? They are feeling the greatness of the soul who painted this fragile bird—this bird that almost surely outlived him.

5

JOHANNES VERMEER

The Fingerprint Beneath the Frame

THE MAN WHO writes this sentence is forty-five years old. He is sitting in the same room to which he came half a lifetime ago, when he was a gawky boy trying to balance a taste for adventure with a strong streak of monasticism. This is the room he chose to begin his adult life. It was a yellow rectangle that almost lacked furniture. It had a big old desk, but it didn't even have a bed, and the walls were piled high with moving boxes.

When he came here, he was still young enough that anything could happen to him. This was sometimes exciting and sometimes terrifying. He wanted to be a writer, an artist, and though he had no idea how to go about this, he felt that this was the right room to start. It was on what he had learned to call the second floor. (It was the third where he came from.) And it was the right room, he thought, because of the windows.

There were two. They faced the street. Each about as tall as he was, six feet plus, and a bit less than half that wide. From outside, he saw them flanked with heavy wooden shutters that were never shut in practice. They were decorative, painted in triangles of the city's emblematic red and white, and covered the bottom half of the windows. A thick wooden cross separated the four windowpanes into oblong rectangles.

The lower two panes were set in little doors, and opened toward the inside. The top two panes, which could not be opened, were covered with a lead latticework in a pattern of squares around a circle. The design was handsome, classic, typical of an old house like this one, which dated to the Golden Age. But what the young man liked about them was that they were the very same windows you could see in the paintings of Vermeer.

The association pleased him. Those windows, and the light that came through them, were an inspiration. They suggested that this was a place where great things could be achieved; and when it felt pretentious or ridiculous to try to measure up to Vermeer, he reflected that he'd rather aim for something more than mediocrity. There was no reason to take a chance on himself unless it was in order to try to do something great.

The association also intimidated him. He was always falling short. The light that poured in through those windows fell on rejection after rejection, bill after terrifying bill, one aborted project after the next. He felt the time passing; and when, to clear his mind, he would go to the Mauritshuis and look at Rembrandt's *Anatomy Lesson* or Vermeer's *Diana*, he would realize that both were painted by men younger than he.

Now, at forty-five, he's fought battles, and won enough to be able to live a contented middle age. He's written some things he's proud of; and though he continues to fall short in more ways than he cares to recall, he knows that one of the advantages of middle age is that this matters less than it did when he was young. Mostly, he hopes for more time. He is already two years older than Vermeer was when he died.

———

BY FORTY-THREE, Vermeer's life and labors were over. He had fathered fifteen children, of whom eleven survived childhood; ten lived at home when he died. It was a lot of kids; and though he was reputed for his slow and deliberate methods, he painted a lot of paintings, of which we have around thirty-five. From *Diana*, his earliest work, to *A Lady Seated at a Virginal*, his last, his career spanned no more than a score of years.

He painted around three paintings a year. This doesn't sound like a lot, until you remember that these were three Vermeers a year, and that the name Vermeer has come to symbolize an otherworldly perfection, and that, beside it, even the most accomplished works of even his most accomplished contemporaries seem to have been daubed with fat, groping fingers. Amid the mayhem of all those kids—and three a year is a lot.

So many of the pictures are so perfect that I was shocked by—and then became morbidly fixated on—a handful of weird Vermeers. Some were just plain ugly, and though the idea of an ugly Vermeer sounded as absurd as an ugly piece by Mozart, there they were: those two paintings in the National Gallery in London, for example, which had every element of the great Vermeers—except the magic.

There was a painting in Braunschweig, too, *The Girl with a Wine Glass*. Once again, it had everything you expected: the window, the richly laden table, the swathes of beautiful textiles, the pretty young woman—but wearing a goofy grin that shatters the contemplative mood, the magical stillness, that is the hallmark of the great Vermeers. Without that enchanted name, the picture would be cute. With it, it's repulsive.

Others just seemed wrong. The histrionic *Allegory of the Catholic Faith* in the Met is so heavily encrusted with symbolism—a bitten apple, a crushed snake—that it might have been painted for Torquemada's private chapel. Here, again, the name Vermeer makes it seem worse than it would be if it were by another artist. We like our Vermeers subtle, indirect. We like them to whisper—and not, like this one, to shout.

My interest in these paintings did not make me despise their maker. To the contrary, they brought me closer, showing me, behind the perennial perfection of the great works, a man struggling, like any other: dare I say, like me. They showed that failures were not the end but the beginning. To see a mind seeking made the eventual finding all the more satisfying. They were, in short, an encouragement to someone starting out.

Without the failures, it would have been hard for me to relate to Vermeer. His personality was so mysterious, his works so few, that it was hard to have any feeling about him beyond awe. He had edited so much out of those paintings, after all. Everything in them was so clean, bright, perfectly composed, with nary a screaming urchin or a dirty dish. There were none of the wrinkles and grub of Rembrandt—of life.

His own life was hardly picturesque. He was born in Delft in 1632.

The city was around a dozen streets wide, maybe five or six broad; it took about thirty minutes to walk its perimeter. An important percentage of its land was given to agriculture. Its claim to fame was the splendid tomb of William of Orange, the "Father of the Fatherland" and the greatest hero of the war against Spain, who was assassinated there in 1582. Still today you can see the holes the bullets left in the wall behind him.

Little is known about Vermeer's early years. He was born at an inn on the Voldersgracht called the Flying Fox. His family were Protestant. He had one sister, Gertruy, twelve years older. When he was nine, his father bought another inn, called Mechelen, near Delft's main square. There, he grew up around what passed for the art world: besides innkeeping, his father also sold pictures. And Gertruy married a frame maker.

From baptism in October 1632 to betrothal in April 1653—twenty-one years, nearly half of his life—not a shred of documentation has been unearthed. With marriage, he steps from umbra into penumbra. His fian-cée, Catharina Bolnes, was Catholic. This required a certain finesse: her mother, Maria Thins, a central figure in his later life, refused to authorize publication of the banns, but neither did she block them.

A record survives of the conversation that produced this diplomatic solution. On the evening of April 4, Leonaert Bramer, an older Delft painter, paid a visit to Maria Thins, together with a captain who had served in Dutch Brazil. The documentation surrounding the wedding places some important figures into relation with Vermeer: Bramer and then, two days after the marriage, no one less than Gerard ter Borch.

Was Ter Borch, fifteen years older, there for the wedding? His sig-nature is found alongside Vermeer's on some unrelated paperwork. It seems a bit too coincidental that Ter Borch, who lived in faraway Zwolle, happened to be in Delft, and happened to have signed this document, two days after the wedding of Vermeer, whose paintings echo his in so many important ways: of course they knew each other.

But how? We know nothing about where, or by whom, Vermeer was educated. Names—Bramer, Ter Borch—are mentioned, only to be dismissed. There is a tempting connection, via the family of Maria

Thins, to Abraham Bloemaert of Utrecht; Maria owned at least one picture by a leading Caravaggist painter from Utrecht. And a picture by Vermeer from 1656, three years after his marriage, shows the influence of this painting.

This is the Dresden *Procuress*. To one accustomed to the small scale of Vermeer's works, its relative hugeness jumps out. It shows four people squeezed into the space between a wall and a balustrade sumptuously decked with an oriental carpet. A young swell hands a gold coin to a young woman dressed in bright yellow. This transaction occurs under the gaze of an older woman in black—the brothel keeper.

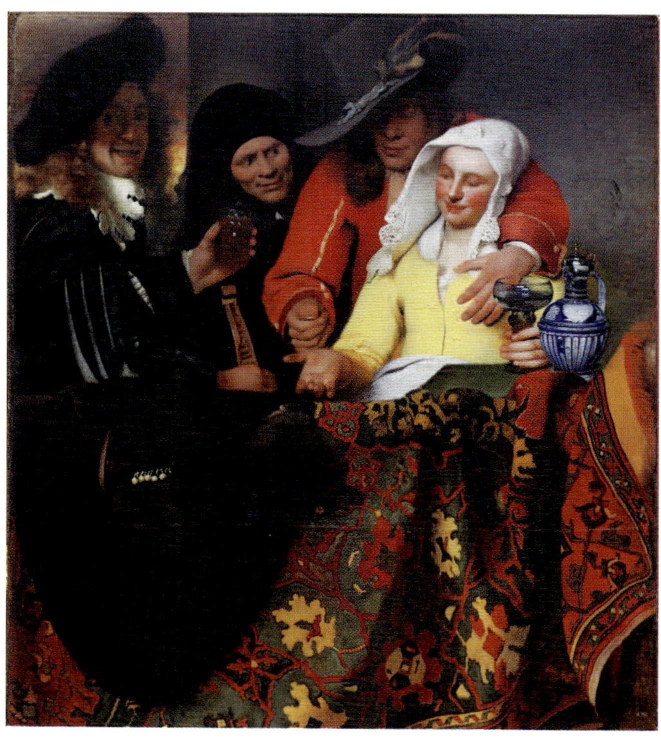

The early Procuress: *soon the wall will be pushed back, the ceiling raised, and the light let in from a window at left.*

The brothel theme was popular in Dutch art, and had been treated in the painting Maria Thins owned. That painting, by the Utrechter Dirck van Baburen—it may be the one now in Boston, though there is at least one other copy known—shows the more direct influence of Caravaggio; Van Baburen reached Rome shortly after Caravaggio's death, and his *Procuress* appears in the background of two of Vermeer's paintings.

Van Baburen's painting is flatter than Vermeer's, and lacks its enamel-like colors. Its faces are sharply delineated, whereas Vermeer's already have that misty sfumato that was a specialty of Leonardo's. But the most uncanny thing about the painting is how alive the people look. Unlike painted faces that have been dated by costume and hair and pose and expression, these people look as real as people in photographs.

On the left, there's a fourth figure. Tradition has it that this young man, whose face is half covered in shadow, is Johannes Vermeer himself. This is possible. But we have no idea what Vermeer looked like, and so, like so much else about him, we can only say that this person is the right age—twenty-four—and occupies a position, on the left side, winking at the audience, in which artists often placed themselves, as commentators.

It's a pleasure to come across *The Procuress*, big and bursting with color, on a wall in dreary Dresden. It's intriguing to speculate whether that is the face of the great Vermeer, and whether someone who looked like that—barely out of adolescence—could really have painted something this beautiful. You have to fill in a lot. As always with Vermeer, people have. Speculation is what we have; nothing else.

———

AT A CLIMACTIC MOMENT of Clarice Lispector's *The Apple in the Dark*, the protagonist decides to write something, only to discover how hard this is. He hesitates, dumbstruck. It shouldn't be so difficult, he tells himself: "For he had an experience, he had a pencil and a piece of paper, he had the intention and the desire—nobody had ever had more than that. Yet it was the most helpless act he had ever performed."

I felt the same helplessness when I looked at Vermeer's paintings. I had the same pencil, so to speak, the same piece of paper. I had the same window, the same room. And once the furniture had been moved in, I even had a bookcase with old blue-and-white Delft and Chinese porcelain. The light coming through the windows would strike it, just so, every afternoon: the same porcelain that turns up in the works of Vermeer.

And when I looked at his paintings, I saw the paucity of their means. This was a surprise. In writing about Vermeer, someone will invariably point out how luxurious his works were, saying that he used the expensive blue pigment called ultramarine, and mentioning how slowly he painted, and how rare his surviving works are, and how he took his subjects almost exclusively from the upper reaches of society.

But if you take a closer look, you see how little, really, he used. He sets his scenes in a corner of a room, lit by that window. At the table, there's a girl, and a wine jug. There's a carpet, a curtain, or both. He seems to have owned a couple of maps, a few paintings: these turn up, too. There is a yellow jacket, surely the same mentioned in a post-mortem inventory of his possessions. There's a Chinese bowl and a Spanish chair.

The subject matter isn't very original, either. Most of it can be traced to the Utrecht Caravaggists or to painters he knew personally: to the older Ter Borch, whose scenes of women in luxurious interiors pre-dated his; to Pieter de Hooch, his neighbor in Delft; or, most enigmatically, to Carel Fabritius, ten years older, who was killed when Vermeer was just twenty-two. Vermeer owned works by Fabritius. But we don't know which ones.

You can see the traces of the explosion that killed Fabritius in Vermeer's *The Little Street*, which shows two houses separated by a double alleyway. Painted just four years after the calamity of 1654, the work features a house belonging to Vermeer's aunt, located just outside the zone destroyed by the "thunderclap." The façade bears visible cracks. Some of the brickwork looks as if it's only recently been touched up.

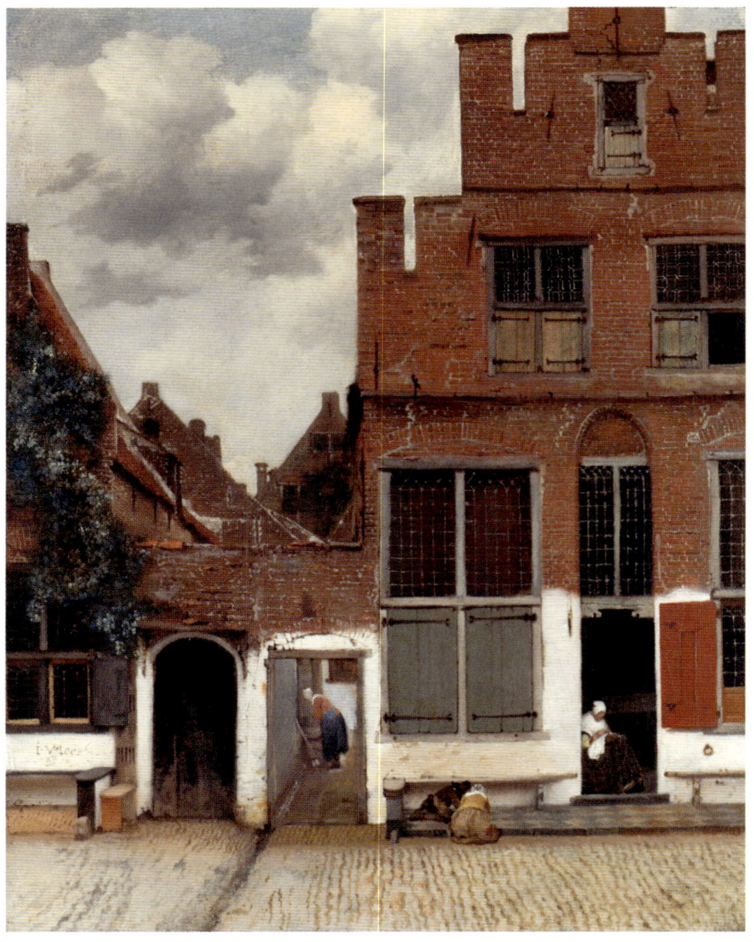

In the freshly patched-up brickwork, a sign of the explosion that killed Fabritius.

NEITHER IS VERMEER a storyteller. The Dutch, in general, weren't. It is surprisingly rare to find depictions of heroic events, such as the episodes of the Eighty Years' War, which in Italy or Spain would have inspired huge canvases; and neither were the Dutch much given to sacred or mythological episodes. Lacking royal or ecclesiastical patronage, they turned to landscapes, portraits, still-lifes, and genre scenes.

Perhaps never before in the history of art had such a great artist devoted himself to such commonplace subjects. It is impossible to imagine Raphael painting a kitchen maid, or Titian a girl reading a letter. But in Vermeer's mostly small paintings, what might be derided as nugatory is raised to the highest art. Not because of what he saw but because of how he saw it, he became the hero of the nonheroic subject.

The question of how he saw is fraught. For a long time, it was thought that he used a camera obscura, a projecting device, though that theory, which had a kind of occult glamour to it, has been mostly discredited. But it is true that the way he saw seems to demand some kind of explanation. The paintings are so perfect that they might seem easier to relate to if we were to learn that the painter has somehow cheated—like a singer caught lip-synching.

Vermeer was born in the same month that Antoni van Leeuwenhoek, who would become perhaps the greatest scientist of his time, was also born in Delft. A pioneer of the microscope, the father of microbiology, Leeuwenhoek's discoveries in the world invisible to the naked eye were often compared to the Dutch discoveries in faraway lands, and he became one of the most prestigious symbols of the nation's cultural achievement.

He was the first to observe bacteria, protozoa, and spermatozoa—the last, he emphasized, acquired "without sinfully defiling myself"—and even the titles of his letters to the Royal Society in London make fascinating reading: *Concerning the causes of the different tastes of Waters and edge of Razors*, for example, or: *concerning the Worms in Sheeps Livers, Gnats, and Animalcula in the Excrements of Frogs.*

A month after the birth of Vermeer and Leeuwenhoek, Baruch Spinoza—who would equal, in philosophy, their achievements in art and science—was born in Amsterdam. Even amid the surplus of talent that marked the Golden Age, this was a rare constellation, and they shared an interest in optics: Spinoza created lenses and microscopes. Inhaling glass dust reputedly killed him, age forty-four, a year after Vermeer.

How exactly Vermeer studied or observed light is not known. But in a small town we can take as given that he knew Delft's other resident genius. We have, in fact, two pictures of scientists, *The Astronomer* and *The Geographer*, Vermeer's only paintings of solitary men. They are the same size, and show the same man in the same room. Is it Leeuwenhoek himself? We can't be sure. But he's the right age, in his late thirties.

What we can be sure about is how strangely, how abnormally, Vermeer saw. His way of seeing is already there in his first paintings:

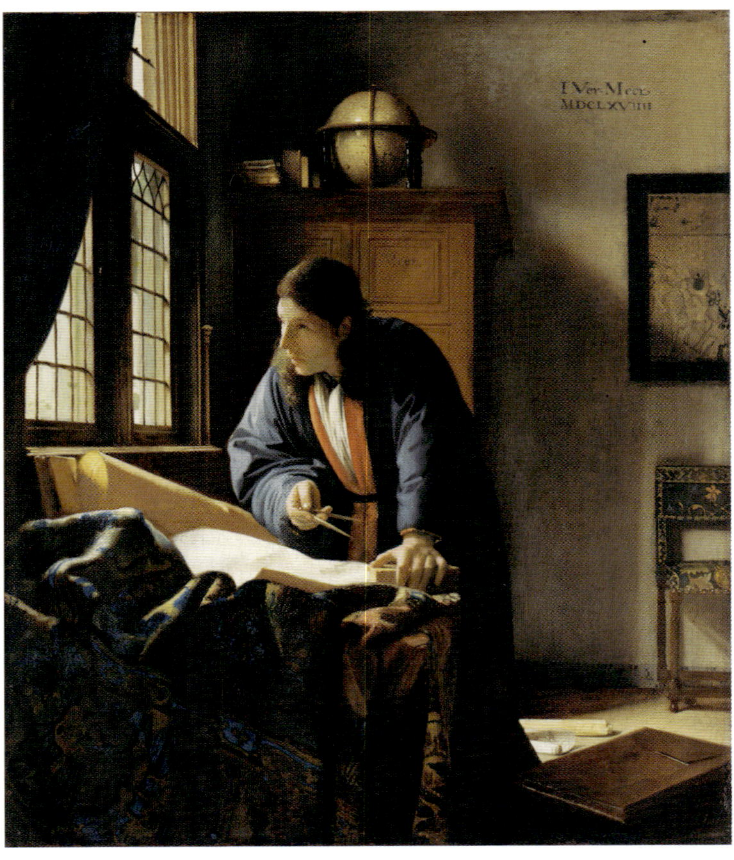

Could this geographer, whom Vermeer also painted as an astronomer,
be his neighbor Antoni van Leeuwenhoek?

the soft-focus fuzziness, the dotted highlights, the way the figures seem to melt into each other, and into the background: the sense that the objects are alive, as in a great still-life, and that the people are "still life," too, so quiet and poised that they hardly seem to breathe.

You can see how he saw by comparing two of the greatest paintings ever produced in the Netherlands, Van Eyck's *Arnolfini Portrait* and Vermeer's *The Art of Painting*. Both show a man and a woman in a richly furnished interior, lit from the left. Each contains an ambiguous portrait of an artist, who may or may not be the actual artist. Van Eyck is a smudge in a mirror; Vermeer is seen from behind.

And each contains a magnificent six-armed chandelier. If you zoom into Van Eyck's, painted two centuries before Vermeer's, you see one of the many wonders of this artist, who was trained as a painter of miniatures: seen from up close, it looks just as crisp, just as perfect, as when seen from a distance. The painting is both a full-size work and a faultless microscopic wonder. The closer you get, the more detail you see.

Zoom in on the Vermeer and you notice the exact opposite. The closer you get, the less you see. The chandelier dissolves into a blur of yellow, brown, and white dots with no real backbone, no real architecture; but step back and the whole thing resolves into an image as perfect as Van Eyck's. There is no substance to an object that is described only in terms of the light that bounces off it. This is "the art of painting."

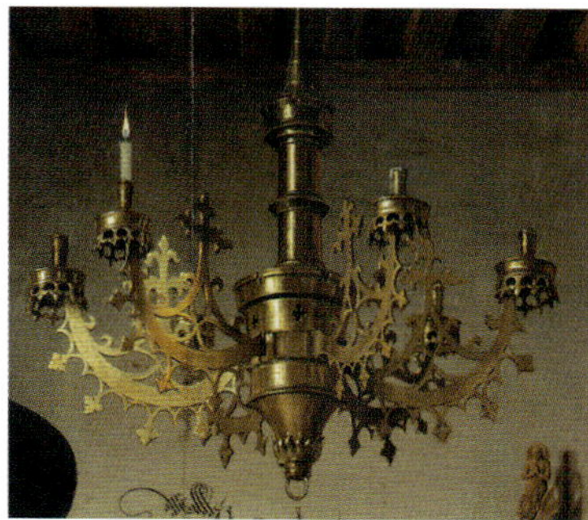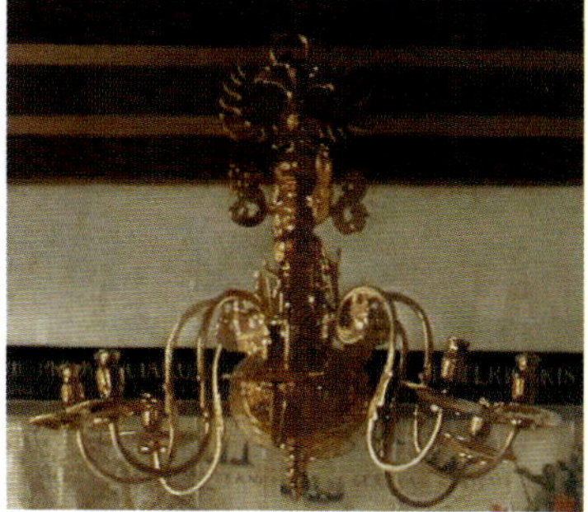

Two great Netherlandish chandeliers, by Van Eyck and Vermeer.

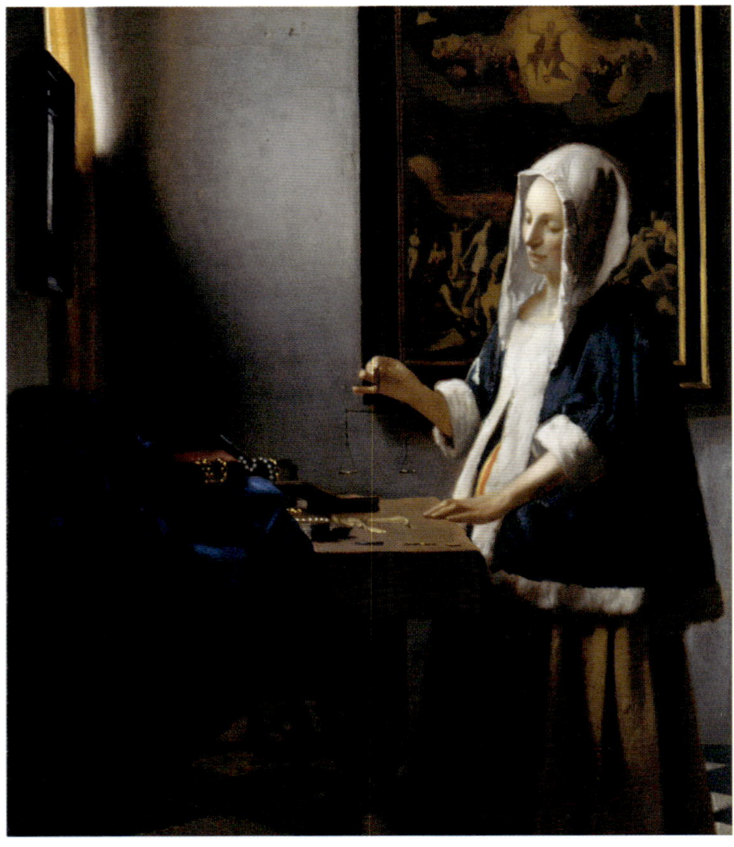

Would we prefer the Woman Holding a Balance *without the
Last Judgment on the wall behind her?*

THE MIDDLE OF Vermeer's career is marked by the so-called pearl pictures. The gems that recur in these works are produced by tapping a dot
of white or gray onto a darker circle. Pearls are worn as jewelry, or they
simply lie on a table, resplendent. They are entirely self-contained, are
not transparent, and do not, like translucent stones, spray light back onto
other objects. You cannot see through them. You can only see them.

Some of the pearl pictures are among the greatest Vermeer ever produced. The silver and blue *Woman Holding a Balance*, for example, shows a woman gazing at a delicate instrument for weighing gold. Behind, surrounding her head on three sides, a large painting of the Last Judgment lends the scene a moralizing meaning, echoing the theme with an allusion to the weighing of souls that will accompany the Second Coming.

Yet we like our Vermeers without a message. Since the 1970s, it had been known that there was a painting of a Cupid—the same that recurs in three other Vermeers—lurking behind the blank wall of the Dresden *Girl Reading a Letter*. It seemed that Vermeer himself had painted it over; but when the top layer became discolored and tests showed it was done after his death, the curators made the decision to reinstate the original composition.

The result was in many ways an improvement. The painting gained the freshness that is a happy consequence of a good restoration. It gained, too, in accuracy, and in respect for the artist: this is how he painted it. But the Cupid is such an explicit symbol—it transforms a letter into a love letter—that we feel a bit disappointed to find it there, as we are dismayed by symbolic overload of the *Allegory of the Catholic Faith*.

Many of his paintings don't, strictly speaking, *show* much. They have the same room, the same window, the same few objects, the same cast of similar faces. They don't need to show much, just as they don't need to be about anything much. What is the narrative in *The Girl with the Pearl Earring*, for example? Narrative in Vermeer is rare, and strikes us as wrong. At their best, the paintings aren't, in fact, about anything.

In many ways, Vermeer is a dead end. He had no imitators, pupils, descendants. One can make a caricature of Vermeer—*The Girl with the Pearl Earring* has spawned a thousand cartoons—but that is all. "A copy after Steen is at least an amusing illustration of some sort," wrote the art historian Max Friedländer. "A copy after Vermeer—characteristically enough, there are hardly any, only forgeries—is nothing at all."

He has proven fertile in another way. As the eye turns dots and dashes into a chandelier, we have constantly provided narratives for

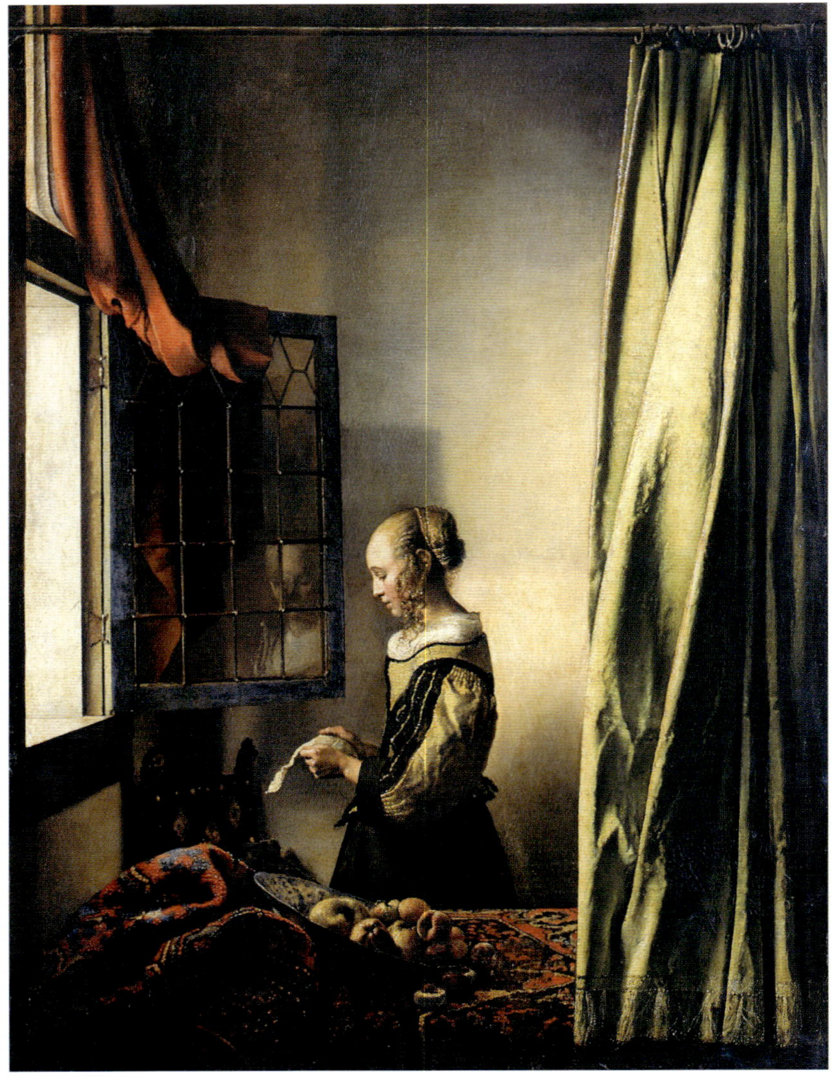

Vermeer direct or indirect: the Girl Reading a Letter at an Open Window *before and after its restoration.*

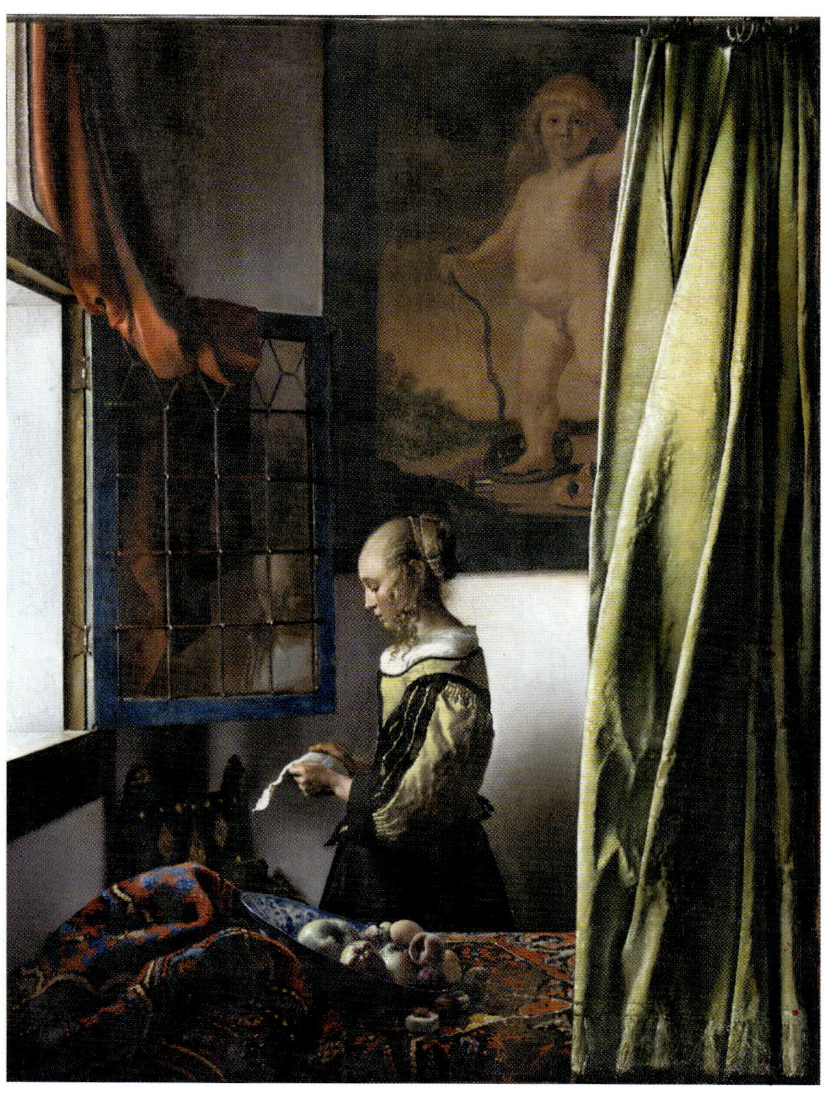

paintings in which, strictly speaking, nothing is happening. No Dutch painter has spawned as many novels, films, and myths. Even with the addition of the Cupid, for example, we know nothing more about the girl reading the letter than our imagination can provide. We are free to fill it in.

Because there is something about Vermeer that makes us want to get closer to him, to understand more of him, it was a spooky thrill when, during the restoration of the *Girl Reading a Letter*, a little smudge appeared in a corner usually covered by the frame. Closer examination revealed that it was a fingerprint—probably the fingerprint of the artist himself. Who else would have picked it up when it was still wet?

———

TOWARD THE END of Proust's *In Search of Lost Time*, the novelist Bergotte leaves his house for the final time. In a review of a show of Dutch painting, he has read that there is a patch of yellow wall in Vermeer's *View of Delft* that was "so well painted that it was, if one looked at it by itself, like some priceless specimen of Chinese art, of a beauty that sufficed unto itself." Bergotte is bothered that he can't remember the yellow wall.

He eats a few potatoes and goes to see the Vermeer. As he climbs the steps of the museum, he is struck by an attack of dizziness, and when he enters he notices the frivolity of so much of the other art. When the old man reaches the painting, "more striking, more different from anything else he knew," he notices "some small figures in blue, that the sand was pink, and, finally, the precious substance of the tiny patch of yellow wall."

> "That's how I ought to have written," he said. "My last books are too dry, I ought to have gone over them with a few layers of color, made my language precious in itself, like this little patch of yellow wall." Meanwhile he was not unconscious of the gravity of his condition. In a celestial pair of scales there appeared to him, weighing down one of the pans, his own life, while the other contained the little patch of wall so beautifully

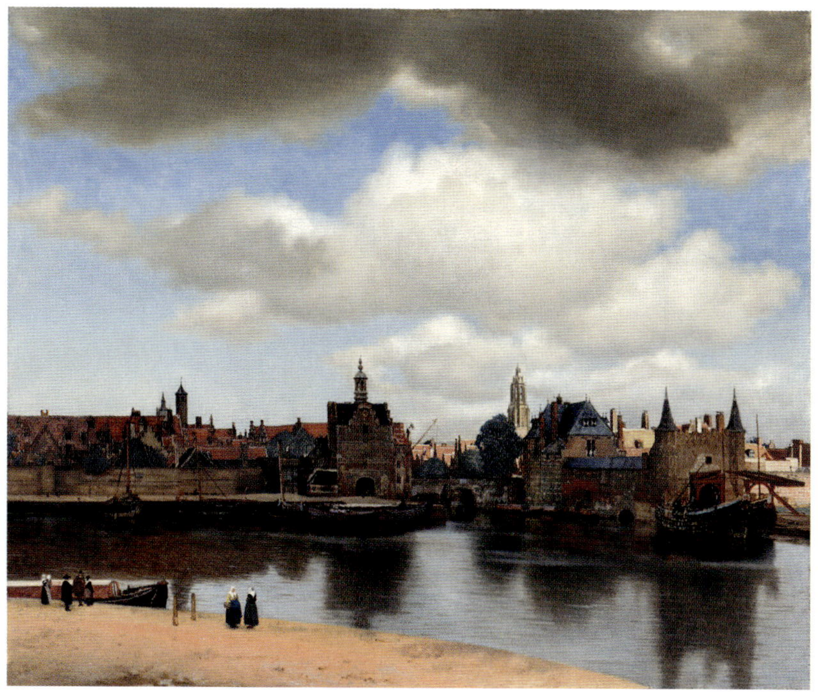

The View of Delft, *which Marcel Proust considered*
the greatest painting in the world.

painted in yellow. He felt that he had rashly sacrificed the former for the
latter. . . . He repeated to himself: "Little patch of yellow wall, with a
sloping roof, little patch of yellow wall."

Bergotte collapses onto the settee, blaming the undercooked potatoes; and as he is trying to recover another attack follows: he crashes,
dead, to the floor.

The story was written almost immediately after Proust's own visit
to the *View of Delft*. He had first seen the painting in 1902, when he came
to Holland and visited the Mauritshuis under the inspiration of Thoré-
Bürger. "Ever since I saw the *View of Delft* in the museum in The Hague,"

he wrote in 1921, "I have known that I had seen the most beautiful painting in the world." Now, the writer was determined to see it again.

The story of his visit is uncannily similar to that of the fictional Bergotte's. As he left his apartment to go to the Jeu de Paume, where the *View of Delft* was on display, the fragile Proust, like Bergotte, fell ill. Shaken by the attack but determined to see the painting, he went ahead to the museum. After lunch at the Ritz, he returned home, and added the story of Bergotte's death to his manuscript. He never left his apartment again.

I thought about Bergotte a lot during the first years I spent surrounded by my own yellow walls. Time passed. The threat of professional failure—which I feared when I started out—began to fade in contrast to another threat, that of professional success. This brought its own demands, its own fears, and when it arrived it posed the question, all the more urgently, of what—time was still passing—I was supposed to do with myself.

Vermeer died at forty-three; Proust, at fifty-one. I had no expectation of living up to their standard, but I still felt encouraged by its existence. I thought it nobler to aspire to their urge to self-sacrifice—to bear in mind those scales. I recalled their admonishment to prefer the little patch of yellow wall to life itself. I didn't; I hadn't. But one oughtn't be depressed by failing to live up to ideals. One ought to be depressed by not having tried.

TO SEE VERMEER'S WORKS together, in a book or in an exhibition, is to wonder what they are really saying. We're always in the same room, beneath that same window, looking at the same handful of situations—a girl reading a letter; a girl and her maid; a girl sitting, or maybe standing, at a virginal. There's nothing, yet he is indubitably among the greatest of painters: the paintings, you think, must be about *something*.

There's something a little tacky about dismissing content entirely. Like someone who admires Chinese calligraphy without knowing what it says, you can derive something from art you don't understand. But if words have a meaning, a painting doesn't necessarily: it can also be experienced sensually, seen and not understood, as music is heard but not understood. You don't need words for painting as you don't need them for music.

At the same time, we feel—we know—that there's a subject beyond the purported subjects. Vermeer's greatness is such that any subject he turned to would be elevated by his regard, but to locate this subject in routine household activities would be a disappointment. There's got to be something else. But these silent, unemotional figures have a way of thwarting anyone who tries to read anything into them.

And then, when you look at the paintings again, the subject pops out so aggressively that you're embarrassed you ever wondered what might be in that love letter. The subject is light. When you get close to a Vermeer—when the chandelier disappears, when the pearls dissolve— all you can see is light, rendered, like Morse code, as a series of dots and lines. Vermeer doesn't try to show objects. He tries to show how light strikes them.

Unlike so many painters, Vermeer seems to photograph well. It doesn't feel like a coincidence that his great fame didn't arrive until the late nineteenth century, once his pictures could be photographed. Walk into any museum shop anywhere in the world, even a museum that doesn't have a Vermeer of its own, and you won't have to look hard to find a keychain, a book, or a postcard featuring *The Girl with the Pearl Earring*.

Yet when you see these paintings in real life, you are always struck by how much more paintlike they are, how much more explicitly artificial, and by how little of this quality can be captured in photographs. Part of it is their pearlescence, the way the painter has trapped light into layers that reveal themselves with the changing light in the room, or with every shift of your head. The light is physically present.

Part of it, too, is how visible the paint is. The closer you get, the less you see "story" and the more you see crushed lapis lazuli. At this level, it doesn't matter that the girl's grin might come across as a little ditzy, or that Vermeer has heaved an encyclopedia's worth of religious allusions at the *Allegory of Faith*. What matters is how those specks on the tapestry resolve, when you take a step back, into a woven horse.

Like the chandelier in *The Art of Painting*, Vermeer himself seems to dissolve the closer we get to him. We clutch at the few scraps that have come down to us: the postmortem inventory of his household that includes "an old beer jug" and "twelve bedsheets, good and bad." We thrill at the glimpse of that fingerprint beneath the frame. But the sparsity of these remains points to the mystery of everything that is missing.

Is that right? Documentary truth is not the only truth. As a person's inner qualities are visible in the face, spiritual truths are visible, too, and made of the same specks and dots. Jacob Spoors, an older neighbor in Delft and relative of Leeuwenhoek, wrote that the light of the sun was the "moral counterpart of shadow." This is the moral light that we see when we stand in front of the paintings of Vermeer.

In that light, we see his personality, too. He eschewed the footling symbolism and cute anecdotes of lesser colleagues in favor of a transcendence that remains appealing because he himself must have been appealing: because he was a creature of light, and not of darkness. Both came through those windows, in his time as in mine. His paintings are the image of a man who saw light and saw darkness—and made his choice.

PART II

THE PICTURE ABOUT ANYTHING

R EMBRANDT HAD students and school, successors and imitators. You can trace his influence as you can follow the descendants of a patriarch down through a family tree. Vermeer is different. He was a dead end—until his rediscovery in the nineteenth century, and his rebirth as the "Sphinx of Delft."

A Sphinx has a question, and a question begs an answer. In Vermeer's case, the answer came with the discovery in France, in the years before the Second World War, of a series of extraordinary paintings. These bridged the stylistic gap between Vermeer's earlier, larger paintings and the pocket-size masterpieces of the "pearl period." They were unveiled with great fanfare. One such treasure, *The Supper at Emmaus*, was sold for a spectacular sum to the Boymans Museum in Rotterdam. It still

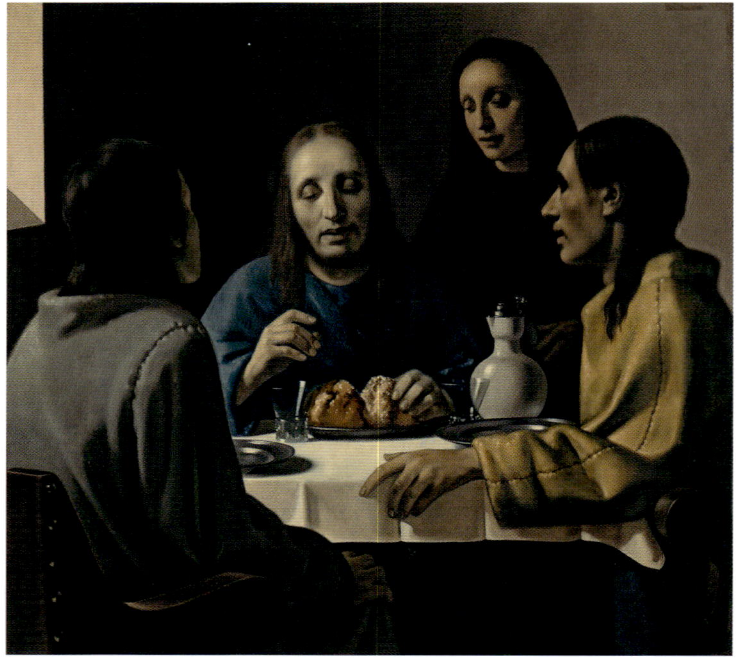

Van Meegeren's "Vermeer" is that rare painting that attracts visitors because it is fake.

hangs there today, one of the museum's main attractions, and one of the most enthralling.

This is because *The Supper at Emmaus* is perhaps the most famous fake painting in the world. If fakes are usually quietly placed into storage, the *Emmaus* still draws crowds—because it's so ugly, for one thing. You can't believe anyone, much less the world's leading connoisseurs, ever thought this bug-eyed cartoon was a Vermeer. But they did. In a passage that I hesitate to quote, Abraham Bredius wrote:

It is a wonderful moment in the life of a lover of art when he finds himself suddenly confronted with a hitherto unknown painting by a great master, untouched, on the original canvas, and without any restoration, just as it left the painter's studio. And what a picture! . . . We have here—I am inclined to say—*the* masterpiece of Johannes Vermeer of Delft . . . quite different from all his other paintings and yet every inch a Vermeer.

I hesitate to quote it because it has been so often quoted before—so often that, for many people, it is the only thing they know of the great Bredius. There is something inspiring about recalling that he, at the age of eighty-three, with a lifetime of service and scholarship behind him, was still able to feel such excitement about a new discovery. He was hardly the only one to fall for this painting, but he fell for it more eloquently than most, and when we see it today this eloquence is part of what makes the painting so intriguing. How? Why? What do we see when we see a painting? If its forger had never been unmasked, would we, too, see it the way Bredius did?

The forger, a failed artist named Han van Meegeren, painted it in 1937, partly as a way to show an establishment that he felt had rejected him that he was as much of an artist as any old master. His success—words like Bredius's—must have amazed him, and when Germany invaded the Netherlands in May 1940, the opportunity of a lifetime was at hand. He pumped out forgery after forgery after forgery, the paintings becoming increasingly sloppy as his drinking and consumption of morphine-laced sleeping pills increased, but by the end of the war he was living in a mansion in the center of Amsterdam, the owner of no fewer than fifty-two houses and fifteen country estates.

He was a bit too successful. After the war, arrested for collaborating with the enemy, he claimed that the priceless national heritage he had allowed the Nazis to spirit away was, in fact, fake. "The painting in Göring's hands is not, as you assume, a Vermeer of Delft, but a Van Meegeren!" he announced, with what one imagines was a mixture of embarrassment and pride.

Convicted of a lesser charge of forgery in 1947, he was sentenced to a nominal prison term but died of a heart attack before going to jail. He remains a Dutch legend, and even received an homage few forgers earn: his fake paintings were themselves later faked, including by his own son.

Vermeer was inimitable. But he was not the only practitioner of an art that flourished among his contemporaries, and that was perhaps the most typical expression of Dutch Golden Age art. This was "genre," and it was not easy to define. Sometimes, in a genre painting, people are doing nothing, representing nobody but a human type, like *The Girl with a Pearl Earring*. Sometimes they are sewing or chatting or dancing or smoking, some every-day activity with no identifiable religious or historical meaning.

Maybe the best way to think of a genre painting is as showing a scene—or a character—from a novel. The first modern novel, *Don Quixote*, was published in 1605, a generation before the birth of the great Dutch genre painters. It took some time for its originality to be felt. But as the novel eventually expanded the subject matter available to writers, so did the genre painting expand the subject matter available to painters. After Cervantes, a novel could be about anything. It could also be about nothing. After Vermeer, a painting could be, too.

6

GERARD TER BORCH

The Human Condition

I N 1882, the grandly named Society for the Study of the Law and History of Overijssel, a local historical association in the eastern Netherlands, held an important exhibition in Zwolle, the capital of the province of Overijssel. The occasion was the society's twenty-fifth anniversary, and the show was ambitious: the catalog included more than three thousand entries.

Among the attendees was Abraham Bredius. In the future, Bredius would become a grand old man: director of the royal picture collection at the Mauritshuis and founder of his own Bredius Museum in The Hague, just across the water from the Mauritshuis. In 1882, he may have been grand—his family was rich enough that he could afford Rembrandts—but he was not old: he was an artsy gay kid, twenty-seven years old, on the verge of the kind of discovery of which young antiquarians dream.

In Zwolle, he fell to talking to a gentleman named Lambertus Zebinden. If Bredius admired the Ter Borchs on display, Zebinden said, he ought to stop by his house, where he had a lot more: he just so happened to be a descendant of Gerard ter Borch, Zwolle's greatest artist. When Bredius arrived, he was stunned to wander in to the art-historical equivalent of Tutankhamun's tomb: the intact archive of the Ter Borch studio.

Nothing like it existed in the Netherlands. Nothing like it existed anywhere: hundreds upon hundreds of drawings, manuscripts, studies, prints, etchings, and documents from the entire Ter Borch clan: the famous Gerard Junior; his father, Gerard Senior; his brothers Moses and Harmen; his sister Anna; his cousin Jan; and his sister Gesina, Gerard's favorite model, who compiled and preserved the collection.

When she died in 1690, Gesina bequeathed it to a sister, and for nearly two hundred years it passed down through the generations. At Zebinden's death in 1886, four years after his meeting with Bredius, most of the collection was acquired for the nation, making Gerard ter Borch's story very different from most other stories of Dutch painters, who lurk in the undocumented shadows. Thanks to Gesina, we have something like a full portrait of the Ter Borchs.

————

IT IS LUCKY that the archive existed in *this* family. They were as accomplished a clan as existed anywhere, and certainly in the middling city of Zwolle. Related to the English "swell," the name refers to a bump in the landscape that protected it from flooding; and Zwolle was not much more than a bump in the cultural landscape. During the war for independence from Spain, it was a garrison town near a dangerous frontier.

Gerald Senior, the son of a tax collector, was born around 1582. It is something of a riddle as to how he became an artist. In his youth, Zwolle boasted only a single artist whose name we know—barely. Gerard Senior probably went to Haarlem or Utrecht for training, and by eighteen was already headed abroad. Unusually and luckily, he spent nearly a decade in Rome: "richly, abundantly maintained," he said in a poem written in old age.

It is not clear why he was being so richly and abundantly maintained; but, like his son, he was a talented social climber, and ended up living in the palace of Cardinal Colonna, one of the most splendid buildings in that city of splendor, and stuffed with a magnificent art collection. On the evidence of Gerard Senior's drawings, he was pursuing something like an extended study abroad—sketching Italian architecture and trying his hand at traditional religious and mythological subjects that he could later work up into paintings.

But the paintings never came, at least as far as we know. (Only one survives.) After a journey home that took him through Nîmes and Bordeaux, he settled into a less glamorous routine, marrying a woman named Anna Bufkens in 1613. In 1617, his first child, Gerard Junior, was born. Around this time, he took up his father's post in the tax collector's office, where he would remain for forty years.

What did he feel about giving up his artistic ambitions? Maybe—like many people—relief. Maybe he felt that public service was a contribution to the effort to build the newly independent and still precarious nation. But he didn't seem to like the job much. Gesina preserved a poem he wrote denouncing the "lords of the greedy city" of Zwolle, whose corruption and venality would, he hoped, incur the wrath of the Almighty God.

Anna died when Gerard Junior was an infant. His father married Geesken van Voerst, who bore him two daughters, Anna and Sara, before dying in turn. Finally, he married the twenty-one-year-old Wiesken Matthys, who bore him nine children and outlived him and all but two of her children. In Gerard Senior, one senses a kindly paterfamilias whose greatest satisfactions were domestic.

He cultivated, and documented, his children's talents, allowing us to get closer to Gerard Junior than to any other major Dutch artist. It is impossible to imagine the drawings of a seven-year-old Vermeer— but we have a sketch of a man on horseback produced when Gerard Junior was that age, and another upon which the proud father wrote: "My Gerrit drew this from life on 24 April Anno 1626. in Zwoll."

With his own background, the elder Ter Borch must have realized he had a prodigy on his hands. Like him, his son would have to head elsewhere to complete his artistic education; he went to Amsterdam and Haarlem and then, most unusually for a Dutch artist of the time, to London, where he was ushered into a milieu of a sophistication and refinement unavailable anywhere in the Dutch Republic.

His stepuncle, Robert van Voerst—the brother of his father's second wife—was an engraver there who worked closely with none other than the Flemish painter Sir Anthony van Dyck, court portraitist to the king of England. (For a middle-class boy from Zwolle, Gerard Junior was, and throughout his life would remain, amazingly well connected.) From this sojourn, a warm letter from father to son survives.

Along with a trunk filled with clothes and art supplies, Gerard Senior offered some practical advice, including to pursue "modarn" themes. "If you do that you will be loved by God, as you were in Haarlem and Amsterdam." After only a few months in England, young Gerard had to go back to Zwolle; the plague had killed Robert van Voerst.

WHAT DID Gerard Senior understand by "modarn"? Nothing less than the great originality of the Dutch: the drafting of commonplace people and their doings into their most refined art. For the Italians, art was exactly whatever was higher than everyday life, and they were often mystified by the Dutch tendency, which Caravaggio adopted, to depict soldiers or prostitutes or housewives. They considered this lowering.

Incorporating these figures into historical or mythological or religious scenes had been controversial enough when Caravaggio did it—but the dirty feet in his paintings still belonged to saints, and his hookers were still meant to represent the Magdalene. In Holland, the soldier in the tavern was meant to represent a soldier, and the prostitute making eyes at a client was meant to show a prostitute.

The term that came to be attached to these scenes was "genre." They were usually small paintings. You didn't need acres of canvas to show a woman writing a letter. These were the same nonheroic subjects in which the Dutch specialized. They were neither fantasies of the hereafter nor commemorations of famous events. Their theme—this was their intellectual, novelistic novelty—was everyday life.

Depictions of routine events in anonymous lives had existed before, but in genre the symbolism that clothed earlier representations was stripped, mostly, and the scene allowed to speak for itself. Scenes of rural life, for example, common since the Middle Ages, could be used to illustrate different months or times of the year. The genre painter showed similar scenes—planting, ripening, harvest—without this symbolic overlay.

This did not prevent later critics from making awkward attempts to interpret these pictures. Of a beautiful Ter Borch of a boy cleaning the fur of an adorable little dog, the Polish poet Zbigniew Herbert wrote: "Those who 'read paintings' cannot agree whether it is in praise of cleanliness or a reproach for preferring unimportant activities to school duties. (Here is an example of the intellectual games of bored elderly gentlemen.)"

For decades, bored elderly gentlemen have scoured genre paintings for symbolism, and the search has delivered uniformly predictable results. Very different pictures by very different artists will be reliably announced to contain a handful of banal and moralistic allusions—to

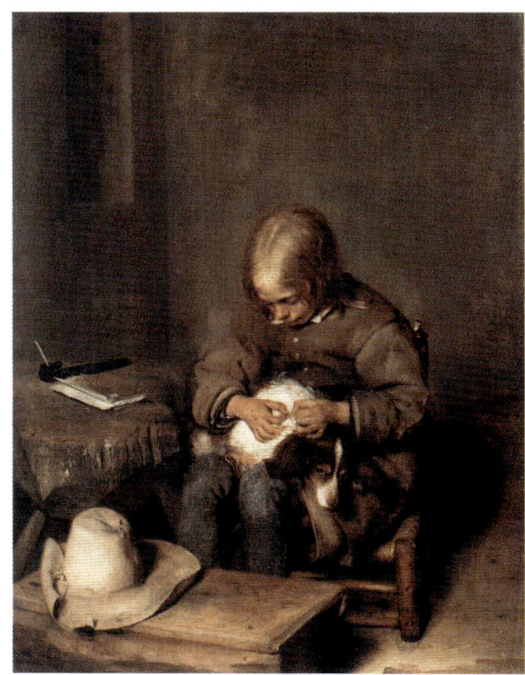

A little boy, Gerard's brother, Moses, plucks the fleas from his patient dog.

sexual incontinence if we're lucky; to the importance of hard work, religious observance, or household cleanliness if we're not.

But it is their lack of specificity that gives genre paintings their timelessness. A picture of a boy and his dog evokes the same sentiments now as it would have then. "The historical picture says: *that* happened once," wrote Max Friedländer. "The genre picture says: *this* happens often, this is how peasants behave at such and such a time in such a such a place; or: this is what happens when belligerent horsemen meet."

GERARD JUNIOR HAD the genre sensibility from his first known drawing, which his father preserved and which shows a man on horseback. His first known painting, produced around a decade on, is of the same subject. A bit later, he painted a picture of a doctor examining a vial of urine—the kind of genre theme that for some painters would occasion a preachy message—a warning against illicit sex—and for others an ironic leer. But a quiet dignity already distinguished him.

That temperament did not mean that he, like his father, would settle into a quiet provincial life. After he escaped the plague in London, he embarked on an even more distant journey. The destination was Spain, the archenemy of the Netherlands. It was a curious choice in national terms—I can't think of any other Dutch painter who followed him—and in artistic terms, too. Why not make the traditional pilgrimage to Italy?

He must have had some connection, since he quickly, and as usual, rose to high positions. This must have been quite a trick: Spain, the great bastion of reactionary Catholicism, rarely welcomed Protestants, and even less Protestants from the fiercest of heretic nations, and a nation with which Spain was officially at war. We don't know how he pulled it off. Ter Borch must have had some talent beyond the merely artistic.

How much political skill, how much backroom maneuvering, is involved in an artist's success? The talent for moving in society is the dirty secret of many artistic careers, and is usually masked from historians. There are many people with artistic talent. But only a handful succeed, and these are not always the most talented. Success requires another talent: the talent to discover opportunities to use that talent.

Ter Borch was a gifted artist. But he was not a Mozartian or Rembrandtian genius. The history of his extraordinary ascension might be as interesting as the history of his artworks themselves—but this history is hidden from us, muffled by a layer of shame or embarrassment, sneered at as climbing. That is one way to look at it. Another way of looking at it is as the history of how, at every epoch, art gets made.

In Ter Borch's case and most others, this history went unwritten. We can only see the results of his skill. A poem records the esteem in which he was held at the Spanish court: the king himself, Philip IV, sat for him. These works have not survived, except for the strongest visible evidence of this journey: a haunting picture of faceless worshippers—dressed, like American Klan members, in white gowns and tall pointy hats.

They are flagellants, beating their backs with spiked whips, staining their white vestments with blood. It is a dark and disturbing picture that inevitably calls to mind another court artist, Goya, who seems to have known this work, and who, 150 years later, painted a similar scene. But if the scene is Goyaesque, it isn't Ter Borchesque. Nothing similar exists in his work. Nothing similar exists in Dutch art.

It is easy to assume that we know what Ter Borch was thinking because we know what Goya was thinking. Goya doesn't leave much room to doubt; many of his works are explicitly captioned. He tells us that he hates cruelty and war, and he uses his art to denounce them. But to read Ter Borch's painting through Goya is to see denunciation in an artist too tactful to denounce.

What is Ter Borchesque is to ask a question and then withhold the answer. To get to know Ter Borch is to meet a born diplomat, someone innately discreet, someone who plays both sides, someone whose stories rarely have a clear moral. At times of plague like the outbreak that had recently killed his uncle, flagellants flourished. For all we know, Ter Borch might have found such a gruesome penance fitting—touching, even.

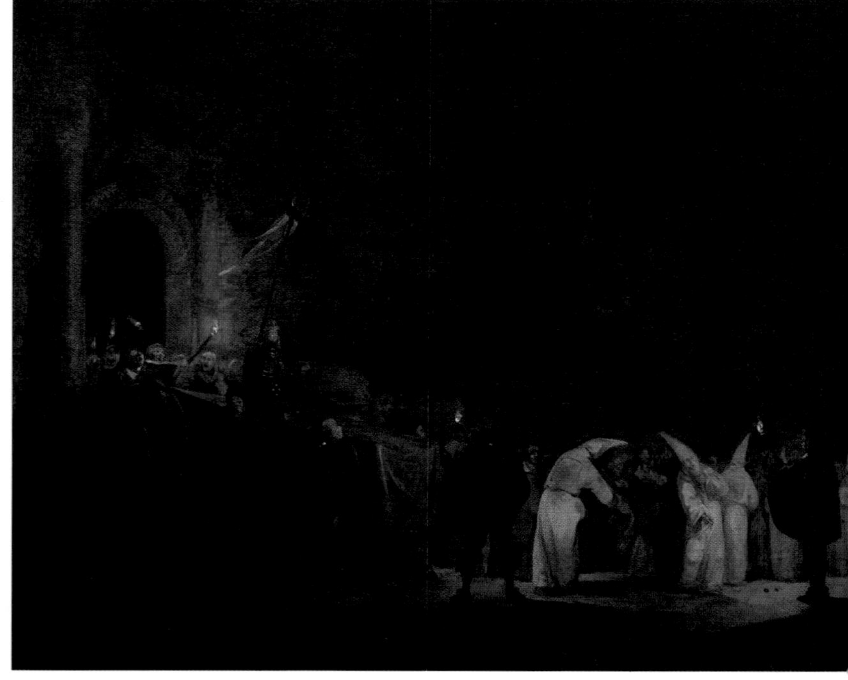

These mysterious flagellants have no parallels in Dutch art; are they a souvenir of Ter Borch's journey to Spain?

SOON AFTER he returned from Spain, he would bring his abilities to the most consequential diplomatic theater in Europe. After nearly eighty years of on-and-off warfare, the Dutch, by the 1640s, were ready to make peace with their nemesis. Both the Dutch and the Spanish were threatened by France. And the Dutch had not only been independent de facto for decades—they had become Europe's leading maritime power.

But to transform de facto independence into official recognition would mean another recognition, which was that the southern Netherlands—Belgium—was irreversibly lost. The Dutch were loath

to do this. The balance of power had shifted; Spain was now vulnerable. Yet the war that began so many decades ago had left little appetite for the kind of heroic sacrifice that would have been necessary to reconquer the south.

The negotiations that got under way in Münster and Osnabrück, across the German border in Westphalia, also aimed to end another war, confusingly named, in this context, the Thirty Years' War. This, the final salvo in the wars of religion, had blossomed into a horrifying world war. It ravaged Germany, tore apart Spain—Portugal managed to secede from Spain in 1640, and Catalonia came close—and eventually killed an estimated eight million people. In some areas of Germany, the population was halved.

Onto this vital diplomatic stage stepped Gerard ter Borch. He stayed in Münster for two years, until 1648, when the final treaties were signed. During that time, and uniquely among Dutch painters, he came to occupy a position akin to that of a photojournalist, producing images of current events and leading personalities: one showed the leader of the Holland delegation entering Münster with the pomp of a king.

Perhaps he spoke some Spanish. Perhaps he had met some members of the delegation during his time in Madrid. In any case, Ter Borch, much as he always seemed to do, managed to ingratiate himself to both the Dutch and the Spanish, and painted delegates from both sides. Most of these paintings are small. But if the faces and clothes are different, the format is the same—like studio portraits made by a single photographer.

These were studies for his would-be tour de force, a group portrait that eventually came to include seventy-seven (!) people. *The Swearing of*

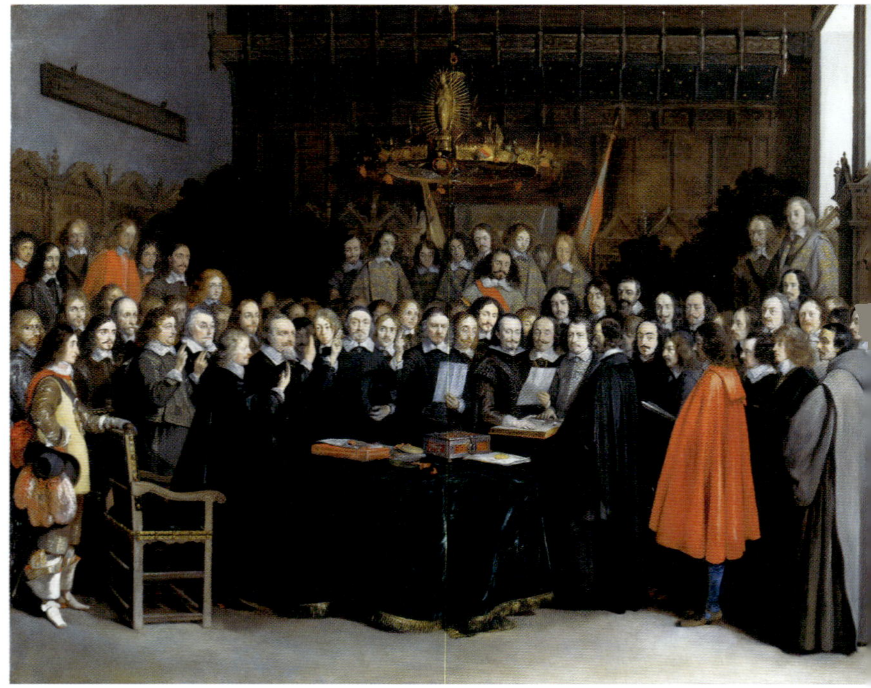

In oddly bureaucratic fashion, Ter Borch's Treaty of Münster *commemorates the triumph of the Dutch in their eighty-year war of independence.*

the Oath of the Ratification of the Treaty of Münster is unique in Dutch art. Considering how many faces are crammed into it, and considering the momentous event it commemorates, it isn't very big, first of all: certainly nothing like the group portraits by Hals or Rembrandt.

It's unique, too, because of its bare-bones treatment. There's nary a naked goddess, nor a trumpeting angel, nor an allusion to the Trojan War. Instead, we meet a group of unassuming men in a glorified conference room, shaking hands at the end of a meeting. If this matter-of-factness might seem Dutch, it is odd in a painting by a Dutch artist, and one designed to commemorate the greatest triumph in Dutch history.

Place it next to Bartholomeus van der Helst's *Banquet of the Amsterdam Civic Guard in Celebration of the Peace of Münster* and you immediately see the difference. Van der Helst's picture is gigantic, for one: so big that it has usually hung next to the *Night Watch* in the most prestigious gallery of the Rijksmuseum. Bursting with gold and swagger, this is a painting that seems worthy of the moment.

Ter Borch's painting is weird, hard to explain, when placed alongside the famous group portraits of the time. It's slightly less weird if you look at it as a photograph: of a graduating class, for example, or of a group of heads of state, neatly lined up, at an international summit. But it's not a photograph—and it's not a genre picture, either. There is no Dutch painting that so clearly states: "*That* happened once."

Ter Borch was proud of this picture—proud enough to demand a fee so astronomical that he couldn't find a buyer. At his death, the picture was still in his family. Maybe the price wasn't the only thing that kept him from finding a buyer. It's hard to disagree with Zbigniew Herbert when he writes that, although "according to general opinion it is a masterpiece," it looks instead like "a World Congress of Insects."

IN THE YEARS that followed, Ter Borch would travel farther still. After Münster, he joined the entourage of the Count of Peñaranda, the leader of the Spanish delegation, who brought him to Madrid, where he was knighted by the king of Spain: the sort of reward that Van der Helst, with his unabashed patriotic triumphalism, was not likely to receive. Arnold Houbraken said that Ter Borch revealed a tic:

> When the Count sat for him for the first time in order to be painted, and he with great zeal according to his old habit started to whistle a little tune, was the Count offended, as indecent in the presence of such a mighty Prince, and stood from the place he was sitting; in order to leave: but when TERBURG realized his error he excused himself by saying: That he was in the habit of doing such a thing without realizing it, when

the brushwork was going along nicely and according to his wishes. At this the Count sat back down, and said now laughing: Keep whistling.

Houbraken says that Ter Borch's stay in Madrid was cut short by the jealousy of certain husbands—he was something of a roué—and that he fled to England, where he made a lot of money, then stuffed his boots with gold coins and crossed to France, where he met with the same worldly success that attended him everywhere, before heading home and attracting, inevitably, the attention of the Prince of Orange.

Houbraken records how Ter Borch got that prince to sit still, and gives us snatches of their repartee. The prince, aware of the artist's reputation, asked "how many mistresses he had had in Madrid. Can his Highness, he answered, tell me how many seas he has sailed on? I cannot recall because they are countless, answered the Prince. Neither can I retorted TERBURG, tell you about my mistresses."

Yet—like his father—this man of the world came home, and there he found his real subject: the private life of a cultivated family. These were genre scenes, but they were unlike any genre scenes that had come before. They were works of incredible luxury—Ter Borch was famous for his ability to reproduce the shimmer of satin—that were, at the same time, suffused with the intimate glow of the happy home.

His discovery of this subject would mark all subsequent Golden Age genre painting, starting with Pieter de Hooch's and Johannes Vermeer's. How Ter Borch knew Vermeer is a mystery; all we have is that document the two of them signed in Delft in 1653, just after Vermeer's wedding: Ter Borch always seemed to know everyone. Both Vermeer and De Hooch would borrow many of his themes.

Vermeer took these motifs—a woman receiving a letter; a lady at her toilette—in a different direction. His paintings are much brighter than Ter Borch's. His take place during the day; Ter Borch's, we assume, at night. Vermeer shows the source of light, often an open window; Ter Borch never does. In Ter Borch's pictures, we are not sure where the light is coming from, as we nearly always are with Vermeer.

One reason may be that Ter Borch did not have an advanced under-

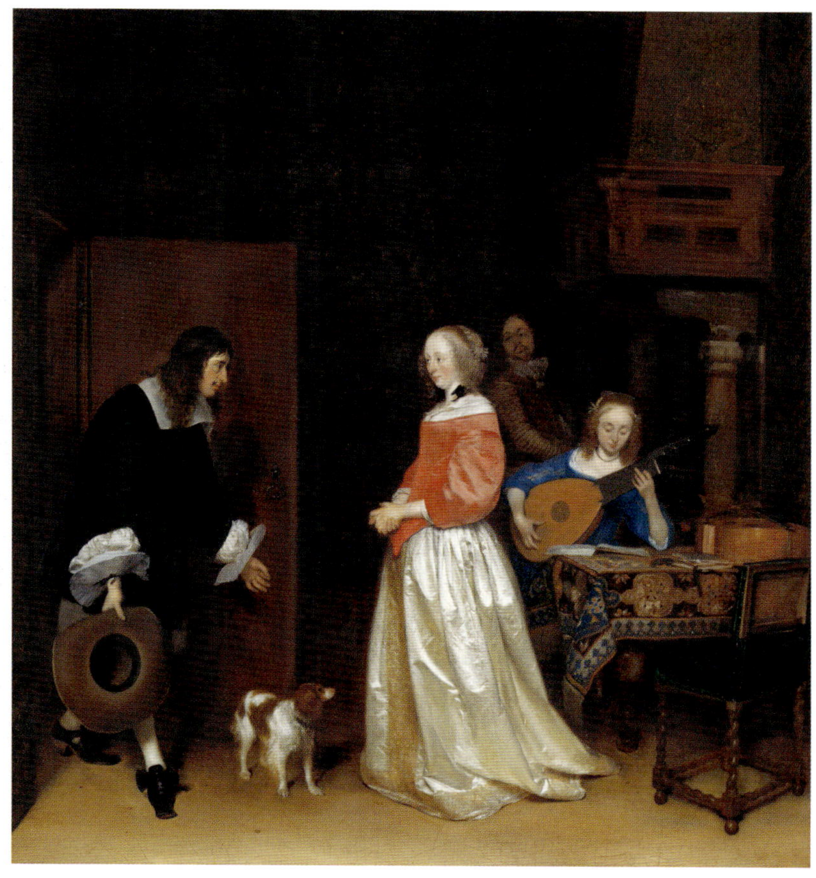

*After the great war, the great peace: Ter Borch showed
the life of a cultivated Dutch family.*

standing of perspective. When Pieter de Hooch takes a Ter Borchian
theme—a mother combing a child's hair, for example—he places it
in an intriguing architectural setting. In a Ter Borch, you rarely see
the back of the room, and much less a view into other spaces. Without
a grasp of perspective, he would have been best advised to keep the
backgrounds shadowy.

The penumbra—the world as seen in the late afternoon, or by candlelight—lends these paintings their intimacy. The Utrecht Caravaggists used flashes of light to illuminate their characters' stagy gestures. Ter Borch's light picks out each figure softly and ushers you into the sanctum of a family in a land that, in large part through such images, became synonymous with tranquil cultivation, with civilization itself.

This is the world of the genre painting, and one characteristic of that world is that the protagonists are anonymous. We are interested in what people are doing rather than who they are. We might see a profession, an age, an activity, a position in life, but we don't quite care about who the models for these paintings might be. At its best, the genre painting shows us something more fundamental: the human condition itself.

Ter Borch's pictures don't need names. In order to appreciate a tender painting of a boy and a dog, we don't need to know the name of the boy or the dog. Yet though we don't know the dog's name, we do, thanks to the archive, know the boy's: Moses, Gerard's youngest half brother. And we know, thanks again to the archive, that Moses was an artist whose drawings, lovingly preserved, reveal a talent no less than his father's or brother's.

We see Moses again in a picture of a boy learning how to read. He is around the same age, seven or eight, as in the picture with the dog. Now the teacher is his mother, and Gerard's stepmother, Wiesken Matthys. The all-black background picks out their heads and the book they are reading, enveloping the whole in an almost sacred atmosphere. The love of mother for child is plain; so is the love of the artist for both.

———

WE ALSO KNOW that the girl who turns up in painting after painting is Gerard's half sister Gesina. She was fourteen years younger; he had missed most of her childhood during his *Wanderjahre*. When he returned, he found a bright seventeen-year-old who became his favorite model,

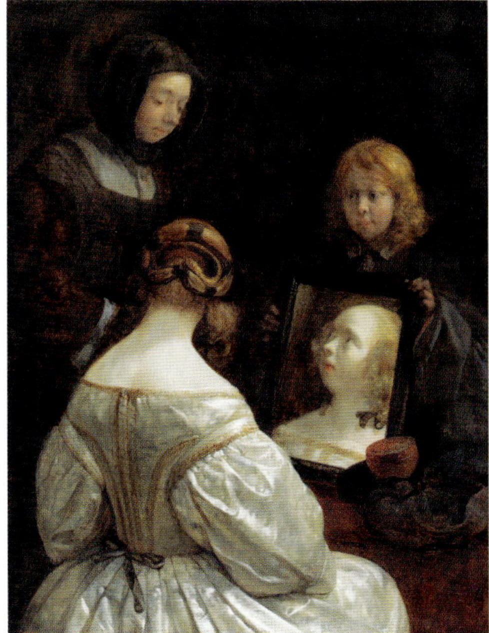

Gesina became her older brother's favorite model, and appears in many poses throughout his work.

instantly recognizable from her slightly upturned nose. Once one learns to spot her, one sees her everywhere in his work.

Here's an innocent Gesina at a mirror, looking up at a maid. Here she is playing the girlfriend of a soldier, their intimacy disturbed by a summons to war. Here she is as a young lady receiving a swashbuckling suitor, in the satins for which Ter Borch was famous; here peering over the shoulder of another sister, Jenneken, in order to sneak a peek at a letter; here, stirring a glass of lemonade, in what might be or might not be a brothel.

Thanks to these pictures, we know Gesina ter Borch's appearance as well as we know that of any woman of her time. And thanks to the albums she collated and preserved, we know a great deal about her mind. Like her brothers, she showed early promise in drawing. Unlike them, she does not seem to have received training as a painter, and was encouraged instead to pursue calligraphy, embroidery, and watercolor.

The Ter Borch collection at the Rijksmuseum contains three books Gesina assembled: the *Materi-Boeck*, a brief collection of her early drawings and writings; a poetry album; and a scrapbook. In this latter, perhaps the only such to survive from the seventeenth century, she chronicled the life of her distinguished family, including its little odds and ends: a receipt from the pharmacy, some dieting advice from the doctor.

It also includes writings from her friends, who praise her virtues and, especially, her intellect and talent. To discover her equal, one man claims that he is forced to reach into classical antiquity. (She must have cut quite a figure in Zwolle.) A temperament emerges from these books.

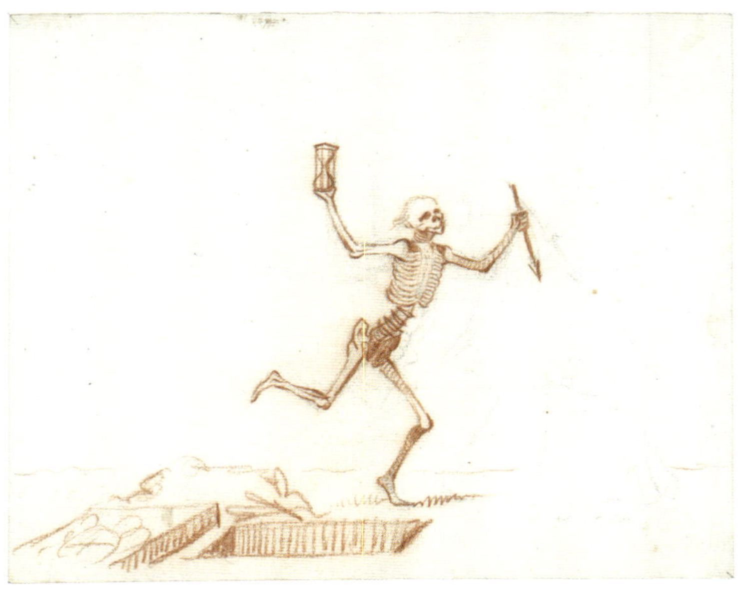

A drawing by Gesina Ter Borch from the albums carefully collected
and passed down through generations of her family.

Gesina's was a highly literary mind. She was skilled in several arts and attracted to the symbolism of death and romantic love.

Perhaps, if she had been a boy and given proper training, she would have grown up to be a professional artist. On the basis of her drawings it is hard to say how far she might have come. The drawings are lively and full of charm but nevertheless lack the refinement of a traditionally schooled artist. There is, however, one portrait that gives a tantalizing glimpse of what she might have become.

IN 1654 Gerard married his stepmother's sister, Geertruyt Matthys. She lived just upriver in Deventer, and it is there that he would spend the rest of his life. Deventer, smaller and more conservative even than Zwolle, was a strange choice for a man who had known so much worldly renown, and his move to Deventer, like his return to Zwolle, would mark a change in his oeuvre. He now dedicated himself to portraits of the city's elite—a group that he would soon join when he was named city councillor.

These portraits are impossible to confuse with any other artist's work. They follow the same formula. A figure stands in a space—not quite a room—that is empty but for a table or chair. The men's feet are in the shape of a T—one pointing to the side and one pointing to the front. Like mounted butterflies, the figures look pinned to the walls behind them. Their clothes make them look uncomfortable.

These weird-looking Deventer notables are so different from anything else in Dutch art that you recognize them immediately, and greet them when you come across them. There are almost sixty today; there once were more. They are small. And though they are good individual likenesses when seen close up, they project, when seen together, a uniformity that seems to underline the unity of a local ruling class.

"Who ordered these unattractive canvasses?" Herbert wondered, and you know what he means. It is hard to imagine a town whose citizens wanted to be portrayed in this way—but there they are, includ-

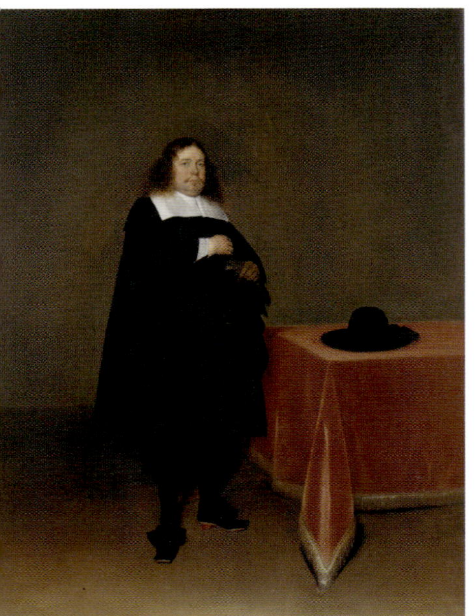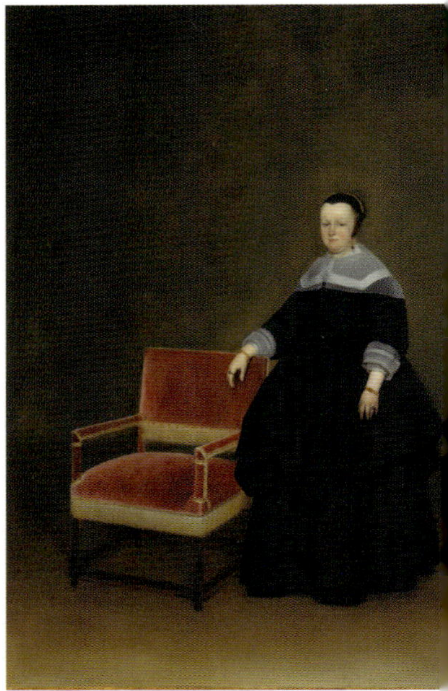

When Gerard married and moved to Deventer, he painted dozens of its leading citizens, including Jan van Duren and his wife, Margaretha van Haexbergen.

ing in a large picture of the Deventer town council that is still in the city. Everyone is identically dressed and has an identical face. The picture makes the Münster insects look almost lively.

How different is one of the most touching works in the Rijksmuseum, the portrait of Moses ter Borch. The little boy Gerard had painted grooming his dog and being taught to read by his mother—the skilled draftsman whose productions we know from the archive—volunteered to fight the English in 1664. He was killed in action at Harwich in 1667, when he was just twenty-two years old. His promise came to nothing.

The next year, Gerard and Gesina painted a memorial portrait. Moses adopts the stance—full-length, in the center of the canvas, one

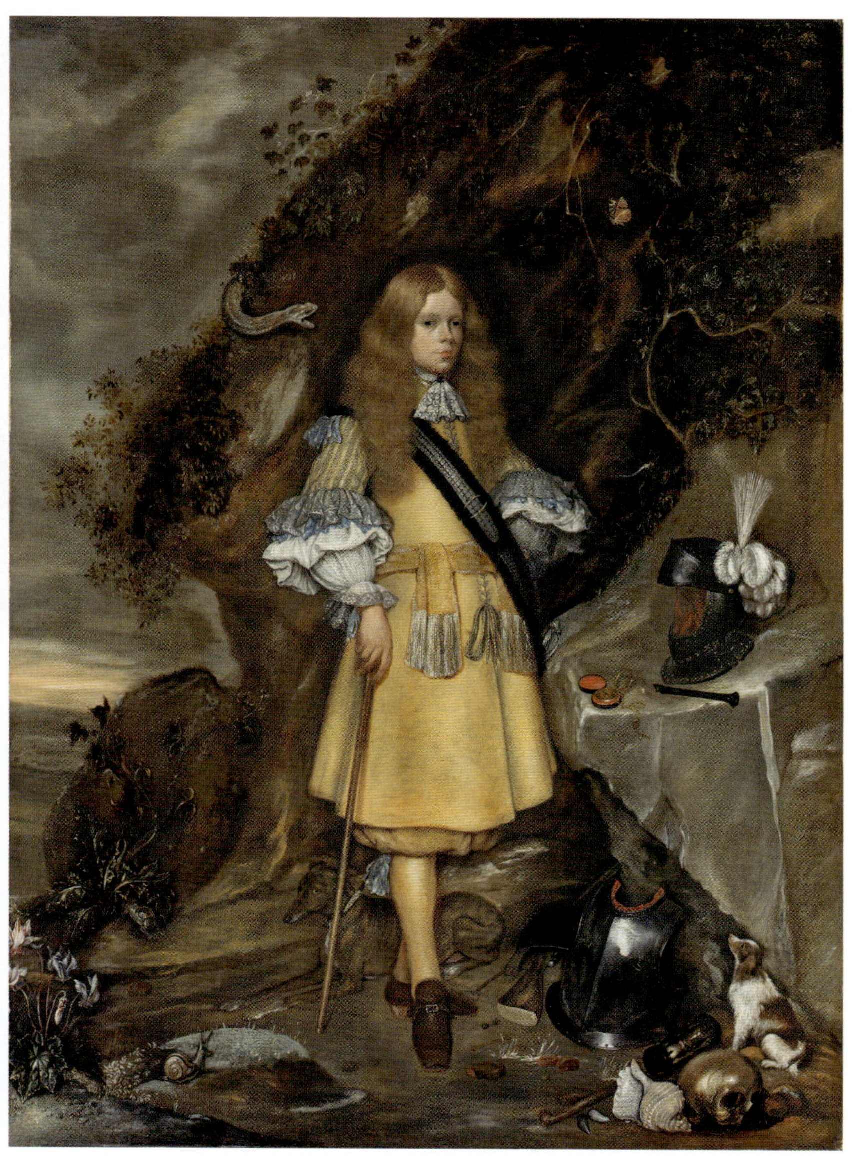

*Gerard and Gesina joined forces to create this memorial
to their slain brother, Moses.*

hip cocked, T-shaped feet—that we know from Gerald's other portraits. He is dressed in a yellow outfit so luxurious that it seems much too grand for a boy this young; the painting was once, in fact, thought to show the Prince of Orange. Otherwise, the work is typical of Gerard.

What makes it so memorable are Gesina's contributions. Where Gerard's portraits are symbols of down-to-earth good sense and the methodical accumulation of capital, this portrait is stuffed with a riot of allusion. It is not subtle—the openmouthed viper, for example, inches from Moses's luxuriant golden hair—but it is intriguing to decipher, and tells a vivid story about a life that ended just as he entered adulthood.

It includes military symbols—armor, a befeathered helmet, a gun. Shells indicate his death in a naval engagement, and the painting contains a veritable almanac of symbols of passing time. And there are two dogs. One of them looks just like the spaniel in the earlier picture, the dog the boy was grooming. Only thirteen years separate the two paintings. It is surely the same dog. As much as his brother and sister mourned him, the dog Moses loved must have mourned him, too.

7

PIETER DE HOOCH

A Peaceful Room in a Peaceful Land

AT SOME POINT between December 17, 1998, and February 27, 1999, I went to visit my sister. I am not sure of the exact date, but I know what those months meant in terms of my own life. In the spring of 1998, I had graduated from college and moved to New York. My sister was a few months from graduating from Amherst College. We met in Hartford and went to see a show at the Wadsworth Atheneum.

It was a retrospective of the paintings of Pieter de Hooch, a painter I had never heard of, and those were the dates it ran. In those years, I hadn't heard of many artists, and the more I learned and studied, the more I realized how much there was to learn and study. In order to continue my education after college, especially after coming to New York, I read art magazines and went to every exhibition I could. It didn't matter what it was.

I don't remember most of what I saw in those years. But I remember the Pieter de Hooch exhibition clearly because it was the first time I had ever felt the charisma of the Dutch. His pictures showed spotlessly clean middle-class rooms where, bathed in warm light, brightly clad people were taking part in some peaceful activity: getting ready for school, chatting with neighbors, playing with the dog.

Those rooms breathed refinement and civilization. Anyone who visits a palace fantasizes about what it would be like to live there, but

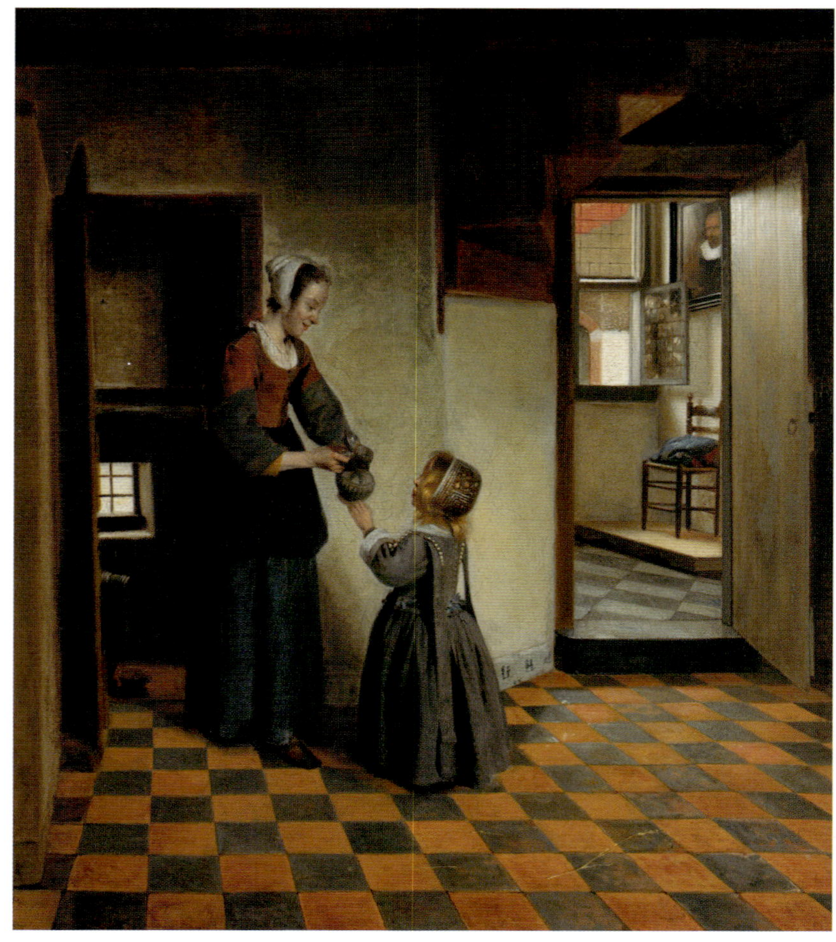

The peaceful interiors of Pieter de Hooch introduced me
to an ideal vision of Holland.

nobody ever thinks that they will ever actually move to Versailles or the
Winter Palace. The appeal of De Hooch's Holland was that you could so
easily see yourself in those perfect rooms. It was a vision so welcoming
that I never forgot it. *That*, I thought, is a place to live.

That weekend in Connecticut, I did not suspect how quickly a series of coincidences would bring me to those rooms—or how much of my life I would spend in them. Before long, I would be living in a seventeenth-century Dutch house, with windows (and beams and courtyards and doors) that looked exactly like those in De Hooch's paintings. Only the people looked different; but the people weren't the point.

At first, it was the fantasy. In later years, the light started to fade. The reality of Dutch life—dreary weather, a bursting in-box, reptilian politicians on television—muscled its way in. It made me forget the silvery light falling through latticed windows onto the blue-and-white ceramics that reminded me of Vermeer. The place became a bit too ordinary, a bit too pedestrian. I remembered Pieter de Hooch.

THERE AREN'T MANY BOOKS about De Hooch. Maybe this is because, as Lievens, Bol, and Flinck suffer in comparison to Rembrandt, De Hooch suffers in comparison to his neighbor and acquaintance Vermeer. Maybe this is because, like many Dutch painters whose radicalism in their own day has grown invisible to us now, he seems so unchallenging—the equivalent, in painting, of a high-end interiors magazine.

There hasn't been another show about him since the one I saw right after college. One suspects that the exhibition was a long cherished dream, since it was put on by the Wadsworth's then director, Peter Sutton, who wrote the catalog and who, nearly two decades before, had written the standard work on De Hooch. In a cruel, curt paragraph in that book, Sutton summed up what was known of the artist's life.

De Hooch was born in Rotterdam in 1629, had moved to Delft by 1652, was employed by a linen merchant and joined the guild in Delft in September 1655. Contact with the painter Hendrick van der Burch was established in these years and after settling in Amsterdam in 1660–1. De Hooch is known to have encountered works by De Witte. He evidently remained a resident of Amsterdam until his death in the madhouse in 1684. Throughout his life De Hooch seems to have been relatively poor.

Those last two sentences brought me up short. Relatively poor— death in the madhouse. They seemed incompatible with his tranquil, composed rooms. In his pictures, you can almost see dust floating in the light streaming through the windows. You can imagine the crackling of logs. You can hear the swish of the maidservant's broom on the floor, the snore of sleeping puppies. These are pictures of a dream.

This is why their titles—*Woman and Child in an Interior*, *A Party of Figures Around a Table*—seem so disappointing. Long after they were painted, when it was felt that paintings needed titles, the barest descrip-

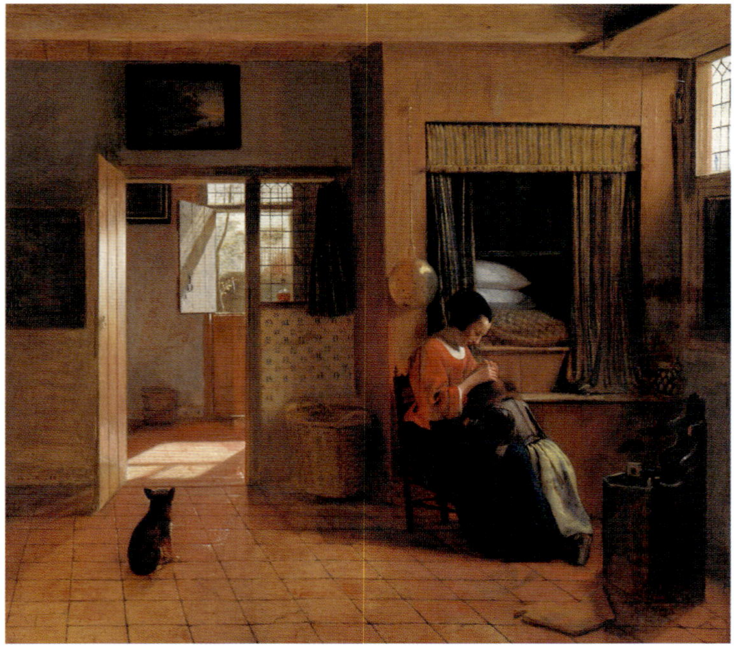

*Thanks to artists like De Hooch, the intimate middle-class home
became a symbol of Holland.*

tions were chosen, their poverty pointing to the embarrassment of putting into words the feelings they really evoke: *A Young Man's Yearning for Love*; *My Beloved Grandmother, Dead These Many Years*.

You could describe them in other ways, too. You could name them for furniture, for atmosphere: *Afternoon Light on a Gilded Wall Covering*, *Study of Bricks and Tiles*. You can omit the people because the people—the people inside the paintings—aren't really the point. The most important people stand outside those rooms and imagine themselves inside. They are the people looking at them; we ourselves.

The world into which De Hooch invites us is rigorously edited. His subject is conviviality, friendship, and family. Like Ter Borch, his deepest feelings seem to have been reserved for scenes of mothers and small

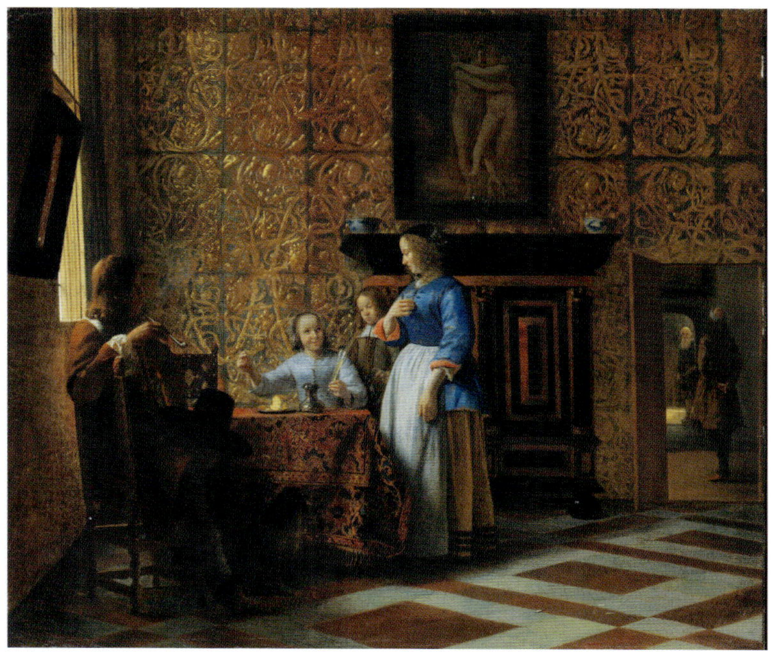

De Hooch's interiors gradually became more sumptuous,
but always evoked the same warm mood.

children; and though he himself was the father of seven, he hardly ever paints fathers. Maybe the men are the ones outside the pictures—men like me. Inside the pictures, men are shown as accessories to women, and the love of couples is suggested mainly by the offspring those unions produce.

Yet it is a world suffused by love. No unpleasantness intrudes. The time and place are instantly recognizable, but the works seem to exist outside of time.

THE WORK OF Pieter de Hooch can be divided into three distinct phases—or, as we shall see, four. The earliest is made of paintings of humble people, often soldiers, in taverns and inns. They're sitting around drinking, playing games, killing time. The setting is the countryside, the village; the rooms are like places where livestock might be kept, with floors of clay or mud or the barest wooden planks.

The tavern and the village gave way to the middle-class urban home in his second phase, a shift that coincided with his marriage to Jannetgen van der Burch, a woman from Delft, in 1654. He had moved there from Rotterdam, a middling city that barely suspected its future destiny as the largest port in the world, and arrived in Delft in the same year as the explosion of the gunpowder magazine that killed Carel Fabritius.

The city's devastation, which attracted other painters, was edited out of De Hooch's works. Nothing intrudes on the contentment of the happy home. His first children were born in 1655 and 1656. If another artist might have experienced such an eruption as an interruption, it was a liberation for De Hooch, and it was in the years of his children's infancy, the late 1650s, that he painted his greatest works.

In these pictures, De Hooch, more than any other artist, created a nation. It was a country where, as all foreign visitors remarked, cleanliness was next to godliness ("One doesn't dare spit in the rooms," a Frenchman marveled in 1651) and where children were cosseted. Foreigners thought they were spoiled: "Never before had a people produced so many images of tender and contented families," Sutton writes.

The prosperous land of clean and happy homes was an artistic invention. The further back one goes in the history of art, the more one realizes how many such inventions there are, and how little we could see or say without them. So many forms and expressions that seem too obvious to have necessitated an inventor turn out, upon closer inspection, to have had one; we often know their names.

"Pliny names the first painter to have distinguished males from females, the first painter to show three-quarter views of heads as well as veins and drapery folds, the first painter to paint open mouths and teeth and expressions, the first painter to depict objects realistically," wrote the art historian Christopher Wood. "Aristedes of Thebes 'was the first of all painters who depicted the mind and expressed the feelings of a human being.'"

In De Hooch's paintings are other inventions, too, including his trademark *doorkijkje*, a window or door that opens onto another space. This trick demands deviousness. The painter needs to fool the brain into combining two separate perspectives into one, as bifocals make us combine a split image into a whole. De Hooch was figuring out the technique right as he began painting mothers and children.

You can see its beginnings in a painting from just before this breakthrough, *Soldier and Serving Woman with Card Players*. The people cluster in the left half of the painting, lit by some light that comes from the place where we are standing. The right half is dark—except for a tiny golden streak, a brushstroke glowing like a painting by Mark Rothko or a zip by Barnett Newman. It would soon expand.

This brushstroke dates from around 1655, when De Hooch would step out of the tavern and head into the home. When he did, the little streak grew. In *Mother and Child with a Serving Woman Sweeping*, the other room suggested in the earlier painting has opened onto a small bright vestibule. In the picture's imperfections, we see how hard it is to unify these spaces, and the different kinds of light that enters them.

By this point, the muddled, muddy floors have become brick and tile. This classes the rooms up a bit. And it gives the painter a neat geometric grid along which to plot his perspective. This is convenient, but the transitions are rough. If De Hooch had simply closed the door to the vestibule, the picture would have been perfect. Because he opened it, the strains show. The little room has come strangely unhinged.

Soon—we can't know how soon, but in the early years of marriage and fatherhood—he resolves this difficult technical question, and his pictures start to burst with views—down streets, through windows, out of doors—that turn some of his paintings into labyrinths. Light streams in from all sorts of unexpected directions, and the pictures take on a warmth and an openness that matches their subjects.

The paintings of the last part of the 1650s are among the most sheerly beautiful that the Dutch produced at the height of their success. Perhaps his own success inspired him to exchange stuffy Delft for the booming capital, Amsterdam, where he moved in the early 1660s. There, he began the third phase of his career—taking families outside their bourgeois homes and placing them in palaces.

———

SEVENTEENTH-CENTURY Holland is fertile ground for novelists, fantasists, and forgers. Easy to envision (thanks to its artists) and meticulously documented (thanks to its tireless bureaucrats), its history is just romantic enough, and contains just enough mysterious gaps, that it invites us to use our imaginations to fill in the unknowable what-ifs. For all we know, some of these invented answers might even be true.

So many pieces have already been found, after all. A whole history has been pieced together from a century and a half of determined sleuthing. Apparently trivial details—notes from village account books, drawings fished out of suburban garages, tests on pigments and nails—have slowly added up, and these small fragments provide such a rich picture of the Golden Age that it is always tempting to add one more.

Some inventors, like the novelists, acknowledge that they are using their imaginations. Others, like the forger Van Meegeren, fill in the gaps in more devious ways. One such question concerns the relationship between De Hooch and Vermeer. We know that they knew each other, and that their art was in dialogue. Like so much else in these scarcely documented lives, the nature of their relationship is cryptic.

Vermeer's fame, surpassed only by Rembrandt's, is so great that any artist in his circle is relegated to staffage. But in Sutton's exhibition—

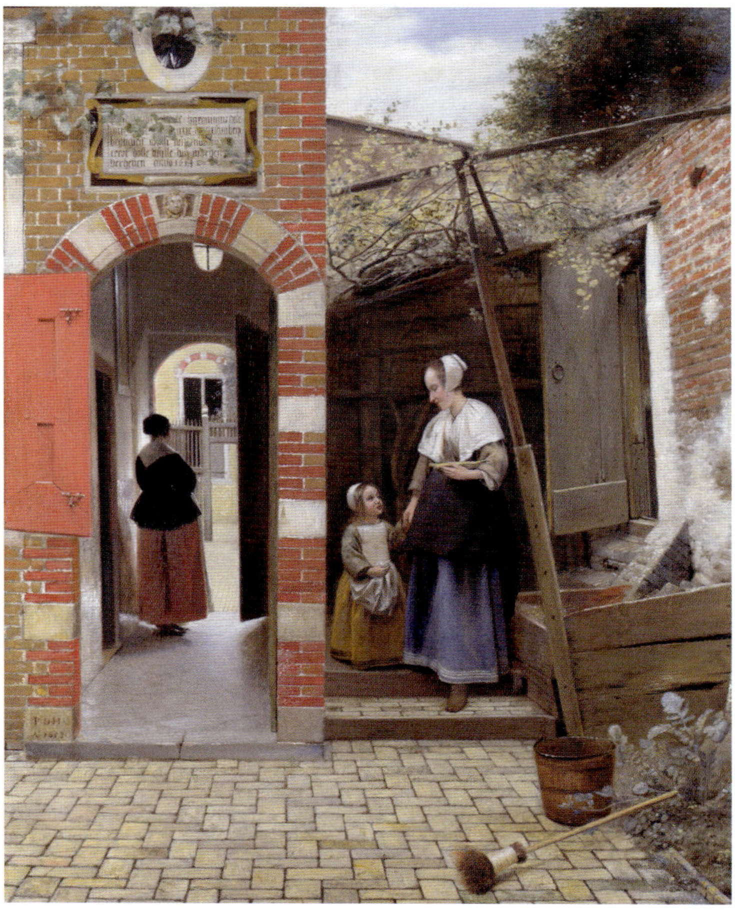

*The loving husband and father's view of his family were combined
with intricate, highly complex perspective and lighting.*

this might have been its thesis—was a claim that De Hooch and Vermeer represented "one of those extraordinary creative partnerships, whether personal or merely professional, which advance the history of art in ways that the two masters might not have achieved individually."

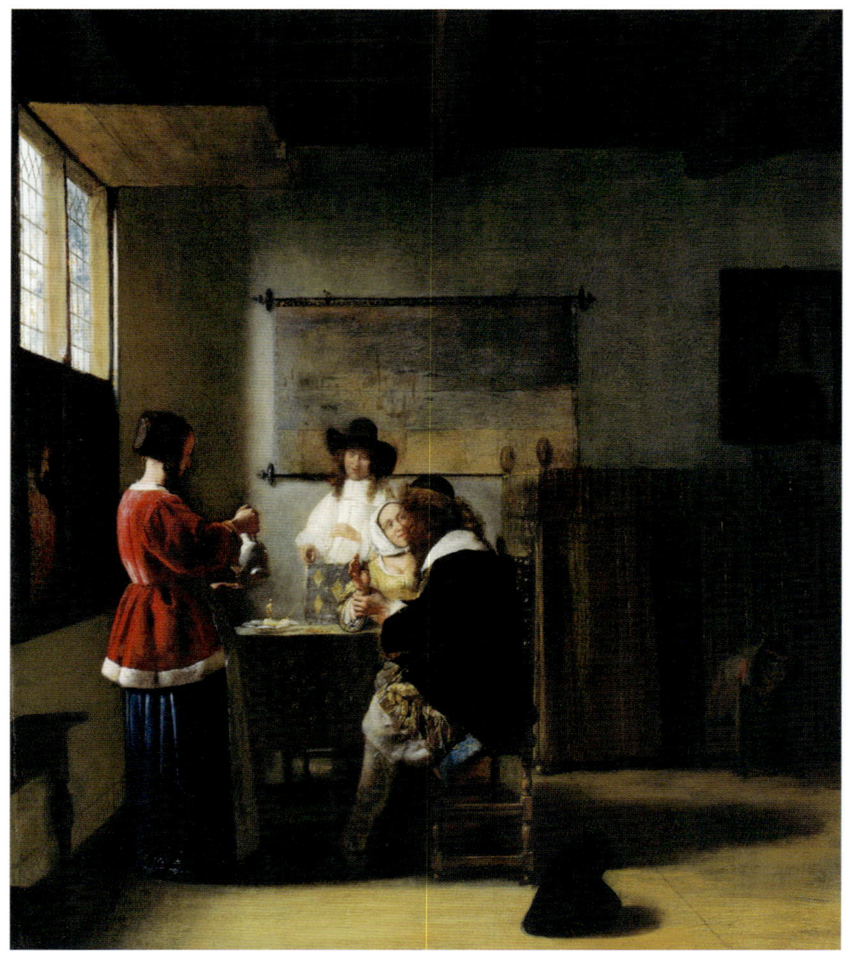

The documents reveal little about the connections between Vermeer and De Hooch. Paintings like this one reveal more.

Vermeer was three years younger. By 1656, when he painted his first dated work, *The Procuress*, De Hooch had already left his own apprenticeship years behind and embarked on the great works of his mature period, whose characteristics were the same kinds of small interior scenes that would become Vermeer's trademark. In paintings like the *Officer and Laughing Girl* in the Frick, we see a clear echo of De Hooch.

The work seems to be derived from a picture of De Hooch's from a few years before. It has been given the typically pedestrian name of *Soldiers Playing Cards*. The design is similar, the differences clear: De Hooch is more expressive and less precise, without that peculiar characteristic of Vermeer's, that uncanny way that his paintings, like a pixelated photo blown up too big, dissolve when seen from too close by.

There are other differences, too: De Hooch's colors are darker, less jewel-like than Vermeer's. But as we see in De Hooch's first real masterpiece, *A Merry Company with Two Men and Two Women*, we are in the same world. As usual, the title tells us nothing except that the picture features four people in an interior; we visualize it better when learning that great connoisseurs once took it for a Vermeer.

The figures are grouped around a table and lit, as in so many Vermeers, from a window whose lower shutters are closed. The light, coming from the gray skies that settle like a blanket over Holland for so many months in the year, creates a feeling of privacy, of intimacy. The scene suggests a land of decent people, and invites us to dream of what life could be in a peaceful room, in a peaceful land, like this.

WHEN DE HOOCH MOVED to Amsterdam around 1660, his pictures gained a new bombast. The pictures from Delft yielded to something befitting the great city's opulence. The floors, once of mud and then of brick and tile, are now of exotic marble. The solid furniture of the earlier pictures is now carved from ebony and inlaid with tortoiseshell, the gray walls now covered with gilded leather.

Many of these scenes are sited within the city's great wonder, the City Hall. Holland had no tradition of kingship or of palatial architecture; and

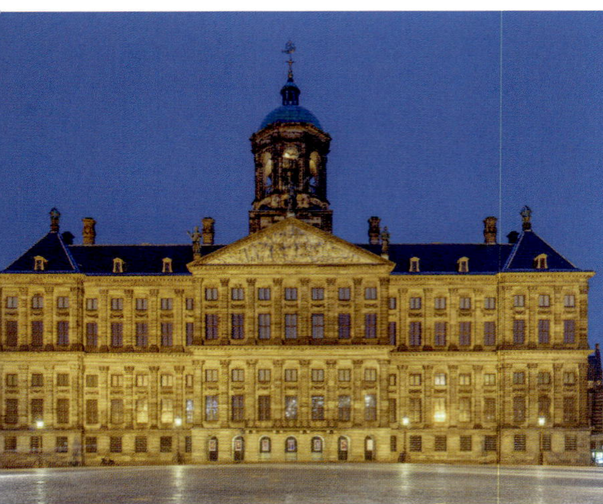

The greatest building built in Europe between St. Peter's and Versailles, Amsterdam's City Hall proclaimed the upstart city's role as the emporium of the world.

if, even today, this building looms gigantically over the low-rise center, we can only imagine how majestic it would have appeared to someone who had just arrived from Delft. The building was in the last phases of construction when De Hooch reached Amsterdam.

Its interiors were as lavish as the palace of a king. (It would become a royal palace after the establishment of the current monarchy in 1815.) But in this merchant's republic, the monarch this architecture honored was Amsterdam itself. De Hooch was the first to paint these interiors. Several of his paintings show impressed tourists, suitably dolled up for the occasion, and accompanied by pet dogs. They walk atop the world: on the huge marble maps of the known universe that are set in the floor.

De Hooch also repurposed the town hall as a fantasy palace. Imagining its chambers as the rooms of a great aristocratic house, he inserted groups, fancily dressed and doing fancy things, in similar positions to the families and friends he painted in Delft. But something has happened. Even the most accomplished of these paintings lack the freshness of the earlier works. The fantasy, now, is a bit too obvious.

DE HOOCH PRODUCED nearly half his known paintings in the last fourteen years of his life, after his move to Amsterdam. It is hard to delineate what might be called the fourth phase of his work, because it runs concurrently with the third. Throughout these years, he was still capable of high quality, and even of the occasional masterpiece. But many of his works from this time were hideous.

Some are so bad that they were later used as an admonishing metaphor to illustrate the decadence of an entire nation—a down-to-earth folk which, bloated by wealth and power, had been lulled into a complacency that precipitated their fall. These works have long frustrated his advocates, and posed an interpretative challenge.

Besides the visual evidence of these paintings, almost nothing is known of De Hooch's last years. Five more children were born in Amsterdam, bringing the total to seven; two died. Four years after he moved and started painting his fantasy palaces, he was not assessed any tax, meaning he was relatively poor. He never found his footing in the metropolis, which was facing economic distress and foreign invasion: the end of the Golden Age.

Rembrandt died in 1669. This was the period in which Vermeer had to move in with his mother-in-law, and Jan Steen had to apply for a license to run a tavern. The brothers De Witt, the country's de facto political leaders, were lynched in The Hague. In 1672, the "Year of Disasters," the country was nearly overrun by France and a coalition of German states. The nation's defenders opened the dikes and flooded much of its land.

Looking at De Hooch's pictures from this time, it is easy to imagine the aging artist pumping out as much "content" as he can, forced to sacrifice the most remarkable feature of his greatest works, their quality of stillness—their distance from the madding crowd. If his earlier works communicate composition, warmth, and restfulness, his later works make you uneasy. Sometimes, coming across one, I felt physical distress.

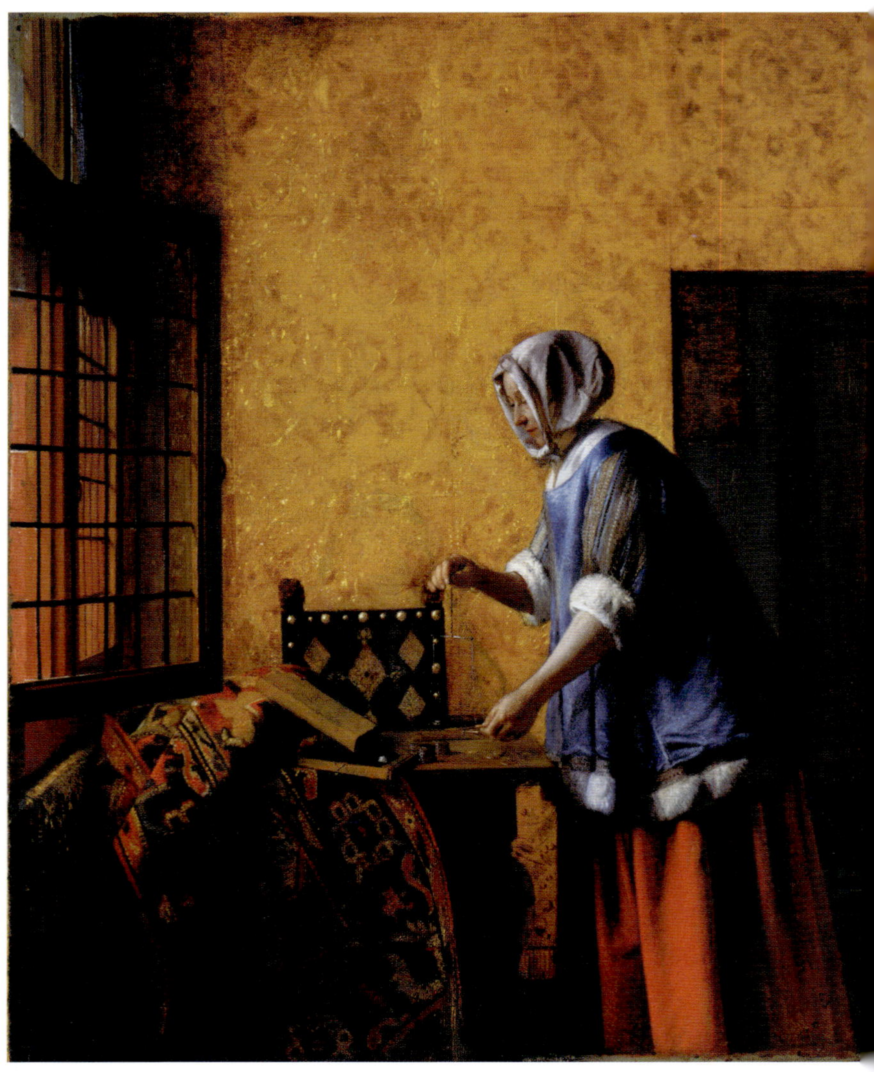

Like Vermeer (and Metsu), De Hooch painted a woman holding a balance, but unlike Vermeer he provided no explicit religious reading.

In 1976, the discovery of a document showing that he had died insane cast an entirely new light on these pictures. Here, at last, was an explanation, though one that raised its own unanswerable questions. What was the nature of his mental illness? When had it begun? Was his illness responsible for his lapses? Or was it his deteriorating economic position—his inability to work as in his younger years—that drove him mad?

De Hooch's late period is not, like that of Frans Hals or Rembrandt, an apotheosis. It is a shipwreck. And when his work is compared, once again, with his neighbor Vermeer's, it raises another question. Attributions vary, but Vermeer left around thirty-five works, and died at forty-three. What if De Hooch had died at the same age, a year or two after he moved to Amsterdam, and painted none of his late work? He would still have painted more than Vermeer—but not by much, especially if we deduct the pictures from his years of apprenticeship. There would be about the same number of great paintings, around thirty. Some of these are better than the lesser Vermeers. If the two bodies of work were placed side by side, not everyone would agree—not instantly—as to which was the greater artist.

MY FATHER WAS in town. A lawyer, he had discovered that the trial of Slobodan Milošević in The Hague was open to the public. He was curious to see how a United Nations courtroom proceeded. I could think of many ways I would rather spend the day than hearing about the mass graves and racist massacres that took place during the breakup of Yugoslavia, but I went because of my own morbid curiosity: there weren't many monsters like Milošević, and few of them were available for close inspection.

In his gray suit, the monster looked as unimposing as the men who carried out the Holocaust. The question being discussed was the makeup of a chain of command that authorized a massacre in Bosnia, and whether the ultimate power resided in Belgrade—with Milošević—or with the Bosnian Serb army in Pale. The discussion was no less boring for being a question of life or death. Afterward my dad and I went to the Mauritshuis.

This was almost exactly the scenario that Lawrence Weschler describes in *Vermeer in Bosnia*, a book I read, attracted by its surprising title, shortly thereafter. In it, Weschler tells of a judge who, after a day of listening to stories of rape and murder, would go to that same perfect museum. The contrast between the courtroom and the museum brought him to an insight, and brought me close to the appeal of those images of conviviality:

> When Vermeer was painting those images, which for us have become the very emblem of peacefulness and serenity, all Europe was Bosnia (or had only just recently ceased to be): awash in incredibly vicious wars of religious persecution and proto-nationalist formation, wars of an at-that-time unprecedented violence and cruelty, replete with sieges and famines and massacres and mass rapes, unspeakable tortures and wholesale devastation. To be sure, the sense of Holland during Vermeer's lifetime which we are usually given—that of the country's so-called Golden Age—is one of becalmed, burgherlike efficiency; but that Holland, to the extent that it ever existed, was of relatively recent provenance, and even then under a continual threat of being overwhelmed once again.

Vermeer's serenity was interrupted by his early death. Would he have been able to keep up the pose if he, like De Hooch, had lived another coarse, hungry decade? The ugliness he kept so carefully at bay crept into De Hooch's later pictures in all kinds of ways: not in direct depictions of the depredations Weschler describes, but in the off-kilter sense they give of how hard it was to keep it together.

———

AS TRAGIC AS De Hooch's death in the madhouse seemed, it was, at least, an explanation, a drama. These spare facts—a once great artist churning out half-deranged pictures for a quick buck, and brought to this pathetic end—delivered us back into the realm of the historical novel, and held out an invitation to fill in the blanks. Even without speculation, these facts offered a kind of redemption for his work.

But in 2008, the art historian Frans Grijzenhout discovered that the Pieter de Hoogh who had died in the Amsterdam madhouse in 1684 was not the artist. It was his son, also named Pieter, who had been committed five years earlier, at the request of his own parents. He was twenty-four, and trained as a painter. His parents undertook to "supply him with linen and wool and wash and change him properly."

No further documentation has been discovered about De Hooch's own death, or that of his wife, or that of the four children who, presumably, survived them. Besides this document, the only information that we have about his last years is the record of the baptism of another son in 1672. The year of his son's death is the year of his last dated painting, so we can probably assume that he didn't live much longer.

When the younger Pieter was sent to the madhouse, the other surviving children were fifteen, twelve, and seven: a young household still. But the man who had painted mothers and children with such tenderness had grown old. He had already buried two children; and his son's illness must have been severe in order for his parents to commit him to an institution as ugly as a seventeenth-century bedlam.

The portrait that emerges from this new information does not, therefore, change much about the artist's decline: a torturous home life, an attempt to keep producing at a time of economic meltdown. He must have known how inferior these later works were. For any artist, it would have been a source of reproach to watch inspiration ferment into drudgery. But he had rent to pay, mouths to feed.

For *this* artist, this fate was especially cruel. His deepest feelings were reserved for scenes of the happy home, of contented women, of bright children. Everything suggests that the man who created these images was a loving husband, a proud father; and if rooms and relationships were surely messier in real life, the emotions these images stir are too convincing for them not to reflect the artist's.

Or a *longing* of the artist's. It was a longing of mine, too. His fantasy of perfectly ordered rooms stayed with me because when I encountered him I was at the beginning of my adult life. I wondered if I would be lucky enough to find such a serene future. Though I could never have suspected it during that weekend in Hartford, that future would take place in Dutch rooms that, with a little imagination—with a little editing out of computers and refrigerators and indoor plumbing—looked so much like his.

I wonder how De Hooch, when he was older and his life was mostly behind him, looked back at the masterpieces from his heroic period. Did he think much about them? Or did he look forward the way so many of us do, imagining himself still in the process of becoming? Artists know their failures as well as anyone, which is why I don't like to dwell upon this painful thought. It is one thing to look forward to happiness. It is something else to look back at it when it is lost.

8

GABRIËL METSU

Mammonomania

IN THE SPRING OF 2009, I found myself in the Hotel Oloffson, a rambling, creaking mansion that looms like a mad dowager over Port-au-Prince. It is a beacon of style in a place too poor for any but the most basic architecture. On its wide verandas, in its lush gardens, you could imagine the lives of the Haitian rich; and when gazing from its breezy rooms at the port seething outside, you could imagine how uneasily they had slept. Home to two presidents, it was a place where the mighty came to bitter ends. Tirésias Simon Sam ruled for six years at the turn of the twentieth century. His son, Guillaume, succeeded him for five months in 1915, before being torn to pieces by an angry mob.

If I were to believe the story I heard about room 11, on whose balcony I slept in a large bed covered with mosquito netting, a more famous president had met his end here, too. In the spring of 1963, the story went, two Americans checked in. One was fat, one thin. They took their meals in the room. They spoke to no one. The thin man sometimes left the room for a swim in the pool. The fat man emerged only when a car turned up to whisk them to the National Palace. A few months later, when President Kennedy was assassinated in Dallas, the occasion was fêted with champagne in the palace. Fingers pointed at a neighboring Caribbean dictator, but Haiti knew who was really responsible. The inscrutable occupants of room 11 had plotted with Duvalier to destroy the American president.

Death, in Port-au-Prince, was never abstract. Its municipal cemetery was not a quiet place to reflect on the passing of time: death lurked here, violent and immediate. The cemetery wall was decorated with a painted mural of the *lwa*, or voodoo spirit, called Baron Samedi, Lord of the Cemetery, whose dress Duvalier had imitated and beneath whose fearsome image the dictator's firing squads dispatched his enemies. Inside, the dead rested uneasily. Certain rituals—nobody could or would say which—required items found here, and the debris crunching underfoot, I realized after walking over it for a few minutes, was human bones.

But like the *lwa*, thirsty for ritual offerings, the internet, even here, must be fed. I was on a deadline. With the dust of the deceased trapped in the treads of my shoes, I returned to room 11 and started beavering away at my laptop. The subject of my essay was, of all things, Jan Lievens. A caricaturist, I imagined, could not have conjured a more perfect image of the ivory tower: Haiti groans as a bespectacled intellectual earnestly discusses the reception of Lievens's and Rembrandt's works, and contrasts their uses of chiaroscuro. Mother Teresa would be defeated by Haiti's immense need; but Marie-Antoinette herself might have drawn the line at pondering Dutch art in Port-au-Prince.

But when I mentioned my malaise to a Haitian acquaintance, he was almost offended. What better place to write about art? he asked. Magnificent art had always flourished here, he reminded me, in large part *because* of Haiti's poverty. Where, after all, was beauty needed more?

TOWARD THE MIDDLE OF the 1650s, Gabriël Metsu painted a young woman weighing coins on a tiny scale. Heavily bundled against the cold, she grasps the top of the scale delicately, between her thumb and index finger, as she gazes into the middle distance, past the coins, her attention diverted by some solemn thought. The colors are dark and the mood is grave: as in other pictures of this kind, the woman and the table are painted in slightly different perspectives, giving the impression that the coins, perched precariously close to the edge of the table, are about to teeter off it.

The atmosphere suggests some operation beyond the merely monetary, an implication that would be made explicit around a decade later by Johannes Vermeer, who borrowed Metsu's theme for his *Woman Holding a Balance*, the same theme Pieter de Hooch had painted, too. A beautiful young woman dangles a scale before an open box bursting with jeweled baubles, while on the wall behind her an image of the Last Judgment shows Christ's weighing of human souls. Whether the weighing of souls is best suggested, as in Metsu's and De Hooch's paintings, or frankly stated, as in Vermeer's, is a matter of taste: for all its blunter symbolism, Vermeer's painting is remarkable, like all his work, precisely because of the calm way it stirs some nameless feeling in the beholder, a feeling different for everyone. The painter might see light and perspective; the Stoic, a reminder of vanity; the Christian, an affirmation of the inevitability of judgment.

Their subtle range of allusion opens these works to many interpretations. What is obvious—so obvious that it hardly seems worth stating—is that these pictures are not about the coins on the table. Yet it is remarkable just how much writing on Dutch art concentrates on the gold, the pearls, the satin, forgetting the feelings, which are harder to define, that the works themselves impart. Perhaps those feelings are too vague, too subjective. But I have often felt that their interpreters were fundamentally embarrassed by the appeal of their beauty to the emotions, the very thing that makes the painting of the Netherlands so enduring a subject. Many writers saturate their essays instead with such insistent discussions of privilege, class, and money that anyone who buries his head in museum catalogs grows a bit anxious. Even without a Haitian slum in sight, he often feels that he is comparison-shopping his way through a mall of ancient vanities, placing in the scale not his soul but the grubby guilder itself.

The origin of this interest seems to be the idea that the art of the Netherlands is an art of exchange, an art of the marketplace, an assumption that, by implication, aligns the Dutch with the consumerism of present-day Anglo-America. "Bourgeois" Dutch paintings are parsed, as "aristocratic" Italian and French paintings are not, for the exact prices of the objects they display. These are "paintings *of* luxury," the catalog of a Metsu exhibition held at the Rijksmuseum in 2010 insisted, and they are, "simultaneously, paintings *as* luxury." The catalog is full of statements that reinforce this idea, some of which reveal a materialism that can border on the obsessive: "Raechgel Rogiersdr. Cortius had a sewing cushion, which she bequeathed in 1637. It is not possible at this remove, however, to establish whether her cushion had a fitted interior, nor that of the green sewing cushion valued at twenty guilders and owned by Maijcken van Steenkiste, a member of the Mennonite elite in Haarlem." Further on, we even learn that "a preference for one colour or another was then, as it is now, a matter of personal taste that could be influenced by social position, religion, age, marital status, financial resources and, last but not least, the prevailing fashion."

When reading about Dutch art, one finds such an overwhelming preponderance of markets, auction prices, values, commodities, carpets, clothes, jewels, and drinking horns that it often seems that historians of Dutch art talk about money with the same doggedness that Freudians insist on sex, a mammonomania that certainly says more about our society than it does about the seventeenth-century Netherlands. That may be why I felt jittery in Port-au-Prince. Until I was corrected by my Haitian friends, I had, subconsciously at least, accepted the lamest and most inescapable canard about my subject: that this art was a middle-class pastime created for and about people who, besides commissioning expensive sewing cushions, didn't have much else going on. If that were true, it would indeed be hard to justify its study in a world so thickly populated with rapists and refugees. But so much of it was created when "all Europe was Bosnia," and in conditions of deprivation that we find hard to imagine today. And this misplaced materialist fixation loses sight of precisely what is beautiful and enduring about Dutch art: about art.

GABRIËL METSU'S LIFE, like that of many of the most distinguished Dutch painters, is poorly documented. He was born in 1629 in Leiden. His parents, most likely Catholics, were part of the vast wave of immigrants to Holland from Flanders, still under Spanish rule, and may have arrived in the north as infants. His father, Jacques, also a painter, died around a month after Gabriël was conceived. In total, his mother would be widowed four times.

He may have begun studying to be a silversmith, but his talents developed in another direction, and by the age of fourteen or fifteen he was already registered in the guild as a painter. Still in his teens, he left Leiden for Utrecht, where he received more training, and from Utrecht, in 1654, he went to Amsterdam, where he would live for the rest of his life. Four years after the move, he married Isabella de Wolff, a woman from an artistic family in Enkhuizen: her mother, Maria de Grebber, was one of Holland's few early female painters, though only two of her pictures are known today.

Metsu's portrait of an older woman painter is presumed to show Maria, and he would portray her daughter Isabella many times. Around the time of their marriage, he depicted her as Terpsichore, the muse of dance, playing a viola da gamba to inspire the husband who sits in front of a blank canvas: the composition may have inspired Vermeer's *The Art of Painting*. A few years later, borrowing that great theme of Rembrandt's, Metsu painted himself as the prodigal son, holding, tipsily askew, a foot-long wineglass, and embracing a bemused but apparently forbearing Isabella. Technically, the subject is moralizing—a confession of sinfulness—but the frolicsome mood, as in Rembrandt's painting of himself and Saskia in *The Prodigal Son in the Brothel*, winks and nudges.

Like Rembrandt, Metsu frequently painted himself. Unlike Rembrandt, who often did so in independent self-portraits, Metsu generally inserted himself, as he did in *The Artist as the Prodigal Son*, into genre scenes: for example, as a laughably self-important soldier whose lush scarlet jacket pops out from its grimy surroundings in *A Cavalier*

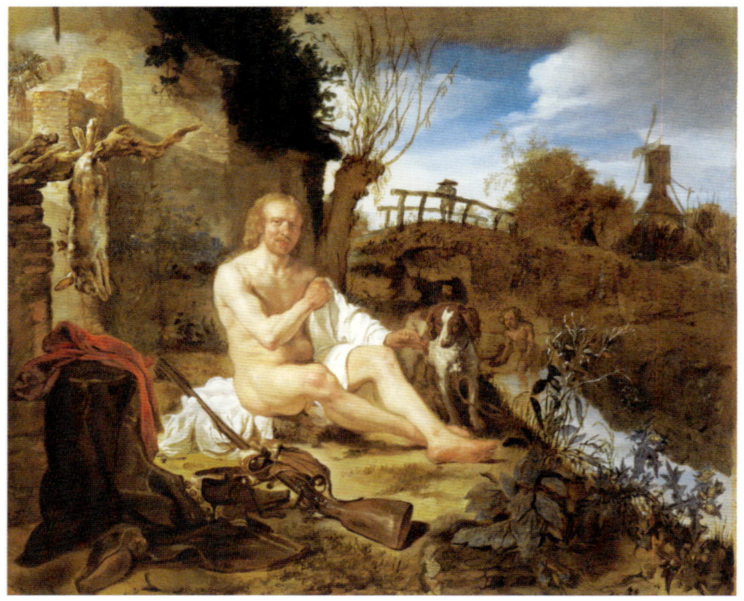

*Metsu, perhaps uniquely among Dutch artists of his time,
portrayed himself naked.*

Visiting a Blacksmith's Shop. Most startlingly, he showed himself naked,
as *A Hunter Getting Dressed After Bathing*, a unique nude depiction of a
seventeenth-century artist.

Vermeer and Metsu both painted women writing letters, looking
out at the viewer with enticing smiles. They have been interpreted as
flirty "poster girls," though no such interpretation has been offered of the
naked hunter who—unlike the neatly dressed, meekly smiling girls—
all but leers at us while flaunting a body that meets all the then current
measures of male beauty: muscular, almost entirely hairless, with "full
calves and clean feet." Metsu may be getting dressed, as the picture's title
claims, but inquiring minds might speculate that he is, instead, taking
his clothes *off*.

The lacuna is striking because similar themes are so widely read into other, less obviously sexual pictures. We learn that a cast-off shoe is "a detail with sexual associations," though the art historian Linda Stone-Ferrier offers a corrective to some more exuberant readings, including to the most clichéd one of all: that any bird in the vicinity of a woman refers to the term *vogelen*, "birding," an old term for intercourse. In discussing Metsu's *Old Man Selling Poultry and Game*—in which a seated old

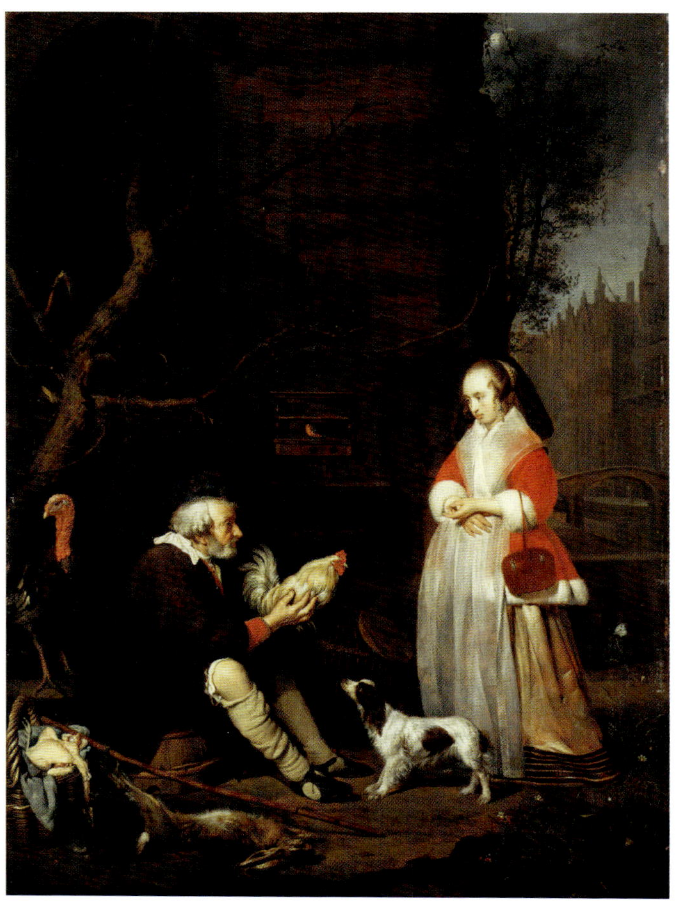

Even for Amsterdam's poshest citizens, misery was only a handshake away.

man, dressed in rags, hands a cockerel to a beautifully dressed young woman—Stone-Ferrier rejects a previous interpreter's notion that it "must allude to the erotic titillation and moral warnings inherent in the double meaning of birding" by pointing out that both parties are "respectable, proper and honourable in effect and costume."

Instead of a cheesy pun, one can also see, in this painting, the full range of Metsu's virtuosity, how he incorporates the techniques of the still-life and the landscape painter into a stirring scene. He shows the woman's long, gauzy scarf falling over her sumptuous red-and-yellow-silk clothing; he contrasts the wrinkled skin of the old man with the young woman's rosy face, and the feathers of the chicken and the turkey with the fur of a dog and a rabbit. There is a moral here, but it is not about sex. Metsu places symbols of age and death on the old man's half of the picture. The tree behind him, branches broken, is wizened and bare; the tree behind her is bushy and bright. The perky dog is hers; a dead rabbit and a plucked chicken, its neck hanging lifelessly from a basket, is his. Her clothes are colorful; his torn and drab. She stands before a canal, the open city stretched out behind her. He is surrounded by cages.

———

TO LOOK AT an exhibition of Metsu's work is to see another of those seamlessly flexible, smoothly brilliant Dutchmen the Golden Age pumped out in quantity, one whose flexible mind managed to reflect almost all the tendencies in the genre painting of his time.

Like Vermeer, who was three years younger, Metsu began his career painting more traditional religious and mythological scenes before he turned to "genre" in the mid-1650s. In 2005, a revisionist show was held in Rotterdam. Its title, "Senses and Sins: Dutch Painters of Daily Life in the Seventeenth Century," used "daily life" instead of "genre," which its catalog denounced as "perhaps the stupidest designation for a type of painting that there is. It is the type that was left over after history and portrait and landscape and all the other types which are true types. . . . It is the unwelcome remainder of figure pieces which simply show people, not people with names but types, and not people in a well known story but in a more or less plausible situation."

Metsu and Vermeer were both inspired by Ter Borch, who was twelve years older than Metsu. His strange and apparently allusive pictures of people courting, writing letters, and making music would profoundly influence the subsequent generation. But Netherlanders had long produced images of "daily life," first in manuscript illuminations and then, parenthetically, in the margins of sacred scenes. Even when these shook off their religious underpinnings and became independent subjects, they still often remained true to their origins by conveying some moralizing message.

These could be rather thinly overlaid, as in certain works of Pieter Bruegel, the sixteenth-century Flemish master famous for his images of rowdy peasants. Over the century that separated Bruegel from Ter Borch—a century marked by the war for independence and the emergence of the Netherlands as a great power—these scenes of the peasantry gave way, though never entirely, to pictures showing the lives of the country's cities.

Sometimes these paintings of people "in a more or less plausible situation" had a clear message, made explicit, as in Vermeer's *Woman Holding a Balance*, by a commonly understood allusion, or simply suggested, as in Metsu's image of the same. In one of Metsu's most dazzling paintings, *A Woman Reading a Letter*, a pretty girl contentedly studies a letter whose contents we are not given to see. Her maid, meanwhile, peels back a curtain to reveal a painting of a tempest-tossed ship—a hint that the relationship between the girl and her lover is, or will soon turn, stormy.

Because enough genre paintings do have such explicit meanings, critics plausibly imagined that there might be clues lurking in others, keys not immediately obvious to present-day viewers: hence the interest in birds and cast-off shoes. Searches for "hidden meanings" were popularized by Erwin Panofsky, the German-American art historian who used contemporary literature to uncover forgotten layers of significance in late medieval religious paintings. Some of his interpretations have

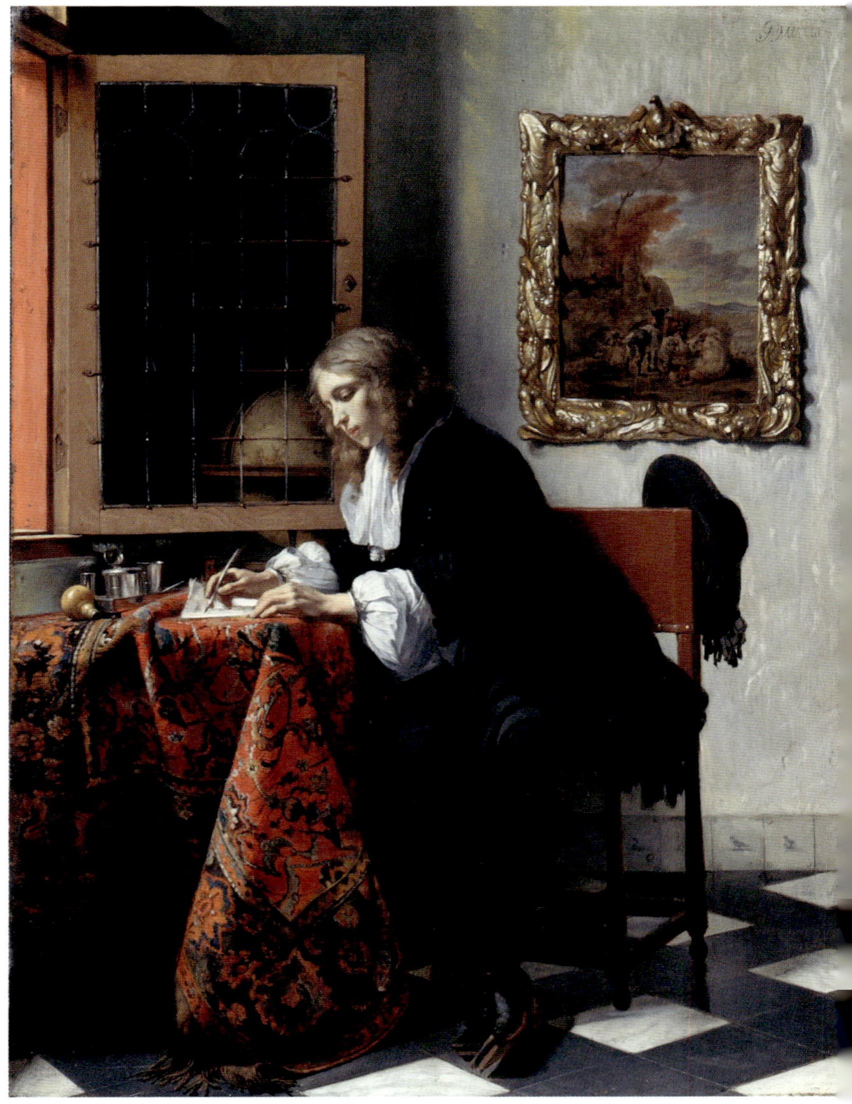

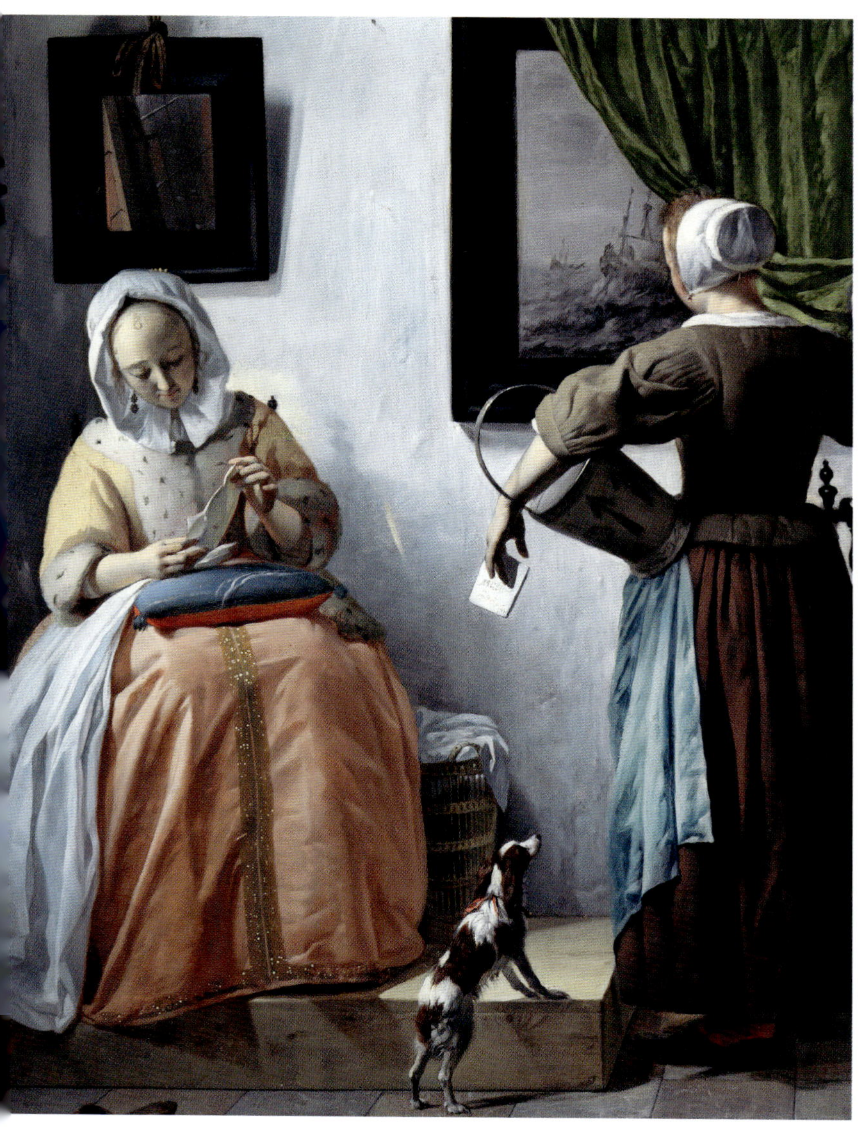

A man writes a letter; a woman receives it;
a maid peers at an image of stormy seas.

been questioned or updated, but his discoveries shape art history to this day, particularly because his basic insistence—that research in literary, religious, and political history could bring us closer to understanding works of art—was so obvious in retrospect.

But the religious art of the late Gothic was always densely symbolic. Artists displayed their mastery by manipulating intricate symbols as surely as they did by shows of technical bravura. In the genre paintings that emerged two centuries later, in the work of Ter Borch or Vermeer or Metsu, symbols can be smudged or entirely stripped. Pictures are no longer necessarily "about" anything beyond their purported subjects—at least as far as we can tell. Instead, they derive their power from a puzzling or suggestive atmosphere.

This has been unsatisfactory to historians trained to seek interpretations, and its limits were illustrated in "Senses and Sins." Of Ter Borch's *Woman Drinking Wine*, one writer asked: "Has the woman just begun to drink, as the carefully held and barely tipped glass would seem to indicate? Or is she about to set the latter down again, having taken her first sip?" The letter motif is similarly mysterious: "Holding a quill, the inkpot seems to signalize that an act of writing has quite recently been or is soon to be carried out. On the other hand, the creases in the paper suggest that the letter was written by another hand and the lady is its recipient." These questions are unanswerable. But an art historian's job is to find meanings, and this is bound to be frustrating. It is much easier to write about a warning against intemperance than about a woman drinking, for no apparent reason, in the middle of the day.

———

FOR THE HALF CENTURY preceding "Senses and Sins," critics had mostly believed that these meanings were there—hidden, perhaps, but there. They assumed that "nothing, absolutely nothing, in seventeenth-century art was what it seemed to be in a dispassionate way, [and] everything had to be seen through edifying glasses."

But the quest for double meanings ran into a dead end. The hidden meanings had been too well hidden, and most of these pictures didn't "mean" that much at all. Yet the habit of scrutinizing objects stuck: Svetlana Alpers's *The Art of Describing*, published in 1983, suggested that the scrutiny of objects was, in fact, the fundamental characteristic of Dutch art. Four years later, Simon Schama's *The Embarrassment of Riches* brilliantly placed money and its discontents at the center of Dutch culture.

The combination offered a way out of the impasse. If the Dutch were obsessed with objects and money, the historian could look at the stuff in a painting and figure out how much it cost. This description may be an oversimplification, but the approach had the virtue of relegating the impossible question of meaning to the field of folklore. And it produced materialist criticism that—though it never described itself as such—amounted to Marxism *après la lettre*, an interest in class and finance more appropriate to a consumerist society dazzled by auction prices than to the world of the Dutch masters.

Shorn of any consequence beyond the economic, genre paintings became the Rolexes of yesteryear: "paintings *of* luxury" and "paintings *as* luxury." The catalog of the Metsu show of 2010 revealed how deeply ingrained this notion became: it included essays called "Gabriel Metsu and the Art of Luxury," "Gabriel Metsu's Street Vendors: Shopping for Values in the Dutch Neighbourhood," "Early Owners of Paintings by Metsu in Leiden and Amsterdam," "Costumes in Gabriel Metsu's Paintings," and an intriguing survey of fluctuating reputations titled " 'Why Buy a Vermeer When a Metsu Is Available?' "

Luxury, shopping, owners, clothes, prices: the organizers have even abandoned hopes of portraying genre paintings as illustrations of "daily life," the key to the "Senses and Sins" survey of 2005. Even then, its curators were a bit self-conscious about its title, because, as the introduction itself admitted, "these images do not reflect reality but were imagined by the artist and have no obvious significance; the title of our exhibition," therefore, "may seem a bit provocative."

It was provocative because even the vague and apparently inoffensive idea that they showed "daily life" was undermined by years of research into the objects within them. Five years later, for example, the Metsu

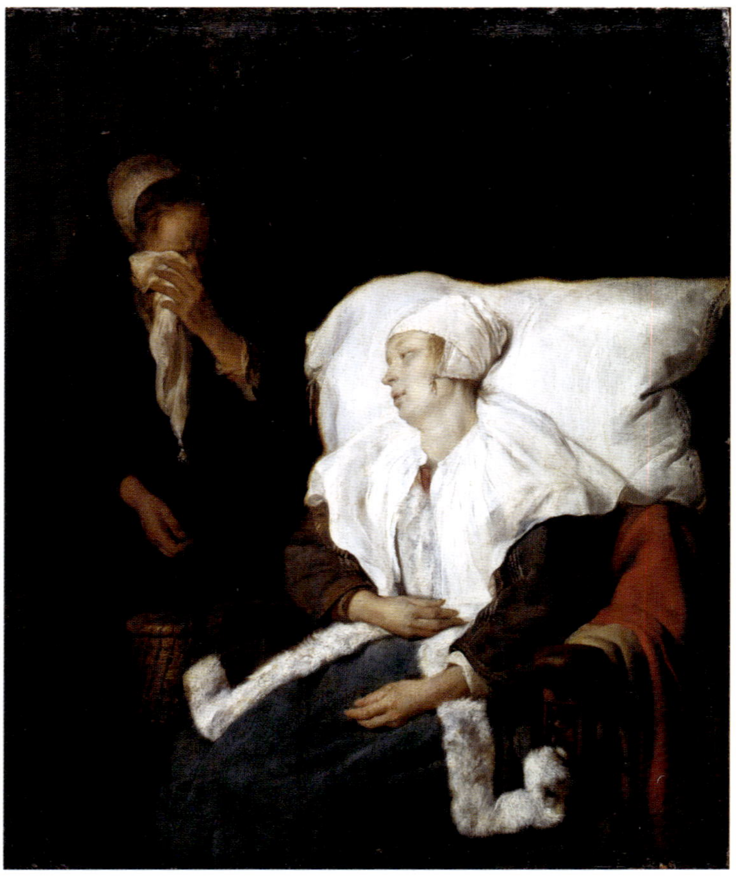

Does The Sick Girl *show a longing for a lover, or a young life cut short?*

catalog stated that "chandeliers are omnipresent in genre paintings, thus imparting the misleading impression that they were essential to household décor. In reality, chandeliers were extremely costly articles most frequently fabricated for churches."

The phrase "in reality" recurs, suggesting a rather grim determination to restore "reality" to obviously fantastic pictures. Even unarmed

with knowledge of the placement of chandeliers in the seventeenth century, anyone walking through galleries filled with paintings by Gabriël
Metsu—or Vermeer, or Ter Borch—will realize that these images are
hardly more "real" than the angels or satyrs down the hall. The maid is
too pointedly contemplating the picture of a stormy sea; the fishmonger
is too decorative; the lady's satin dress too swooshy.

Indeed, the prominence of curtains—painted curtains swept back
to reveal the scene playing within; covering the paintings shown inside
the painting itself; attached to the frames to protect the pictures—offers
a clue that this is an art of the theater, designed to heighten and refine
daily life, an art whose very essence is its artificial and artistic nature:
the opposite of daily life. It is an art of escapism. And an art of escapism
makes one wonder what its creators wanted to escape.

IN 1661, Gabriël Metsu painted a large and ambitious work called *The
Visit to the Nursery*. It shows group of five figures, a baby, and a dog.
The room is luxurious beyond the real domestic arrangements of even
the richest Amsterdammers. It includes a gilded bed, an ostentatious
silver service, marble floors, an ornate mantelpiece with red marble
columns like the one that had been installed at Amsterdam's colossal City Hall, inaugurated six years before. Above the mantelpiece,
another storm-tossed vessel.

The painting was presumably commissioned by a great patrician ("with a net worth amounting to the then astronomical sum of
230,000 guilders") named Jan Jacobsz. Hinlopen, who was so impressed
by Metsu's work that he commissioned the noted poet and playwright
Jan Vos to praise it; and who, about a year later, commissioned from
Metsu a picture of himself, his wife, and their four children in a similarly
opulent environment.

This picture shows the great Dutch bourgeoisie unembarrassed by
its riches: the plump patriarch, the magnificently dressed children, the
virtuous-but-perhaps-slightly-smug lady of the house, in a posh setting that includes paintings, gilt-leather wall coverings, and a classical

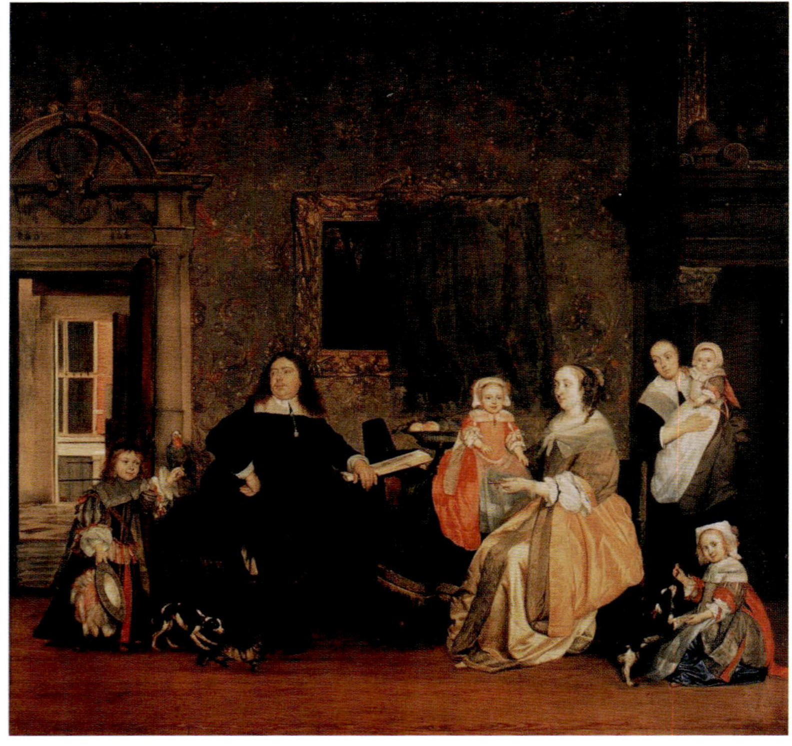

The opulent family who posed for this picture had no idea—
no more than anyone ever does—what fate had in store for them.

doorframe, along with a nurse, two dogs, a cat, and a splendid and exotic parrot, perched on the little boy's outstretched hand. The painting at the center is mostly obscured by a large curtain, but it does not seem to show a stormy sea.

We can imagine easily enough why Hinlopen would commission a picture to celebrate a birth or a family. But these two paintings belie a world of hardships that has little to do with economic standing. Childbirth, celebrated in the first picture, was dangerous to a point that we, in our age of antibiotics and ultrasounds, cannot easily imagine, often fatal to both mother and child. Those who survived, as the exhibition catalog maintained, "struggled to stay alive. Women, too, had a hard time staying healthy. If they managed to survive their numerous confinements, they often had to provide for their families, if their husband abandoned them, died of some disease, probably contagious, or had enlisted on one of the countless ships that were away from home for years at a time." (Metsu's mother, four times a widow, was among these abandoned women.) Given these grim circumstances, it is startling to read that "representations of ill women were always meant to be humorous, as the women are not genuinely sick, but suffering from *minnepyn* (love sickness)."

That is not what I see in Metsu's *Sick Woman and a Weeping Maidservant*, which might just as well show the moment of death: the maid's disconsolate gesture makes her mistress's gorgeous clothes seem nearly ironic. So many of Metsu's paintings, even the funny ones, feature sick children, sick women, and the elderly poor ("rarely cared for by their married children or other relatives [and] expected to live unobtrusively and modestly as befitted the last stage of life"), though life was not only hard for the poor and the old, or for women and children. The stormy sea in *The Visit to the Nursery* was no more a merely sentimental or romantic symbol than it was for the men on the "countless ships away from home for years at a time."

CONSIDER THE posh, proud Hinlopens. Only a year after Metsu painted them, the plague struck Amsterdam. Geertruyt, the baby the maid holds on the right side of the picture, died in August; Jacob, the boy holding the parrot, followed in October; their mother, Leonora, joined them in the first week of November. Jan, the father, shown here in the ripeness of his middle age, would survive only three more years, dying at forty. In Amsterdam as in Port-au-Prince, the mighty met bitter ends.

Here, too, death was never abstract. The plague outbreak that decimated the Hinlopens killed nearly 10 percent of Amsterdam's population:

the fourth time in the century that a similar proportion of the population had been wiped out by this one disease. Amsterdam may have been the richest city in the world, but its catastrophes were Haitian in their recurrence and extent. A quick sampling of famous Dutch painters reveals a world as fragile as Port-au-Prince. Willem Drost died at age twenty-six, Dirck van Baburen and Paulus Potter at twenty-nine, Carel Fabritius and Adriaen Brouwer at thirty-two, Willem Duyster at thirty-five, Jan van Kessel at thirty-nine, Hendrick ter Brugghen and Jan-Baptist Weenix at forty. In this context, Johannes Vermeer, who made it to forty-three, was a ripe old man.

Metsu himself was buried in Amsterdam in 1667. He was thirty-seven.

OUR PAINS SOFTENED by our fabulous anesthesia, our lives extended beyond the imaginings of our ancestors, our houses glutted with infinite, and infinitely expanding, consumer choices, we probably cannot imagine how these elaborate theatrical fantasies appeared to people whose lives were so harsh, vulnerable, and short, who lived in a world where the rich, beautiful young woman was only a handshake away from the broken old man. No matter how much Amsterdam, with its churches and canals and elegant houses, looks like the city of the classic paintings, that city is gone, and the architecture is only décor: the contentedly shopping Amsterdammers of today, worrying about germs and whether to send their kids to private school, cannot imagine the fleeting, floating world of their fathers. To get closer, they might imagine Haiti, where death, in the form of Baron Samedi, is a gentleman in a natty suit, lurking on every street corner. There, they might ask why art is important in our short lives. What did all this beauty mean to those who made it, and to those who saw it? How did these colors stand out amid the cemeteries and the slums?

9

JAN STEEN

The Airborne Peacock

O N THE TOP FLOOR of the Rijksmuseum, take a right at *The Night Watch*, away from the crowds in the Gallery of Honor, and walk until you see a small balcony on your left. There, beneath a huge glass vault, a bibliophile's dream unfurls: the glorious Gothic cavern, three stories tall, of the museum's library. Down at the bottom, at the tables, researchers sit hunched over books, indifferent to the eyes of tourists.

Viewed from on high, this space seems like another of the museum's paintings. Like one of Vermeer's or De Hooch's houses, it looks like a place you might fantasize about but never enter. The difference is that you can enter this one. It's not even hard: you register on the website, request whatever it is you want to see, and the curators and librarians will wheel it out. Now you're the one the tourists are looking at.

When you're sitting there, it seems unbelievable that someone would let you flip through Rembrandt's drawings—but someone will, and even encourage you to do so. In my career as a researcher, I have always been impressed by how welcoming librarians and curators have been, and how different their hospitable spirit is from their fearsome reputation—and been sad about how that reputation keeps people away.

One morning, I came to see drawings of Jan Steen. Not *by* Jan Steen—there are only two such, firmly attributed, in the world—and

PRENTEN-MAGAZIJN VOOR DE JEUGD. No. 125.

LEVENSBESCHRIJVING.

JAN STEEN. — Geb. omstreeks 1640, Overl. 1678.

Jan Steen brengt leven in de brouwerij.

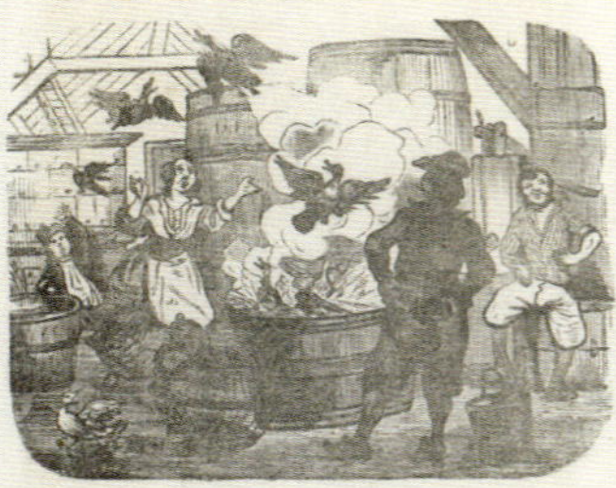

«Jan Steen!» dus sprak zijn vrouw, «het gaat niet als voor dezen:
» Men vraagt vergeefs om bier: er moest meer leven wezen
    » In onze brouwerij.» — «Wees maar gerust!» zei Jan,
    » 'k Zal toonen, dat ik dit zeer spoedig maken kan.»
Weldra verzint hij wat, om Grietje te bedriegen,
Laat' in de brouwerij een aantal eenden vliegen,
    En voegt zijn vrouw nu toe: » wat zeg je thans van mij!
    » Is 't nu niet levendig in onze brouwerij?»

De Huishouding van Jan Steen.

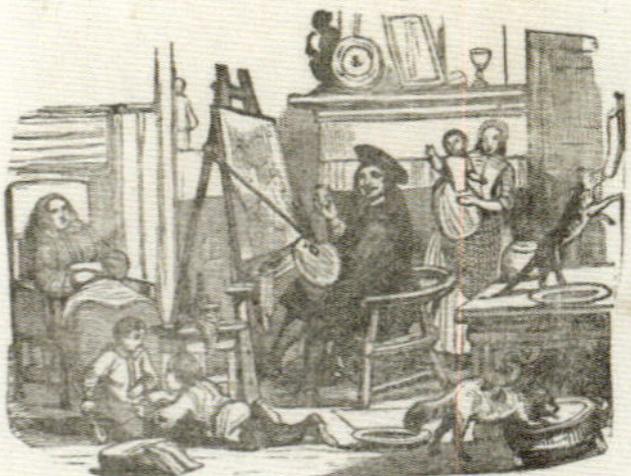

Het eerste schilderstuk van onzen snaak der snaken,
Door 't welk, als schilder, hij een' grooten naam mogt maken,
    Toont u zijn huisgezin. Ei lieve! zie hoe zot:
    De kat steelt van het spek; de hond snoept uit den pot:
De kindren haveloos, hun ell'boog door de mouwen;
De vrouw zit in haar' stoel dit goede werk te aanschouwen;
    Jan drinkt zijn glas, terwijl hij vrolijk om zich ziet,
    En op den schoorsteen de aap, die 't gansch tooneel bespiedt.

Jan Steen heeft aan den arm van het portret zijner vrouw eene
mand met schaapshoofden en pootjes geschilderd.

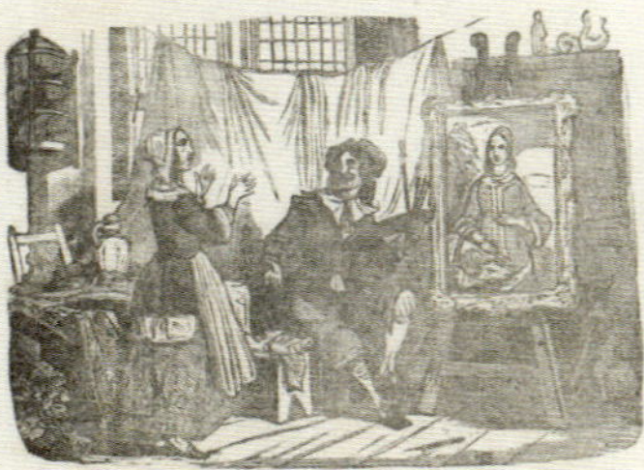

» Neen Jan! nu ben ik boos: gij hebt het gansch verkorven;
» Verminkt gij mijn portret? het is geheel bedorven.»
    Dus duwt zijn vrouw hem toe; doch Jan zegt: «'t is niet waar!
    (De snaaksche vent toch had zijn woorden altijd klaar)
» Juist deze mand, beladn met schapenkoppen, pooten,
» Moet uw portret gewis in waarde zeer vergrooten:
    » Gij wont daarmede uw brood, thans kent u elk, mijn schat!
    » 't Is daarom, dat ik dit er bij geschilderd had.»

Het Sint Nicolaasfeest van Jan Steen.

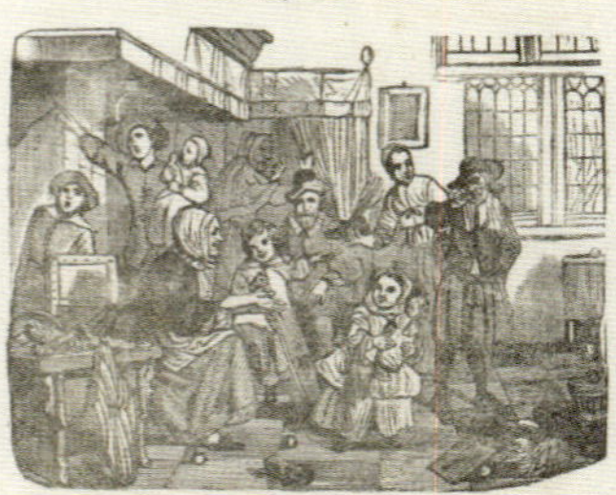

Dit fraaije schilderstuk, op 't Trippenhuis te vinden,
Van dezen schildersbaas moet de aandacht trekken, binden
    Van ieder, die 't beschouwt. Ei! zie dien slungel staan:
    Een roê steekt in zijn schoen; dit staat hem gansch niet aan:
Hoe leelijk huilt de knaap; hoe vrolijk daarentegen
Ziet elk der andren, die wat beters heeft gekrogen.
    Der andren blijdschap is meé sprekend afgebeeld;
    Terwijl het gansch heelal onze oogen boeit en streelt.

Prenten-Fabriek van **J. SCHUITEMAKER** te Purmerende.   (6.)

*Of the great Dutch painters, only Rembrandt and
Jan Steen never needed to be rediscovered.*

though one of them is here, its main value is as a curiosity. What I want to see is how Steen himself was depicted. So many Dutch artists have a story of being forgotten and rediscovered, but not Steen. Along with Rembrandt, he was the only major artist who never went out of style—but not necessarily as an artist.

As I work through a pile of cheap nineteenth-century prints, I encounter Jan Steen again and again. These prints—the ancestors of baseball cards and comic books—were meant for kids, and often contain a moralistic ditty. Steen, figure of folklore, fits right in among images of the princes of Orange and the "Pet Museum," cut-out domino games and Old St. Nicholas, images of boats and of funny animals from Africa.

In one series, Jan Steen takes his place alongside such eminences as Klaas Bierbuik ("Nicky Beerbelly") and Hans Altyddorst ("Johnny Alwaysthirsty"), "Chairman of the Beer Drinker's Club." In such images, a heroic if unidimensional Rembrandt is depicted as a dignified and uplifting example for the young. He refuses distractions; he subsists on bread and herring alone. Steen is a buffoon. And he seems like a lot more fun.

Three anecdotes recur. In the first, his wife, Margriet, begs him to settle down and get back to work at their brewery: "Jan, trade is dwindling. . . . You are meant to keep the brewery lively." Steen promises to. He fills the coppers, dumps the rest of the malt in, buys some live ducks, and plops them in the water. They flap and squawk and cause such a ruckus that Margriet rushes into the room; despite herself, she laughs.

To that, Jan says: "The brewery is lively enough now, isn't it?" The phrase, *leven in de brouwerij*, is common to this day: "We need some life in the brewery," you say of a dull party, or, when a fun person walks in: "Here comes the life in the brewery." Few Dutch people attribute the phrase to Steen, but the same is not true of another staple of the old prints: *een huishouden van Jan Steen*, a Jan Steen household.

"The room was in complete disarray, the dog slobbered from the pot, the cat ran off with the bacon, the children rolled about wildly on the floor," according to an early biographer. When the name Jan Steen is mentioned, this is the image, preserved in his most famous paintings,

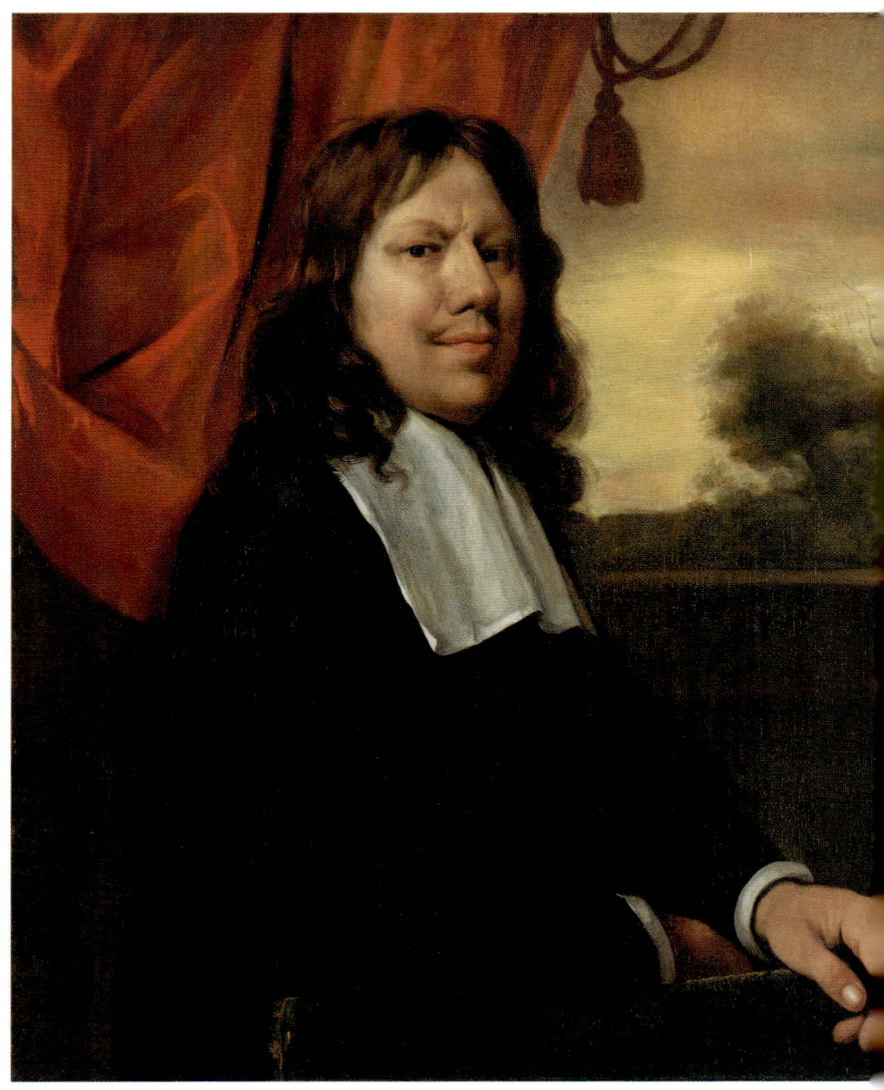

Steen could be a gentleman; he could also be a buffoon.
Dutch popular culture has mainly remembered him as the latter.

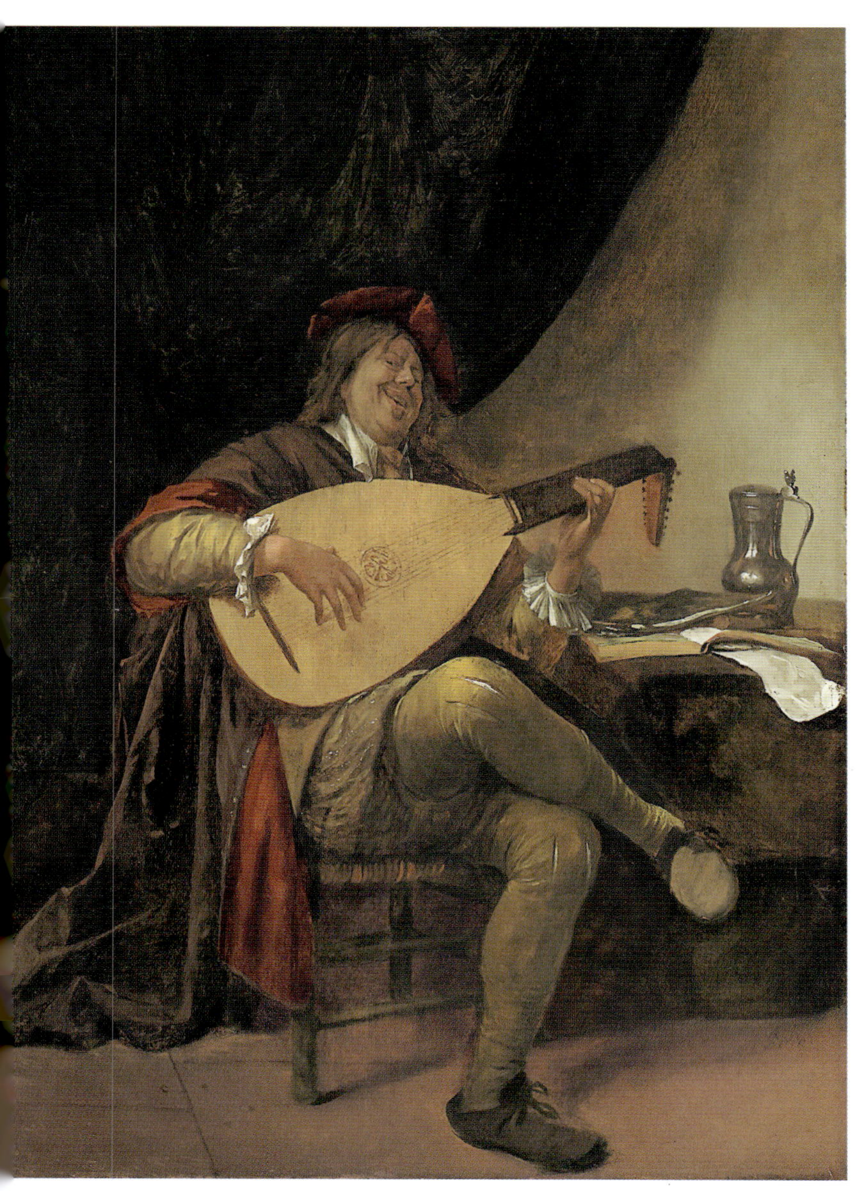

that instantly pops into the Dutch mind: "This bedroom looks like Jan Steen's household," a parent might say to a slovenly child.

Another story is about his second wife, Maria. Steen often included himself and his family in his paintings. Maria understandably tired of being shown "as an indecent object, sometimes as a horny tart, or sometimes as a match-maker or a drunken whore," and so Jan painted her in the stately way she desired—then couldn't resist alluding to her former job, a seller of offal, by adding a basket of boiled lambs' heads.

THE FOPPISH cartoon character that lived on in popular memory when Vermeer, Fabritius, and Hals were forgotten was Steen's own creation—an outgrowth of the zany figure that appears in his own paintings. Like an instantly recognizable actor in different roles, there he is, in picture after picture, with his silly grin and hippie hair and straggly moustache and a jowly chin that tumbles down, ring by ring, into his neck.

Few artists made less of an effort to look attractive, you might think: but though he's not pretty, Steen *is* attractive. Once you recognize him, once you start picking him out—as a naughty father teaching his kid how to smoke; as an old dunce, dressed in a funny costume, having his pocket picked by a fetching hooker; as a laughing drunk sliding down a ladder—you start to look for him, and are happy when you find him.

More than the irretrievable Vermeer or the olympian Rembrandt, Steen feels close, when you get to know him: more so, probably, than any other Dutch painter. A few decades after his death, Arnold Houbraken, the eighteenth-century biographer of the artists, wrote that Steen's "paintings are as his way of life, and his way of life as his paintings." This feels right—but only sometimes, because the paintings do not show a single way of life.

Despite his many walk-on roles in larger scenes, only two proper self-portraits are known. And they are so different from each other that, without all those other images of his face, they would be hard to identify as showing the same man. In one, a grinning Steen, in a floppy red beret, strums a lute. In the other, soberly dressed, he poses without a trace of self-mockery. One shows the painter as knave; the other, as a gentleman.

Both feel exaggerated. Both also feel true—and why not? None of us, we know, are one single thing. We know how different we can look at different ages, or at the same age, in different photographs. Neither is right; both are. Yet the Steen that was remembered, the one who made it into those prints and into the language, was the fool, not the gentleman: the bohemian, to use a word that wouldn't be popularized for two hundred years.

The bohemian was the opposite of the artist who conversed learnedly with potentates and popes, the artist-as-courtier that Rembrandt showed in his self-portrait as Castiglione. Steen was the artist who had to climb out of the window of the whorehouse, who—as one nineteenth-century painter imagined—sent his son out to hock his pictures in exchange for beer. This was not the artist who upheld decorum, but the artist who mocked it.

In perhaps his most famous painting, *As the Old Sing, So Pipe the Young*, Steen shows himself as the paterfamilias of a riotous brood. He paints his first wife, Margriet—daughter of the landscape painter Jan van Goyen—leaning back in her chair, helping herself to another glass of wine. He himself holds out a long clay pipe to his son, Cornelis. This, the painting warns, is what happens when parents set a bad example.

Yet this admonishing moral, which after all is not very original, is undermined by the elegant way it is painted. There are show-offy artist's tricks (Margriet's luxurious dress; an illusionistic nail, like Fabritius's, casting a shadow on the wall), and the painting's rigorous diagonal lines are the opposite of the unruliness that the picture describes. And it's undermined even more because the artist makes the sins involved look so fun.

———

OF THE MAJOR Dutch painters, Jan Steen might have issued from the most comfortable background. Born in Leiden in 1626—six years after the Pilgrims, who lived in his neighborhood, departed for Massachusetts;

twenty years after Rembrandt was born nearby—he descended from the small core of old families in a city that, with the influx of thousands of Flemish refugees, had become the second-largest in Holland.

His father was a brewer: a cultivated member of the upper-middle class. The family were Catholic, which excluded them from certain civic functions, but Steen attended the same Latin School that Rembrandt did, and enrolled at the university at twenty, though he never graduated. It is unclear where and when he trained as a painter, but by the age of twenty-two he was already registered with the local painters' guild.

His relations show just how intimately connected was the cultural

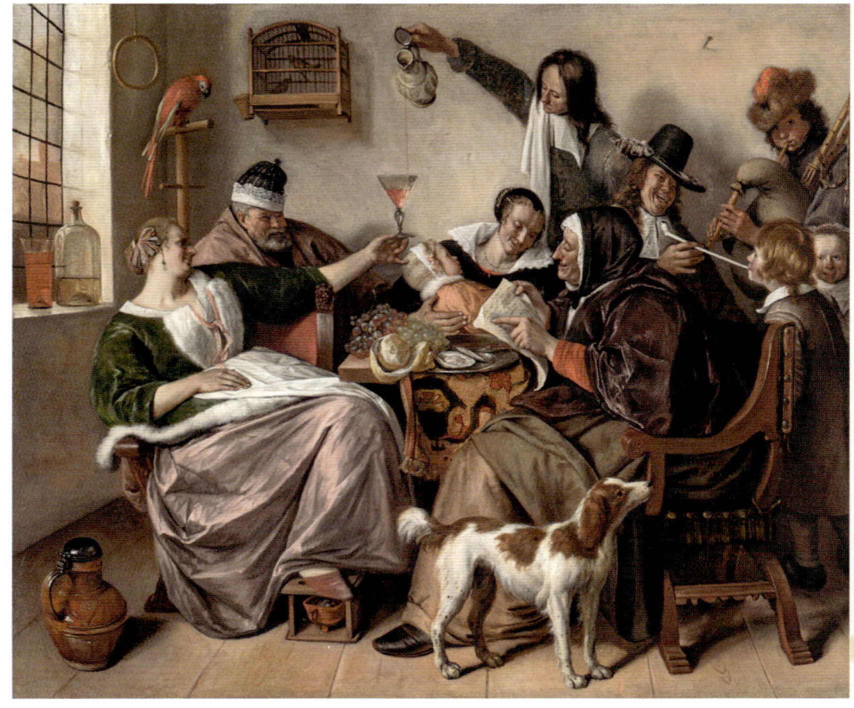

*The chaos of the scene—the old corrupting the young—
is undercut by Steen's neat diagonal composition.*

and artistic world of the time. His aunt was married to Jan Lievens's brother. He himself would marry the daughter of Jan van Goyen, who later sold to Steen's father a house at Paviljoensgracht 74, in The Hague. This was the same house where Spinoza would spend his last seven years, write his great *Ethica*, and die in 1677.

Paulus Potter, Steen's near-exact contemporary, moved down the street when he was just three. Later, Steen would be close to other artists, including Frans van Mieris, Jan Miense Molenaer, and Judith Leyster, who was Molenaer's wife. In Delft, he seems to have known De Hooch, Fabritius, and Vermeer. Later, in Haarlem, he knew Frans Hals well enough to include one of his paintings (*Peeckelhaering*) in one of his own.

For everyone in a country of just a million people, Holland was a small world; it's not surprising that Steen knew these people. What's striking is how liberally he borrowed from them. His work, seen end to end, is like flipping through an anthology of Golden Age painting. As for so many other artists, the base note was Bruegel, whose scenes of rural life and popular amusements resonated throughout the century.

Almost everyone else passes by as well. The sixteenth-century painter Lucas van Leyden turns up in Steen's religious paintings. Ter Borch's posh ladies stop by, too, sometimes as decorously as in Ter Borch and sometimes—as never in Ter Borch—passed out drunk. Some of his portraits resemble Bol's, and some of his interiors De Hooch's. Some of his trees look like Potter's. Some of his skies look like Van Goyen's.

In a winter landscape, he borrows two figures from Avercamp, another follower of Pieter Bruegel's. In a *Dismissal of Hagar*, he quotes Metsu—who is in turn quoting an etching of Rembrandt's. Steen produced works in the highly polished "fine" style of Leiden painters like Gerrit Dou and Frans van Mieris, and produced even more in the style of Adriaen Brouwer, who preceded him in depicting carousing lowlifes.

And yet for all this stylistic diversity, Jan Steen remains instantly identifiable. It's not so much that his features are recognizable. (Only Rembrandt, who painted dozens of self-portraits, is as familiar, and though Rembrandt occasionally placed himself in a crowd, his face is best known from his formal self-portraits.) Steen is recognizable from something else, harder to define than a face: from a voice, from a *mood*.

———

THIS MOOD WAS what made him legendary. A mood was what a scene of peasants in an inn, or of princes celebrating a feast, allowed you to capture; a mood was what infused a picture of a rowdy family or of a lovesick girl. In creating a recognizable feeling that rises above style—above the particulars of whatever was being shown—Steen was akin to a novelist: something could be Steenian, as it could be Dickensian or Proustian.

So many of the witticisms that amused his contemporaries seem a little embarrassing now, like the various symbols of the female pudenda (oysters, mussels, stockings) that are scattered throughout his comic works. Even once their meanings are elucidated, they still strike us as somewhat less hilarious than they might have once. You feel a bit annoyed when they are explained. You don't need them. What you need is the mood.

It's the mood that has been impervious to four centuries of trends, the mood that kept his name alive. Fifty years after his death, Houbraken noted that his works cost ten times more than they did in his lifetime. His work entered the major aristocratic collections early. And when museums sprouted up at the turn of the nineteenth century, his pictures filled them. The Mauritshuis has more works by him than by any other artist: fifteen.

Yet a mood is hard to define. For someone who painted in as many different manners, it wasn't a matter of style. Certain nineteenth-century Dutch critics, embarrassed by the dodgy reputation of one of the country's leading painters, tried to rebrand the frolicsome drunk of the popular imagination as a moralist, and in a way they were right: there is a moral in most of these paintings. But it is not always clear which one.

Take *A Woman at Her Toilet*, a picture so graceful that it was sold to the king of England in 1821. Behind a large stone doorway, a woman is sitting on her bed, pulling a stocking over her naked legs and looking at the viewer—presumably a male viewer—in the eye. Come hither? Not so fast. Consider the warnings lurking everywhere. There's a skull wrapped in a vine, for instance, and a lute with a broken string.

You have to study the painting closely—and have a firm grasp of

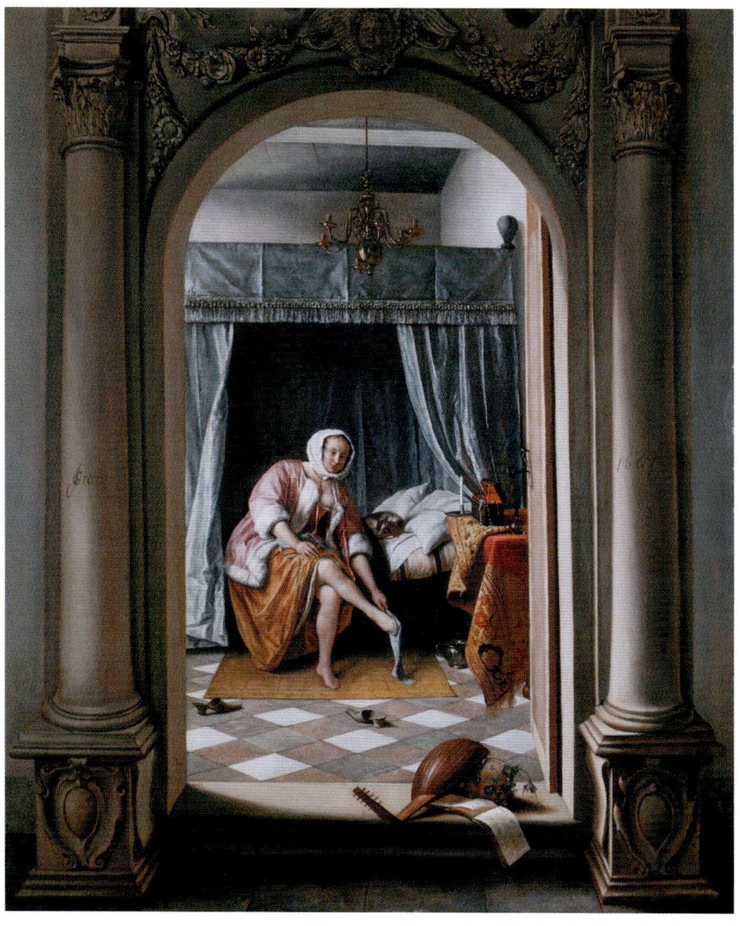

"Come hither," whispers the woman at her toilet:
ignore the pro-forma warnings the painter has appended.

iconology—before you notice other admonitions, including sunflowers ("a traditional symbol for constancy," one scholar notes) and grapevines ("Eucharistic associations"). The painter might be protecting himself. He might be making sure that, if ever summoned to the witness stand, he can defend his painting against charges of encouraging immorality.

So he's unambiguously stated that you're not supposed to walk through this door. At the same time, as so often in Steen's work, the atmosphere says something quite different. He's warning you, and in no uncertain terms, not to head toward that—now that you mention it—extremely attractive, scantily clad, and very welcoming young lady: the one who is slyly beckoning you to join her in her rumpled bed.

Sleeping with her is a terrible idea. (And don't even *think* about pouring yourself another drink.) Any tedious preacher would remind you that life is fragile, and pleasures fleeting. But Steen's understanding of human character is far more subtle than that. In picture after picture, he appends a pro forma warning against vanity and vice—and then, knowing perfectly well that you're going to do it anyway, he winks.

CONSIDERING HIS TALENT, relations, and renown, it is something of a mystery that no contemporary descriptions of Steen survive. It wasn't until long after his death that a few snippets were recorded by Houbraken, that indefatigable interviewer. He tracked down one Karel de Moor, "artist and knight," who recalled that Steen "held forth so reasonably about every aspect of art that it was a pleasure to be a witness to his speeches."

One mystery is how and where he learned "every aspect of art." Like Metsu, Steen may have studied with Nicholas Knüpfer in Utrecht. He may have spent some time with Adriaen van Ostade in Haarlem. But whatever training he had had to have been brief. This is reflected in his paintings, which sometimes show little technical errors: feet twisted into impossible relationships with legs; heads a bit too small for the bodies they adorn.

Houbraken chalked this up to partying. A more recent critic,

Lyckle de Vries, attributes it less excitingly but more probably to the brevity of Steen's apprenticeship—and to something else, too: his experimental personality. "The artist could have surmounted his short-comings by setting himself a narrow task and striving for perfection within those self-imposed boundaries, but he seems to have chosen other priorities."

And this is what is most striking about Jan Steen: his energetic refusal of the "narrow task." As he absorbed influences from almost every notable painter of his time, he tried his hand at nearly every genre, and the more action-packed, the more sweeping, the better. Alongside his comic pictures, he also painted the kinds of history and religious paintings that were then considered the pinnacle of sober and serious art.

These pictures posed a problem for criticism, since they seemed a bit less sober and serious than the sober and serious works of other paint-ers, and since the mood of his light works is very similar to the mood of his "serious" works. If the comic paintings start to look more serious the longer one looks at them, the history paintings often seem more comic. Steen is always saying one thing, and then saying something else.

Take a *Wrath of Ahasuerus* in Birmingham. While taking an extrava-gant meal with Esther and his minister Haman, the Persian king learns of Haman's dastardly plot to destroy the Jews. He clenches his fist in rage—and leaps from his seat so brusquely that he sends the table's con-tents careening to the floor. The pièce de résistance is about to explode: a silver platter containing a gigantic pie made of a stuffed peacock.

The story of Esther is as exalted a theme as exists in the classic rep-ertoire. It was always popular with painters. Set at the court of a distant, nearly unknown land, it offered the ambitious artist opportunities to conjure an exotic setting: oriental landscapes, gorgeous costumes, opu-lent still-lifes, and a whole range of emotions, from the love of Esther and Ahasuerus to the plotting—and then the satisfying demise—of Haman.

It is hard to know how to describe Steen's treatment of this tower-ing and complex subject. In the criticism on Steen, the word "theatrical" recurs. Theatrical doesn't have to mean fake or indecorous. The painting

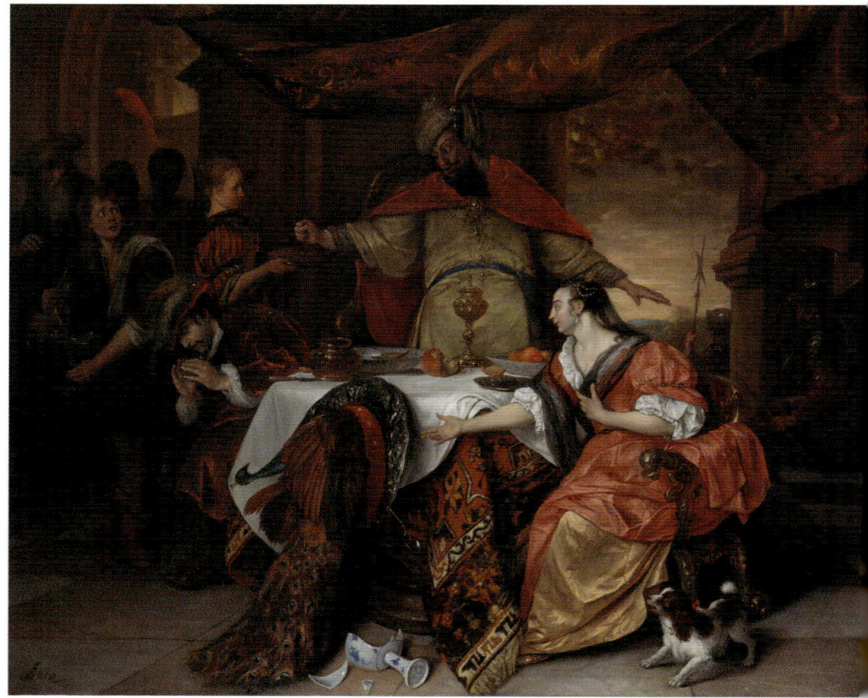

When Steen painted this flying peacock, there wasn't quite a word for this style, which Susan Sontag would popularize centuries later: camp.

is neither jocular nor offensive. And though the flamboyant gestures—along with the curtain at the top and the side, and a landscape view that looks like a backdrop—seem to justify the word, it still feels off.

"Theatrical" might be a better description of a huge painting of Rembrandt's in Bucharest, in which Haman kneels, begging for his life, at the feet of the resplendent Esther. She turns away from the suddenly humbled petitioner—the kindhearted queen forced to be cruel; the genocidal ghoul forced to be meek. The moment is decisive, but the scene is serene. The atmosphere, bathed in shadows, is inevitability, tragedy, doom.

———

CRAMMED WITH COLOR and action, Steen's picture has a much different mood—and that airborne peacock offers a clue to how it might be described. "The essence of camp is its love of the unnatural," wrote Susan Sontag, "of artifice and exaggeration." And to read "Notes on 'Camp,'" her essay of 1964, is to find a full account of Steen's aesthetics. The essence of camp, Sontag writes, is the subordination of content to style.

Steen's fascination with style—with the texture of the peacock's tail, with the swoosh of Esther's dress, with the two-foot-long plume in Ahasuerus's bejeweled turban—overwhelms whatever "content" he diffidently tries to infuse. This fascination explains, too, how well he absorbed different styles, and seamlessly incorporated them into his own. It also accounts for his attraction to certain stories.

He painted Esther and Ahasuerus at least three times. He painted the same number of versions of the banquet of Antony and Cleopatra, the tale of the Egyptian queen who bet the Roman general that she could spend a fabulous ten million sesterces on a single banquet. The meal was nothing remarkable—until dessert, when she removed one of her priceless pearl earrings, dissolved it in her wine, and drank the concoction.

(She won the bet.)

"Camp is a woman walking around in a dress made of three million feathers," Sontag writes; and she traced this "spirit of extravagance" to the late seventeenth and early eighteenth century, "because of that period's extraordinary feeling for artifice, for surface, for symmetry; its taste for the picturesque and the thrilling, its elegant conventions for representing instant feeling and the total presence of character."

Steen's works precede those Sontag cites by at least a couple of generations, but the mood is unmistakably the same. Likewise another aspect of camp, its awareness of "a double sense in which some things can be taken." This is the sensibility one finds time and again in Steen, "susceptible of a double interpretation, gestures full of duplicity, with a witty meaning for cognoscenti and another, more impersonal, for outsiders."

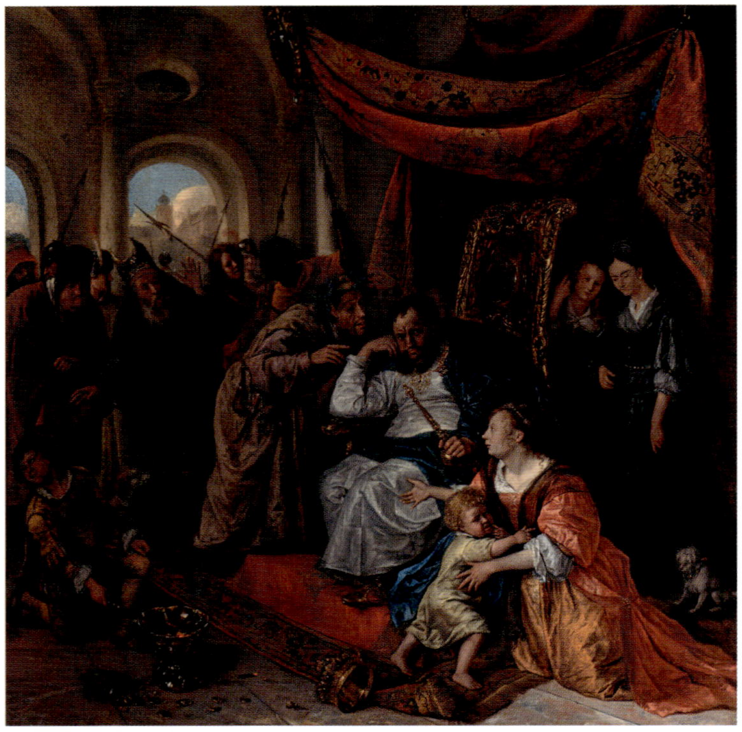

*One of the great camp themes is hierarchy overturned,
as when the infant Moses knocks off Pharoah's crown.*

Four hundred years on, though, the operation Sontag described is reversed: the witty symbolic meanings, veiled to the uninitiated, have grown tedious, the inside jokes hard to explain; and to append a footnote to every broken eggshell or ladies' stocking is to disrupt the mood. We feel instinctively the spark in Steen's eye, making the same transgressions he is supposedly condemning seem more than enjoyable—irresistible.

Yet it's remarkable how many of his subjects relate to mocking. Haman is humbled; Samson is taunted; Pharoah's crown is knocked to the ground by the toddler Moses. The theme is common in Dutch art—

the "upside-down world" of hierarchy overturned—but it is also what Sontag calls camp: "The whole point of camp is to dethrone the serious," she writes. "One can be serious about the frivolous, frivolous about the serious."

Ultimately, camp isn't mocking. Seriousness is what separates it from kitsch. "When something is just bad (rather than camp), it's often because it is too mediocre in its ambition. The artist hasn't attempted to do anything really outlandish." And even when their subjects are comical, Steen's pictures are too beautiful, too carefully painted and composed, to be dismissed as merely zany or prankish.

This is why a critic expecting serious works to be serious and comic works to be flippant will be wrong-footed. Those who have tried to understand why Steen's serious pictures seem so offbeat, so melodramatic, have long forced themselves into complicated explanations that we instinctively feel are not quite right—even though they might not be quite wrong. The usual ways of understanding such works are always a bit off.

He troubled the categories, and because there were no contemporary writings to explain how he had been understood in his own time, the key would have to wait until nearly three centuries after his death, when Sontag divided art into three categories. The first, high culture, was "basically moralistic," she said, recognized by "the seriousness and dignity of what it achieves." Into this category she placed Rembrandt.

The second was "art whose goal is not that of creating harmonies but of overstraining the medium and introducing more and more violent, and unresolvable, subject-matter." In this category she placed Bosch, Sade, Rimbaud, Kafka, and Artaud. These were the creators of an art of dissonance. Their art broke with conventional language and forms, and formed the dominant mode of the twentieth century.

The third was what Sontag calls "the sensibility of failed seriousness, of the theatricalization of experience." Into this category we can place Steen: not, like Rembrandt, moralistic; nor, like Bosch, in that limbo between moralism and aestheticism. Instead, Steen is wholly aesthetic, which is exactly what Sontag calls camp: "a victory of 'style' over 'content,' 'aesthetics' over 'morality,' of irony over tragedy."

———

IF STEEN WAS in fact given to drinking and low company—and there's no reason to think he wasn't—that makes his productivity even more stunning. He produced works in almost every genre, and lots of them: the exact number has yet to be established, but by any measure he was, for a painter of his time, highly prolific. Perhaps none of his contemporaries produced works in as many styles and registers as he did.

Despite his heroic labor, Steen's later years were difficult. Some of this was surely due to indulging his extravagant personality. Some was also due to living in a collapsing economy, at a time when the Golden Age was reaching its finale. When his wife Margriet died in 1669, he couldn't pay the apothecary who delivered the medicines on her death-bed: another of the facts that lurk in the archives to humiliate, posthumously, so many great artists.

Like Hals, he was left with a passel of children—five—and when he remarried he acquired his new wife's two. Together, they had a son, making a total of eight. When he died in 1679—he was fifty-three—two of the children were independent, leaving his widow six. And when she died in 1687, "many of the children and grandchildren either died young, ended up in the Leiden orphanage, or left for the Dutch East Indies."

It is a sad ending. It is not, alas, atypical, even for artists who indulged themselves less than Steen. What was atypical was his afterlife—the afterlife of the character he created. As a character, the different Jan Steens are ancestors of Fernando Pessoa's heteronyms or Cindy Sherman's self-portraits. These show a single personality—but one that is continually fractured and continually reconstituted.

It makes no sense to ask which of these self-presentations is the "real" Jan Steen. For such artists, all are; none are; and the self is not a single essence; it is an aesthetic phenomenon, most real when cast in a role, existing through, and thanks to, its external presentation. "Camp is the glorification of 'character,' " Sontag wrote, "a key element of the theatricalization of experience embodied in the camp sensibility."

So whatever we learn about Steen through the reality encoded in a handful of verifiable facts, we will be missing something essential if we try to see him in the terms of reality—of some definable essence. Once we see Steen's characters as aesthetic productions, we understand that they could later be converted into cartoons, and that he—the lovable loser, the no-account boozer—was the greatest character of all.

To ask who Steen really was is like asking if a great opera singer is "really" Carmen or Norma. The character is what matters. The character is what survives when the four-hundred-year-old humor has withered: when a woman putting on a sock has started to look like a woman putting on a sock rather than a naughty allusion. Such facts—the truths the historian or biographer is taught to seek—are beside the point.

If it's hard to imagine Steen's works adorning a church or dignifying a courthouse, that's because of that ubiquitous winking, always undermining whatever "message" other painters might include: because they don't care about messages. Their message is their miraculously intact mood, which never scolds and never condemns; which remains light even when showing sacred histories or bloody revenge.

The mood is of friendliness, of savoring life. "Camp taste is, above all, a mode of enjoyment, of appreciation—not judgment," Sontag said. "A kind of love, love for human nature. It relishes, rather than judges, the little triumphs and awkward intensities of 'character.'" That brilliant way he registered our little awkward triumphs is what makes us love Jan Steen, even when everything else has fallen away.

PART III

WALL POWER

I N ORDER TO PINPOINT a location where Jan van Eyck had stood, my friend Hugo van der Velden once hired a crane, parked it in a suburb of The Hague, and hoisted himself several stories into the air.

People laughed when he told the story. But I understood why he did it. Sometimes, when you discover where an artist stood, you find a pile of bricks. Sometimes, though, something unexpected happens. To Robert Caro's advice to researchers, "Turn every page," I'd add a corollary: "See for yourself." When I stood outside Clarice Lispector's house in Recife and heard the fruit sellers in the square shouting exactly as she had described their shouting in her girlhood a century before, I felt a thrill of closeness to her. And when, early on a jet-lagged morning, I saw the tiny house where Susan Sontag lived in Tucson, I was suddenly back in the middle of nowhere, and felt how frantically a bookish girl would have longed for a cosmopolitan life.

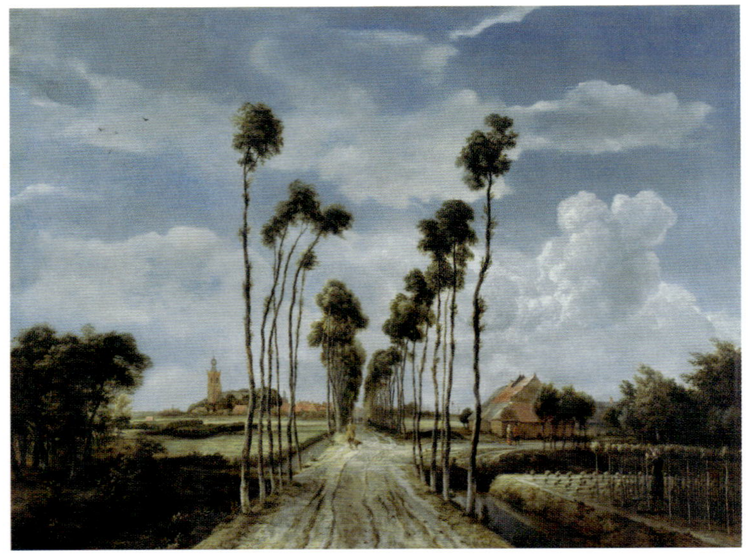

*No reproduction can capture the majesty of the swaying trees
in Hobbema's* Avenue at Middelharnis.

When I discovered the Dutch museums, I wanted to see where these artists had lived. I wanted to see what they had seen. I started taking short trips around the country. If the view was unchanged—on a few lucky occasions I found the country that the old paintings teach the foreign eye to seek—I could see what they had done with that view, how they had modified or elevated it. If it was changed, I would get to go see some new corner of the country, traveling as a researcher does, seeing places I otherwise never would have seen, and meeting people I otherwise never would have met.

That's how, in the spring of 2011, 321 years after the creation of Meindert Hobbema's *Avenue at Middelharnis*—one of the glories of London's National Gallery, praised by an eminent Dutch art historian as "the finest picture, next to Rembrandt's *Syndics*, which has been painted in Holland"—I arrived in the small town of Middelharnis. The National Gallery's website told me that "the view is remarkably accurate and has hardly changed since the seventeenth century." Most things, we know, have changed since the seventeenth century. But maybe in this out-of-the-way place the landscape might be the same that Hobbema saw. I drove beneath skies as bright as those in the painting, which shows a lane of ash trees, wiry as palms, lining a country road.

I was five months late. On December 1, 2010, along that same avenue, a new Gamma had opened. This was a big-box store selling building materials, surrounded by a huge parking lot: the kind of structure that, all over the world, we associate with the words "sprawl" or "blight"—the same kind of building that has wrecked the edges of cities and towns everywhere. Still, the avenue, called the Boomgaardweg or Orchard Lane, was there. With a bit of imagination, I could see the place in Hobbema's painting.

The Avenue at Middelharnis, with the ironic defiance of the most reproduced pictures, reproduces poorly. No photograph can capture the balletic sway of the trees. In the picture, besides the trees and the sky, there's a hunter, some dogs, a man and a woman talking, a man pruning his orchard: the orchard remembered in the road's name? But no written description accounts for how such commonplace elements can come together to make a work of such surpassing majesty.

The painting is made more mysterious by its date, 1689. Around three decades before, Hobbema, an orphan from Amsterdam who was the only known pupil of Jacob van Ruisdael, created a series of landscapes that were the equivalent, in that genre, of the magnificent still-lifes that showed the loot gathered by the Dutch Republic, and that departed from their more solemn antecedents as much as Hobbema's landscapes did from the work of his moody teacher.

The landscapes from Hobbema's heroic period have a feature

that is hard to reproduce. Their swagger—"wall power," in museum jargon—can be so overwhelming that one can imagine building an entire mansion, an entire garden, around a single example. These are the works of an impatient virtuoso. And as with Carel Fabritius or Paulus Potter or Gabriël Metsu or the countless other painters who died in their twenties or thirties, one irresistibly speculates about what maturity would have made of Hobbema. But his case is different. When he was thirty, in 1668, he married, and eventually had five children. He continued to paint for another couple of years, but his production soon ground to a halt. Most writers attribute this decline to his taking the job of *wijnroeier*, or wine gauger, measuring imported alcohols. Though he lived another forty-one years, he almost never painted again.

There are romantic explanations for this caesura, and there are practical ones. The year after his last dated painting, 1672, was the Year of Disasters, in which his country was invaded and its great estates—where his paintings would have hung—ransacked. Prices for luxuries crashed. Artists were ruined. Some chose to emigrate. Amid this calamity, many might have envied Hobbema's civil service sinecure. For nearly twenty years, he busied himself gauging wines. Then, suddenly, he appeared on the island of Goeree-Overflakkee—of all places—to create a work of art that would assure the permanence of his name. And then, in the two decades of life that remained to him, he would never, as far as we know, paint again.

The romantic explanations—Hobbema is a romantic painter—begin here. Was his personality torn, like Goethe's Faust, between the imperatives of the artist, thirsting for freedom, and those of the regular man, longing for comfort and security? "Two souls live, ach, inside my breast!" he may have emoted, like Faust, before finally laying down his brushes. And then, twenty years later, he shows up in the small town of Middelharnis, and paints a single picture. It is a great one, as he surely knew. Then he lays down those brushes once again, this time for good.

Why this place, and why this painting? It was in the town hall of Middelharnis until the early nineteenth century, which suggests a local commission. But such clues lead only to a chain of maybes. Maybe some patriotic citizen came across a token of the artist's youthful glory. Maybe he sought out the aging Hobbema and tried to lure him, with a generous fee, to the island. Why did he agree? Maybe he needed the money. Maybe he hesitated, fearing that his style was outmoded, and he himself out of practice. Or maybe he had kept working in private, fantasizing about going back to painting once his kids were older, or once he'd saved a bit more money. We don't know. We don't know what he felt while he was painting. Maybe the picture came to him in an ecstatic rush. Maybe it was a slog, a reminder that the work of which he'd dreamed during his bureaucratic days was—at least on most days—as tedious, as routine, as any other. All we know is that he came to Middelharnis and painted the picture—and then never painted again.

In this story—or lack of story—you could see even more questions. You could see a mighty personality, an individual vision: call it inspiration. You could see how this personality, this vision, clashed with social pressure: call it money. Was it a tragedy that Hobbema stopped painting? Maybe, for him, it wasn't. Maybe a steady job offered a serenity that art never does. Maybe he had willingly chosen domestic tranquillity, and maybe, when he no longer painted, he still thought of himself as an artist. How much do you have to produce in order to claim that title? Do you have to go to the end?

Maybe what you needed was wall power. You needed that personality, that vision. And you needed to figure out, artistically but also practically, how to convey them. The great museum was a monument to people who had managed to do it. They reached across the centuries, and made us feel their presence, and see what they saw. How had they done it? What had it cost? I don't know. But I did know that everyone who had succeeded had done so in a different way. If there had been a formula—there are a lot of technical formulas in art—the answers on the wall would not have been so different, and artist's lives would not have been so fraught with danger.

Painting is no guarantee of happiness. Neither is not painting. When Hobbema was young, his talent may have seemed like a promise of happiness. It didn't turn out that way. The civil service job may have seemed like a promise of an easier life; it didn't turn out that way either. After he created his final painting, he returned home, another obscure widower bound for a pauper's grave. Did he recall his neighbor in the Rozengracht, Rembrandt, who, forty years before, had died in the same circumstances, on the same canal, having pursued his vocation to the bitter end?

Whose was the greater courage?

And if you painted *The Avenue at Middelharnis*, did it matter?

10

HENDRICK AVERCAMP

The Mute Muse

ONE OF THE MOST oddly compelling works in the annals of art history was published in 1933. It is odd, and it is odd that it is compelling. Its very title, *Hendrick Avercamp 1585–1634, Known as "The Mute of Campen," and Barent Avercamp 1612–1679 "Painters in Campen,"* seems almost deliberately confusing. Its florid Dutch is somewhere between archaizing—its author has a highfalutin style—and actually archaic: the book is nearly a century old, and deals with documents from the sixteenth and seventeenth centuries. Even so, the style seems perversely designed to thwart potential readers: "It was these banneret-cies of Bronkhorst and the Precinct of Steenre, belonging to the Reeve of Zutphen, which in 1817 were united with the township of Olburgen, belonging to the Precinct of Doesburgh, from which three unequal parts was created the present-day municipality of Steenderen," a typical sentence reads. It is even less comprehensible in the original.

Yet a current of emotion runs through it. Its author, Clara Welcker, was the municipal archivist of Kampen, a small city in the province of Overijssel. From the beginning of the book, she announces the excitement—the grave responsibility—she felt when a local association, the same Society for the Study of the Law and History of Overijssel that put together the exhibition where Abraham Bredius discovered the archive of the Ter Borchs, invited her to write a study of the city's most illustrious painter, Hendrick Avercamp. She was "overwhelmed by the spontaneity of an offer by which I was honored," she writes; and the rest of the book proves that this was not the kind of polite formula often found in the acknowledgment section. You feel she had been waiting all her life for this chance—that this was the most important thing that ever happened to her—that she was determined to make this book everything it could be.

She struggles with a difficulty known to any biographer. Proud of her research, she hates to lose any fact that her painstaking work has unearthed. But she also knows that the facts that so excite the biographer are often far less exciting for the reader. She excuses herself. "Not to digress," she writes; "Not to bore anyone," she goes on; "Not to get too tedious," she says—all on the very first page of the book, when she is reaching deep into the Middle Ages to discover the family's origins, finally locating the precise field from which the ancestral Avercamps sprang. (The name means "land, strewn with oats.")

Yet her dazzling investigative vigor carries you through those knotted sentences. Less for tale—almost impossible to follow—than for teller. Less for Avercamp—snowed under a blizzard of genealogical trivia—than for Clara, whom you start to imagine. You see the hair tied into a practical bun; you see the smudged glasses through which she peers at some indecipherable scrawl. You imagine decades in that archive, in that sleepy workaday town: unmarried, childless, with few people to share her interests in history and literature. Perhaps there was a schoolteacher—a pastor—a notary who lived in Amsterdam in his youth—but most of the citizenry, you imagine, must have regarded her as an eccentric old maid. The great event of her month was the meeting of the historical society. You imagine what it meant when they invited her to write this book.

And then, as you read on, you feel another struggle, also so familiar to the historian or the biographer. On the one hand, the academic, who must buttress every assertion with a fortifying footnote. On the other hand, the writer, the artist—who, when the archives are silent, wants the freedom to fill in the gaps. Precisely because her book is so exhaustively documented, it comes as a surprise to see the artist start to get the better of the archivist. I first noticed this in the captions underneath certain drawings. "Beatrix Peters Vekemans, widow Avercamp, with three sons, presumably from l. to r. Everhardus, Beatrix, Lambert, and Hendrick"—a fascinating degree of specificity for an artist about whom virtually nothing was known. I was curious how she discovered this information; but I waited in vain for an explanation, and scoured the footnotes, also in vain. Through many such details, I slowly started to realize that—despite the veritable jungle of documentation—I was in the hands of an unreliable narrator.

Perhaps more than any other writer, the biographer is supposed to be discreet, all but invisible—in his or her own books. I don't think this expectation exists in any other branch of literature: because a biography is "about" someone else, any intrusion of the biographer will be quickly whacked down by chastising reviewers. But as a poet reveals himself in a poem and a novelist in a novel, biographies are full of personal revelations, sometimes advertent, sometimes not, and these are often the most interesting part of the book. They are when the writer is trying to break free of the subject.

So I sought information about this obscure, long dead archivist. I knew that there had to be some clue, somewhere, as to what it was about her that made her book both so bizarre and so extraordinary. I wanted to locate the source of that current of emotion, since I was sure there had to be one. I felt that there was something she wasn't saying, but I didn't know what it was.

I spent a morning digging around on the internet.

That was when I discovered that Clara Welcker was deaf.

So was Hendrick Avercamp.

———

LONG BEFORE I knew his name, I knew Hendrick Avercamp's paintings. They show a merry Christmassy world of funnily dressed people disporting themselves on frozen canals: paintings I knew from jigsaw puzzles and holiday cards. Here was a young couple gliding over the ice, love in their eyes; there were people exercising picturesque professions: a skate sharpener, a bird catcher, a chestnut seller. If you kept look-ing, you found a good-natured scabrousness. Behind that spidery tree was a man taking a dump; and over there was a woman who'd slipped and exposed her red buttocks; and there, beside the village inn, was a drunken fool being fished out of the ice. No artist ever captured winter fun as well.

Like the interiors of Pieter de Hooch, the winter scenes of Hendrick Avercamp were so iconic, so Dutch, that I felt a bit bereaved, when I moved to the Netherlands, to realize that the world they showed was gone—and that, thanks to climate change, it wouldn't be coming back. Even the Elfstedentocht, the skating race through the eleven historic cit-ies of Friesland that is one of the most beloved national traditions, was

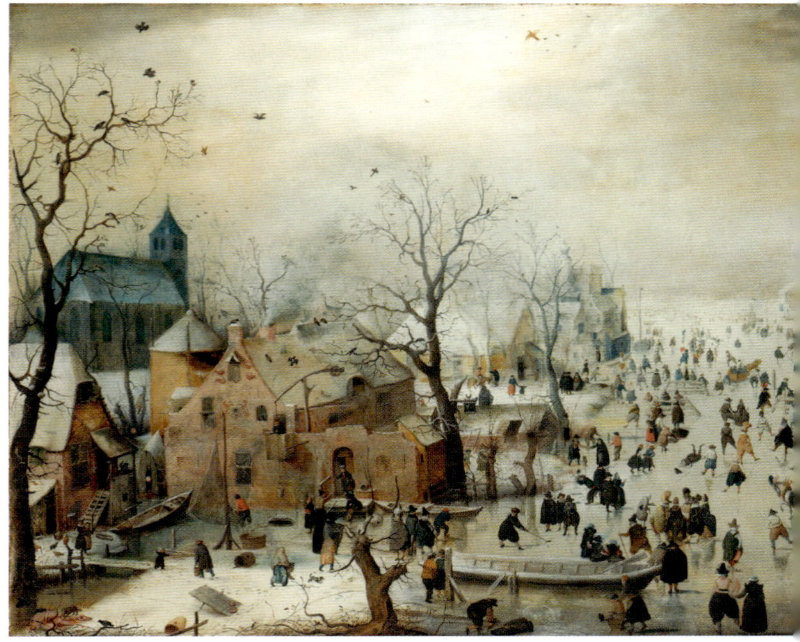

passing from memory. The ice has to reach a certain thickness in order for it to be safely held, and the ice no longer reaches that thickness: the last race was held in 1997, a few years before I arrived. What I found, in place of the sparkling white winters of the old paintings, was month after month of tepid drizzle.

As it turned out, Avercamp's life coincided with an unusually cold period known as the Little Ice Age. The medieval world—when Greenland could be colonized and wine produced in southern England— had been much warmer. The first notably cold winter was in 1564–1565. The vast Scheldt froze from bank to bank at Antwerp, and a huge iceberg formed at Delfshaven, the port from which, fifty-five years later, the Pilgrims left for Massachusetts. A rather primitive painting of the ice- berg survives, the first such winter scene to be painted in the northern Netherlands. In the same year, in Flanders, Pieter Bruegel created his

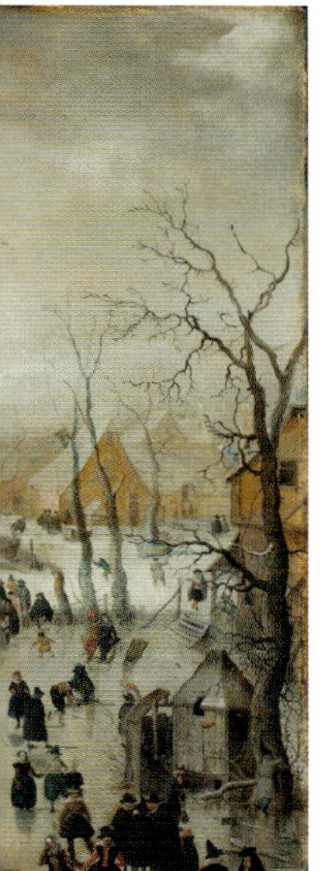

own first such work, called *Winter Landscape with a Bird-Trap*. This painting became so famous that no fewer than 127 copies are known: an example that would echo throughout the next century.

At a time when the painting of landscape was emerging into a genre of its own, free of religious or allegorical symbolism, these dramatic winters offered a novel theme. But the Netherlanders had always loved the ice and the diversions it offered. Frozen water was like carnival, an upside-down world when, for a few days, the conventions of daily life relaxed. "Here," wrote the famous jurist Grotius, "nobody speaks of rank; here we are open and free." All of society, from the beggar to the countess, headed outside. It was a whole human comedy unfolding in a magnificent setting: one ripe for an enterprising painter.

Four hundred years on, Avercamp's pictures of winter fun have never been excelled by any other painter.

THAT THIS PAINTER WOULD be Hendrick Avercamp is something of a surprise. In his own day, according to the records that Clara Welcker discovered, he was usually referred to as "de Stomme" or "de Stom." In Dutch as in English, the word means "dumb" in the sense of "mute," as well as "dumb" in the sense of "stupid." Welcker is proud of "the Mute of Kampen," who brought "the fame of his family all the way into our time."

This may have been an overstatement. In Welcker's time, little was known about Avercamp. He goes entirely unmentioned in the classic biographical works. Not until 1767, 130 years after his death, does his name first crop up in a scholarly work—though, inexplicably, he is mentioned the very next year as someone whose fame is "immortal." In 1816, another writer says that it is "remarkable that we find nothing about him in the writers who have described the lives of the painters; since he has from olden days been known to connoisseurs, and his art has remained in high esteem." Perhaps it was his work that was cherished, though the specifics of his personality had been lost: again surprising, since it seems noteworthy that an artist who, in Welcker's words, "entered the world with a handicap," would have occasioned so little comment. His deafness must have been unusual.

Welcker's book has a hero, Hendrick's mother, Beatrix. "Only those who themselves have had to take charge of the upbringing of a child disfavored by nature can fully realize what was involved in this task," she wrote. "In earlier centuries the fate of the handicapped, without the institutions we have today, which try to make them into useful members of society, was endlessly crueler. A child who could neither hear nor speak was simply lost to the community. That from the unfortunate child of Barent Hendrickszoon Avercamp and Beatrix Peters Vekemans came an artist whose name after centuries is known and spoken with honor is thanks to his natural talent, but surely in the first place to the efforts his parents took in his upbringing, and, because of his father's early death, to the thirty-year-long, unfailing care of his mother."

Born in Alkmaar, in North Holland, Beatrix was the daughter of a learned man named Peter Vekemans. During the siege of Alkmaar in 1573, which ended in a spectacular Dutch victory over Spain and helped consolidate national independence, Vekemans, "who had a feeling for art and antiquities," rescued a quantity of manuscripts from Egmond Abbey. Thanks to him, these survive today in the library of Leiden University. But his wife, Beatrix's mother, did not long survive the siege. She died in 1577, leaving him to raise five children, the oldest of whom was fifteen. He moved the family to Amsterdam, where he took a job at a school and where, in 1583, Beatrix married the pharmacist and teacher Barent Avercamp. In 1585, their first son, Hendrick, was born.

Barent soon got a job as the apothecary in the former Hanseatic city of Kampen. This was a middling place whose prosperity had declined since the River IJssel, a branch of the Rhine, began to silt up, cutting it off from the wider world upon which its trade depended. By now, the city lacked a fully qualified doctor, so the apothecary did everything from selling marzipan and candied limes to offering basic medical care. His was a prestigious position in the city, and he was personally held in high esteem, Welcker found, by both church and state. Barent and Beatrix would have seven children after Hendrick, two of whom would die young. It was a family that could afford to take good care of its surviving children. They were well educated. Like his father, two of Hendrick's brothers became pharmacists; another became a physician, and was trained in France.

This meant that the family would have kept up with modern scientific developments, including in the education of the deaf. The idea of lipreading was first described by no one less than Leonardo da Vinci, who considered the deaf masters of movement, since they could follow conversations without words—through gestures and expressions alone. The first book on the education of deaf children was published in Spain in 1620, by which point Hendrick was already thirty-five. But there is evidence of the use of sign language in the seventeenth century, including of a hearing mother who would use sign language to "read" the newspaper to her deaf son. Perhaps Barent and Beatrix Avercamp did something similar; in any case, they took expensive pains to educate Hendrick.

In the early years of the new century, when he was in his teens, the plague raged in Kampen. Clara Welcker noted how many wills from this time were preserved in her archive, and how often they were witnessed by the apothecary, whose duties brought him to the houses of the afflicted. On one of these visits, to a man named Abraham van Neer, he himself caught the pest and soon died, leaving Beatrix a widow with six children—and her suffering, writes Welcker, was "by no means at an end." The archives show a staggering loss. First, in 1602, she lost her husband, and then, in the same year, a third child—and then, in 1603, her father, whose will "witnesses the noble character of Peter Vekemans" in the passages regarding Beatrix: in the "fidelity and care" he took to make sure she and her children would be provided for; "in the sadness about the disaster that had struck his oldest child."

——⋅——

AMONG THE HARD FACTS of the archives—births, marriages, deaths—is a lacuna that invites the novelist. In *The Mute of Kampen*, the classic children's writer Thea Beckman imagined the shock of Hendrick's parents when they realized he hadn't noticed a noise that startled everyone else. And Welcker wrote: "We need to imagine him as a child heading outside all by himself, armed with a bit of chalk or a pencil and a sketchbook, taking down whatever remarkable things he noticed, whatever interested him."

The only recorded fact of his childhood is his baptism in Amsterdam in 1585. He does not reappear for another twenty-two years, when, at the auction of the estate of the painter Gillis van Coninxloo, five words record the purchase of a lot of drawings by "de Stom tot Pieter Isacqs," "the Mute who lives with Pieter Isacqs." Upon these five words, Welcker and her successors have erected an impressive edifice. They show, first of all, that Avercamp had been sent to the capital. They show that he was handsomely provided for, since the works he purchased were not cheap. They show where he lived, in Amsterdam, on the north corner of the Jodenbreestraat and the Zwanenburgwal, a couple of steps from the house that Rembrandt, born the year before, would purchase in 1639. And they show with whom he lived: with Pieter

Isaacz, a painter born to Dutch parents in Denmark. Welcker describes him as follows:

> To a teacher born on far shores—according to Van Mander he had wandered through Germany and Italy—to a man of broad horizons, not from a narrowminded, petty, provincial background but cosmopolitan for the time, was confided the care of the [deaf]mute, talented Hendrick.

It is not hard to read in this sentence ("narrowminded, petty, provincial") the author's own longing for broad horizons. But Avercamp's paintings don't look much like Isaacz's. They look Flemish, and his presence at the Van Coninxloo sale hints at a genealogy. Van Coninxloo owned an astonishing seven pictures by Pieter Bruegel—only forty survive today—acquired directly from the great man's descendants in Antwerp. He himself was Flemish, and from Flanders he brought the tradition of the "world landscape," which zooms in to the figures in the foreground and then zooms out to reveal—miraculously, majestically—entire cities, entire provinces. Their canny handling of perspective allows them to be packed with casts of thousands, which first made them useful for illustrating episodes from sacred history, and which would later be secularized by Bruegel. This was the tradition in which the young Avercamp worked. In a round painting in London, he placed a few figures on a little outcropping at the bottom of the picture. Behind and beneath the outcropping, we look down at a landscape: an entire village come out to frolic on the ice surrounding a sugary pink castle.

My first art history teacher observed that one way to define a successful painting was to see how long people stood in front of it. An artist himself, he made ironic use of this observation by packing his own paintings with long texts; in a gallery, people were forced to read the small print, and thus to make his work look more intriguing. Nowhere, in subsequent years, have I recalled this observation more often than when looking at pictures by Hendrick Avercamp. In the London tondo, grandly beribboned men lead women in elaborate skirts past more practically dressed peasants. A fancy sleigh is pulled by a horse adorned with feathers in the

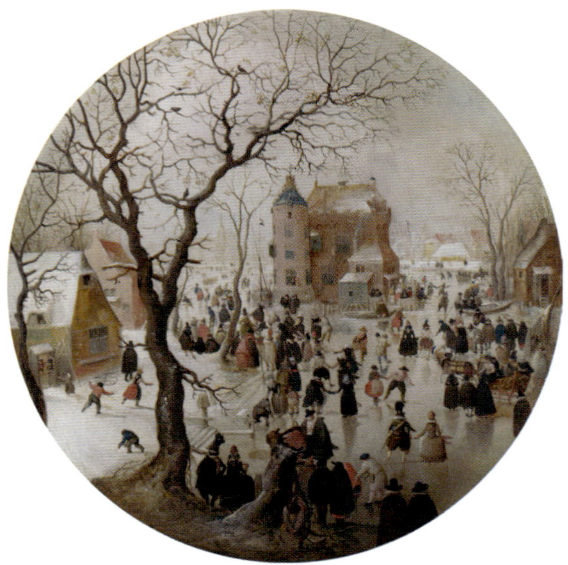

A clever Flemish invention, the technique of the "world landscape" allows little details to be shown alongside broad panoramas.

patriotic colors of red, white, and blue—while a couple, skating closer to the pink castle, are flung in the air, in the middle of a spectacular wipeout. There is no end to these details. But because the scene is seen from slightly above, it doesn't feel crowded. There's room to wander around here, and the frozen river's meandering shape follows the round format, drawing you deeper and deeper into the distance, all the way to the village church.

YOU CAN TRACE the sources of this work to ancient depictions of the four seasons, to Bruegel, to Van Coninxloo, to Flanders, but you can't trace the most outstanding characteristic of Avercamp's work: his charm. Though Old Man Winter sometimes pops up, and though there are Dutch proverbs that warn against skating on thin ice, his paintings aren't necessarily deep, nor do they much lend themselves to allegorical readings.

When placed alongside other depictions of winter, this becomes especially obvious. Unlike other painters, Avercamp shows very little of the rough struggle to stay warm, eat, survive. The paintings are full of activity—but not of work. Other painters show the harshness of the dead land, and show people outside because they have no choice. Avercamp shows people who are there because they want to be. This must have been a deliberate choice, a reflection of a personality that, because of his handicap, is nonetheless often supposed to have been sad. Welcker imagines "how entirely outside of daily life he must have stood." Another historian writes: "Avercamp creates in painting what must have been virtually excluded to him in life—the infectious interaction of human beings at ease with each other in relaxed, festive circumstances."

There was another reason—five more words—to assume that Avercamp must have been wretched. In December 1633, as Beatrix lay dying in Kampen, she made provisions for *haren stommen ende miserabelen soen*, her dumb and miserable son, to be cared for after her death. This seemed to ratify the idea of a difficult life: his work, after all, declined in subsequent years. Those perfectly observed figures became stiff, more caricatural, and the bright, crisp atmosphere that illuminated his winters grew muddier—dimmed. What was missing from these later paintings was that quality that made his earlier works so wondrous. What was missing was their charm.

Critics noted this deterioration. "Here," wrote one, "Hendrick Avercamp for once fell short; here he showed himself to be the archaic artist who knows nothing about the developments that come with time; once advanced, he became a has-been. We'd rather have no Avercamp from 1663. It's sad to see the old artist who has exhausted his talent." He was just another of those competent but ultimately second-rate artists that the Dutch Golden Age churned out—or so it seemed until Clara Welcker made her great discovery, announced in the italics she deployed to make sure the reader was paying attention: Avercamp had died in the spring of 1634, soon after his mother.

For Dutch art history the discovery of the burial records of Hendrick Avercamp "the Mute of Campen" after nearly three centuries is an important moment.

With Welcker's discovery, a mighty scholarly edifice could once again rise on the foundations of a handful of words. His mother's reference to Hendrick as "miserable," coupled with his own death just four and a half months later, might refer to a temporary, rather than a permanent, state. The works that for so long had clouded his reputation turned out to have been made by his nephew Barent, a timber merchant who painted in his style. Barent's works are not bad—you would happily hang them on your walls, and they are in many museums—but there is no denying that they lack his uncle's vigor and originality. The critic who noted that they are dated was correct: Barent more or less repeated Hendrick's themes for the next forty-five years.

His dedication to his uncle's themes over so many decades must have meant that there was a market for them. People liked them then as much as we like them now. We know that Hendrick left a huge store of drawings. The wealthy marine painter Jan van de Capelle owned no fewer than 883; George III bought another group, kept today at Windsor Castle; and

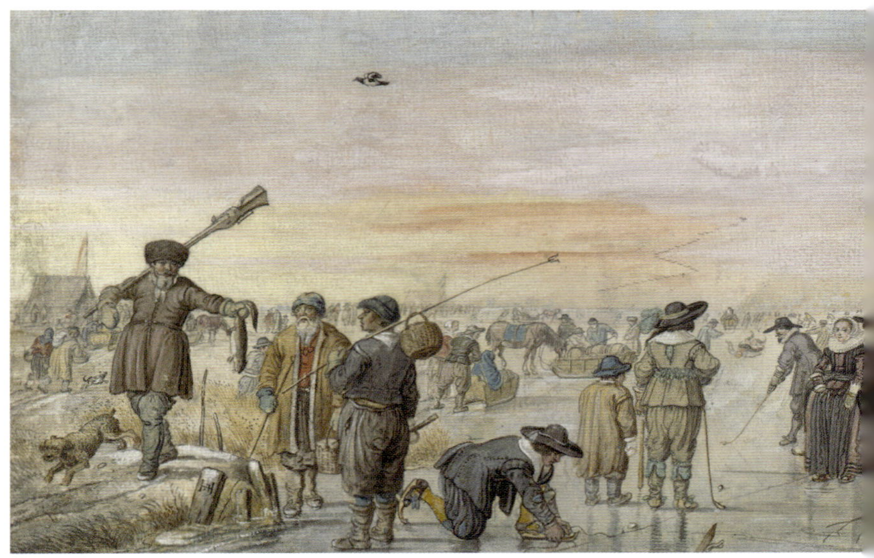

From Avercamp's hundreds of surviving drawings emerges a novelistic portrait of a whole society.

in 1816 they were described as "more highly esteemed and expensive than his paintings." They range from sketches—like a quick drawing of a fancy carriage that has crashed through the ice, horse, passengers, and all—to masterpieces painstakingly outlined in clear black strokes of the pen, then filled in with watercolor. These drawings are so refined and detailed that, we feel, they must have been intended for sale and display. Avercamp is one of the finest draftsmen of the seventeenth century, and to flip through page after page of his drawings is to see something wondrous emerge: a broad novelistic view of an entire society, like the works of Balzac or Dickens—but one made, unlike theirs, entirely of pictures.

That so many of these drawings were kept together suggests that they formed part of a studio archive; and in fact we come across many of the figures in the drawings in the paintings. Hendrick and later Barent must have drawn from this archive to create their paintings, and when we consider that they produced works on broadly similar themes for almost seventy-five years, we can imagine that, rather than isolated and

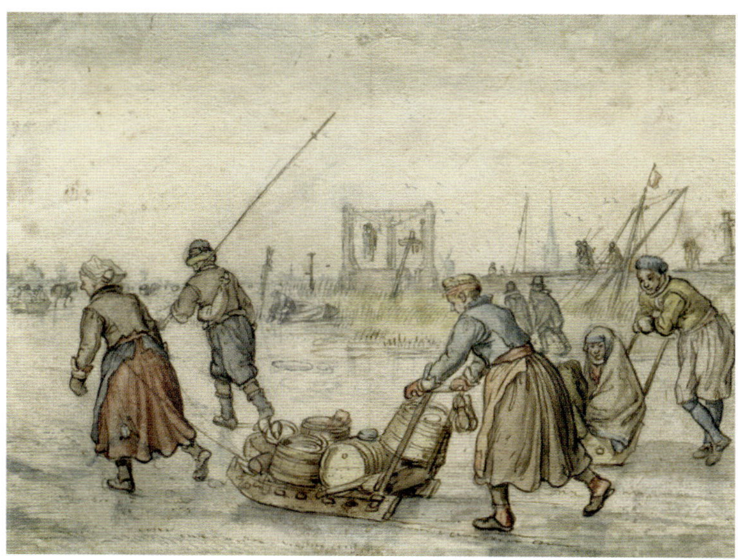

"miserable," Hendrick was in fact the founder of a successful business that survived him for decades. It's also remarkable that, though he spent nearly all his life in Kampen, he did not, at least as far as we know, paint portraits or still-lifes: the bread and butter of the small-town painter. Perhaps his family took such good care of him that he didn't need to. But it seems even more likely that he was well paid for his work, and that collectors sought him out. His works seem to have mainly been sold—or to have ended up—in Amsterdam. Even Clara Welcker couldn't find any records for commissions in Kampen. The only time he appears in the city archives is a single sentence from 1622, when he was paid to paint some horses on the municipal stables.

———

HOW ISOLATED WERE the deaf in the seventeenth century? Before the advent of specialized education, they might have been less unusual, less pushed into separate communities, than they would be later. Like other children, they would have been taken care of well or badly according to the families in which they happened to be born. Like hearing children, some would have been smarter, quicker, better at communicating, than others; some parents would have taken more pains with them than others. They lived in a world in which physical calamities were dramatically more common and less treatable than today, and in which deafness, considering the many other handicaps available, was perhaps just another difficulty with which people had to contend. A bright deaf boy born into a family willing and able to educate him could have been, like Avercamp, quite successful.

But because of his deafness and muteness, we can know even less of Avercamp's inner life than we know of many other artists of his time. Their voices occasionally speak through the archives; but though Avercamp couldn't speak, we can't assume that he was miserable. Perhaps someone like Clara Welcker was unhappier. A woman of energy and talent, she planned to be a teacher until, in her teens, her hearing worsened. This forced her into the relative isolation of the archives. She was only the second Dutch woman to take charge of a municipal archive, and she published quantities of articles about genealogy and local history. When she arrived in Kampen in 1917, she reorganized and modernized the archive, working entirely alone until, in 1922, she was assigned a volunteer. In 1927, she was allotted a paid employee.

"Not only her difficulty in hearing made contact with others difficult," wrote J. ten Hove in a brief biographical notice: "Her high

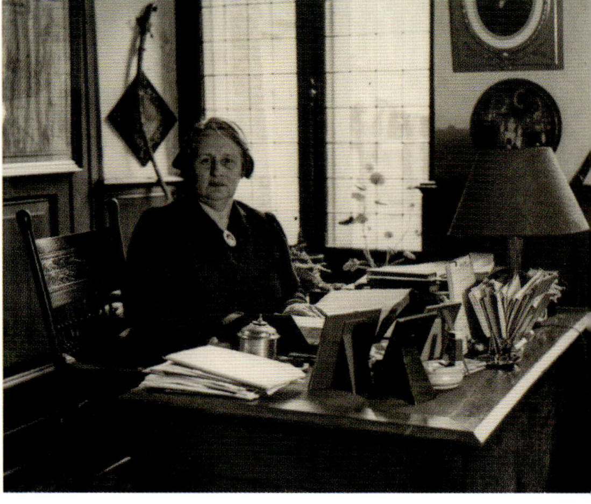

Clara Welcker, the deaf Kampen archivist who brought Avercamp back to life in one of the strangest works of Dutch art history.

scientific demands and the fact that she determined who got into the Kampen archives" led to tensions, which ended up being formalized in an official break. Kampen has the unusual distinction, for a town its size, of possessing two archives: besides the one Welcker administered, another was founded by a local captain of industry. Its collections benefited from Welcker's prickly reputation. Perhaps she—bright, energetic, ambitious, but deaf and consigned to an old archive in an unimportant town—projected her own feelings of isolation onto Avercamp, even as she allowed his work and his personality to be understood and remembered at last.

In return for her kindness, Avercamp performed one of his own. Centuries after his death, he gave Clara Welcker the chance to be a writer—to be an artist herself.

11

FRANS HALS

At the Crossroads

THE "WAR AGAINST WATER," the Dutch struggle to wrest their country from the sea, is strangely invisible now. Concerns about global warming are just that, global. The little local struggles—the rush to get the livestock to higher ground, the nervous pacing along the village dam—belong to dangers from olden days, like getting shipped off to suppress a tribal uprising in Sumatra, or contracting cholera from the shit in the canal.

Only the ancient, now, recall the last time things went wrong. The North Sea Flood of 1953 occasionally resurfaces in black-and-white photographs and television documentaries. Every Dutch person has seen these images, but they look as remote as the folk costumes the people in them are wearing. Almost nobody has experienced the old ancestral terror: that ominous water, always underfoot, waiting to whisk you away.

This is because the flood of 1953 was the last of its kind. In its wake, the government embarked on one of the most elaborate engineering projects in history, the Delta Works. The River Rhine reaches through Germany like a long arm, splitting into fingers just across the Dutch border. Big and small and under different names, these fingers spread across much of the country: the source of its wealth, and its greatest threat.

The most watery part of all is in the south, and is appropriately called Zeeland, Sea-Land, where the Delta Works were constructed. But the challenges for which this system of dams and gates was designed are not the challenges, then barely envisioned, of global warming. To ask whether those enormous barriers can withstand the wrath of a new age of weather is to wonder how long the Netherlands can survive.

With every freak hurricane and unexpected drought, we find ourselves, like every generation past, dwelling on eschatology. And when we imagine the collapse of dune and dike, among other things we imagine are the cultural losses such a cataclysm would bring. If the western Netherlands—all those cities, with all those museums and libraries—were swept into the sea, which treasures would we miss the most?

For me, the answer is surprisingly easy, and is to be found along a quiet street in Haarlem. There are many reasons for the art pilgrim to come to this city, halfway between Amsterdam and the ocean. Today virtually a suburb of Amsterdam, a few minutes' train journey from its central station, Haarlem has a cultural tradition as distinguished as nearly any in the world. That tradition is honored in a museum named for its greatest painter.

To see Frans Hals in his own place is to realize that not every artist travels well. Some can be seen anywhere. You can appreciate Titian better in Madrid, Paris, or Washington than in his hometown of Venice, where his works blend too seamlessly into the ambient splendor. Yet you'll never understand Carpaccio outside his own city, where his mythological tableaux glow with Egyptian mystery.

The Dutch, for the most part, are transportable. Most painted for living-room walls, and those can be found anywhere: one reason that, since medieval times, their works have been exported by the tens of thousands. If Holland suddenly disappeared, the achievement of its painters would still be visible all over the world, and we would know their Golden Age as we know those of Greece and Rome: from noble fragments.

Enough Rembrandts and Vermeers would survive. But though many of Hals's greatest works are in foreign collections, you still, as I learned, have to come to Haarlem to see him. There, in eight gigantic

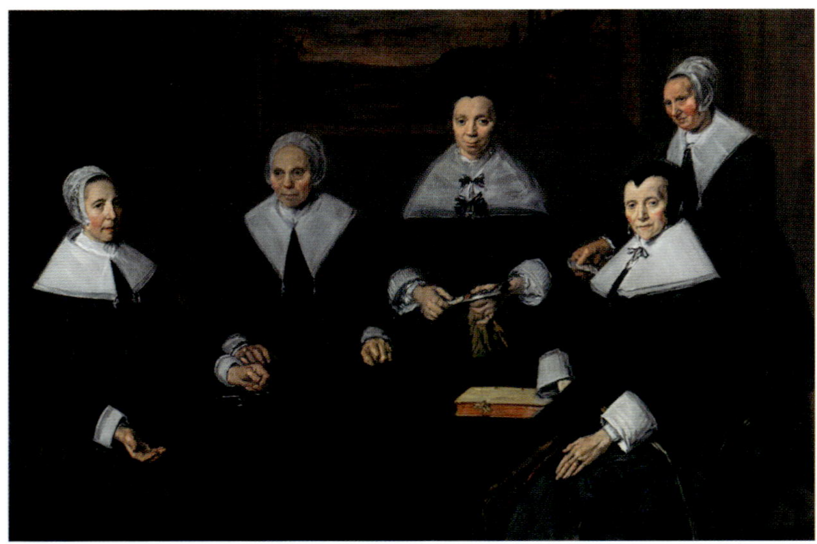

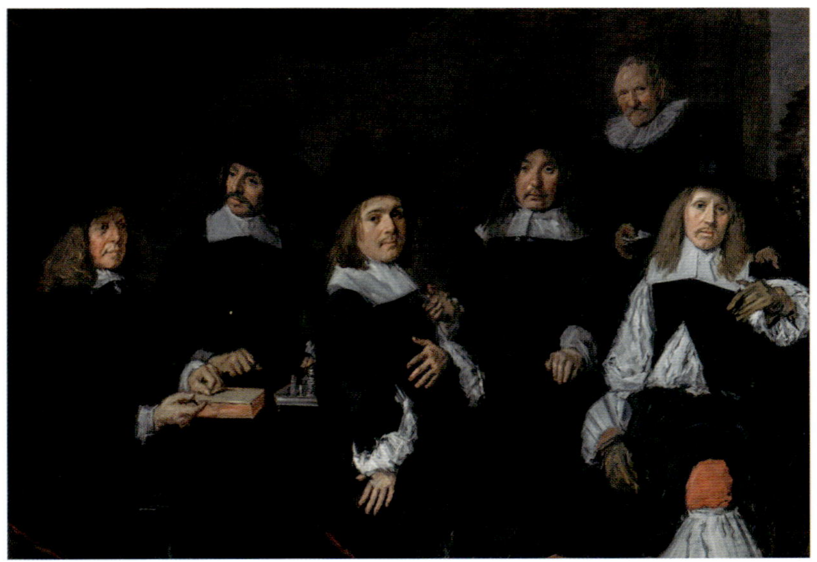

Painted just before Hals's death, the regents and regentesses of the building that houses the Frans Hals Museum today have attracted generations of artists to Haarlem.

paintings—placed end to end, they are twenty-three meters long—the Dutch Golden Age unfurls in portraits of members of Haarlem's charitable and military institutions: eighty-four people in all, painted over half a century.

———

IN JUNE 1902, to escape construction noise next door to his house in London, the American painter James Abbott McNeill Whistler fled across the North Sea. In The Hague, he met the German painter Georg Sauter, who was dismayed to see the state of Whistler's health. A drive to the beach at Scheveningen sufficed to exhaust him; and when Whistler spoke of going to nearby Haarlem, Sauter thought he was too frail.

The next day, he was amazed to find Whistler in Haarlem. They strolled past the pictures, from the earliest, painted in 1616, when Frans Hals was young, to the *Regentesses*, painted in 1664, when Hals was nearly as close to death as Whistler was now. "Certainly no collection would give stronger support to Whistler's theory that a master grows in his art, from picture to picture, to the end, than that at Haarlem."

The elderly painter warmed to the subject, and slid under the railing in order to view the pictures from closer by. The guard forced him to take a step back, and Whistler determined to wait until the other visitors were gone. At last, wrote Sauter, "We were indeed alone with Franz Hals. Now nothing could keep him away from the canvases; particularly the groups of old men and women got their full share of appreciation."

Whistler clambered onto a chair, "absolutely into raptures over the old women, admiring everything; his exclamation of joy came out now at the top of his voice, now in the most tender, almost caressing whisper: 'Look at it—just look; look at the beautiful colour—the flesh—look at the white—that black—look how those ribbons are put in. Oh, what a swell he was—can you see it all?—and the character—how he realised it.' "

Then he moved his hand so close to the picture that it looked that he wanted to caress it. He screamed with joy, Sauter recorded: " 'Oh, I must touch it—just for the fun of it,' and he moved tenderly with his fingers over the face of one of the old women." The guards indulged the sick painter—who miraculously managed to make it back to London. He hardly left his house again. The construction banged on. Soon, he was dead.

———

THE CARE LAVISHED ON the building that now houses the Frans Hals Museum seems at odds with its original purpose, a nursing home. Such splendid buildings amazed foreign visitors, who were more used to seeing such outlays reserved for princes or bishops. If the Old Men's Alms House was an expression of dedication to the infirm, it was also—not accidentally—an advertisement, in mortar and brick, for Dutch moral excellence.

Hals was young when construction began, in 1607. With its spacious rooms and tranquil garden, the Old Men's House still speaks, centuries later, of wealth sagely deployed, of a well-ordered civilization. So does the collection's centerpiece, Hals's group portraits. Swooshing with silk, dripping with lace, they nonetheless convey a dignity that, even at its most celebratory, is never ostentatious: these are people who deserved their golden age.

Yet the life of the artist who created the pictures—the person for whom the building is named—speaks of a poverty so extreme that the modern mind struggles to fathom it. Rembrandt died poor but enjoyed long periods of affluence, even magnificence; Hals, from before his birth till after his death, was trailed by such destitution that most of what we know of his life comes from the annals of the small-claims court.

When he was born, his father was involved in a lawsuit arising from his brother's estate. The question, which dragged on for nearly a year, involved a rapier, a doublet, six shirts, and a pair of stockings. The records of this dispute survived. The record of Frans's birth has not, because though we do not know the exact date, we know he came into the world in Antwerp toward the end of 1582: amid a holocaust.

The Dutch Revolt that began in 1566 had been centered in Antwerp, the mercantile and banking capital of Europe, which was being reduced to a colonial tributary. The Spanish repression was, among other things, unwise, as this was by far the richest part of the Habsburg Empire; but the grim Spanish king was determined to roll back the grudging not-quite tolerance that had kept the peace since the beginning of the Reformation.

The cruel response from their foreign rulers inflamed the Netherlanders. When religious oppression was joined to economic and military oppression, they rose up under the leadership of William of Orange. The revolution would later be seen as the triumph of Protestantism over Catholicism, republicanism over monarchism, and capitalism over feudalism, and thus the forerunner of the French and American Revolutions.

But around the time of Hals's birth, it mainly meant poverty and slaughter. Antwerp had been reduced by wave after wave of destruction. In 1566, the Protestants purged the churches of what they saw as idols, an act of defiance against king and church that was answered, ten years later, by a sack of the city: eighteen thousand people were killed in three days. The "Spanish Fury" meant the end of Antwerp as the entrepôt of the North.

In personal terms, for the survivors, it meant nothing good, especially if they, like Hals's parents, were poor to begin with. His father was a shearer—a man who cut wool from sheep—one of the many artisans in a clothmaking industry that never recovered from the attacks. In an economic and military context that made six shirts and a pair of stockings a treasure worth fighting over, more violence was to come.

Around the time of Frans Hals's birth, another Fury broke out. The Prince of Orange invited the brother of the French king to lead the liberated provinces; but the Duke of Anjou, unwilling to be a constitutional monarch, attacked his own city of Antwerp. The coup resulted in a humiliating defeat, and hundreds of troops were hacked to death by the outraged citizenry. But the "French Fury" weakened Antwerp still further.

The next summer, the Spanish returned. After a year of starvation and horror, the city fell. From then on, the northern and the southern Netherlands were severed. For two centuries, the Dutch blockaded Antwerp. Over half its population fled, and among them were the Hals family. They settled in Haarlem—also besieged and plundered by the Spanish. But the Spanish left Haarlem in 1577, and never returned.

———

BY THE TIME THESE thousands of Flemish immigrants arrived, Haarlem was being rebuilt. The skills these sophisticated people brought revitalized the city's trade, including the cloth trade that employed Hals's father, Franchois. The city prospered. The Hals family did not. In 1599, to make good a debt incurred by purchasing half a cow, Franchois was forced to cede the entirety of his household goods.

A pair of stockings, half a cow: the tone was set. Frans Hals would be sued, in 1624, for payment for a jacket (three guilders and six stuivers). In 1627, he would be sued for seven guilders for a delivery of butter and cheese. In 1629, a baker sued him for five guilders and seventeen stuivers. In 1631, he was sued over his failure to pay for some meat for which he had agreed to pay forty-two guilders; thirteen were still outstanding. In 1634, he was sued for twenty-three guilders for bread. (He had exchanged a painting for the bread, not enough to cover the debt.) In 1636, another baker sued him. In 1640, he was sued for thirty-three guilders for rent. In 1642, he was sued for five guilders for a bed. In 1644, he was sued for five guilders and two stuivers for the purchase of canvas. In 1647, he owed his shoemaker fifty-nine guilders and eight stuivers. In 1649, two of his grandchildren were admitted to the orphanage, their parents deceased and he and his wife unable to care for them. The next year, a local innkeeper sued him. The year after that, his wife was sued for four guilders for not paying for a box. When his ailing son Claes made a will in 1656, he allowed his parents to choose among his gray coat, his "worst outfit," or one Flemish pound (six guilders).

So it went. If one knew this man only through the scarce documents that chronicle his life, one would be utterly unprepared for the glorious paintings that deck the halls of the museum that bears his name. If his life was petty, his work was lavish. Perhaps more than any other Dutch painter of his time, his impulse was celebratory, and as notable for everything it omits as for everything it includes.

There are no still-lifes. There are no landscapes or seascapes or cityscapes or—surprisingly for a man with something like fourteen children—nudes. Notwithstanding the odd skull, his pictures are bereft of allusive symbols; we vainly comb them for memento mori. And though a pair of paintings of evangelists turned up in the basement of a Ukrainian museum in the 1950s, they bear not the slightest whiff of religion.

FRANS HALS'S SUBJECT was the citizens of Haarlem. His first known portrait—still in his museum—shows Jacobus Zaffius, a Catholic who, in 1578, witnessed the destruction of Haarlem's holy images and was imprisoned for protesting. In 1611, when this picture was painted, Zaffius was a figure who looked to the wars of religion and independence—to the nation's past. The man who painted him pointed to the future.

Hals was not quite young—almost thirty—when he painted Zaffius. It was a late start. At that age, the animal painter Paulus Potter was dead; Fabritius had two years to live. Despite the hurdles he faced in his life, Hals would live far longer than any prominent Dutch painter. He died in 1666, aged about eighty-four, fully twenty years older than Rembrandt was when he died—and Rembrandt was considered old, and outlived most of his colleagues.

The vitality that propelled Frans Hals through a long life is visible, already, in this work. The paint is laid on in liberal quantities. Though the colors are few—black and brown for Zaffius's clothing, yellows and reds and whites for his face and beard—Hals wrings every nuance out of them. "He doesn't have a single black, but twenty-seven different blacks," wrote another painter, who thought Hals was Rembrandt's equal.

That painter—Vincent van Gogh—was one of many modernists who found a model in Hals. Whistler called his painting of his mother *Arrangement in Grey and Black No. 1*, a title that could have served for any number of Hals's paintings. Only Rembrandt and Hals placed such unembarrassed emphasis on the artifice of their art, a break with tradition that would not be taken up again until the nineteenth century.

Yet all these whorls and scratches inevitably resolve into Haarlemers who, though centuries dead, illustrate the paradox that makes Hals's work so fascinating. Blatantly artificial—yet so alive that his subjects always seem to have been snapped in flagrante, as if by a canny street photographer. Roman Vishniac's Warsaw, Vivian Maier's Chicago, Henri Cartier-Bresson's Paris, all descend from Hals's Haarlem.

IN HIS TECHNIQUE, the modernists found a lineage—and in his subjects, too. After a visit to Haarlem, Manet made up his mind to become a painter of his own time. Hals had discovered the range of humanity even in a small city, and alongside the grandees and the flush merchants he showed the common *volk*: a barmaid tallying her customers' drinks on the wall; a series of fishermen's children; a sly streetwalker.

The city was small, but its citizens reflected the Dutch Republic's worldliness and ambition. Isaac Massa—a fluent Russian speaker who was ennobled in Sweden, became the first Westerner to publish maps of Siberia, and wrote an account of the False Dmitry, the impostor who claimed to be the son of Ivan the Terrible and ruled Russia for a year—puts in an appearance; and so does a man attired in one of the rare kimonos that the Dutch were allowed to export from Japan.

The first person to paint the landscape of Brazil, Frans Post, sat for Hals as well. So did a man who, though born in France, became as much a symbol of Dutch cultural achievement as Hals himself: René Descartes, who spent his adult life in Amsterdam. There, in a climate of intellectual freedom that had no equal anywhere in Europe, he composed his philosophical works, and was painted by Hals shortly before his death in 1650.

Alongside these eminences are people one would cross the street to avoid: a man who played an instrument that squawked so obnoxiously that neighbors would bribe him, with a coin, to get him to move along; and Malle Babbe, "Crazy Babs," known in local legend as the sorceress of Haarlem. Malle Babbe clutches a pewter mug of beer while an owl—a symbol of drunkenness, of the nightside—perches on her shoulder.

Is she laughing? Grimacing? She is one of Hals's most ambiguous characters. Some find her *gezellig*—an overused word that means "fun, sociable"—the type of kindhearted drunk you might spend a memorable evening with down at the bar. Popular songs have been written that portray her as a prostitute, which seems unlikely. Others see a terrifying madwoman in the grip of addiction and mental illness.

She was a real person, Barbara Claes, who appears in the records of the same asylum to which Hals's own son Pieter was committed. (Another of the tragedies that filled his life, recorded in the dry prose of bureaucracy.) In an age without euphemism, this institution was known as Het Dolhuys, "The Madhouse." In an age without specific diagnosis of mental disabilities, it is hard to know what ailed her.

Whatever her story, she surely never dreamed that she would remain a symbol of Haarlem centuries after her death, or that the city would honor her with a statue, complete with her owl. Her name and face are still known thanks to Hals's portrait, which—in our image-soaked world, in our dutiful trudges through "encyclopedic" museums—is that rare picture that, once it has been seen, can never be forgotten.

"*El sueño de la razón produce monstruos*," Goya wrote on an etching: the dream of reason produces monsters. Owls descend on a dozing man. They land on his shoulder as they did, 150 years before, on Malle Babbe's. Amid all the attainments of civilization—Goya showed the man respectably dressed—it is enough to close one's eyes to see the madhouse, the bailiff, the orphan, the drunk. (Enough, too, to open them.)

YOU ENTER THE Frans Hals Museum through a monumental gate, take a right, buy your ticket in the bookstore, and then walk, counterclockwise, around the courtyard. The great Haarlem artists before Hals file past on the right side of the quadrilateral—and then, in the wing opposite the entrance, the first of the works that have attracted generations of artists to this city, the eight heroic group portraits, appear.

No matter how many other pictures by Hals you have seen in real life—no matter how many times you have seen these particular pictures reproduced in books or on screen—you will not be prepared for their

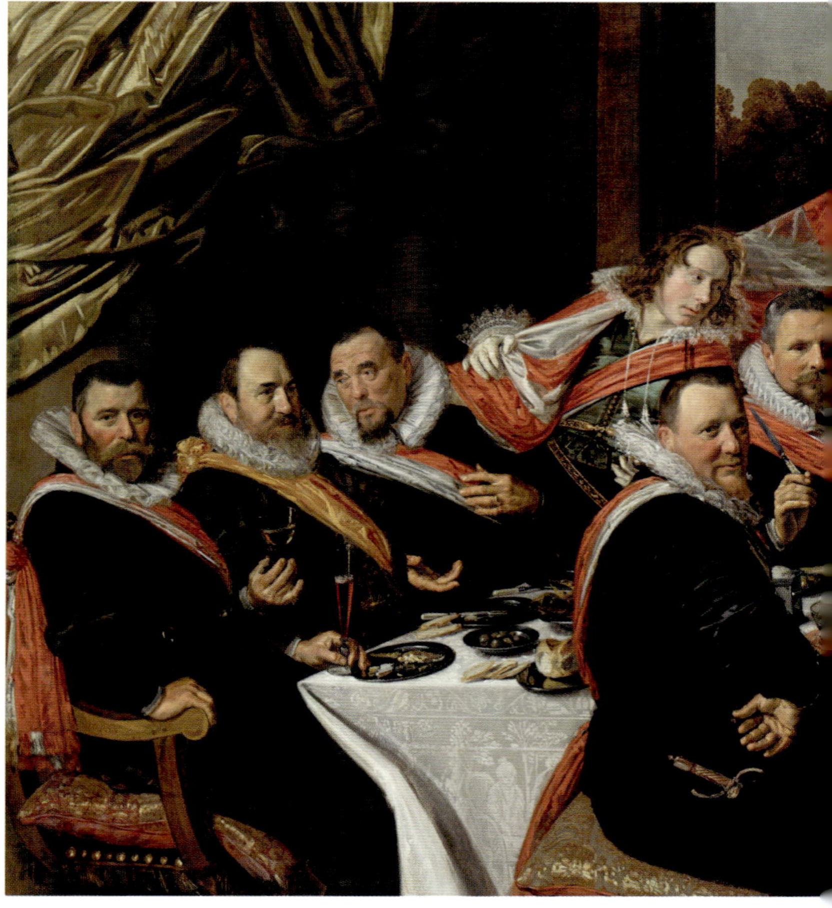

The earliest of Hals's heroic group portraits, painted in 1616: a series that would be added to for half a century.

size and impact. The nebulous idea of inspiration, of the artist's pleasure in his work, crystallizes here. To see Hals paint is to see a graceful young animal bounding and jumping, delighting in everything he sees.

A fork!! A hat!!! A moustache!!!! There are no dull passages; everything is climax. The flash of the feasting militiamen, seated at their richly laden tables, clad in their fabulous garments, is rendered by a man who

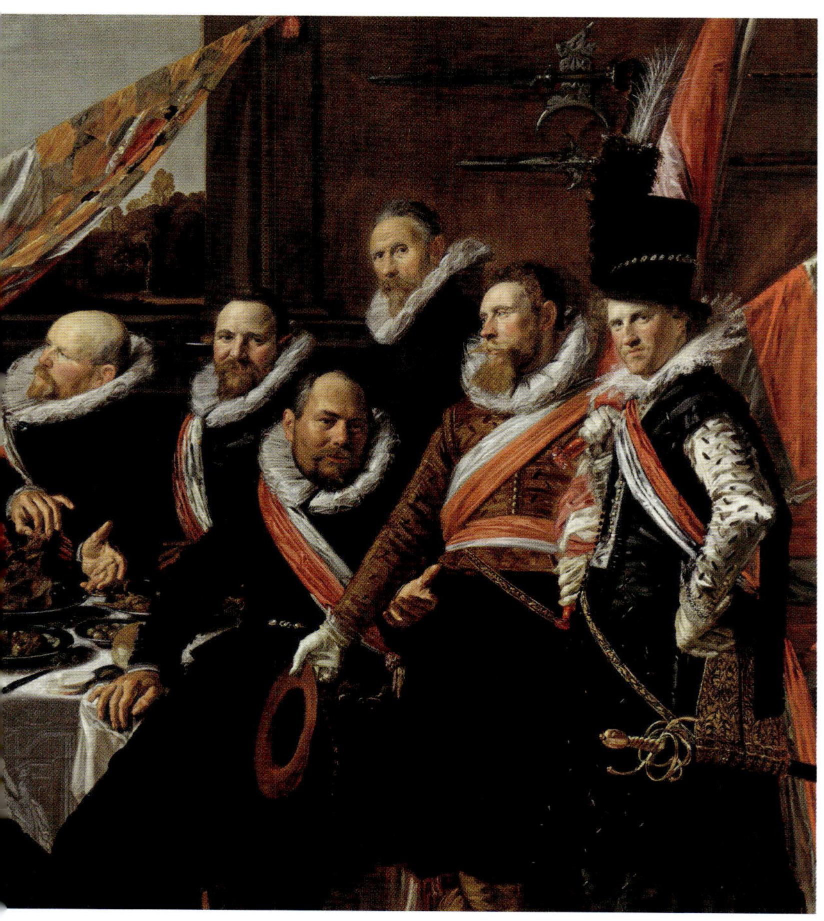

wields brushes as they wield swords, and whose technique matches his
subjects so perfectly that it is impossible to separate one from the other.
The militiamen flaunt their pride, and so does the painter.

The earliest, *The Banquet of the Officers of the St. George Militia Company*,
dates to 1616, the beginning of Hals's career. Its colors are bright and
cheerful, showing young men—many younger even than Hals—the

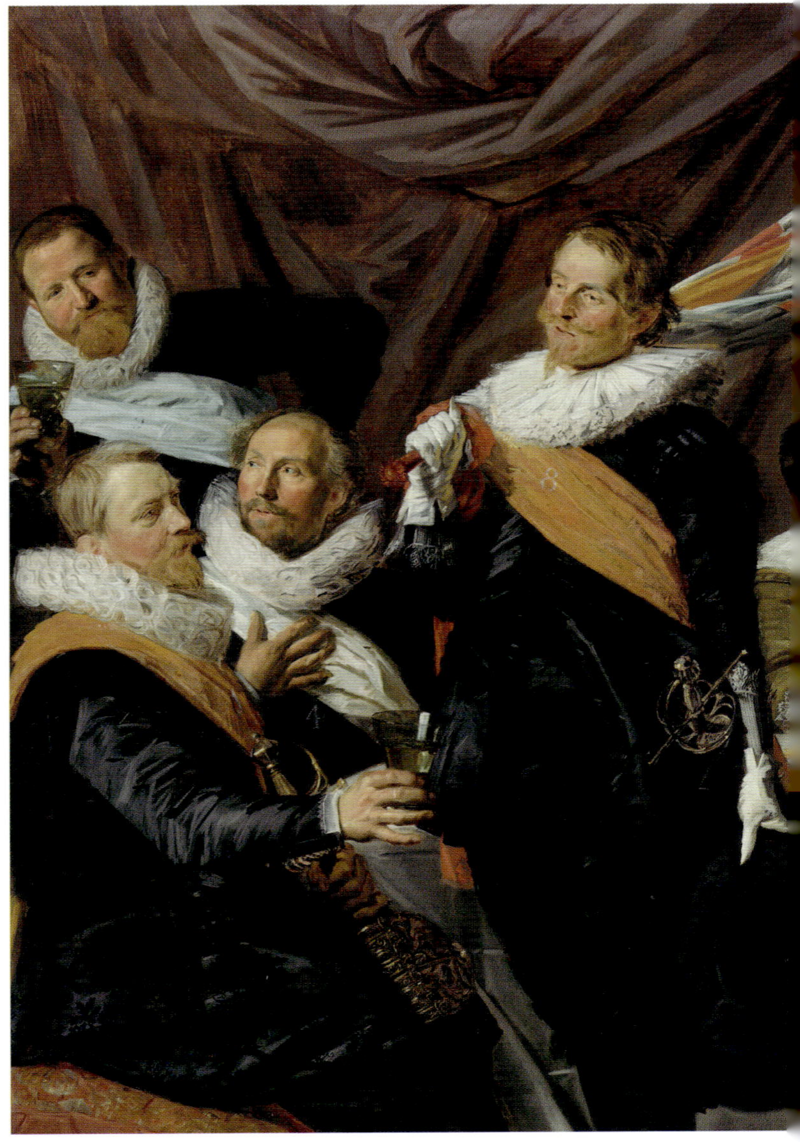

In 1627, eleven years after the first group portrait, Hals painted two banquets of the Haarlem civic guard (here and on the following pages).

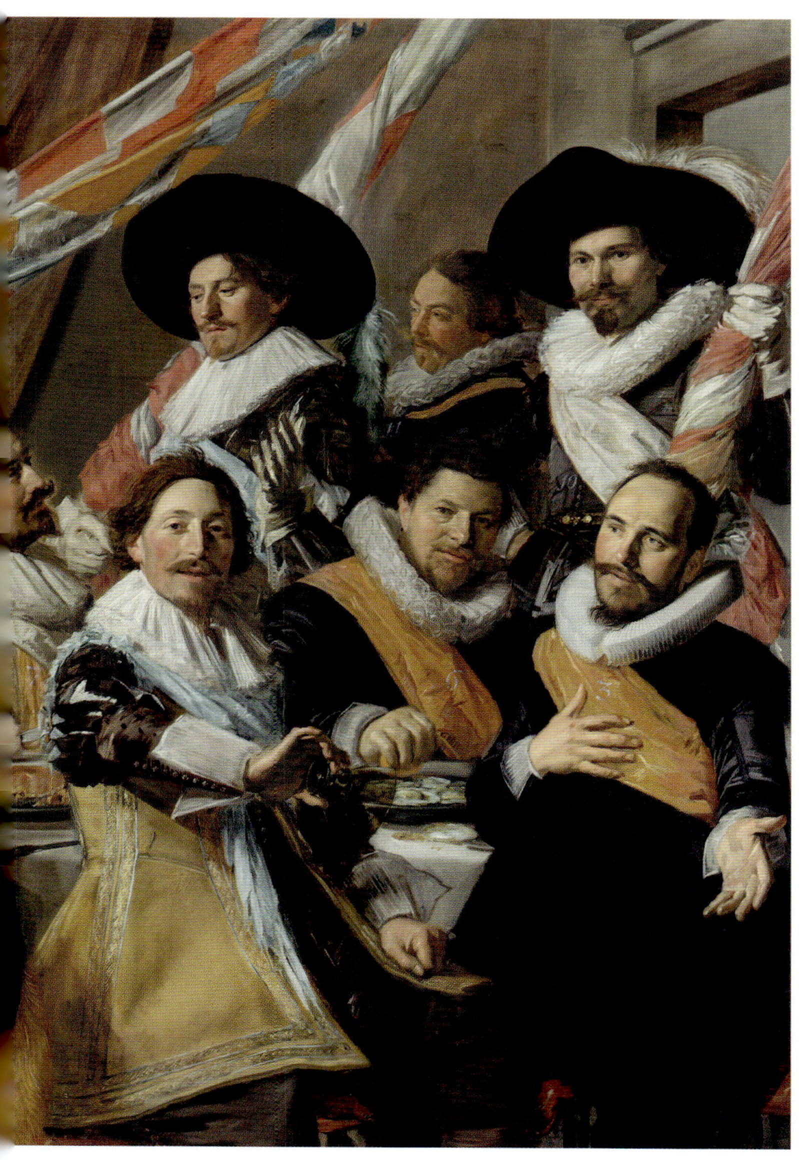

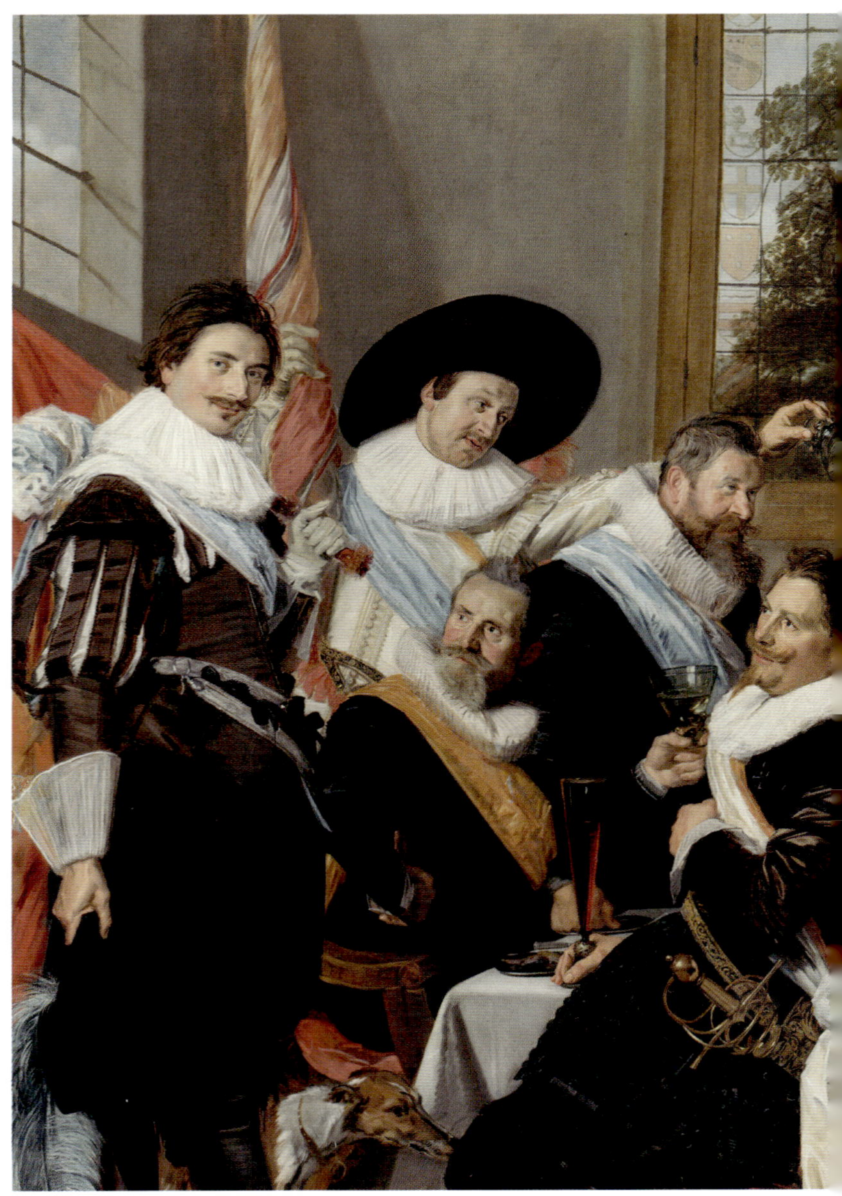

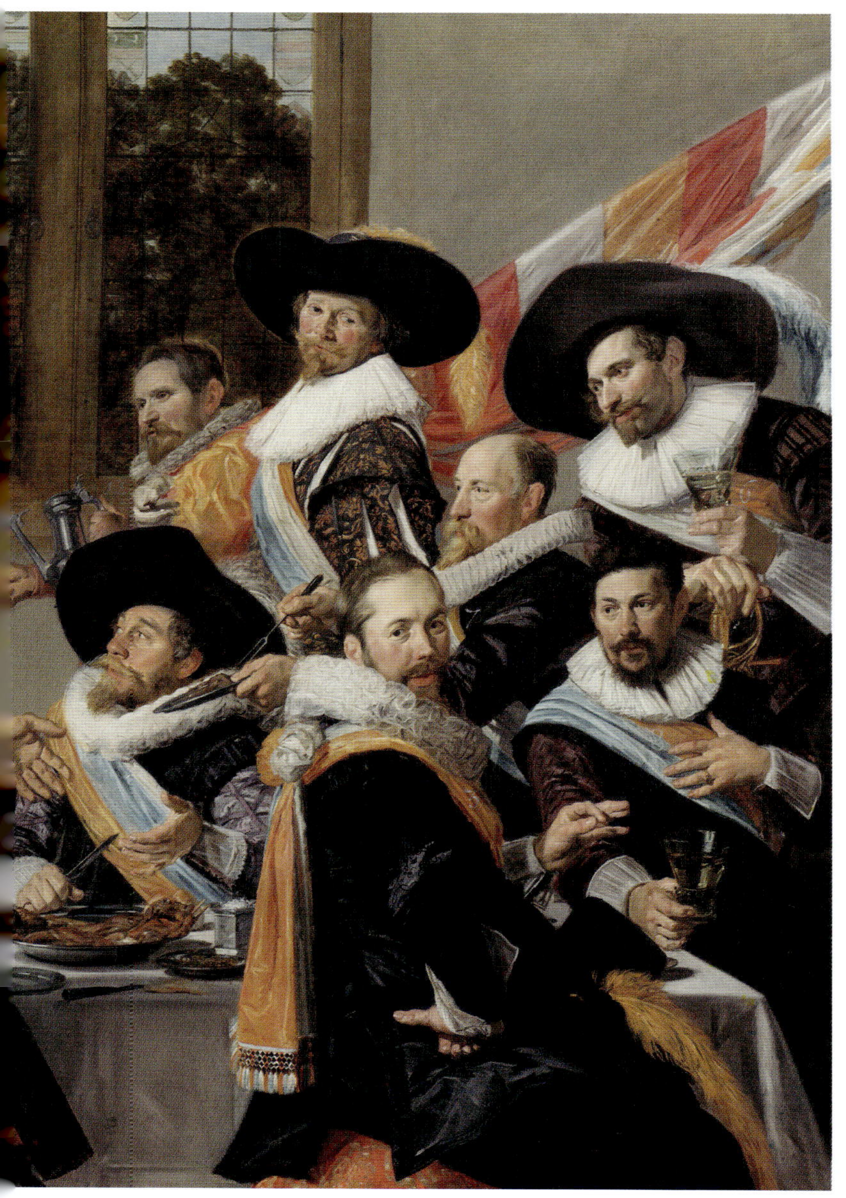

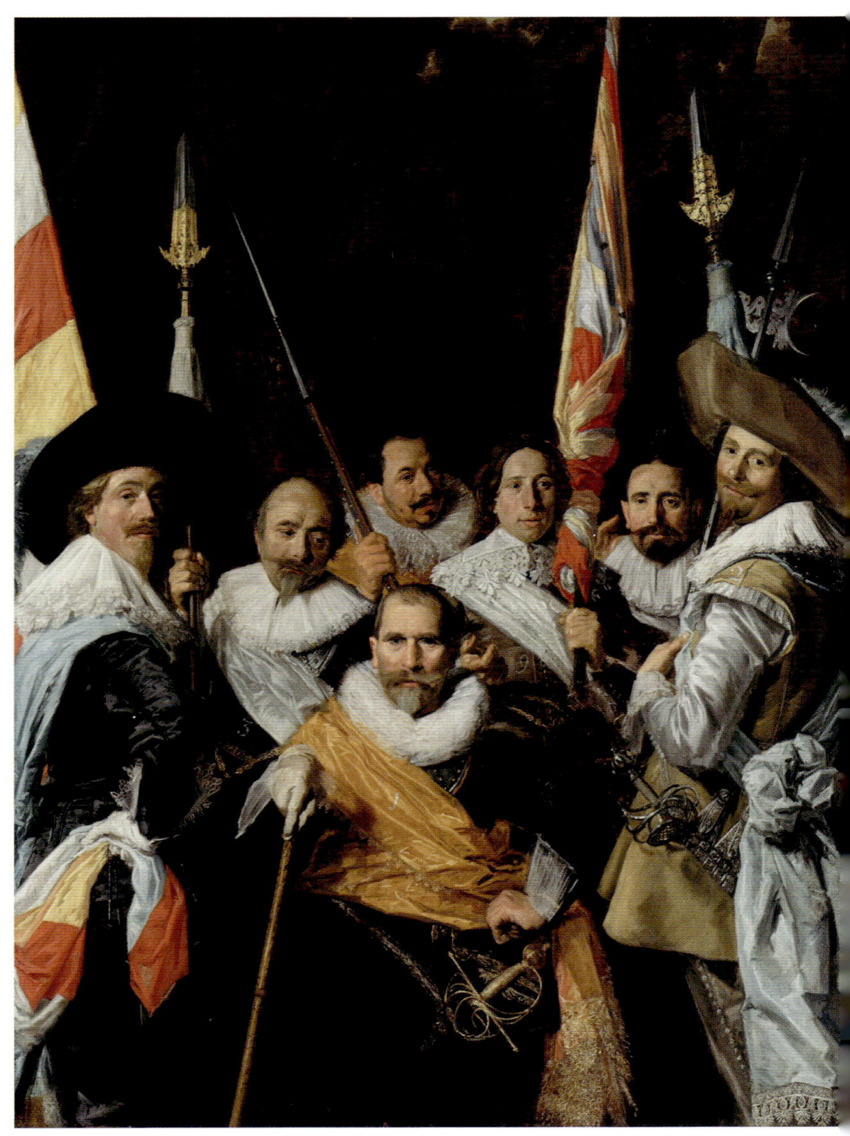

In 1633, when he created this huge and spectacular portrait,
a middle-aged Hals was at the height of his powers.

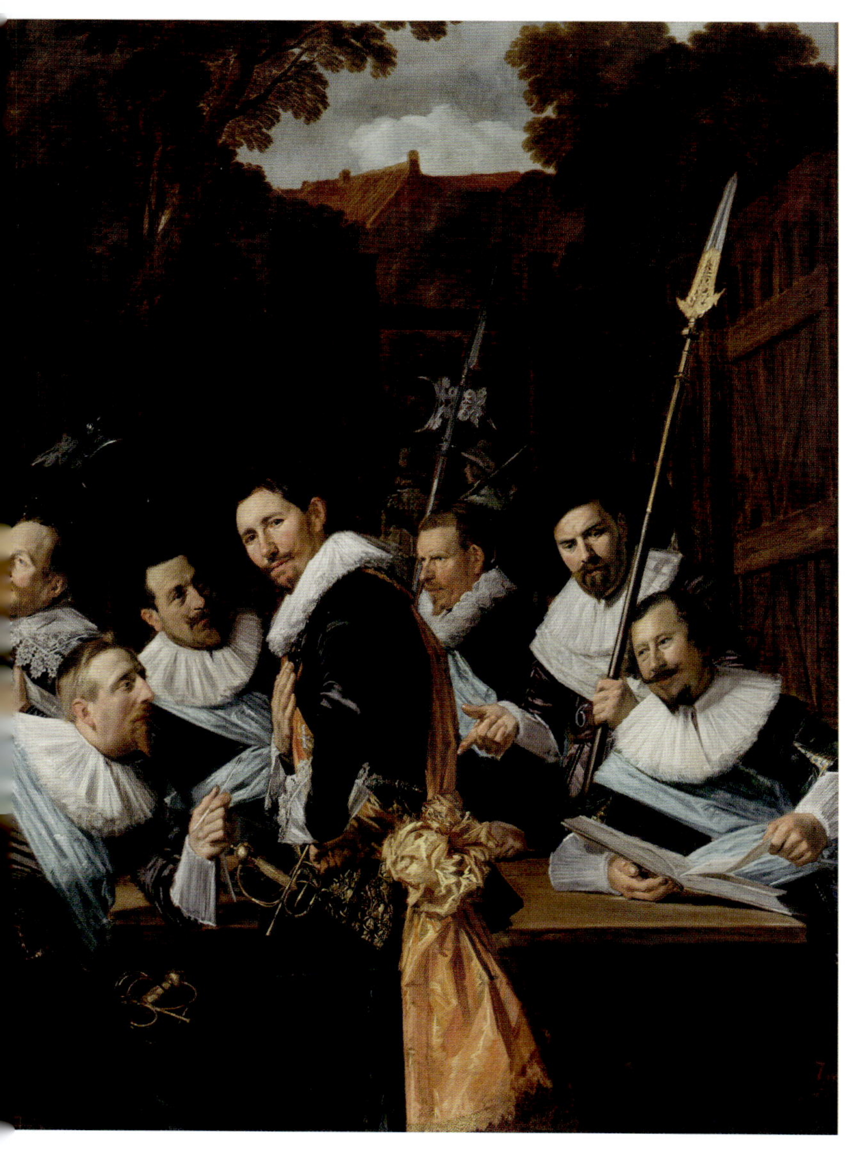

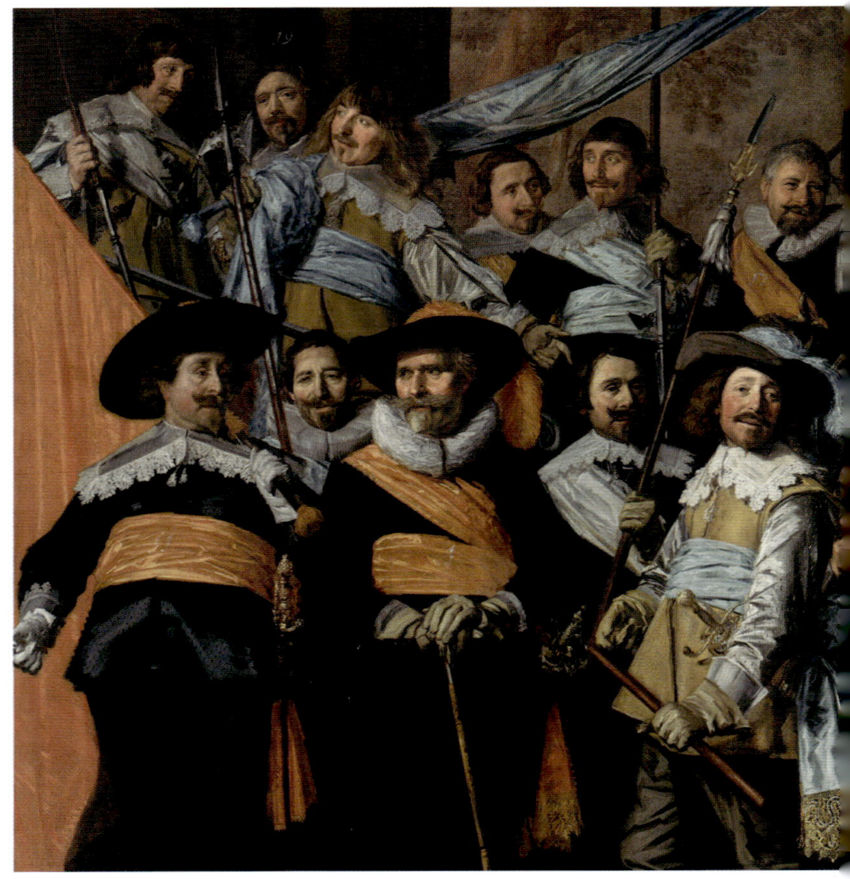

In 1639, nearing sixty, an age when many of his colleagues were long dead, Hals included a man—top row, second from left—traditionally thought to be the painter himself.

flower of a triumphant nation. The iconoclasms and religious wars, the sieges and massacres, would have been, for them, thrilling stories they had heard, as children, from the greatest generation.

Twenty-five years, another generation, later, Hals, now middle-aged, painted the regents of St. Elizabeth Hospital, an institution housed directly across from the museum. The colors have sobered,

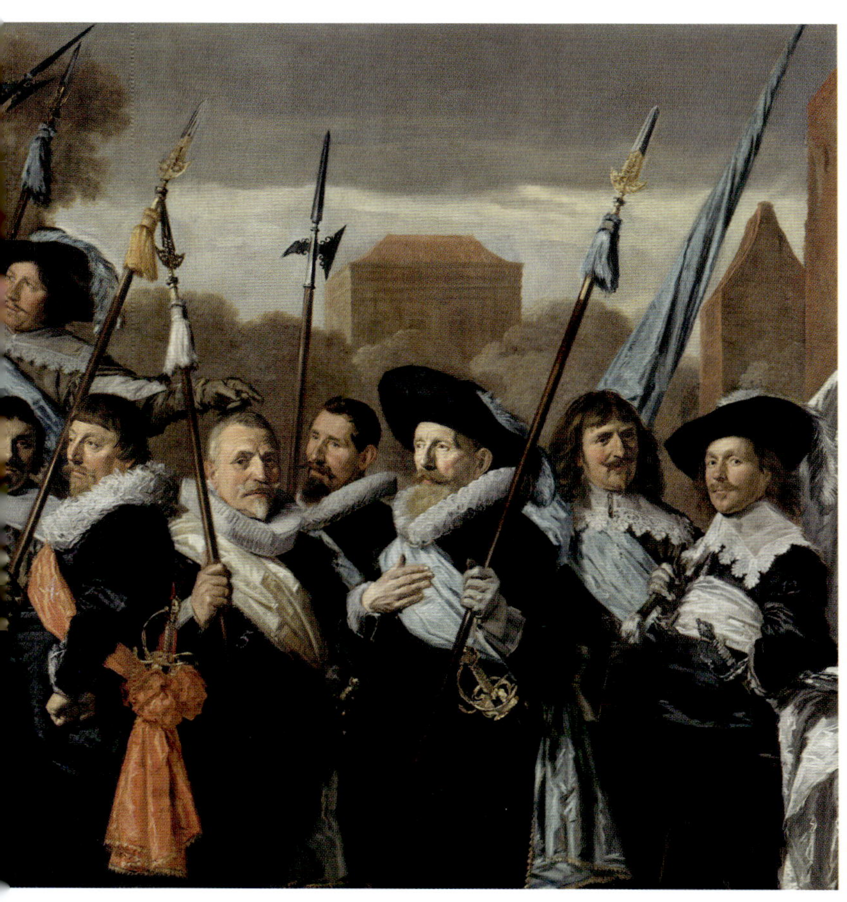

and the subject is different: the directors of a charitable foundation, the first such group painted in Haarlem. Gone is the sparkling silver-ware; the only metal visible is a clutch of coins dedicated to the care of the infirm.

Here are people scratched together in paint—those twenty-seven shades of blacks—who seem far more real than the smoother creations of other artists: lifelike, and life-size. The man closest to the viewer is seen in profile, cocking an ear toward some invisible interloper who has walked in on their gathering. Through that gesture, the group acknowledges the viewer, and through their gestures they acknowledge one another.

Like a pianist whose fingers never allude to the deprivation that preceded his performance, or like a pirouetting ballerina whose dainty smile betrays no hint of the blood in her shoes, his travails—his quibbles

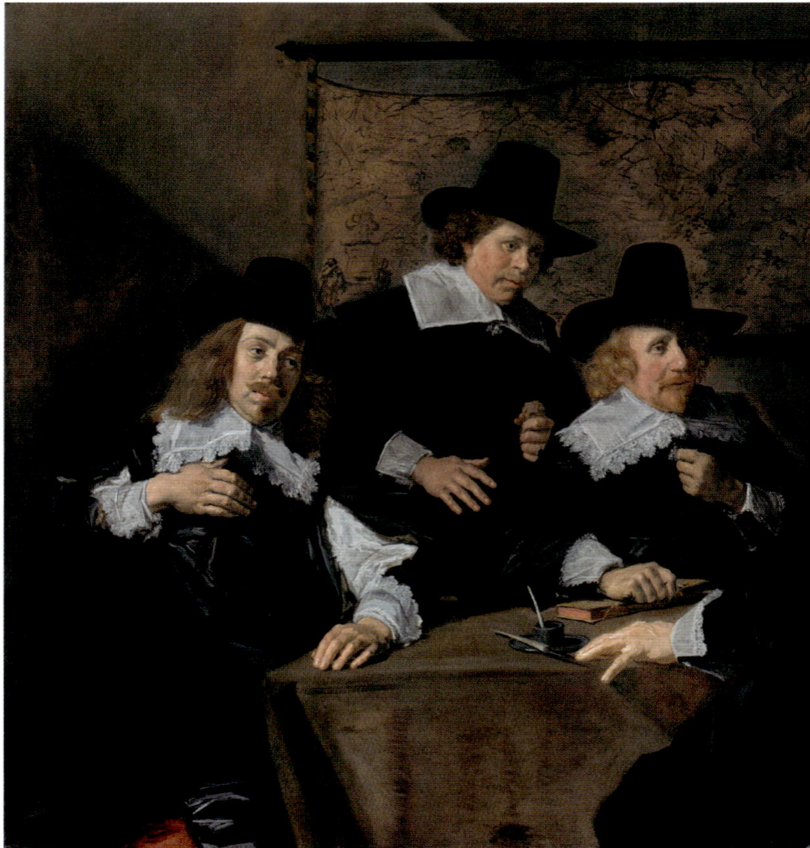

In 1641, Hals painted the regents of the St. Elizabeth Hospital, across the street from the Frans Hals Museum: a sober monument to a people who, these paintings proclaim, deserved their golden age.

with the tailor, his dead children—have been pushed offstage. He is entirely at the service of an art that does not show daily life but that, by rising above it, elevates it. All the spectator sees is the sprezzatura of the prodigy.

His light touch disguises something only his fellow painters can fully appreciate: nobody else can do this. His works are all of a piece, so much so that they seem to have been dashed onto canvas in a single inspired

explosion. Technical research shows that these works took years. But the appearance of effortlessness—of a balance so refined that it seems inevitable—is the miraculous illusion of the virtuoso.

YET THE GREAT VIRTUOSI are not always the great artists. These are often those who, alongside their mastery, have that creepiness, that slightly-off-ness, that getting-under-your-skin-ness, that Freud called *das Unheimliche*. One feels the tension between spontaneity and obsession even in Hals's earliest works, but only as one is nearing the exit of the museum does "the uncanny" burst into full funereal flower.

Here we find the regents and the regentesses of this very building, the Old Men's Alms House, staring at us from across the ages: five women and six men, gathered in two gloomy paintings. These are the works to which the dying Whistler paid homage, and they are so strikingly weird that it is no surprise he dragged himself here to touch them, or that a legend grew up around them. These pictures demand explanation.

The man with the floppy hat and the hangdog face is drunk, for example; and the portrayal of the crones was Hals's revenge for their forcing him to spend his last years in this institution. The stories, however charming, are myths. An inebriated regent was unthinkable in a formal portrait, and Hals never lived in this building. But they thrive because we know there is more to these pictures than a meeting of the board.

We know for certain that these pictures were created by an octogenarian, and that, if eighty is elderly now, it was ancient then: given the life expectancy at the time, most residents of the Old Men's House were presumably much younger. We know that these were the last pictures Hals made. And we know that another twenty-five years—another generation—have passed since the St. Elizabeth's portrait.

Something has changed. If the earlier portraits are cohesive internally (the figures relate to one another) and externally (the figures relate to the viewer), the regents and regentesses interact with nobody. As if sliced from other paintings and pasted into an amateuristic photomontage, they stand uncomfortably, pinned to a background, looking right and left, and above, and below—never at one another, and never at us.

In a traditional novel, one sentence leads to the next, one thought to another. In a sonata, an initial theme is coaxed into a more elaborate development, then brought back to a recapitulating conclusion. To see Hals's final, fragmented pictures is to understand that the earlier portraits were akin to fictions, in which the chaos of experience has been pressed into a readable narrative, an artificial form.

No matter how wild Hals's pictures seemed, they respected the classical order. Eye met eye; hand led to sleeve that led to elbow; one color led harmoniously to the next. Here, though, the colors seem to have been frightened off. All that remains are the twenty-seven blacks, and an equal number of whites. Hands and heads emerge from darkness; and the people, especially taken together, look disembodied, ghostly.

"A LONELY PRINCE of a realm of spirits, from whom now only a chilling breath issued to terrify his most willing contemporaries, standing as they did aghast at these communications of which only at moments, only by exception, they could understand anything at all": thus Thomas Mann imagined Beethoven at the end of his life. Abandoning his audience, the artist created a style that was half breakdown and half liberation.

The German philosopher Theodor Adorno was obsessed with this style, and for decades plotted a book about it. (Of it, appropriately, only fragments remain.) Late Beethoven did not show fullness or resolution; he showed, instead, the preposterousness of the very idea of unity, totality, narrative. The works he created at the end showed him in the face of the dissolution of death, their broken nature suiting an artist who had outlived his time.

Such late works do not display a failure of unity or narrative. They display a willingness to transcend it. "Objective is the fractured landscape, subjective the light in which—alone—it glows into life," Adorno wrote. "He does not bring about their harmonious synthesis. As the power of dissociation, he tears them apart in time, in order perhaps, to preserve them for the eternal. In the history of art, late works are the catastrophes."

The shattered illusion of totality is the catastrophe we see in the Black Paintings of Goya or the last plays of Ibsen. Our perplexity and discomfort in the face of such works show that aesthetic needs (for narrative, for visual unity) are grounded in emotion, and show that, as with incorrect punctuation, untuned instruments, or clashing colors, disjointedness upsets us—even physically—far more than we realize.

When we do realize it, another displeasure arrives. It feels pathetic to be so troubled by a lack of harmony or synthesis. We know that our own lives don't add up, and that such totalities are artificial, and that the fractured landscape is, indeed, the objective one; but that may be precisely the reason we expect art to provide that neatness and consolation. Looked at head-on, the fracture is unbearable.

"The maturity of the late works does not resemble the kind one finds in fruit," Adorno wrote of Beethoven. "They are . . . not round, but furrowed, even ravaged. Devoid of sweetness, bitter and spiny, they do not surrender themselves to mere delectation." These were the fruits Hals painted; and when we try to taste them, we discover how prepared we are for delectation, how uncomfortable in the absence of sweetness.

This discovery opens the door to a more accurate appraisal of the world and our place within it. Such knowledge dispenses with devices that link one thought, one person, one figure, to the next, and that understand one phase of life as a positive evolution toward another. As in the Kabbalah, this view understands us as fragments of shattered vessels; but this most secular of painters withholds the prospect of redemption.

THE *REGENTS* AND *REGENTESSES* are thrice late. They are painted by a man who has outlived his generation and buried his children. They show older people: not as old as the painter, but none quite young, and one of whom—the man rumored to be a drunk—seems to be disintegrating. These people, painted by an old person, are in charge, furthermore, of a home for old people—the building where these pictures still hang.

In the wilting flower, the fleeting days, the sunset, thousands of works ponder decline. They are melancholy, but they can be produced by young artists; and even when produced by older artists, they do not necessarily need to be composed in the fractured or antiharmonious manner suggested by Adorno with the term "late style." Not every elderly artist develops—like Beethoven, Ibsen, or Goya—a distinctive late style.

"His late works," Adorno wrote of Beethoven, "constitute a form of exile." In that word, "exile," lies a possible key to these paintings: not the exile we usually imagine, an expulsion from city or country. One might always—at least theoretically—return to a place. These paintings show something more irrevocable. There is no going back for one who has outlived his own time; Hals was an exile from time itself.

A home for the aged is a home for people alienated from whoever they once were. Its residents could once feed and wash themselves, walk without effort, sleep without soiling the bed. Now they find themselves in a building that, no matter how lavishly appointed or caringly staffed, is the antechamber of death; and Frans Hals, no matter whether he lived in this building or a few streets away, inhabited the same room.

This is the institution over which the regents presided. In their spookiness, they resemble other representations of guardians of the crossroads. These are lords of the threshold, at the junction of this world and the next: liminal deities like Janus, who looks in two directions; St. Peter, who keeps the keys to the Christian heaven; Papa Legba, who watches over the gates to the voodoo underworld, Guinee.

Malle Babbe shows the vicinity of sanity to madness. The *Regents* and *Regentesses* show a more unbridgeable distance. No landscape is more fractured than the region between life and death. As the old master wanders along this path, he is freed—if he wants to be—from the restrictions that held him back before. Nothing matters; everything matters. It is not a time to be timid, or respectful of convention.

Beethoven's late works resolved into trills; Hals's, into the tears and fissures of brushstrokes alone. The portraits of these eleven people add up to a portrait of a single man standing between this world and the next.

These paintings loom at the junction between religion and art, evoking a response that more explicit religious art seeks, but often fails to elicit, and it is their very indirectness that lends them their mystic voltage.

Perhaps the reason that I would save these works first, the reason that they appealed to so many modern artists, is that they show how, in a churchless age, we might yet capture the feeling that was previously the province of religion. We are not really looking for answers. We know that truth can be glimpsed only in fragments, and feel defrauded by fiction, by harmony; we sometimes want to taste those bitter, spiny fruits.

12

PIETER SAENREDAM

Infinity in the Making

I N 1662, three years before his death, Pieter Saenredam returned, one last time, to a drawing he had made twenty-six years before. The journey it commemorated was a turning point in his life. Though the journey had not taken him more than fifty kilometers—from his home in Haarlem to the nearby city of Utrecht—it was perhaps the greatest adventure of that life, and its memory stayed with him to the end.

When he embarked from Haarlem, he had just turned thirty-nine. He was no longer young. His own father, a distinguished engraver, had died at forty-two. Perhaps now was the time for him, who until that point had produced worthy but not spectacular work, to strive to meet his father's standard; and so, during the eighteen weeks he spent in Utrecht, he labored furiously, like someone whose time was running out.

When he returned home, he brought the products of that labor: a sheaf of highly detailed drawings of the Utrecht churches. This was his specialty—church interiors—and the old ecclesiastical capital had the richest collection of such monuments in the country. In Utrecht an architecturally minded visitor could see vaulted hall churches and Romanesque basilicas and a cathedral in the French Gothic style.

Is that why Saenredam came, and why he stayed so long? He reached the city before June 18, 1636, and left sometime after October 23. In

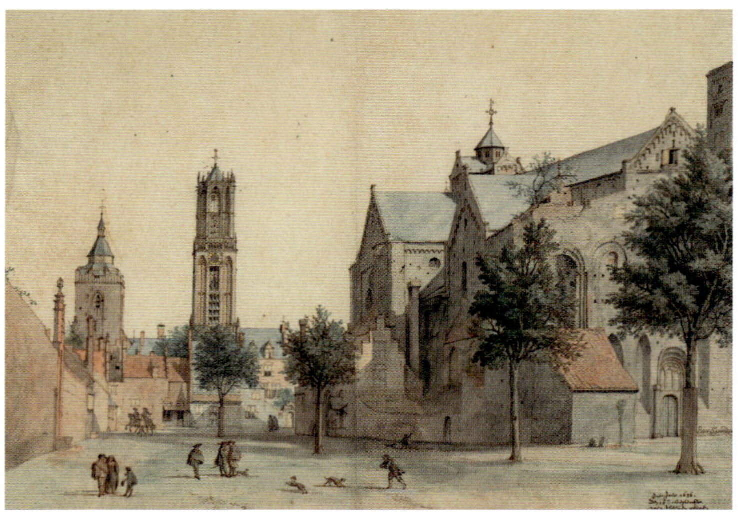

Saenredam drew the Mariaplaats in Utrecht in 1636.
Twenty-six years later, he pulled out this sketch to create his final painting.

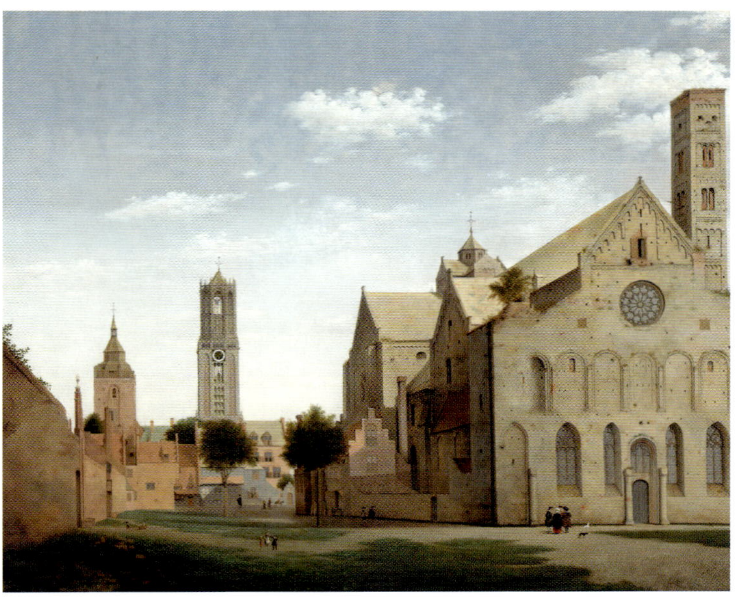

that time, he produced twenty-six church interiors, five church exteriors, and full architectural plans of seven churches—an extravagantly detailed record of the city's architecture. It wasn't everything. But it was nevertheless a more complete record that exists of any other Dutch city.

He must have known he had a lot. But did he know that he had enough to occupy him for the rest of his life—or that, as it turned out, a lifetime wouldn't be enough to complete all the paintings he had planned during his stay? The works he extracted from the material he brought back emerged with agonizing slowness, demanding an investment of time and expertise that made them ruinously expensive to make.

By 1662, when he started this newest painting, he had been using his drawings for twenty-six years. The works that resulted were a dream of purity, and in them Saenredam created a new kind of religious painting. They showed sacred buildings instead of sacred histories, buildings that were as composed as still-lifes, as bursting with personality as portraits—and suffused with a deep, but never spoken, religious feeling.

They look simple, but it is a characteristic of art to disguise its difficulty. Like a dancer who makes an exhausted body soar, Saenredam hid the torturous technical challenges in his work so well that his paintings became bywords for purity, and appealed to modern viewers intimidated by arcane symbolism, and trained to admire minimalism. The key to what made them so beautiful was lost. Their beauty, however, was not.

The drawing he took out now showed three churches from the outside. On the right, taking up nearly half the picture, is the Mariakerk, a dilapidated Italianate pile in and around which he spent most of his time. In the center distance is the symbol of the city: the tower of the cathedral, which still bears the Latin name of Dom, is the highest in the Netherlands. On the left is the more modest tower of the Buurkerk.

It feels as if the aged painter is taking one last backward glance. The life that was then in the future is now in the past. To place the scene next to the drawing from which he prepared it is to see an ideal imperturbability. Everything has changed for the painter. But nothing has changed in his memory. In another drawing, birds perch on the tower. Twenty-six years later, in the painting, they are perching there still.

—·—

I WAS LONG INTRIGUED by Saenredam's stay in Utrecht, because Utrecht was where I lived: where I have now lived longer than I have lived anywhere else in my life. When I first moved there, in 2002, it seemed to be the ideal place to live, and it still does: the Brooklyn to the Manhattan of Amsterdam. It takes about as long to get there as it does to go from Midtown to Park Slope, and the change of atmosphere is similar.

It's the fourth-largest city in the country, but Utrecht still retains the feeling of a college town—cafés, bookshops, head shops. I live in the center of the city, and two of the walls of my garden touch property owned by Utrecht University. A three-minute walk brings me to its library, where I did most of the research for this book, and I don't have to walk much farther than that to find almost everything I need.

The tourists who have made much of Amsterdam nearly uninhabitable (at least on holidays or on weekend nights) have never heard of Utrecht, for which I am forever grateful. On summer evenings, the ancient canals (the one called the "new canal" was dug in 1392, a century before Columbus) are quiet, and you can peer into the windows of the peaceful houses that line them. Here, I thought, is a place where I can write.

From the moment I set eyes on it, I loved this city. I felt clever when I exchanged New York and London for Utrecht: like someone who'd figured something out about how to live, something that had eluded my friends. It's true that they were baffled by my choice to live here, and nobody rushed to join me; but anybody who came for a visit understood its attraction, and understood why it was the right place for me to live.

At first, life here seemed like an adventure. But somewhere along the way, real life set in, with all its deadening routines. And I started to wonder if this was the place where I was going to spend my entire life. It wasn't very challenging, for one thing. And the things that had made it so attractive—its comfort, its ease, its loveliness—could also make it seem lazy. A place couldn't be this pleasant and at the same time still feel like an adventure.

Was this going to be it for me? History recorded crueler fates than living in a beautiful old Dutch house. But I was young when I got here. And as I felt middle age setting in, I started wondering, as I hadn't before, if the rest of my life was going to be more than just a continuation of what had come before. And I started thinking about Pieter Saenredam, who, at around my age, also found himself trapped in Utrecht.

ON JUNE 18, 1636, the earliest date on an Utrecht drawing, Saenredam began recording the architecture of the Mariakerk. The proportions were not yet precisely recorded. (For the highest points, one author has mentioned, he must have had help from the whitewasher or the glazier.) On Monday, June 30, he started in the nave. He then moved through the transept, the exterior of the choir, the north transept, and the aisles.

He spent more time in the Mariakerk than anywhere else. By the

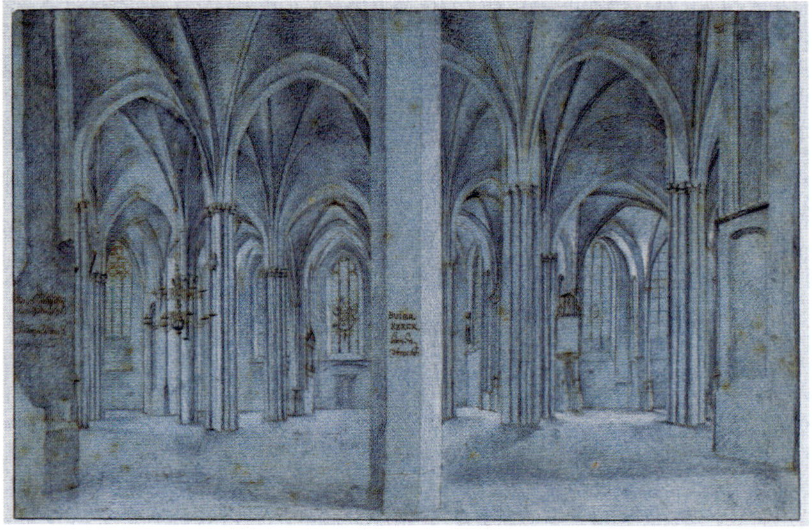

Saenredam's drawings (here of the Buurkerk) demanded an amount of a mathematical knowledge considered "beyond the grasp of normal human beings."

end of July, when he moved on to the other churches, he had established a rhythm of three interiors per building. Looking at the sketches chronologically, you see him gaining confidence. He would no longer dither, as when he first reached Utrecht, over rough sketches. From now on, he would measure everything first, and only then start to draw.

Today we see these drawings as the works of a great artist, and among the most refined drawings ever produced. They exude the same feeling of restfulness and control that his paintings give, but they also contain a stunning amount of pure architectural data: he measured columns, noted the height of vaults and towers, and sometimes added information about the colors of the furnishings. He dated his drawings, too.

And they contain data about his movements—so much that, in a study from 2002, *Pieter Saenredam: The Utrecht Work*, we learn where he sat ("on the wall bench in the bay immediately to the left upon entering via the new entrance") and stood ("the upper storey of the house at 1 Zadelstraat") and stayed ("Saenredam made the drawing from an upper floor, and more specifically from the claustral house number IX opposite the [Mariakerk].")

We can follow his movements to the minute:

> The shadow line on the roof above the entrance to the choir is that of about 8 am. The shadow on the roofs of the sheds shows that the sun has moved several degrees southwards (1 degree=about 4 minutes). The sun is still further southwards and higher at the crossing tower (towards 9 am) and the stepped gable of the offices (just after 9:15 am). Saenredam evidently finished his drawing in this order—from left to right—and at this pace.

Because of this unsurpassed documentary value, we think, when we look at a Saenredam, that we are seeing what he saw. Accustomed to photography, we accept the idea that the world can be transferred into a two-dimensional rectangle so naturally that it doesn't even occur to us that that rectangle is a mental creation. Such images are so ubiquitous that we assume that it was always possible to make a flat image of anything.

But according to his biographers Gary Schwartz and Marten Jan Bok, the device he used, perspective, was reputed to be "a recondite science beyond the grasp of normal human beings." Until 1628—just one year before Saenredam committed himself to practicing this then reconcite branch of art—"the notion of creating perspective depictions of existing buildings on the basis of *measurements* was completely novel."

An earlier Haarlem master, Maarten van Heemskerck, declared that "a painter who wants to prosper will avoid ornament and architecture." The painting of architecture was professional suicide. "Who," wondered a contemporary of Saenredam, "would pay me the premium for the extra work? If a painter has any sense, he will always see to it that he survives, in order not to shortchange anyone by dying insolvent."

Perspective is so devilish that it took whole generations to grasp, and then to codify, its rules. Later, this "recondite science" enjoyed a status among art historians that echoed the prestige it enjoyed among artists. For a certain school, tracing the development of perspective from the Middle Ages into the Renaissance was almost the whole point of art history—a development that lent the discipline a progressive bias.

You might ask what, exactly, was gained by this development. Most cultures, including European cultures, have produced great art without it. But the possibility of using mathematics to create elaborate illusions was so tempting, and so difficult, that great minds were attracted to the challenge—and were starting to solve it around the same time that cartographers were making the first accurate maps of the world.

If a flat image of a complex space seems as natural to us as a flat map of the world, that is because in both cases the perspectival view has triumphed so completely. But perspective was an intellectual, not a natural, development: a product of the mind, a construction, a symbolic form. By studying perspective, the German-American art historian Erwin Panofsky wrote, you could see "the concept of infinity still in the making."

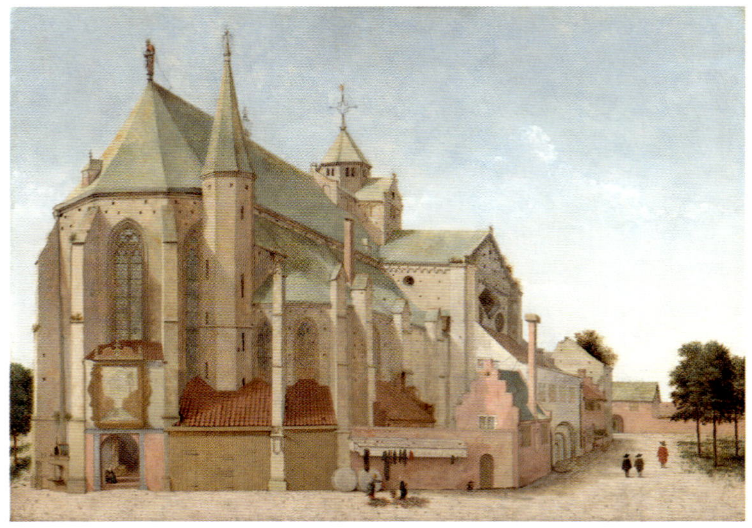

At the Mauritshuis, this view of the Mariakerk usually
hangs next to Vermeer's View of Delft.

TO GET AN IDEA OF the problem, imagine removing the peel of an
orange in one piece. Slit it down one side. Now flatten it out. The edges
will tear, and if you press down the bubbles in the center you will only
distort it more. You can avoid the problem by slicing off the ragged edges
in order to create a rectangle, but in drawing this will sharply limit the
amount of space you can show, and you will only be able to show objects
close up.

The larger the space encompassed, the harder it is to give it the
appearance of unity. Many of Saenredam's contemporaries skirted the
question by placing figures in front of an undefined background, or by
zooming in on them so tightly that the question doesn't come up. The
Utrecht Caravaggists and Gerard ter Borch, for example, got around this
problem by showing their figures from very close by, and painting the
shapeless space behind them in neutral colors.

Others used similar workarounds. Every child knows how to represent objects farther away as smaller than those in the foreground. But

perspective does not represent things. It reverses the traditional means of showing objects by representing—and this is its great innovation, as well as its magic and mystery—the light that falls on them. As in Vermeer, objects are nothing more than the light that lets us see them.

The world of the ancients, Panofsky wrote, was "still by no means a perfectly unified world, a world where bodies and the gaps between them were only differentiations or modifications of a continuum of a higher order." They did not attempt to create that "perfectly unified world" by depicting the spaces that connect one body to another, and the light that comes off them. Perspective means painting light and air.

Saenredam's use of perspective can be compared with the distortions employed in illusionistic ceiling paintings or anamorphoses, which were highly popular—not to mention highly ostentatious—in his day. But where those effects are exciting, Saenredam's are subtle, and—unless someone points them out—you hardly even notice them. What you notice is the light. In the Mauritshuis, the Saenredams hang next to the Vermeers.

SAENREDAM WAS BORN IN the village of Assendelft, a few miles north of Haarlem, in 1597. His father, Jan, had been a student of the Haarlem master Hendrick Goltzius. He became an outstanding engraver and was connected to the area's leading families, but died when Pieter was nine—not, like so many artists, insolvent. His financial prudence made his son's career possible, and allowed him to choose a demanding specialty.

Jan's most handsome legacy was a single share of stock in the Dutch East India Company. That share would pay out regular dividends throughout Pieter's life; in turn he would bequeath a part of it to his daughter. This did not make him rich by the standards of the rich. But it made him rich by the standards of artists. It gave him a steady middling income that freed him from having to work at anything besides his art.

Pieter and his widowed mother moved to Haarlem, the city where he would spend the rest of his life. At first, he followed his father into engraving and illustration, and did not specialize until he was quite mature: he was thirty-one in 1628, when he dedicated himself to the genre of "perspectives, church halls, galleries, buildings, and other things, both interiors and exteriors."

In the British Museum is a small drawing of Saenredam by his friend Jacob van Campen. Made in the same year as his decision to dedicate himself to perspectives, this object has given rise to a great deal of speculation about his life. Saenredam sits in a chair, his arm thrown over its back; he wears an outfit that looks a little uncomfortable. But there is nothing very remarkable about the drawing or the face.

Or is there? In 1937, no one less than Albert Welcker, Clara Welcker's brother, a doctor in Amsterdam, offered a remarkable diagnosis to the historian P. J. A. Swillens. In it, Dr. Welcker issued the same kind of far-reaching verdict that had made his sister's work so improbably compelling. "Saenredam was not physically favored by nature," he pronounced. "Van Campen's portrait drawing leaves not the slightest doubt."

Saenredam, Dr. Welcker saw, was a hunchback. "The big head is pressed onto a short trunk between high shoulders. The right arm thrown over the back of the chair also indicates a very short body." Armed with this information, I look back at the drawing, which is small and doesn't seem to indicate much of anything beyond a rendering of Saenredam's face. I wonder how Dr. Welcker can see this without the "slightest doubt."

And then, in the broad

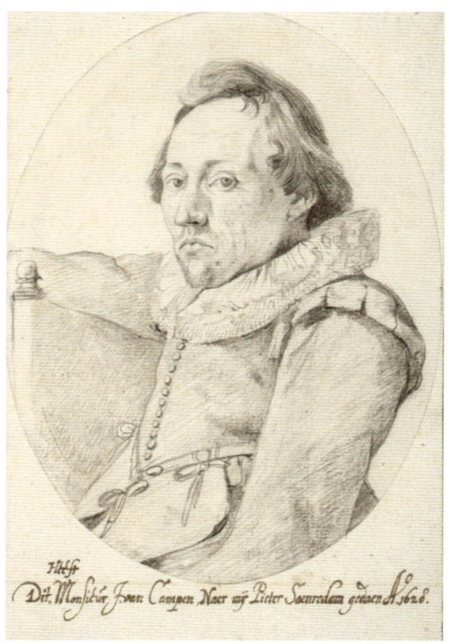

In Jacob van Campen's small portrait of Saenredam, an Amsterdam doctor discovered an entire novelistic drama.

conclusions he draws from this observation, I recognize the family style. "This fact is anything but inconsequential for his work. Such hunchbacks are, besides their fine and sharp minds, all too often also known for being very precise, indeed finicky. Moreover, because of their deformity, they are often reclusive, and seek to work in solitude, where they find compensation for their alleged inferiority."

The advantage of such psychobiographical analyses is, as in his sister's work, their novelistic sweep: the pernickety, awkward hunchback, hiding in quiet churches, far from the gaze of his pitiless fellow man. The disadvantage, as with many of Clara's conclusions, is that these picturesque ideas have little empirical basis—Saenredam may indeed have been short—and make it hard to see what was really extraordinary about him.

His early works mostly show St. Bavo, the main church of his hometown. This vast and venerable building, which looms like a great ship over the city, attracted so many painters that it might be the most frequently portrayed edifice in Dutch art: once you can pick it out, you see it everywhere. Saenredam made a few trips to nearby cities, too. The pictures he made had the composure that comes from a mind that knows what to include, and what to leave out.

When he reached Utrecht, he had been working on perspectives for eight years. But it was in that moment that he crystallized into an artist of whom his biographers Schwartz and Bok can write: "His drawing, brushwork and color changed so little after the mid-1630s that chronology has always been considered almost irrelevant in the study of his work." Until he went to Utrecht, he was still developing. After he came home, he was complete.

———

UTRECHT WAS FOUNDED BY the Romans as a military post—a *castellum*, or castle—along their northernmost border. Unlike Amsterdam, Rotterdam, or The Hague, it is not located at or below sea level, or on reclaimed land. Though only a few meters above the sea, that is enough, in the Rhine delta, to offer protection from the flooding that threatened the more westerly provinces. It was a strategic location, and one that was fought over from ancient times.

The city has the distinction of being built in the shape of the body of Christ. Its pattern is known as the Cross of Churches. On the site of the *castellum* is the Dom, that French Gothic cathedral, which denotes the heart of Christ. The Pieterskerk stands for his head; the Mariakerk his feet. His left hand is at the Paulusabdij, partially demolished in the sixteenth century, and his right hand at the Janskerk.

I live roughly at Christ's right elbow. I see the tower of the Dom from the window of the room in which I am writing this, and feel the wonder, impossible for most Europeans to imagine, that a boy from Texas feels in the presence of thousand-year-old buildings. I love visiting these churches—stepping away from my phone and into the Middle Ages—and whenever I do, I feel the peace I imagine I see in Saenredam's pictures.

Like his pictures, these churches are pruned of everything extraneous. Like Zen gardens, they have been reduced to the essentials; and next to these buildings, the churches of the Mediterranean countries seem congested, tacky, *too much*. Shorn of the hysterical flounces of Catholicism, Saenredam's churches seem to embody an ideal Protestantism: the temples of a pure religion that offers a light-filled path to the divine.

In their austerity lies much of the appeal of Saenredam's paintings. Like the dustless houses of Vermeer or Pieter de Hooch, Saenredam's churches advertise the Dutch virtue of cleanliness, and elevate the notion of hygiene to the status of a religious principle. God appears in these buildings without mediating tchotchkes—saints and crucifixes, incense and altarpieces—streaming through the windows as light alone.

Yet a closer look reveals disquieting suggestions as to how that cleanliness was achieved. Visit the Dom today, for example, and in a small chapel in the right aisle you'll see a delicate Gothic sculpture in which seven figures gather around the Virgin and Child. There are nine figures in all—and all nine of their heads have been brutally hacked off. After nearly half a millennium, the hatred and violence are still palpable.

———

THE DOM CONTAINS several such mementoes of the iconoclasms, a series of attacks that came in the wake of the Reformation and the Dutch war to wrest themselves free of Spain. Like other nations that embraced the Reform, the Dutch attacked the symbols of the Catholic power that oppressed them. John Lothrop Motley, whose books I devoured when I reached the Netherlands, described the transubstantiation thus:

> Those statues, associated as they were with the remorseless persecution which had so long desolated the provinces, had ceased to be images. They had grown human and hateful, so that the people arose and devoted them to indiscriminate massacre.

We no longer see sacred images this way. Because we see them as art, we no longer fear their vengeance. We regret that they were so remorselessly *gezuiverd*—cleansed—in a burst of political rage, however justified that rage might have been. We look differently at the pure light coming through the windows when we learn that it once fell through acres of stained glass. We don't feel bad for God; we feel appalled for humanity.

You could say that the times were different—and they were. You could say that the Spanish tyranny was unbearable, and the Dutch resistance heroic: they were. You could even say that it is a perverse homage to artists that they could create works powerful enough to grow human and hateful—that they could deserve the kind of "indiscriminate massacre" you can still observe in this little corner of the Utrecht Dom.

You could say all that. But when I look at this sculpture, I see the Taliban, and remember my first years in Utrecht, which followed a rise in Islamist terrorism, and coincided with a moral panic in the Netherlands. The upshot was that Muslim immigrants were dangerously unassimilable, more barbarous and uncivilized than we—and I, a white member of a respected allied nation, was unwillingly drafted into that "we."

This autoerotic puffery—how pervasive it was in those years!—made it hard to explain that tolerance was not the only lesson one could derive from Dutch history. (True, by the way, of every nation's history.) But many Dutch politicians considered their hands uniquely clean, encouraged, in part, by foreigners who saw the Netherlands as the birthplace of liberalism and tolerance. And this part was only partly true.

It didn't seem true while these debates were raging every night on television. The tedium of these discussions, the self-righteousness that hung in the air, made me realize that I would like this country much better if I tried more zealously not to pay attention to its politics—but one feels that one should read the newspaper. It was a rookie mistake. A few years later, when I had no idea who was in the cabinet, I was far happier.

All through those years, tourists were wandering through the Dom. Nobody was looking too closely at those broken sculptures, or wondering what they might reveal about a history that was far from the tolerance that Americans saw as either a dignified ancestor of our own, or as a dangerous warning of how far we had strayed. As I tried to avoid current events, I tried not to think too much about the hacked-off heads.

So, it seemed, did Saenredam. The iconoclasms took place within living memory, and the churches were full of evidence of their "cleansing." (As they still are today, if you know where to look.) In his work, the absence of references to this violence is remarkable. Perhaps the subject was taboo even then—especially considering that when he visited Utrecht in 1636, Saenredam, of Protestant origin, had long flirted with Catholicism.

The religious aspect of his life is a mystery. Until 1646, certain of his paintings would contain Catholicizing elements, seemingly made for Catholic clients. If we look to Saenredam's work to find an idealized Calvinism—already in the eighteenth century a German landgrave bought a Saenredam as a Protestant counterweight to an explicitly Catholic church interior by Hendrik van Steenwijck—we might want to look again.

TODAY, UTRECHT IS less than an hour from Saenredam's home in Haarlem. The old religious capital was a natural place for a painter of churches to want to visit. There was perhaps more interesting ecclesiastical architecture in Utrecht than anywhere else in the country. Until Amsterdam boomed and Utrecht stagnated in the seventeenth century, it was, and always had been, the largest city in the northern Netherlands.

But eighteen weeks is a long time. Saenredam arrived in June, when the bubonic plague—a disease of the warm months—was just starting to break out. Seventy-two people died of the plague in his first week, and it would rage all summer long, claiming more and more victims. Quarantines were enforced. Even easy journeys to nearby cities were no longer easy, and sometimes forbidden. Those were eighteen long weeks.

Over his stay, about three thousand Utrechters—more than 10 percent of the population—would die of the plague. It was a ghastly way to die—the fevers and the chills, and then the stinky breath, and then the grotesque swelling of your lymph nodes, and then your fingers and toes and nose turning black—and the authorities nailing the doors and windows of your house shut, and forbidding its inhabitants to leave.

Once your body had been wrapped in vinegar-soaked paper and stuffed into a coffin sealed with tar, those same authorities would come by and nail a large "P" to the door, locking its surviving residents inside for another six lightless weeks. These houses would have been visible throughout the city. Less visible would have been the fear that stalked its inhabitants. The plague was an old, intimate enemy. Who would be next?

Yet Saenredam's drawings and paintings reveal nary a trace of this slaughter or fear. What kind of concentration did it require, at a time like that, to focus only on the beauty of the city's architecture? Plague victims were being buried beneath the floors of the very churches whose windows he was measuring. Forty people per week were being buried in the Jacobskerk alone—but when he painted it all he showed was a man and his dog.

The serenity of his paintings, their perfect composure, is all the more remarkable when we realize the conditions in which they were created. He was haunted by the same fear as everyone else. His

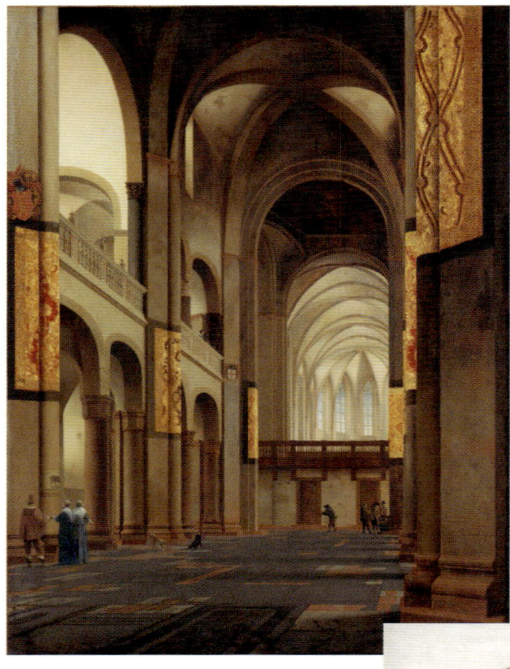

When Saenredam looked at the Mariakerk, he saw something infinitely more sublime than the squat pile another artist depicted: compare this façade with the same building shown on page 226.

library—a single catalog of its posthumous sale was discovered in Germany in 1976—included six treatises on the plague, two of which were published in the year of his visit to Utrecht. The plague was on his mind.

It is a characteristic of a graceful conversationalist to avoid controversial or offensive subjects, and of a mature mind not to allow itself to be deflected or distracted. Instead of surrendering to the pervasive fear, Saenredam worked restlessly, measuring, sketching, taking notes, gathering enough material, whether he realized it or not, to allow him to spend the rest of his life transforming it into paintings.

He did not know how long that life would be. Every day was a day his breath could start to stink. Yet he proceeded as if he had all the time in the world. How did he muster the self-control required to embark on a project that would occupy so many years? Was he aware, at the time, of the enormity of the task—or did he, like so many artists, only realize the magnitude of the project once it was too late to go back?

SAENREDAM TRICKS THE EYE into believing that it is seeing a unified space: the eye, singular. When viewed with both eyes, or from the wrong angle, the edges of certain Saenredams can appear bloated or uneven—irregularities that disappear if you stand in the right place, and close one eye. A painting of the Mariakerk in Hamburg that looks odd when seen with both eyes magically acquires a third dimension when seen with one.

These are the mathematical distortions involved in perspective, and his last known painting, the large view of the Mariakerk, the Dom, and the Buurkerk now in Rotterdam, includes these as well. The artist's lack of idealization—that large bush sprouting from the roof of the Mariakerk, for example—makes us believe that we are seeing what he saw all those years before, when his great achievements were still ahead of him.

We know from his drawings that there have been some tiny changes. The wooden sheds he shows as attached to the façade have been tactfully erased. The people strolling around have been made a bit smaller, in order to make the church loom more impressively. And though we are in the middle of what was until recently the largest city in the Netherlands, the atmosphere is so still that we might be in a village.

Yet we see Saenredam best when we place this view beside another, which Schwartz and Bok include in their biography: a drawing of the Mariakerk by the Utrecht antiquarian Arnoldus Buchelius. In this drawing, Saenredam's soaring Italianate Mariakerk has been transformed into a squat, ugly heap whose eventual demise, in the nineteenth century, must have been greeted by the citizenry with relief.

We see how his eye elevated a scene that must have been dull enough for the people who walked past it every day. We see his eye itself, and how—as some eyes see dates or facts, and some ugliness and decline—his eye saw the beauty of old things. Now he was an old thing himself, and probably sick: though he would live another couple of years, he would not paint again. Did he know that this painting would be his last?

He wasn't the type to say. Instead, by dint of carefully measured detail, he evoked emotions that are all the more intense because they are indirect. He hints at his own impending end, and in this apparently tranquil picture we feel the passing of days, the decay of ancient orders, the scrapping of great ships! And we feel the values that animated his life: circumscribed by discipline and dedication, the finite human task.

We feel ourselves in the presence of a great mind, one that has cultivated discretion, indirection; and as his religious feelings are suggested but never bluntly stated, his feelings about his impending end would be far less moving if he had made them more explicit. Saenredam is a reminder that, at least in art, documentary and commentary seldom age as well as visions of ideals.

By selecting only beauty, Saenredam created a perfect world. He produced paintings that are pure in the way that Greek bodies are pure: purged of unsuitable hairs, undirtied by wrinkles and fat. He disguised the difficulties so well that we don't see, unaided, what was added, and what was elided. And when we do—do we care? Everyone knows, after all, that any perfect world must always, necessarily, be distorted.

13

PAULUS POTTER

The Innocent Eye Test

YOU CAN BESIEGE a museum: stake it out, scrutinize every label, listen to every audioguide explanation, brandish your phone at every notable object, check off every single gallery—and then straggle into the café, feet shattered, eyes bleeding, as if finally furloughed from a military campaign. The campaign is doomed. You can no more absorb the Louvre than you can the Library of Congress.

Or you can wander through the galleries as through a forest, reading nothing, pausing only when something catches your eye, absorbing an energy that—like that of trees—is, in some undefined way, good for the soul. This is the aura that pervades the museum, the library, the ancient church, emanating from objects that have been saved from the wreck of centuries.

It is the same aura that explains why I dread monographs. First of all, they are often—for lack of a more diplomatic word—boring, the products of art history's factory of facts. The detritus heaped up in their footnotes is the evidence—bills, wills—of those most uninspiring sides of everyday existence, the same sides of existence I long to leave behind when I seek the museum and its aura.

Yet since I came to Holland I have accumulated hundreds of these books. If I wanted to know more about the things I was seeing, I would have to start somewhere, and this was the somewhere. My fear of ignorance—of being stranded ignominiously abroad—was so powerful that it propelled me through more of these books than almost any Dutch person has ever read. It was a slow and painstaking apprenticeship.

This reading often felt like a duty—self-imposed, like all the most onerous duties—and as the names in the Dutch galleries went from crashes of unpronounceable letters ("Wtewael") to familial figures, the aura became less satisfying. The time that burnishes art can also strip something from it, and just as once clear handwriting eventually becomes indecipherable, an artwork eventually becomes illegible.

I came to mistrust my love of the aura. It is still the strongest feeling I connect with art, but it was not enough. A work conveys a meaning, and communicates that meaning in a certain way—and, above all, conveys it through the sensibility of a certain person. Someone had wanted us to know something, including something of himself. But the centuries had taken away our ability to see what.

Art historians try to discover that meaning, to show us what, exactly, we are seeing. And as they do, they show me how little, even on the most basic level, I see. I have often felt humiliated to realize how appallingly bad I am at seeing—how reliant I am on simple factual descriptions—how hard it would be to see anything in those galleries without other people's eyes.

One example: Paulus Potter's *Boar and Deer in a Landscape*. In a packed museum, I would surely not pause long enough to discover the boar camouflaged in the undergrowth, nor understand that he was making some sound—chomping or ripping or digging—that was causing the deer to look up, ears pricked, neck erect. If I hadn't spotted him, I would have missed the whole point of the painting.

It is hard to think of a simpler narrative than this. Take another, slightly more complex example: a portrait. If beautiful enough, it will not quite matter that time has gradually absorbed its once illustrious subject into the legions of the anonymous dead, and that we no longer know whom it shows; but the nature of a portrait is to commemorate an individual, and not knowing who it was strips from it a layer of meaning.

Original meanings are not, of course, the only ones. You can admire the portrait as that person who knows no Chinese admires calligraphy; but those stylish swirls form a language, and intend to communicate something, and not knowing how to read it is an impoverishment. Insisting that the only important qualities are formal—that there is no point in learning how to read it—is anti-intellectual: barbarous.

Art history deciphers those meanings, and chronicles the new meanings time brings. It tells how a painter fallen into desuetude (Vermeer; so many others) was resurrected; or why another, once beloved, was denounced as hideous or reactionary; or how yet another, once famous, found his work in a crate downstairs. The sum of views determines what is on the museum wall: how, and whether, that aura is constructed.

To delve into art is to delve into history. And to delve into history, in the case of art history, is to wonder at the near total ignorance from which it emerged. If the tone of monographs is often dry and technical, like something one would encounter in a textbook on engineering or disease, that is because art history comes from the same nineteenth-century positivist science—the same movement to unjumble the world.

AND TO DELVE INTO art history is to discover an odd category of artists. These are not those famous names that were later forgotten, but those whose once tremendous reputations have never quite been lost—who have never been forgotten or, worse, disgraced—but whose former popularity seems puzzling, slightly inscrutable, today. One such is the animal painter Paulus Potter, whose *Young Bull* takes up an entire wall in the Mauritshuis.

This is a life-size painting of a bull—in fact, two bulls—along with a family of three sheep, and a proud farmer standing behind them. Flies swarm; drool collects in the bull's mouth. Beneath its back hoof, unmissable because at eye level, is a large turd. The painting's princely scale seems to contrast with its humdrum subject, and though it is striking, one has a hard time imagining how famous it once was.

After its creation in 1647, when Potter was just twenty-two, it seems to have led a homebound existence. It was not mentioned by Arnold

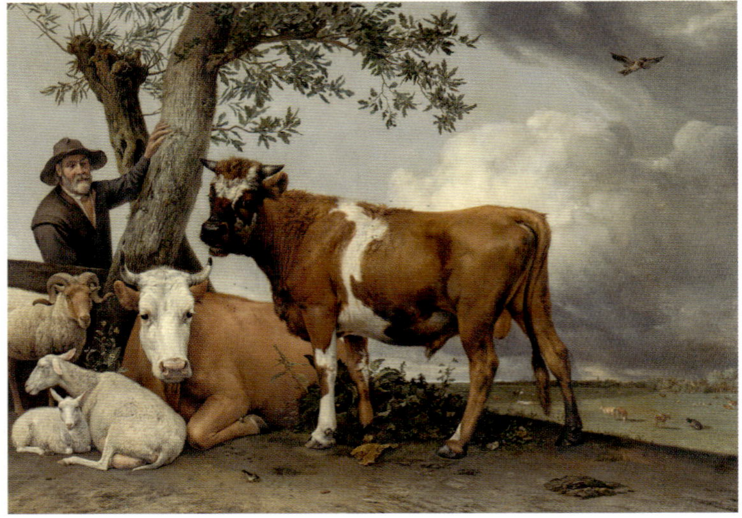

The worldwide fame of The Young Bull, *with its eye-level turd,
can strike us as a bit mystifying today.*

Houbraken in 1718—or, it seems, anywhere else. It hung in a private
house in Haarlem until it was auctioned in 1749, and purchased by no
one less than William IV, the head of the House of Orange. His son,
William V, expanded the collection and, in 1775, opened it to the public.

But it would take a revolution and a world war to bring *The Young
Bull* to the prominence it enjoyed in the nineteenth century—and that
revolution included a revolution in how art was to be seen. Among the
French Revolution's most enduring consequences was the idea of the
modern museum. The Louvre was opened in 1793, on the first anniversary of the abolition of the monarchy—opened to all.

Its founders emphasized the same connection between freedom and
art that, they said, existed in Greece. Their duty to protect and foster the
works of genius expanded significantly when wars brought French armies
into distant countries. Their generals dispatched the art they found to
Paris—for its own good. "By despoiling Greece, the Romans conserved
superb monuments for us," one deputy said. "Let us imitate them."

Art could not be left in the hands of tyrants; it must be taken under the protection of free men. Following the French conquest of Belgium in 1794, one painter claimed that the proper place of the Flemish cultural treasures was "in the fatherland of arts and of genius, in the fatherland of liberty and of sacred equality, in the French Republic." To these were added, in 1795, the treasures of conquered Holland.

Never mind that Holland was already a republic. Its art was not as spectacular—or, with a few notable exceptions, as huge—as the treasures pouring in from Napoleon's Italian conquests. But for that very reason it found favor with the simple folk who, for the first time, were allowed into the palace that had been the seat and symbol of the kings of France. Many of these people appreciated one work in particular.

"I saw two French peasants taking a good long look at Potter's large Bull," the Dutch traveler Adriaan van der Willigen wrote in 1806. "Their natural and correct judgment pleased me particularly, and came down to their opinion that they thought this was the best painted and loveliest picture in the whole gallery. After they had spent a while this way, as if in bliss, they left the object not without regret."

This was not only the opinion of the uneducated. Paulus Potter came to be reckoned among history's greatest. "Rome had its Raphael, Parma its Correggio, Venice its Titian, Bologna its Carracci, Florence its Michelangelo, Brabant its Rubens," a French painter wrote in 1803, "but Holland had its Potter." After Waterloo, twelve years later, the painting was welcomed back to The Hague with a solemn parade.

It became the greatest attraction of the Mauritshuis. Few visitors to Holland neglected to see it. Some were ecstatic: the Italian Edmondo de Amicis deemed it worthy "to be placed in the Vatican beside the Transfiguration by Raphael." Some Americans were confused: one wrote that the "scrubby eight-months-old bull calf . . . would not be permitted to invade the Panhandle of Texas."

Today, both praise and condemnations seem extravagant, and not a little mystifying. There is, after all, something somehow inoffensive about Potter. If it's easy to imagine your grandmother working a jigsaw puzzle of one of his barnyard paintings, or hanging a brownish reproduc-

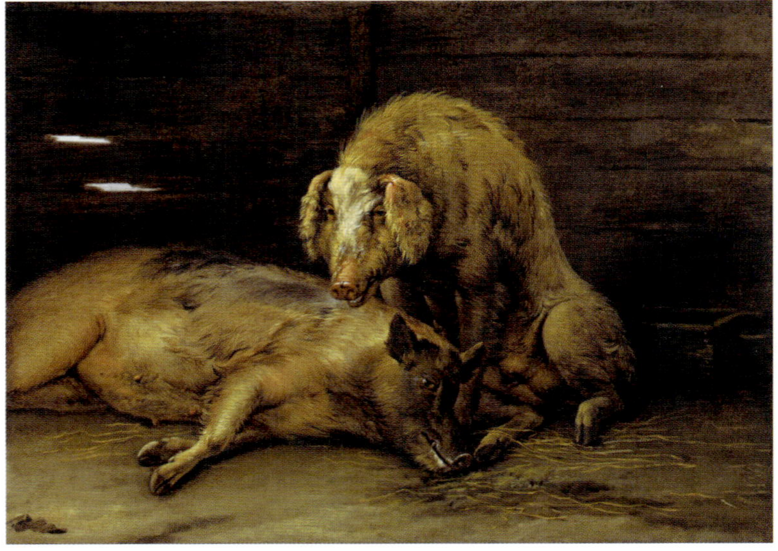

Potter lent an elevation to common barnyard animals that no artist
had ever granted them before.

tion of his famous bull on her wall, it's hard to imagine her, or anyone, having a passionate opinion about him.

PAULUS POTTER WAS born in Enkhuizen in 1625. His father was an artist issued from the prosperous bourgeoisie; his mother descended from the counts of Egmond. Before he was three, the family moved to Leiden, where they lived in the Nieuwsteeg, close by the Pieterskerk, where the English dissenters known as the Pilgrims worshipped. In 1628, many had yet to make the journey to Massachusetts.

The family, which eventually counted eleven children, did not stay long. When Paulus was five, the family moved to the Sint-Antoniebreestraat in Amsterdam, the street to which another artist, Rembrandt, would move from Leiden in 1639. In this milieu—which

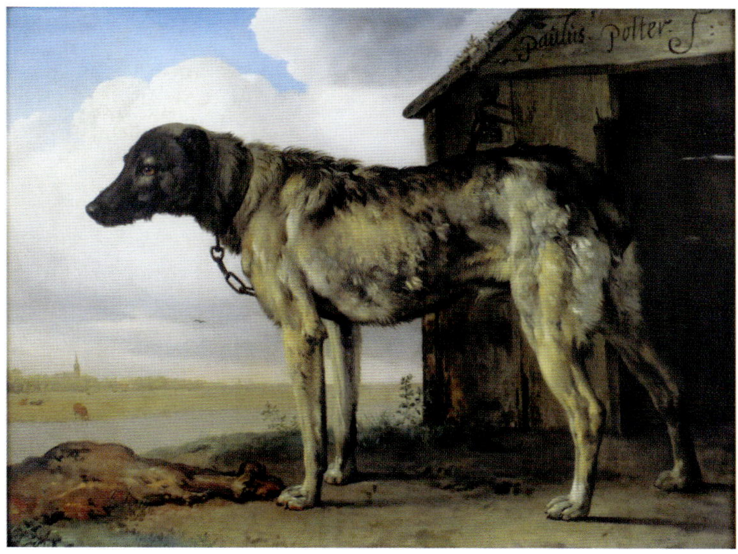

gathered in a few streets one of the most extraordinary collections of artists that history records—Paulus had his education.

Even by the standards of that place, he must have stood out. In 1641, aged fifteen, he signed his first work, a detailed drawing of a boar hunt. It is an incredible achievement for one so young, packed with figures of men and animals—and full, too, of the excitement of a prodigy clearing his throat, finding his voice. Looking at it is like hearing a great singer's scratchy teenage recordings.

But to become the kind of artist an adolescent of this talent and ambition wanted to be, he would have to try his hand at mythological, historical, and religious subjects. These were considered the realm of the most sophisticated painters, and another drawing, from the next year, shows just such a traditional subject: Mercury luring hundred-eyed Argus to sleep with his music from his flute.

Jupiter had set Argus to watch over a maiden, Io, whom he had transformed into a cow. And it was this part of the story—the cow—that clearly appealed to Potter. Whenever he painted a scene from mythology, he chose scenes he could populate with animals. In a later painting of Orpheus, the hero is nothing more than a pretext—smaller than the camel, the elephant, the unicorn, and even the goat.

These exotic animals soon stepped aside in favor of representatives of the more common run of beasthood, the workaday livestock of the flat and featureless Dutch countryside. This was a world that lent itself with far greater difficulty to the elevated abstractions of myth—including because few countries, at least in Western Europe, have less to show of the glorious antique past than this one.

The country is located in the deltas of the rivers that rush down the Alps and meander through Germany before finally petering out in the swamps of Holland. Reclaiming this uninhabitable land began early, and continued until recently: the polders that make up the new province of Flevoland were not completed until 1968, when environmental concerns made further works undesirable.

Everywhere, this landscape is divvied up into rectangles surrounded by shallow moats, forming a countryside so uniform that after a few months in this place it is hard to remember what a technological triumph the landscape represents. Only when landing at Schiphol, itself located on land drained from 1848 to 1852, can one take in the full panorama, and see what a uniquely human creation this country really is.

Flights from the United States land early in the morning, as the sun is rising. When I look out the window, I am always amazed to see the entire country sparkling. Little water-filled ditches, many of which are so narrow that you can easily jump over them, separate one parcel of reclaimed land from the next. Nearly invisible when seen head-on, those slender lines of water catch the morning sun, and the country flashes, that light showing that almost no part of this country was not man-made.

Yet it is an industrial landscape. Like the Beemster where Fabritius grew up, it was created by engineers, at the behest of politicians and corporations. It is not the kind of landscape associated with romance, and not, therefore, the kind of landscape many people bothered to paint. In Potter's

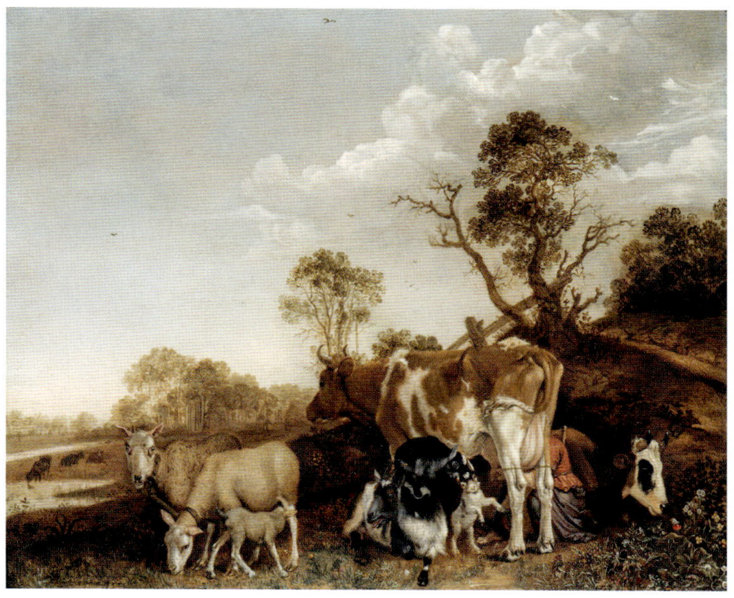

*On the rare occasions when Potter painted humans, they often lurk,
like this milkmaid, behind the animals.*

time, landscape painters tended to journey to the coastal dunes, the inland forests, the hills along the German border—or farther afield, to Italy.

Potter stayed home. His pictures, like *The Young Bull*, show this flat landscape, sometimes broken by a few perfectly aligned trees, sometimes with the steeple of a nearby town. They show overcast skies and sober colors, unpretentious farmers and unpretentious animals. It is not a dreamy place. The romantic patina would come only after his death— another involuntary accretion of time.

TO SEE POTTER'S PAINTINGS together is to see one of the most characteristic aspects of the artistic personality, one that is often more powerful than any other force in an artist's life—often powerful enough to destroy that life. This is the obsessive desire to follow one's own course, even when that course guarantees personal calamity and commercial failure. To see Potter is to see an inner necessity.

Potter was interested in animals to the exclusion of everything else. But animal painting was considered such a lowly specialty—it barely outranked the very lowliest, still-life—that when he asked for the hand of a girl named Adriana Balckeneynde, her father, a contractor who had become a successful architect, scoffed: "If he painted men, all right!—but an animal painter, you've got to be kidding."

The rare accounts of his personality reflect what we can tell by looking at the approximately one hundred pictures he created in the course of his life: that he was driven, restless, obsessive. One anecdote, which has come down to us through a son of Adriana and her second husband, recalled Adriana's saying

> that she had never seen her husband idle; that, whenever he had a spare hour to spend with her strolling outside, he always had a notebook in his pocket; so that if he saw something remarkable that he could use in his work, he could always immediately sketch that object.

Some of these drawings survive, still so fresh that it is easy to imagine Paulus and Adriana strolling around the environs of The Hague or Amsterdam as he sketched pigs, cows, dogs—but not people, who never rise above the level of desultory staffage. In a *Landscape with Livestock and a Milkmaid*, the milkmaid is almost entirely hidden behind the cow. The cow, not the woman, is always the point.

IN 1653, Potter painted a rare portrait of a human. The subject was Dirck Tulp, son of the Dr. Nicolaes Tulp whose anatomy lesson Rembrandt had painted twenty years before. (Today that picture hangs near *The Young Bull* in the Mauritshuis.) It is a great portrait—but not of Dirck, who looks lost beneath the curly heaps of his wig. The picture was originally meant to show someone else, whose face was painted over and replaced by Dirck's.

The real portrait is of his mount, a rearing gray horse. The horse has personality; not so the man. Drab Dirck is perched like a parrot on an admiral's shoulder, a whimsical touch that serves to showcase the horse's stylishness, and a studious reversal of the usual hierarchy, in which animals are reduced to a handful of symbolic roles—the faithful dog, the mischievous monkey. Most painters allot a complex personality to humans alone.

In most of Potter's work, this reversal is subtle. It is a simple matter of showing an animal as itself, without inappropriate anthropomorphizing or blunt allegorizing. Potter's animal portraits show strongly individual presences, but—as the image of a person can convey a living presence, or a still-life painter can place a lifetime of suffering into a strawberry—they also suggest something more.

That something more appears in its least subtle form in a painting in the Hermitage, *The Life of the Hunter*. It is a complex picture, composed, comic-strip-like, of fourteen separate scenes. The twelve smaller pictures around the border show a hunter pursuing different animals, including exotic animals—sometimes for sport, sometimes in allegorical scenes borrowed from religion and mythology.

Some of these scenes are unbearably cruel, including one in which playful monkeys are caught by being tricked into smearing their eyes shut with glue. Yet these scenes are not too different from hundreds of other hunting scenes produced at this time to decorate the houses of blood-sport practitioners throughout Europe. This is the country life, spiced up with the occasional lion or nymph.

They show the expected order—and then, in the two large central rectangles, its reverse. There, the brutal hunter is taken prisoner by the animals, brought before a tribunal, and sentenced to death: roasted on a spit as the animals dance and rejoice. His dogs, his hunting companions, are hung from a tree. One is so terrified that he has lost control of his bowels; his shit drops to the ground.

One is not sure whether to be amused or horrified. Even one most sympathetic to the animals—to animals in general—is troubled by the cycle of violence depicted, the cruelty repaid in the same coin. Unusually in Potter's work, these animals are not really animals; they are symbols,

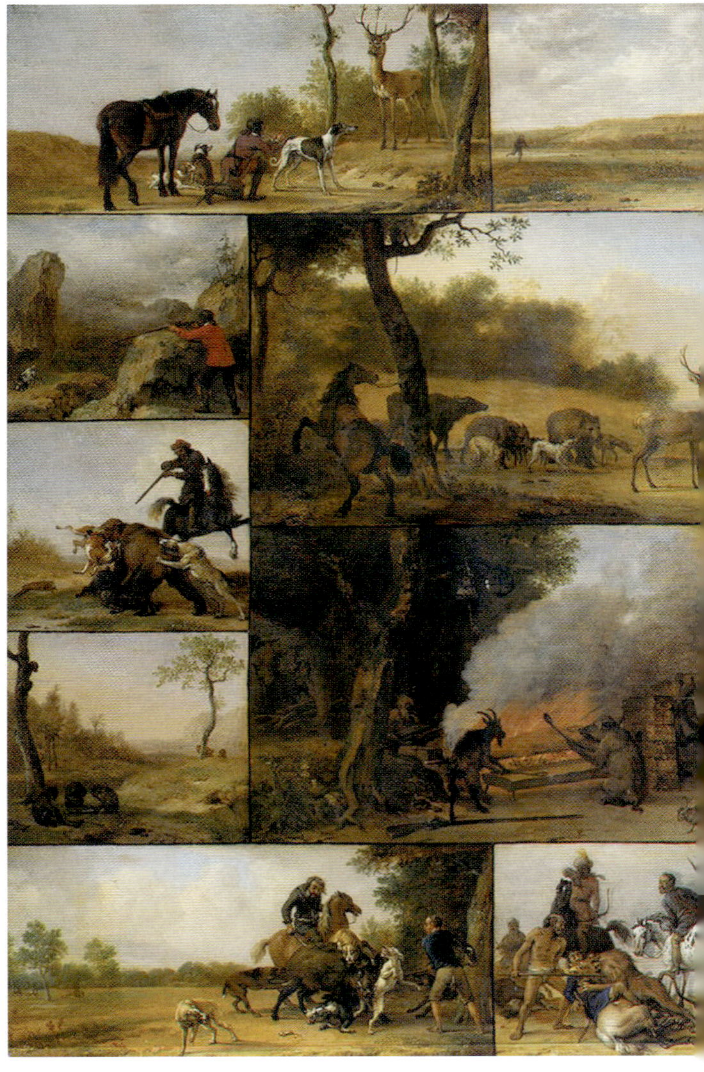

Potter's Life of the Hunter *shows, comic strip—like, a reversal of the normal
order: the upside-down world.*

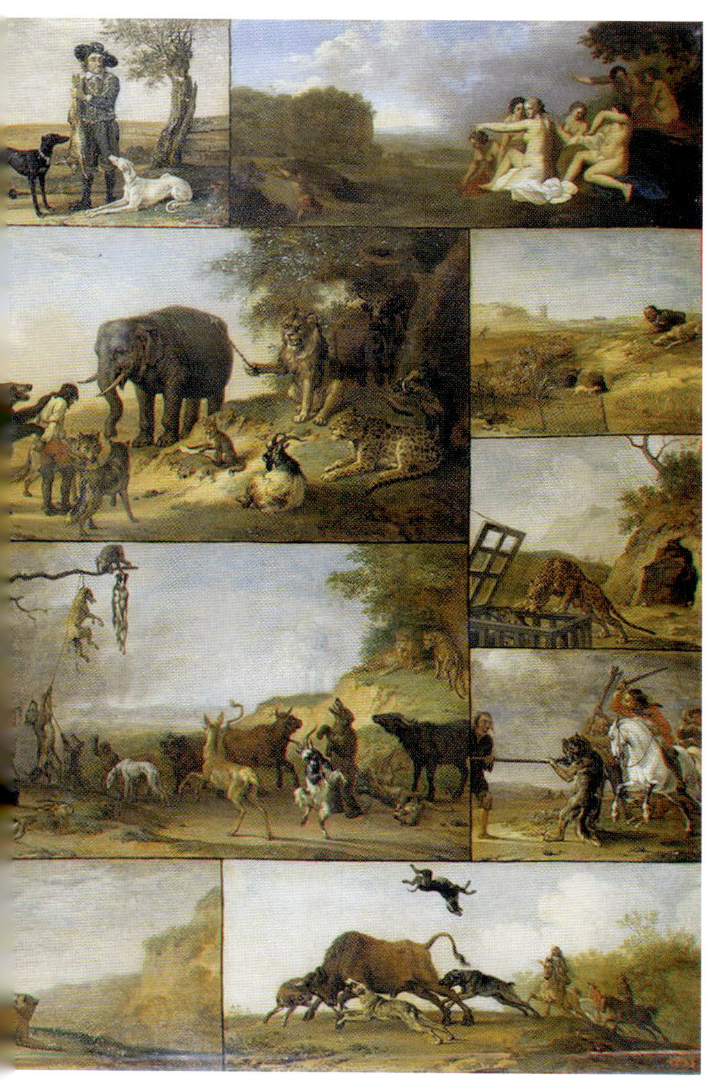

standing in for people. The scene seems to be a comment on contemporary politics—a warning to rulers to beware the wrath of the oppressed.

(Was there another view in Potter's art? He was obsessed with animals, but was he, for example, a vegetarian? Some people, and among them many artists, have always refused the needless cruelty of meat.)

With *The Life of the Hunter*, we are back in the upside-down world, scenes that showed a comical reversal of roles: a pig slaughtering a butcher, children punishing their parents, even—recalling the picture of Dirck Tulp—horses riding men. A peasant and a prince might switch places: shows of flexibility, for example during carnival, that served to strengthen existing arrangements. The presence of this painting in the collection of the tsars shows that the warning against despotism was not considered too threatening.

Still, it is a wonderful painting: "a painted poem," Goethe called it in 1817. Yet Potter was not at his best when, on rare occasions like these, he showed animals being tortured. His campy *Bear Hunt* features a dog whose paw has been torn off: the gory stump lies a couple of feet from the howling animal. Neither was he at his best when he tried to deploy animals as allegories.

Instead, his finest works portray animals with strong individual presences, whose characters emerge as fully as people's. They seem natural, their behavior unvarnished. As with the shitting dog, Potter deliberately included scatological details. One of his greatest paintings seemed a bit too real for its intended purchaser. *The Pissing Cow*, too, was bundled off to Petersburg.

THIS REALISM ENDED UP making Potter a favorite in the nineteenth century. The second monograph about a Dutch painter was not about Rembrandt or Vermeer or Hals but about Potter, written by a part-time artist named Tobias van Westrheene. (The first, by the same author, was about Jan Steen.) Published in French in 1867, *Paulus Potter: sa vie et ses œuvres* begins with a sigh of exhaustion that any researcher will recognize: "What useless troubles this unhappy author has taken!"

The book is just over two hundred pages long. It is modest in appearance. But one of its charms is its author's determination to expose the troubles it caused him. These are the trials all writers pass through, the trials that most writers determine to dissemble. Van Westrheene's moaning gives us a palpable sense of his own personality, and of the difficulties he faced when reconstructing this life and work.

Locating the pictures—Van Westrheene traces 106, nearly as many as the roughly 120 recognized today—was a tremendous task in a day when most were scattered in private collections from England to Russia, and in a day when the Dutch archives were seldom more than heaps of yellowing paper. With great effort, he reconstructed much of Potter's life.

This "humble and grueling work" aimed "to wrest from the past a few stones necessary to construct the edifice we call the History of Art." The research was only one difficulty. The greater one was in inventing a new genre: the artistic monograph, which includes a description of known works; the history of their reception and collection; a compilation of relevant biographical documents; and a general critical interpretation.

Why were more obvious candidates passed over? Because, Van Westrheene writes, "More than any other painter he represents *the naturalist element*," allowing us to address "the question of realism in art." The italicized words are often taken to mean the opposite of abstraction. For Van Westrheene, realism was the enemy of "idealism," which reduces natural forms to mere symbols. This was the view, and the moment, that saw the demotion of artists like Bol and Flinck.

The true realist is "attracted by nature and its beauty." He does not seek to deform it by making it something it is not. In a scientific world becoming steadily less devout, nature started to take the place of the church, and transforming it inappropriately was viewed as sacrilegious. It had to be shown as it was, and not distorted, as the idealist did, by shaping it into a reflection of his own preconceived notions.

The idealist paints according to his own subjectivity, and that subjectivity is false if not derived from nature. An artist must not arrogate "the right to modify and to bend to his own taste the forms, the color, and the proportions—in a word, everything—borrowed from the visible world." Disengaging from nature "leads to symbolic art," Van Westrheene wrote. "The paintings of this artist will be vague as dreams."

That is a good description of many works by the French symbolists and the English Pre-Raphaelites in vogue at the time Van Westrheene was writing. Alongside their inscrutable Sphinxes and bejeweled oriental courtesans, Potter's turd-strewn barnyards certainly seem to show "the extremely simple reproduction," a critic wrote in 1859, "of an unsurpassed verity, of the prosaic pastoral life of the north."

From the French peasants gaping at *The Young Bull* during its brief residence in the Louvre to the most learned writers decades later, this is the note usually sounded in the nineteenth century, even by the picture's enemies. The Frenchman Eugène Fromentin found it "too full without being filled," though he admitted Potter's "skill, taken all the way to its limits, for the imitation of things."

Critics, whether realists or idealists, saw the same thing in Potter's *Bull*. Where detractors saw a dutiful, mechanical lack of inventiveness, admirers saw a faithful mirror of nature. The painting became something of an ideological litmus test, and the word "test" was borrowed for the title of a canvas the American artist Mark Tansey painted in 1981. He called it *The Innocent Eye Test*.

In it, a group of black-clad, balding experts, taking careful notes, have removed *The Young Bull* from its frame and placed it on the floor. They drop the concealing curtain to reveal the life-size bull to the ultimate authority: a cow. Will Potter's amazingly lifelike creation pass her muster?

One wonders how she will express her approbation.

And one wonders to which innocents the title refers.

"HIS KNOWLEDGE, his love, his conscience forbade him to hide, and especially to transform, the slightest trait that he had observed," Van Westrheene wrote. But more than a century after his book was published, critics started noticing something else about Potter's bull—something that brought to mind Tansey's eye test. The eyes that had looked at it had missed something important.

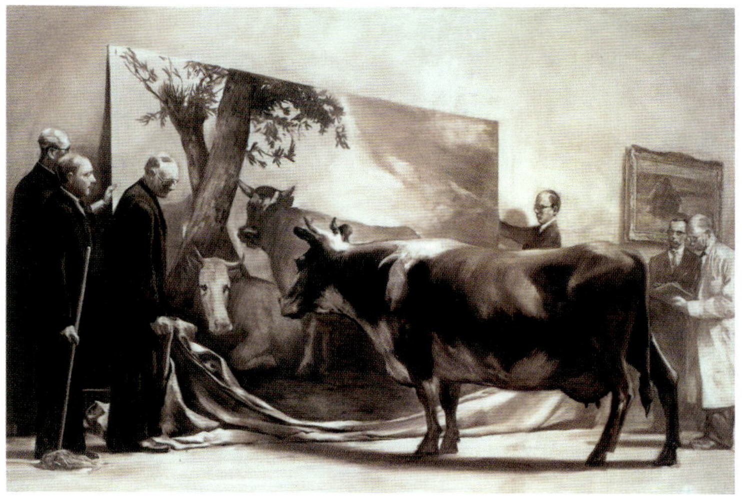

"Nothing is less real than realism," Georgia O'Keeffe said,
and Mark Tansey's painting mocks the theorists of realism
who found in Potter their greatest exponent.

The bull was traditionally thought to be a year old. A closer examination, however, published in a monograph for a Potter retrospective in
1994, revealed that "the dewlap, the hanging fold of skin beneath the
throat and upper chest, is too big for a bull of that age. The horns too are
quite developed and suggest an age of around two years." The teeth, on
the other hand, suggested that he was between four and five.

Upon closer examination, the animal's body came to seem almost
unglued. The highly developed front part contrasts with the back half,
especially the thighs, whose muscles seem flaccid and weak. When
examined closely, the perspective, too, is nearly impossible. The bull
stands in a twisted, almost balletic position, head, middle, and back each
painted from slightly different angles.

The artist had taken a bit from one animal and a bit from another.
The "realistic" bull was a pastiche, not an accurate representation in the
least. With flies, drool, and poop, Potter had misdirected both peas-

ants and experts. One is glad that Van Westrheene did not live to see his almost religious veneration of Potter's "knowledge, his love, and his conscience" obliterated by this careful research.

Rather than a manifesto of realism, *The Young Bull* was a manifesto for the cleverness the Italians called *ingegno*. And rather than an image of "reality," *The Young Bull* was as much of a fantasy as the most overheated imaginings of Gustave Moreau, Arnold Böcklin, Dante Gabriel Rossetti, or Odilon Redon. The only difference is the subtlety with which Potter disguised his.

Without the assembly of detail found in the monographs—all that research into dewlaps and bovine dentistry—that subtlety would have been lost. The praise for the perfect photographic reproduction of a reality Potter discovered simply by wandering around an unblemished countryside would have rung faint indeed. To see only rural folkways would be to see very little of a painting like this one.

———

TO PLOW THROUGH the art-historical monographs, with their addresses and sales figures and measurements, is often, as in the case of Potter's bull, to see something magical happen. Those apparently dry heaps of statistics crystallize. They strip away the things we thought we were seeing when we weren't looking closely enough, and give us something we would not otherwise have seen. They layer a work with a new mystique.

But if *The Young Bull* is a fantasy, whose is it—and of what? Van Westrheene tallied up Potter's works in the collections of the princes of Orange, the dukes of Bedford, and the tsars of Russia. This might have hinted that they reflected the realities of Dutch rural life about as accurately as Marie-Antoinette's idyllic hamlet at Versailles reflected the realities of the French peasantry.

Alongside the aristocratic fantasy of the shepherd and his flocks, they also reflect the fantasy of Potter and people like him, middle-class city-dwellers. He spent most of his life in crowded places like Amsterdam and The Hague. In such places, it would seem natural to dream about the unhurried countryside: about the kinds of warm sunlit afternoons that Potter showed in his paintings.

As his paintings reflect a reversal of the usual relationship between humans and animals, they also show another reversal, but one that Potter did not invent. In Holland, the countryside meant something it did not in other places. If most cities emerge from the countryside, the countryside here emerges from the city, in the same way that suburban subdivisions do. Like Fabritius's Beemster, Potter's landscape was financed by bankers and commissioned by real estate barons.

When first built, this land was made of featureless green rectangles. The passing centuries have filled them with villages and trees, and with suggestions of a lost arcadia; forgetting they were man-made, people eventually thought of them as "nature." Still, for the painter, they presented another problem, so much so that the Dutch, who painted everything, rarely painted these. The problem was that they were too flat.

When viewed from eye level, a flat green expanse collapses into a uniform color. Unbroken by any natural features, the polders stretch in every direction; a village or a house on the horizon shrinks into a clump. One needs a central focal point, like the trees in Hobbema's *Avenue at Middelharnis*, or a way to view the scene from above, which is why the dunes by Haarlem became such a popular subject for landscape painters.

Just behind his bull, Potter did paint a polder landscape. It is a sweeping and accurate view of the dairy pastures of Holland, a view made possible by placing the animal on a hill or an outcrop. The problem, from the point of view of the realist critics, is that, in this perfectly flat country, such outcrops do not exist. In order to look real, this landscape—like this animal—had to be made up.

"NOTHING IS LESS REAL than realism," Georgia O'Keeffe said in 1922. "It is only by selection, by elimination, by emphasis that we get to the real meaning of things." Potter's selections, eliminations, and emphases are so subtle that it feels odd to point them out, including because, when we do, we realize that all artists do this, and that the way they make their choices is what makes them artists.

We don't need to measure the dewlaps to know that there is more to art than imitation. Resemblance is no measure of greatness; many great works look nothing like the objects they purport to represent. Nor is size: Théophile Thoré-Bürger, the nineteenth-century critic, pointed out that there was no more point in painting a life-size bull than there was in painting a life-size house. Quality is in the how—not in the what, or in the how big.

There is another reason there is a false choice at the heart of Van Westrheene's argument. Symbols and language are as real as turds. We do not need to choose between the physical and the metaphysical, the concrete and the metaphoric. Potter's works enhance "reality" by combining physical description with symbolic meaning—as portraitists of people had always done.

The difference was that his subjects were animals. Like portraits of people, his speak of an individual life—and they also speak, more generally, of life. And rather than some minutely descriptive "reality," life, enhanced and magnified and improved, is what we often seek in art. I studied all those catalogs because I wanted to learn something about art. And I wanted to learn something about art because I wanted to learn something about life.

Part of the aura of the museum is the idea that we can come here to improve ourselves, that we can step out of the realm of what we are and glimpse what we might want to be. They are real places—but their reality is different, and this reality was the one that interested me. That sense of something higher in the world—that appeal to something higher in ourselves—is one source of the magnetism of the museum.

———

A SERIES OF five etchings Potter did in 1652, at the very end of his life, shows horses from young to old, all the way to one ragged horse staring at another, who lies dead. With brisk observations of changes in their coats and muscles, Potter shows the toll life takes on these hardworking animals, and renders the textures of their bodies as Ter Borch could render satin, or Vermeer could render pearls.

Some critics have rejected metaphorical interpretations because there are five images. For this kind of series, four—seasons, elements,

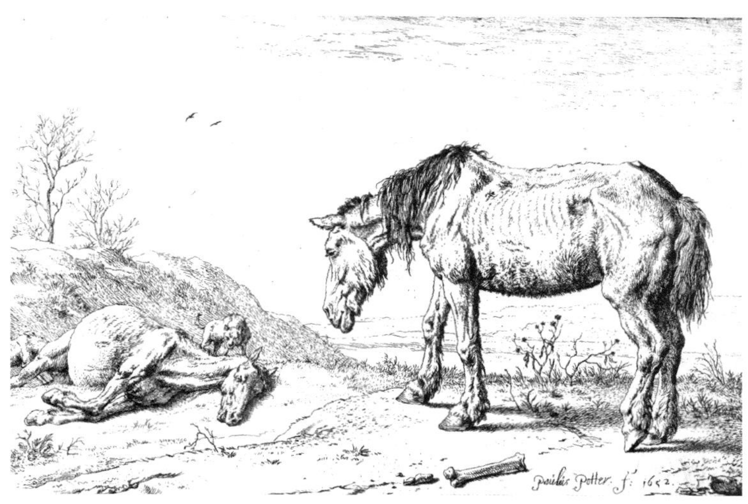

Potter's life-cycle of the horse mirrored his own.

cardinal directions—is the traditional number. But, traditional or not, we immediately know, looking at these animals growing up and growing old, that their lives are our own, and that when we are looking at them we are looking at ourselves.

As when looking at an especially beautiful portrait, we do not need many facts: to know exactly who we are looking at, or who painted it, or when, or for what price. Facts enhance, but cannot create, the uncanny recognition we feel when looking at these horses. This is the recognition that creates the aura that survives the centuries, and rises above individual circumstances.

On January 2, 1653, shortly after the death of his father, Paulus and Adriana drew up a last will and testament. She was pregnant. He had tuberculosis, and knew he didn't have much time left; this, presumably, was why he made the will. Their daughter, Dingenom, was born on January 23. On January 17, 1654, less than a year later, Paulus Potter was buried in Amsterdam. He was twenty-eight. Looking at these horses, we are looking at ourselves—and looking at the artist, too.

14

JACOB VAN RUISDAEL

A Tragedy for Trees

DURING THE COVID PANDEMIC, there was a boom in pet adoptions. For a while, there was even a puppy shortage, as people who had long dreamed of adding an animal to their households found themselves more or less locked into their homes, with the time on their hands that a pet, especially a toothy maniacal puppy, requires. It turned out that lot of people had been waiting for just such an opportunity: I was one of these people.

A few months into lockdown, Basso, a Lagotto Romagnolo with floppy ears and dirty blond curls, entered our household. He was a truffle hunter by breed; by birth, less romantically, he was from the Rotterdam suburbs. A proud parent, I was convinced that there had never been a softer, cuter, smarter puppy in all the history of puppies. He was the sweetest thing that ever chewed a shoe.

Lagotti are athletic: they need at least three nice long walks a day. For owners if almost never for dog, this can get repetitive, and so, in order to avoid circling the same few blocks, we started taking Basso into the countryside, or what passes for the countryside, near Utrecht. This was dispiriting. In one of the most densely populated countries in the world, you could always see or hear a freeway, a railway, a power plant.

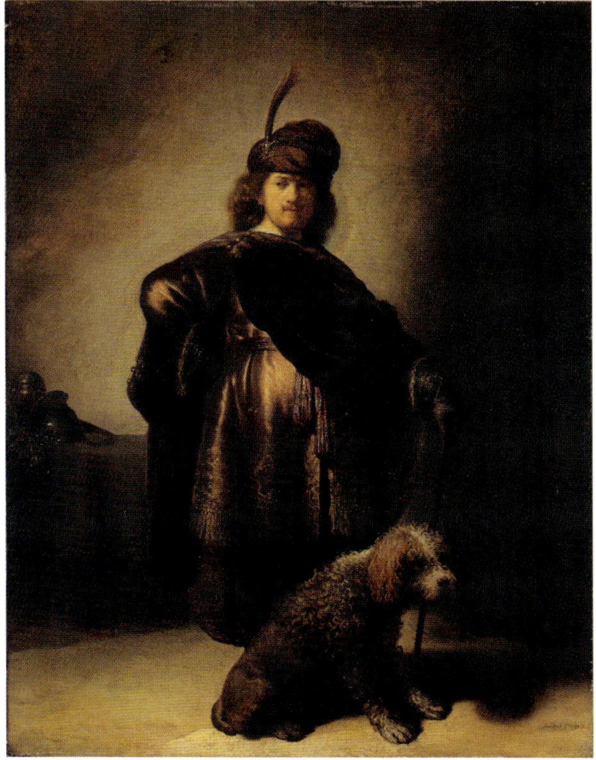

In 1641, Rembrandt painted himself in oriental costume,
with a Lagotto Romagnolo.

As Basso ran through forests whose trees all stood in straight lines or along the shores of rectangular lakes, I thought about the energy you need, in this country, to imagine something natural here, to edit those man-made things out of the frame. The neatness and organization foreigners have noted for centuries—so pleasant in Dutch cities—is less pleasant in the countryside, and starts to feel oppressive and inescapable.

At its most wild, Holland is no more wild than Central Park—but without the glacial outcroppings, grassy knolls, or wide vistas. There is more nature in the middle of Manhattan than there is in most of this country. At its best, Dutch nature is a nice park, good for taking a jog or throwing a stick to your dog, but it's not what most people imagine when they hear the word "nature." If you stay long enough, this becomes an absence you feel physically.

There's something disquieting, for example, about how pristine Dutch produce is. It's been years since I bothered to wash vegetables: they come wrapped in plastic, labeled with scannable bar codes, and in regulation sizes that, once you start observing them, start to seem creepy. Shouldn't potatoes have a little dirt on them? In Holland, they don't always—or only if you seek out a Turkish shop, or an ecological supermarket.

Much produce—the agricultural sector is stunningly productive, and this small nation is the world's second-largest exporter of agricultural products—comes from a series of greenhouses in the west of the country, around Schiphol. If your plane lands at night or in the morning, you can see a construction, glowing under acres of orange light, whose extent is larger than some cities, and can be appreciated only from the air. In them, plants grow that are never watered by rain, or see the unmediated sun.

But even without the accretions of modern ugliness, the Dutch countryside's most striking feature, its flatness, makes it a challenge for painters. The challenge Potter faced was the same that all landscape painters faced. On an unvaried surface, only nearby things can be seen, and everything else fades into the distance. You need a little height, a little variation, in order to arrange a view into something worth looking at.

Yet it was in this country where, at the beginning of the fifteenth century, landscape painting arose. The medieval artist painted bodies to look like sculptures, setting them against backgrounds of gold. But once the need was felt to make them look more real, convincing décors had to be devised. This was the "naturalism" of the Dutch. But it was no more natural than a bar code on an apple. Like the invention of perspective, it was an intellectual revolution.

Any child can draw a thing—a flower, a house, a person. This is the beginning of art. Tens of thousands of years ago, on the walls of the caves of Spain and France, people drew animals, individually or in groups: but they never placed them in a landscape, and wouldn't for thousands of years. The Romans attempted it, but it would be a millennium after the fall of Rome that artists would understand how to arrange figures in large spaces.

The next time you're in a chronologically arranged museum, keep an eye out for the way, between the fourteenth and the fifteenth centuries—around the time of the discoveries that culminated with Columbus—the world starts to be knitted into a coherent whole. On wood and on canvas, you can see it happening. The world the artists depicted starts to explode into different dimensions: into the distance, into the air.

FROM ANCIENT TIMES, huge tracts of Holland were wrested from the sea. This was an ongoing process, and continued until recently, but though the story of a people who created their own country is heroic, it was a matter of mud and pipes, and therefore not one that lends itself to painting. Neither did the resulting land. In the seventeenth century, the newer polders must have resembled postwar American suburbs. Clean and pleasant, but a bit too fresh to have that magical quality—call it soul—that passing time bestows.

The country was man-made—shaped—and this is the relationship of "land" to "landscape." Land is land. Landscape is "land-shaped," an etymological relationship that is more intuitive in Dutch than in English. Shaped by its creators, the land was then reshaped by its painters: shaping is the task of the artist. And the lack of ready-made subjects made that shaping all the more interesting, all the more challenging.

I felt how challenging it was when I was walking Basso. I tried to think myself into the mind of the great landscape painters, trying to mold what I was seeing into something striking enough to hang on the wall. It was not easy. Not because the land was hideous—it had a certain charm—but because it simply lacked much in the way of drama or romance.

There was not a lot you could do with this land of square fields and flat horizons. But people had. I started thinking about Jacob van Ruisdael, reputed to be the greatest of the landscape painters. In museums, I rarely lingered in front of his pictures, since there was almost always something more exciting than his trees and clouds. "Exciting": it was an embarrassing word to use in connection with art. It was embarrassing to want excitement, but never more than when looking at a Ruisdael did I realize how wholly I was a creature of the age of entertainment.

I had walked past Ruisdaels in the greatest museums. And though I had heard them praised by the greatest critics ("Whoever has the good fortune to see the original is penetrated by the insight into how far art can and should go"—Goethe) and read of their influence on the most eminent artists ("It haunts my mind and clings to my heart"—John Constable), I realized that I had never really looked at Ruisdael as I ought to have.

And when I did, I started to see what he had done. Because I knew what this land looked like, I could see how he had shaped it. He had infused a flat country with something like majesty—and majesty is not a quality that naturally belongs to the Dutch countryside. It is not, in any event, an external quality. It was an internal quality—one the artist projected onto his subject. The majesty was his. I wanted to know its source.

———

THEN: the wall.

Almost nothing is known of his life. How many times, in the course of writing about artists, have I typed the same phrase? You don't always know this in advance. You go to the library and find dozens of books about a painter. But only as you study them do you realize that, despite all that has been written and thought about their work, little

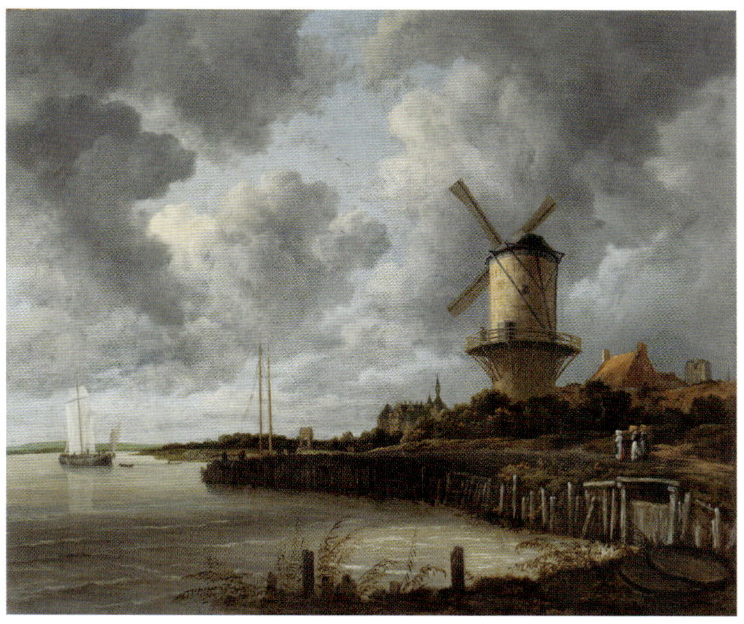

In paintings like The Mill, *Ruisdael gave the flat Dutch countryside
a grandeur that it does not come by naturally.*

is known beyond a name, a few facts, and whatever fragment of their
work survives.

In the case of Jacob van Ruisdael, the missing facts are not trivial.
His year of birth, and the identity of his mother, and where he died,
for example, are all unknown. There is no portrait of him, and no self-
portrait. No letter has come down to us. None of his contemporaries
wrote about him. What we had was a couple of paragraphs, written long
after his death, in Arnold Houbraken's eighteenth-century encyclopedia.

Short as that account was, it turned out to contain errors that subsequent researchers have debunked, making it even shorter. What we
know is that Ruisdael was born in Haarlem. His father was a frame
maker. He worked in Haarlem and Amsterdam. He never married and
was buried in Haarlem. From other sources, we know that his father,

Isaac, was a painter of landscapes. His uncle, Salomon, ditto. They were presumably his teachers.

They were talented, but he was a prodigy. In the single year of 1646—he was about seventeen—he painted more than a dozen canvases. Some are huge, and testify to the young man's ambition. They combine an attention to the most minute botanical detail with an unerring feeling for the monumental: that nearly impossible marriage of microscope and telescope that was a hallmark of the early Netherlandish painters.

In the twists of the trees, in the stormy clouds, they have something brooding, something romantic, that would have appealed to Goethe: not the sun of the Italians—or of Ruisdael's French contemporary Claude Lorrain, whose landscapes are dotted with fantastic temples and washed in the warm pink light of the south—but the range of black and gray and green that characterizes rainy northern marshlands.

In these meetings of water and clouds and brick, you get the *mood* of Holland. The effect these paintings have is on you, the viewer, and not on whatever tiny painted people might be wandering through them, doing this or that: it never matters what they are doing, and though Ruisdael could paint figures—staffage, in the language of art—he often farmed them out to other painters. They are only there to provide scale.

Personality is reserved for trees, which he paints as Paulus Potter painted animals, or as Frans Hals painted the citizens of his hometown. If people are staffage, trees never are: they are pompous or humble, depressive or optimistic, tired or vigorous, with as many shades of feeling as they have tones of green or brown. Ruisdael's trees have the monumentality, the individuality, of people in great portraits.

Look, for a moment, at this blasted elm. It looms over the town of Egmond aan Zee, a town up the coast from Haarlem that, like Haarlem, is protected by beachside dunes. Atop one dune, a tree rears toward the sky, like a dying soldier falling from his horse. It is still alive, barely—a few

A tree like a dying soldier on the dunes above Egmond-aan-Zee.

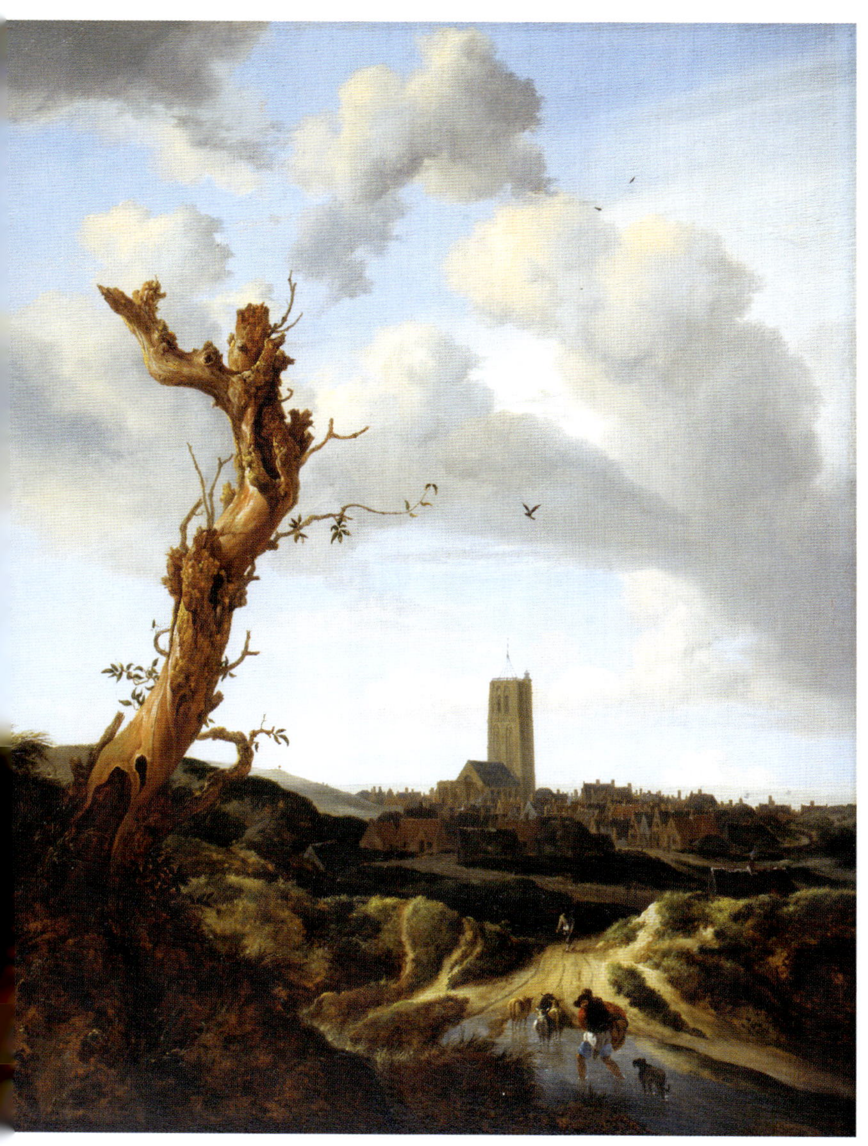

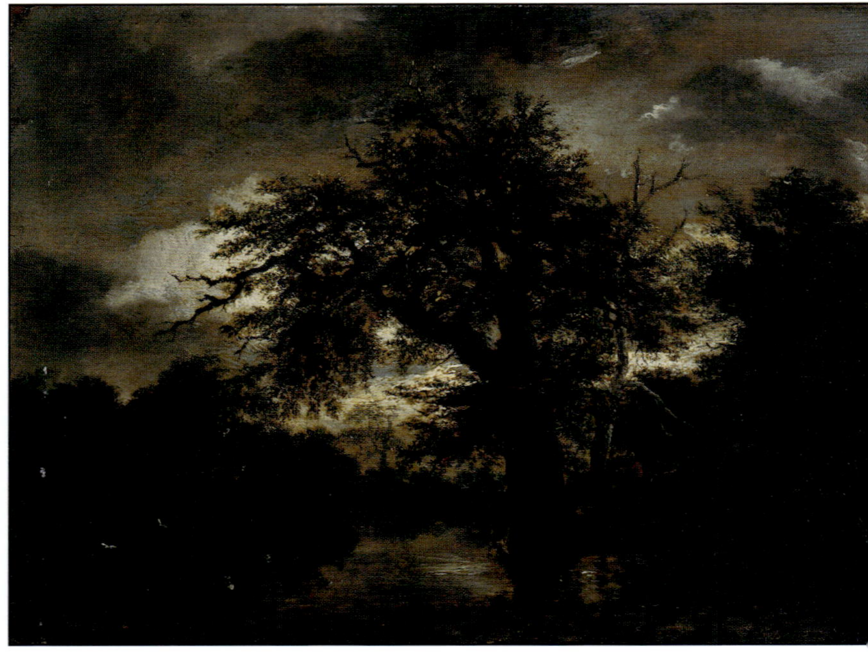

Ruisdael's moody trees evoke—never directly—powerful emotional states, and make us wonder about the artist's own.

green leaves cling to its twisted branches—but to look at it is to feel a pathos that only the greatest painter could evoke in a picture of a dying person.

Or look at my favorite Ruisdael, *The Wooded Marsh* in the Hermitage. The foreground is water dotted with lilies. Like the floor of a cathedral, the water recedes in a rough triangle that points deep into the background. At the farthest edge of the water, a minuscule fisherman—you have to strain to locate him—throws into relief the enormous trees that crowd out almost all the light from the strip of sky above.

The word "cathedral" seems unequal to the scene. Yet its hushed grandeur—those trees lined up on either side of the triangle like the columns of an ancient temple—conveys an unmistakable religious feeling: a counterpart, in paint, to the pantheism of Spinoza, who equated

God with the world. Ruisdael is not one for moralizing messages, but this might be the most moving portrait of passing time that I know.

There, in the right foreground, is the trunk of a once mighty tree, collapsed, headfirst, into the water. Behind it is a gnarled oak. It is still erect, but not for long: if it were a person, it would be an old baron, a haughty magnate, humiliated by the indignity of age. Just behind it, a tender white sapling is fighting its way toward the light still denied it by the elderly oak. This is a tragedy—in which the only actors are trees.

———

TODAY, the municipal authorities would have whisked away the fallen trunk as soon as it hit the water, and the aging baron would have been chopped up posthaste in order to make sure its rotting branches didn't crush a commuter on the neighborhood bicycle path. But *The Wooded Marsh* shows the same land that I see on my walks with Basso: green and dark and spongy, stretching out to a low, distant horizon.

There's another kind of land in many other Ruisdaels, and I recognize it, too. According to the earliest chronicler of the Dutch artists, Karel van Mander, who published his *Schilder-Boeck* in 1604, around a quarter century before Ruisdael's birth, the Dutch landscape originated in Haarlem. Haarlem had a venerable artistic tradition, but there is another reason, a geographical reason, for landscape art to have emerged in this small city.

On its western side, Haarlem abuts a series of forested dunes. Separating the low country behind from the beach a couple of miles away, these dunes are an asset whose value cannot be overstated: a high natural dike that stretches along the Dutch coast, and that is today the best hope for this fragile country to survive in an age of rising oceans. These dunes are an escape from the usual flatness. The Dutch love them.

This area was always considered enchanting. Images survive of well-dressed tourists strolling through the Haarlem dunes. In the seventeenth century, the fields below were decked with bright cloth from the local bleaching industry; and the effect, with light flashing off the windblown

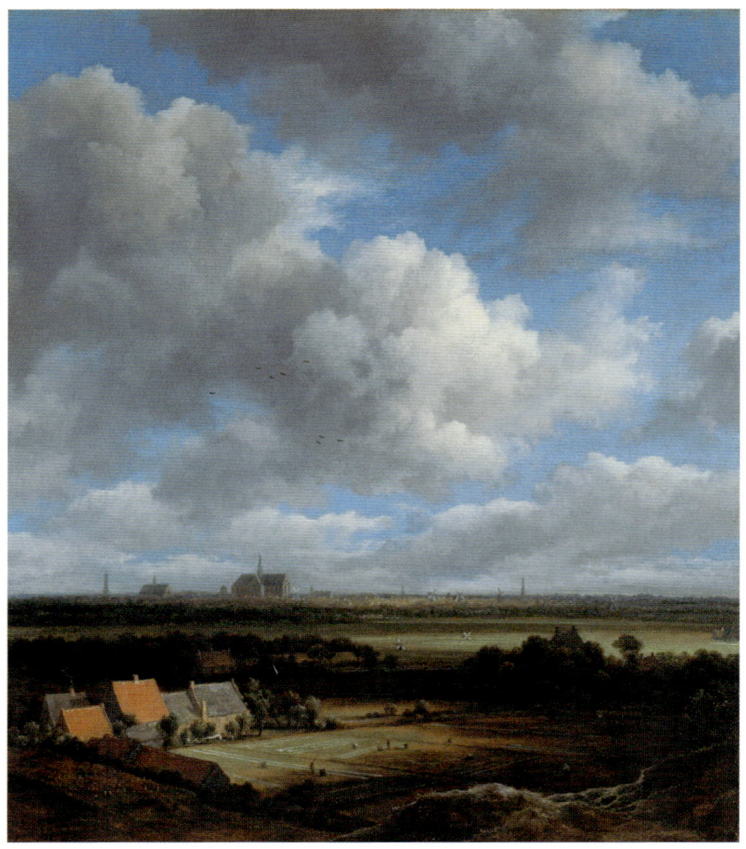

The view of Haarlem from the dunes let landscape artists show sky meeting earth.

cloth, must have been like seeing a work by Christo and Jeanne-Claude. Ruisdael painted the fields—not, needless to say, the tourists.

Without these dunes, the history of landscape painting is unthinkable. Nowhere else in Holland offers any elevation at all, any of the staggered relief a landscape painter needs. Only here does the countryside look a little bit feral, and allow you to gaze into the far distance. The light that falls on the hills is different, too, and knits together objects—from leaves of grass to entire cities—into a coherent whole.

The dunes recur in Ruisdael's works, as they do in the works of virtually all Dutch landscape painters. He understood how useful these topographical accidents were and, often, when depicting an identifiable site, he added a little outcropping of his own. In his paintings of the Portuguese-Jewish cemetery of Ouderkerk-aan-de-Amstel, for example, or of the ruins of Egmond Castle, high and impossible hills loom in the background.

Because so little is known about him, historians seeking to fill the gaps have learned a bit about his travels from identifying the places he depicts. He had a predilection for Scandinavian waterfalls, but never went to the north; he borrowed the motif from another painter, Allart

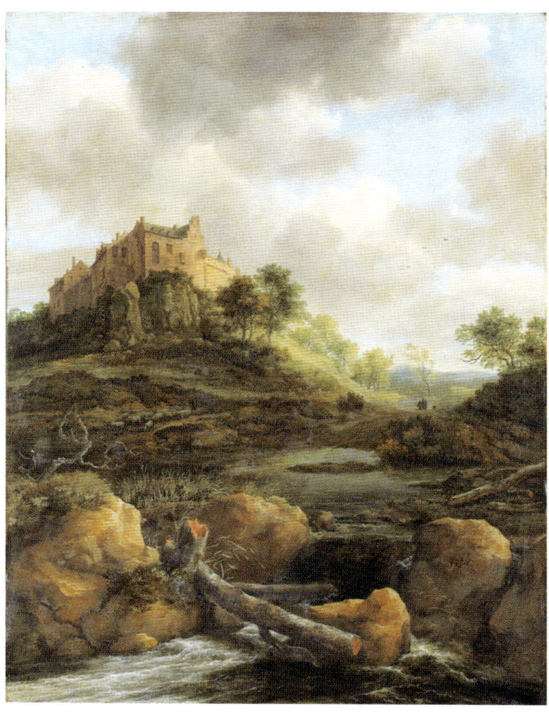

Ruisdael saw Bentheim much as Saenredam saw the Mariakerk: what did this place mean to him?

van Everdingen, who did. He traveled up the North Sea coast, and visited areas southeast of Amsterdam.

And he visited the rural region of Twente, in the east of the Netherlands. On this trip or trips, Jacob made his only documented journey abroad, though the German town of Bentheim hardly qualifies as abroad: it is a short walk from the Dutch border. Bentheim boasts a rough old castle that Ruisdael painted in several versions. In them, it is perched upon a craggy mountain, looming heroically above a green valley.

The actual Bentheim Castle, however, is not perched on much more than a wrinkle—a wart—in the surrounding flatness. Here, more than anywhere else, we can see a literal expression of Ruisdael's need for elevation. This is something that we sense in all his paintings. His every thought is lofty. There is not the slightest trace of vulgarity. There is nothing lowering: no plot, no humor, no attempt to charm, no attempt to entertain.

———

NO FACTS, either: but a sensibility more palpable than facts emerges. "He is the first of the Dutch to express his feelings in pure landscape so positively that we can hear the personal, the unmistakable voice of the man himself," wrote Max Friedländer, more attuned than most to such voices. "We get to know him, although we know little enough of him and glimpse nothing beyond the country he saw in just that way."

Eugène Fromentin, the nineteenth-century French writer-painter, believed that Ruisdael was second only to Rembrandt in the whole of the Dutch school: "He warns you that you have before you the soul of someone of high race, and that he has always something important to tell you," he wrote. "This is the only reason for the superiority of Ruysdael, and this reason is sufficient: there is in the painter a man who thinks."

Though Jacob's paintings show nature and not humanity, they also show moral qualities—elevation, dignity, thought—that are not to be found in amoral nature, and thereby leave a strong impression of the man who made them. His season, Friedländer wrote, was "high summer, already somewhat autumnal, vegetation in full bloom but near to the fall, seldom winter, never the youthful freshness of springtime."

"We imagine Ruysdael not very young nor very old," wrote Fromentin of the man who, at seventeen, was already a master. "One of the *solitary ramblers* who fly from the town, frequent the outskirts, sincerely love the country, who feel it without exaggeration and describe it without phrases, who are made uneasy by distant horizons, charmed by large plains, affected by a shadow, and enchanted by a ray of sunshine."

Houbraken's biography, which is only a bit more than two paragraphs long, mentions that he was "a great friend of [Nicolaes] Berchem," a landscapist whose works, usually set in some sunny Italian clime, are not as moody, not as melancholy, as his friend's. It was with Berchem that Ruisdael traveled to Bentheim. The year was 1650. Ruisdael was in his early twenties, and Berchem was nearing thirty.

For both, the journey was memorable. Both painted many versions of the castle. Why? The building is handsome, but it is just one of many impressive castles in and near the Netherlands that might have attracted young painters. Something about this place meant something to Ruisdael and Berchem, who returned to it again and again, embellishing it and then—as you do with a precious memory—romanticizing it.

———

HOUBRAKEN'S SKELETAL TEXT mentions something else, too. "He remained unmarried until the end of his life; it is said, in order to be of greater service to his father." Maybe. But there might have been another reason Jacob remained unmarried. Of all the painters of the Golden Age, there are few—maybe none—whose heterosexuality is in question. Perhaps because the alternative was unmentionable, it therefore went unmentioned.

How many prostitutes do we find in the paintings of the Dutch—how many drunks and thieves and madmen? Dutch artists were famed—and either admired or denounced—for viewing humanity and its passions with the clear-eyed perspective called "realism." This meant viewing the world as it was, not as it ought to be. This was the opposite of the view taken by the idealizing Italians.

But one human trait, which must have been as common there as it was anywhere else, was omitted. As far as I know, there are no depictions of homosexuality or homosexuals anywhere in the Golden Age: none, neither in painting nor in the mountains of prints and drawings they produced. Neither are there any Dutch artists—a Leonardo, a Michelangelo—whose homosexuality was so much as rumored.

(The Flemish artist Michael Sweerts, born in Brussels, briefly worked in Amsterdam, where he influenced Ter Borch. He led a highly itinerant life, visiting Rome, Jerusalem, Syria, and Persia before dying in Goa, apparently mad. He was given to painting muscular young men, often naked. To us, these pictures look gay. But given the absence of sources, it is hard to know how they looked to Sweerts's contemporaries.)

It is a strange lacuna. As you walk around a museum, you think: *someone* around here had to have been gay. Someone must have at the very least alluded to homosexuality. Perhaps these references are encoded in a way we can no longer read—though we can read a lot, and the Dutch loved sexual allusions. It seems their tolerance stopped here, and that homosexuality was considered too repulsive even to mock.

Right before Houbraken's announcement that Jacob never married, there is another sentence in his note on the artist: "I cannot say he had luck as his friend." As so often, he doesn't elaborate. In a context in which gayness was unmentionable—and until recently any reference to a person's sexuality was considered disrespectful, and would cloak them in the odium of perversion—this indirect reference might be a clue.

There are others. In a painting of the renovation of the manor of Kostverloren, Ruisdael included three naked men bathing in the river alongside the house. The art historian Seymour Slive wrote that "in Dutch pictures of the period naked male figures who are not gods, saints or classical heroes are almost as scarce as hen's teeth." Moreover, Ruisdael, who usually farmed out the staffage, painted these himself.

As with his friendship with Berchem, this is nothing more than a hint. But there is something in his sensibility. Fromentin describes a man

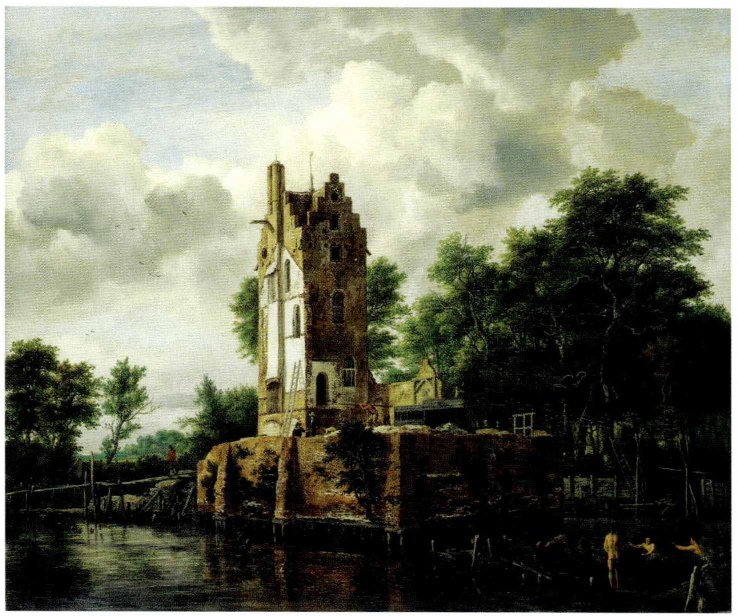

Ruisdael painted a group of naked male swimmers in the Amstel.

"of precocious maturity, very serious, master of himself very early, with the sad reflections, the regrets, the reveries of one who looks back and whose youth has not known the oppressive uneasiness of hope. . . . His melancholy, for he is full of it, has something very manly."

Many gay men would recognize something of themselves in this description, as well as in the similar note Friedländer strikes: "A poet of 'sensibility'—in the eighteenth century sense—seemed to be raising his voice in Ruisdael, a sensitive 'nature' which, weary of the bustle, sought refuge in the solitude of the woods and, sunk in reveries far from the madding crowd, followed with longing eyes the procession of the clouds."

Toward the end of his portrait, Fromentin gets close to providing a key to this shadowy personality: "What had life done to him that he should have so contemptuous or so bitter a feeling for it? What had men done to him that he should retire into solitude and should, to such a point, avoid having anything to do with them—even in his pictures? . . . Did fate give him an opportunity of loving anything besides clouds?"

YET I CAN'T FIND anything contemptuous or bitter in Ruisdael. As Basso and I walk through what passes for the Dutch countryside, I see the generosity with which he looked at this land, the way he lifted it up, turned it into something it doesn't quite deserve to be. I notice his paintings' mood of introspection and meditation, and of a stillness that, in some way, lets you feel the movement of air and earth. I feel close to this invisible man.

Then I notice something that I am embarrassed not to have noticed before. I sought their subjects in trees and waterfalls and dunes— looking down, at the bottom of the pictures. But when I raise my eyes, I see that their real subject was—had to be—the clouds. The skies have all the relief, the drama, that the land lacks, and are all the more vis- ible because of its flatness: a more varied land would push them into a supporting role.

The sky gives this country layers, depth. And because so little inter- feres with the view of the sky, and because the watery land reflects so much light back onto the clouds, the skies in Holland have an animation they lack in countries at similar latitudes, in the gray drizzle of England or Germany. Neither does Holland have the constant glare of the south. Here, the sky flashes: the instantly recognizable "Dutch light."

In Ruisdael, people may be staffage. But trees aren't, and neither are skies. Many of his pictures are nearly all cloud. In some, the skies take up three-fourths of the picture, and make the very word "landscape" ring false. These are pictures of the sky in which the land is often only inci- dental, and they reflect the pantheistic feeling that pervades his paint- ings: nature as a temple, and skies like the vault of a cathedral.

As light streams through stained glass, it tumbles through Ruisdael's clouds. Far below, the doings of man—including me, the man looking at them—are never reduced to pettiness or inconsequence. As in a cathedral, we are elevated by this superior construction, and to see Ruisdael studying it is to be reminded of the peace that comes, in a world saturated with images, from the contemplation of a great subject.

When I think about the energy with which this solitary wanderer painted these skies—nearly seven hundred paintings survive—I feel how wrong I was to seek these views amid the mud and dirt of the external world. These are views of a spirit, of a mind, that let you see the man who painted them, and let you to feel as he did: that the world will go on with or without you—and that, just maybe, love of clouds is love enough.

15

ALBERT ECKHOUT

The Past in the Land of the Future

IN 1578, King Sebastião I of Portugal decided to re-Christianize Morocco. The crusade would have been a dubious proposition in the best of times. With this leadership, however, it would have taken a miracle. The king was little more than a boy, and a boy so inbred that he only had four great-grandparents, one (or two) of whom, Juana, Queen of Castile, was known as "La Loca." After the Portuguese army crossed into Africa, events took a predictable course. Sebastião's forces were smashed at Alcazarquivir, south of Tangiers. The young king simply vanished.

His death was so ruinous for Portugal that two years later, when Cardinal Dom Henrique, Sebastião's elderly successor, died, King Philip II of Spain, asserting a dynastic claim, managed to attach Portugal and its oversees possessions to the kingdom of Castile. The united empire—all of Latin America, much of northern France, the northern and southern Netherlands, Spain, Portugal, large parts of Italy, chunks of Africa, the Philippines—was far too big to administer or defend. There was less to it than met the eye. One contemporary remarked that "the skin alone was of a lion; the flesh was of a lamb."

That flesh was being devoured by ceaseless wars with England and France. But the most costly was the war against the United Provinces of the northern Netherlands, which had begun with the Dutch Revolt. Once they became a power in their own right, the Dutch were always seeking creative ways to hit their old Catholic nemesis, and eventually resolved, in the 1620s, to take the battle to Spain's rich sugar colony, Brazil. They conquered Recife and Olinda, the principal cities of Pernambuco, in 1630, and eventually extended their control across the whole northeastern hump of South America. The possession of part of Brazil—and of Elmina, in today's Ghana, and Luanda in Angola, conquered in expeditions that departed from Recife—meant that the Dutch dominated the world sugar market: the labor supply in Africa, the plantations in Pernambuco, and the refineries in Amsterdam.

The Dutch transformed Recife, located near the easternmost tip of Brazil on a series of islands in a river estuary, into perhaps South America's richest city. It was populated by Africans and Indians, Dutch and Portuguese, Germans, Italians, Spaniards, Englishmen, and Poles. Because a greater degree of religious freedom was allowed in Netherlands Brazil than anywhere else in the Western world—including in Holland—Jews flocked there: so many that at one point they may have outnumbered white gentiles in Recife. One priest muttered that Recife and its twin city, Olinda, were *"como a Sodoma, & Gomorra."*

That the Dutch period has remained widely known in Brazil is mainly owing to the achievements of its greatest figure, Count Johan Maurits van Nassau-Siegen. His governorship, from 1637 to 1644, sparked a brief golden age, a reflection of the renaissance at home. He reorganized the colony politically—the New World's first parliament convened at Recife—and temporarily reconciled the local Portuguese planters to Dutch rule. He planned cities and built forts and conquered new territory both in Brazil and in Africa.

But the count's most lasting achievements were scientific and artistic. His court included two painters, Albert Eckhout and Frans Post, imported from the Netherlands to document the country's landscapes and populations. Johan Maurits sponsored research into tropical medicine; one of his palaces had an astronomical observatory and a marvelous zoo. His botanical gardens gathered species from all over Brazil, and from Africa and Asia as well. The books his "expedition" produced remained the standard works on Brazilian natural history for two hundred years. In much of the historiography, the count is described as the model of the enlightened humanist prince.

Despite Johan Maurits's efforts, the situation had changed dramatically by 1644, when political intrigue at home forced his recall. The cultural and scientific endeavors we find admirable were often, then, found to be merely expensive. And a revolution had occurred in Europe. In 1640, after sixty years of captivity, Portugal finally regained its independence. The new king understood very well how fragile his restored kingdom was, and tried desperately to keep the peace all around, especially with Spain and Holland. He couldn't risk new attacks; he wanted to survive.

In order to solve the Brazil problem and ensure friendly relations with Holland, the king offered several times to pay the Dutch to respect the frontiers of 1641, which included peripheral areas where the Dutch had long since lost de facto control. This would have meant permanently renouncing Portugal's claims to northern Brazil. But it would have protected the south. Portugal could afford to lose Pernambuco—the reasoning went—but its existence as an independent nation hinged on keeping the province of Bahia, a sugar producer as important as Pernambuco. Without Brazilian revenues, the poor, struggling kingdom would almost certainly have been swallowed up by Spain once again.

In contrast to Lisbon's careful diplomacy, the Portuguese in Brazil were taking matters into their own hands. By the end of the 1640s, local attacks had drastically trimmed the extent of the Dutch domain, and the Dutch colony began to fall apart after Johan Maurits left. Many in the Netherlands demanded tough countermeasures: an attack on Bahia and a blockade of the Tagus River, which would have starved Lisbon. Both were militarily feasible and, if carried out simultaneously, would have triggered the collapse of Portugal. Cooler heads understood that this would be a calamity. The Dutch quarrel, they said, had never been with the Portuguese. To help Spain reunite Iberia would be a debacle of the first order. An independent Portugal, eager to trade and allied against

Spain, had far more advantages. Why bother with a huge restive colony, endlessly sucking up money and men?

Behind this explanation lies another: the Dutch politicians, consumed as ever by domestic squabbles, couldn't make up their minds. Meanwhile, events in Brazil had escaped their control. The Dutch were expelled in 1654. In that same year, in acknowledgment of political and diplomatic favors, including appointment to the Order of the White Elephant, Johan Maurits van Nassau-Siegen presented to the king of Denmark a group of paintings by Albert Eckhout.

———

THE HISTORICAL IMPORT of Eckhout's paintings, and of Johan Maurits's patronage, can be best understood in the context of what came before them: pretty much nothing. Eckhout's paintings were the first convincing European representations of Native Americans, in North or

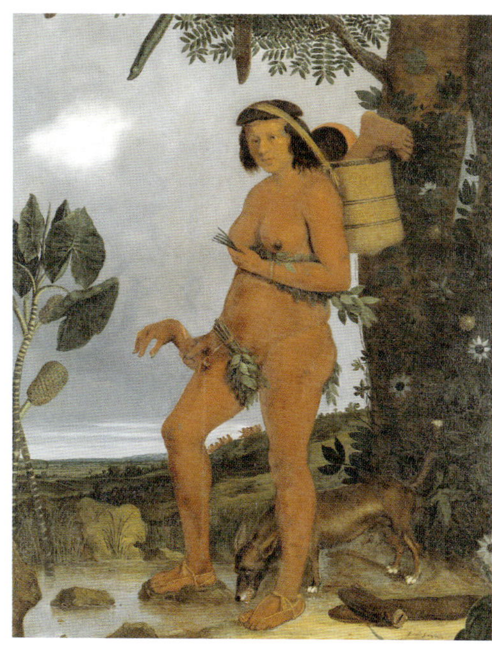

The portrait of the Tapuya woman includes a basketful of human body parts.

South America. Neither had there been any careful ethnological depictions of the peoples of southern Africa, India, or the East Indies.

When one considers how much time had elapsed between the first explorations of America and Eckhout's Brazilian career, this is shocking. Eckhout disembarked at Recife about 150 years after Columbus. This is roughly the same amount of time that separates us from Stanley and Livingstone. Yet from a scientific perspective America was still a dark continent. On the margins of its maps were headless barbarians, men with the faces of dogs, and creatures whose exceedingly large feet could double as umbrellas.

Until the Dutch arrived in the 1630s, the New World had never been examined scientifically. Its flora and fauna had never been cataloged; its peoples had never been systematically described. Nevertheless, the Dutch effort was soon forgotten in Europe. By the eighteenth century, America, like the Jews, had become a "debate," a "question." In France, the leading scientific nation of the day, the learned view of America was something like this:

> A dark immensity, less hostile than repellent, less terrifying than desolate . . . [where] colors faded and edges blurred and lines disappeared over foggy horizons. Ocean, land, lagoons: everything was indistinct and hazy. The confused, slithering vegetation grew in great tangled heaps. Animals were shifty and lacked a fixed physiognomy. The dogs didn't bark; the tigers were cowardly; the people dim-witted.

But Johan Maurits and his artists would not change this. They were a dead end; scientific exploration ceased, and it was not until the voyages of Captain Cook, beginning in 1766, that Europeans dignified a new quarter of the world with an equivalent record of its ethnology and topography, its medicine and botany, its zoology, ichthyology, and entomology. Brazil itself would not be examined so precisely until the nineteenth century. Even then—even now—most Europeans would be interested in the New World only to the extent that it reflected their own preconceptions.

Eckhout paid Brazil the compliment of taking it seriously, rendering the place so scrupulously that an observer of his Brazilian paintings can only think: it is as it was. It is no exaggeration to say that when we look at the pictures of Albert Eckhout, we are seeing a world as it had never been seen before—and would never be seen again.

———

ALMOST NOTHING IS KNOWN about the life of Albert Eckhout. He seems to have been born between 1608 and 1612 in Groningen, a provincial capital in the northern part of the country. He was in Recife in the early 1640s. By 1646 he was back in the Netherlands, where he remained until leaving for Dresden in 1653. In 1663, he reappeared in Groningen as a burgher, a member of the St. Luke's Guild, the association of painters, and of the Reformed Church. He was buried, at an unknown date, in the cemetery of St. Martin's Church in Groningen.

In the absence of biographical data, what remains of Eckhout are eight full-size portraits of the inhabitants of Brazil; twelve still-lifes of various fruits; and a *Dance of the Tapuya Indians*. These twenty-one paintings have resided in Copenhagen since 1654. In addition, Eckhout's known oeuvre includes one painting of two Brazilian tortoises in The Hague, four drawings in Berlin, and seven books in Kraków that form a compendium of Brazilian natural history and include hundreds of other drawings by Eckhout.

The eight pictures of Brazilians consist of pairs: four men and four women representing the mestizos, Africans, Tupis, and Tapuyas. These "ethnographic portraits" are of a size usually reserved for portraits of royalty—almost ten feet tall—and they are crammed with detail. Every basket and earring and feather and shell is rendered with the arresting accuracy that distinguishes the productions of Johan Maurits's court. The figures appear with characteristic attributes. The African man is holding a sword typical of the Akan of Ghana, and the African woman basketry with Angolan motifs. The Tapuyas appear naked, the woman bearing the group's most outrageous crowd-pleaser—sliced human body parts, ready for the dinner table. The Tupis—pastoral Indians that the

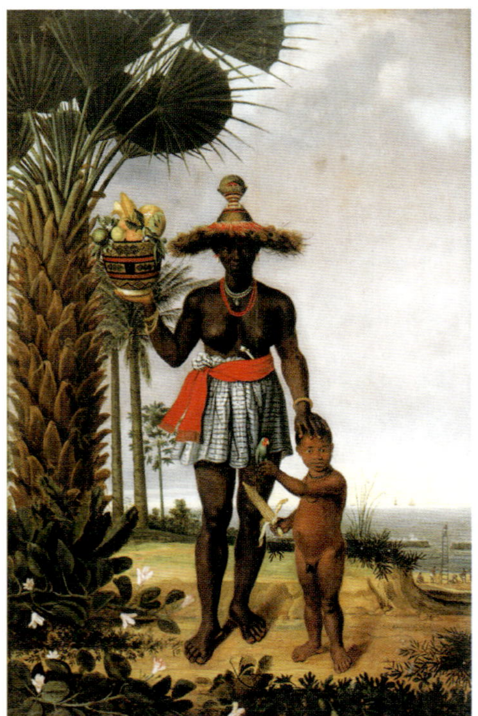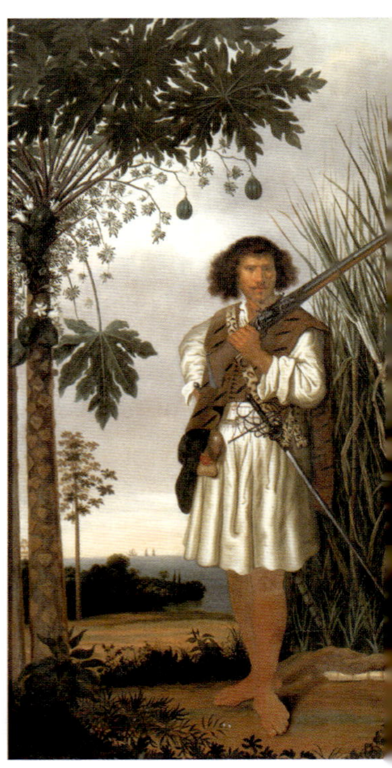

Eckhout painted the inhabitants of Brazil in formats usually reserved for royalty.

Europeans considered the most civilized of the aborigines—are shown half clad, the man holding arrows and the woman posed with a child in front of a sugar plantation. The fourth group is a mixed pair of mixed race. A mameluke woman—of mixed Indian and European ancestry—is dressed in a flowing white robe, holding a basket full of flowers. The elegant mulatto man, whose firearm indicates that he was not enslaved, stands between papaya plants and a grove of sugarcane.

If you've spent any time in northeastern Brazil, these people, despite their antiquated dress, will seem familiar. You know the faces. Tapuyas, who supposedly died out in the early nineteenth century, still walk the streets of Recife, alongside mamelukes and mulattoes and blacks. And their behavior is unmistakably Brazilian: behind the portrait of the Tupi man, Eckhout includes a scene of Indians bathing in a stream. Dutch observers in the seventeenth century were as struck by the Brazilians' remarkable devotion to personal cleanliness as foreigners are today.

The twelve still-lifes are unique in that they are the only Golden Age still-lifes painted against the open sky. This may not sound very impressive, but when you see them, the shifting clouds and varying light make them look like visitors from another planet—radically unlike any other of the thousands of Dutch still-lifes. Like most of Eckhout's paintings, their huge size is overwhelming, and the scale of the works gives a sense of how strange the produce of the New World would have seemed when it was first presented to Europeans. This is the first place many people in

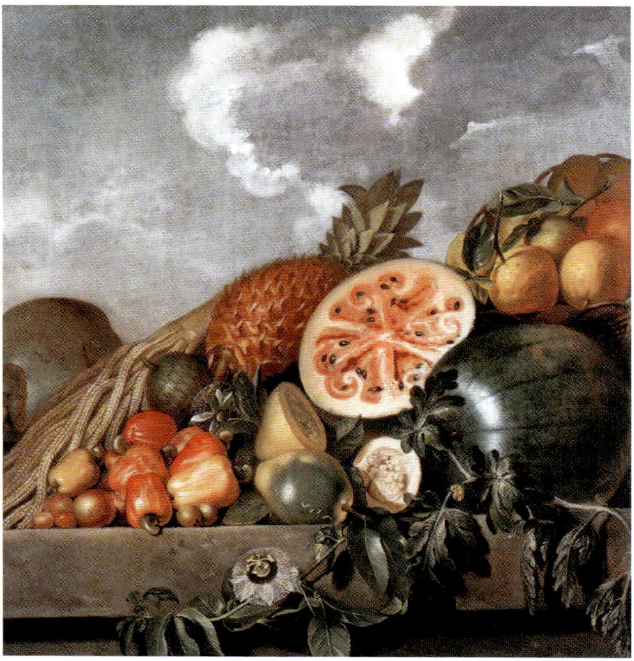

In Eckhout's still-lifes, we can imagine how New World produce would have looked to Europeans encountering it for the first time.

the Netherlands would have seen watermelons or pineapples—alongside plants, like sweetsops or dogbanes, that still look odd to us today.

The largest and most enigmatic painting in the group is the *Dance of the Tapuya Indians*. Eight naked men are dancing in a circle—the chronicler Barlaeus said the Tapuyas liked to sing for hours on end about their prowess in war and the Portuguese they had killed. The men have pierced cheeks and ears filled with large wads of cotton. Eckhout hardly shows their genitals—a strange prudishness, considering that his portrait of the Tapuya man details that race's proclivity for penile adornment. The dark painting is animated by the bright red slashes of macaw feathers, held in the hands of the dancers or worn as headdresses. At the far right, two women covering their mouths with their hands seem to be gossiping or laughing, a contrast to the solemn dancers.

In a standard art history text, Frederick Hartt wrote: "Although the [Dutch] painters' skill was seemingly unlimited, their variety copious, and their number legion, their productions, exhibited today in endless Dutch galleries in leading museums, tend to become monotonous." Even Dutch painting's greatest aficionados must reluctantly agree. It is therefore all the odder that the works of Albert Eckhout, which are so splendid and which show such a different side of the Dutch, should traditionally have been considered a slightly wacky hors d'oeuvre. One survey of Dutch painting calls his work an "exotic intermezzo." Many call him nothing at all.

Perhaps this is because the paintings are so few (but paintings from many great masters are rare!) or because they are concentrated in one place, in the National Museum in Copenhagen, which is a museum of culture and anthropology rather than of art. When I saw them there, they were bunched up together in a small room, and surrounded by South American artifacts (pottery, baskets) that made it hard to see how spectacular they are.

(How different they looked when they were put on display in the Mauritshuis! This is the secret of the curator, as of the photographer: much of what we see in art, or at least so much of what we think we are seeing in art, is not the object but its display. Until you see the same paintings hung somewhere else, you don't think you're noticing the lighting, the color of the wall, the frame.)

Still, these paintings are different. They don't quite fit into the broader history of Dutch painting—and yet they do. I have long fantasized about placing the prancing cannibals of *Dance of the Tapuya Indians* alongside some of the other group portraits of the period: Rembrandt's *Anatomy Lesson of Dr. Nicolaes Tulp*, for example, or the *Regentesses* of Frans Hals. It seems that Eckhout's images, even in their own time, did not have the impact that one might expect. References to them surface in a few isolated instances, mainly in the designs of tapestries. But they seem to have been quickly shuffled off to the cabinet of curiosities. They certainly never gave rise to a new idea of America for Europeans, who preferred more sensationalist depictions. They were too new; they needed time to be absorbed and understood.

THERE IS one place where they are well-known, however. The Dutch period has long been a Brazilian preoccupation. "No period of national history possesses such abundant literature as the troubled Dutch domination of eastern Brazil," wrote the historian Alfredo de Carvalho in 1898. This preoccupation endures, though the reasons for it have constantly shifted. For many years, the historiography described the expulsion of the Dutch as a providential assurance that Brazil would remain unified, Catholic, and Portuguese. The large numbers of Jews in Dutch Recife also meant that the tone of these criticisms was often antisemitic. As late as 1979, the nationalist historian Gilberto Freyre could approvingly cite an earlier historian who saw the war against the Dutch as a struggle between "the cross and the shop counter."

Yet another tradition in Brazilian historiography, one that is largely triumphant, defends the Dutch. One writer compared the two colonial powers: "[With the institution of the Inquisition] the Portuguese expelled the classes that had freed themselves from feudalism . . . while the Dutch shook off old systems and embraced private initiative." Today, nostalgia for Dutch rule is nowhere more palpable than in Johan

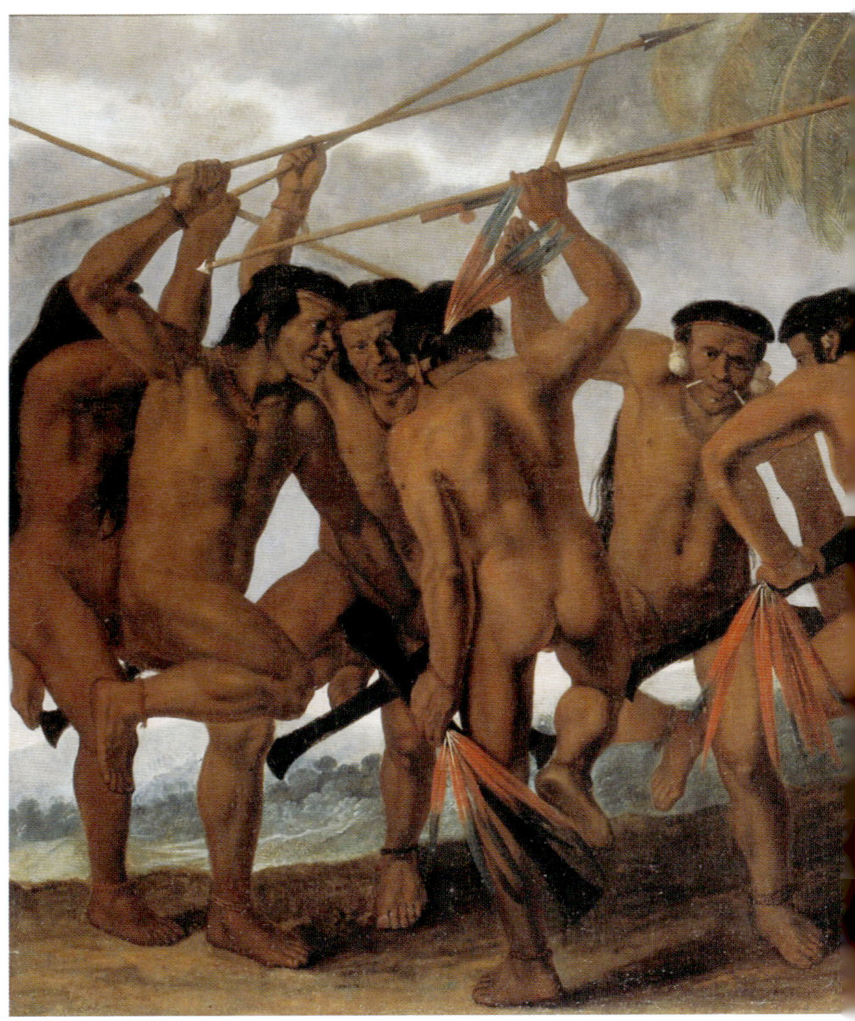

Eckhout's Dance of the Tapuya Indians *has traditionally been hung alongside anthropological collections, and never alongside the contemporary group portraits.*

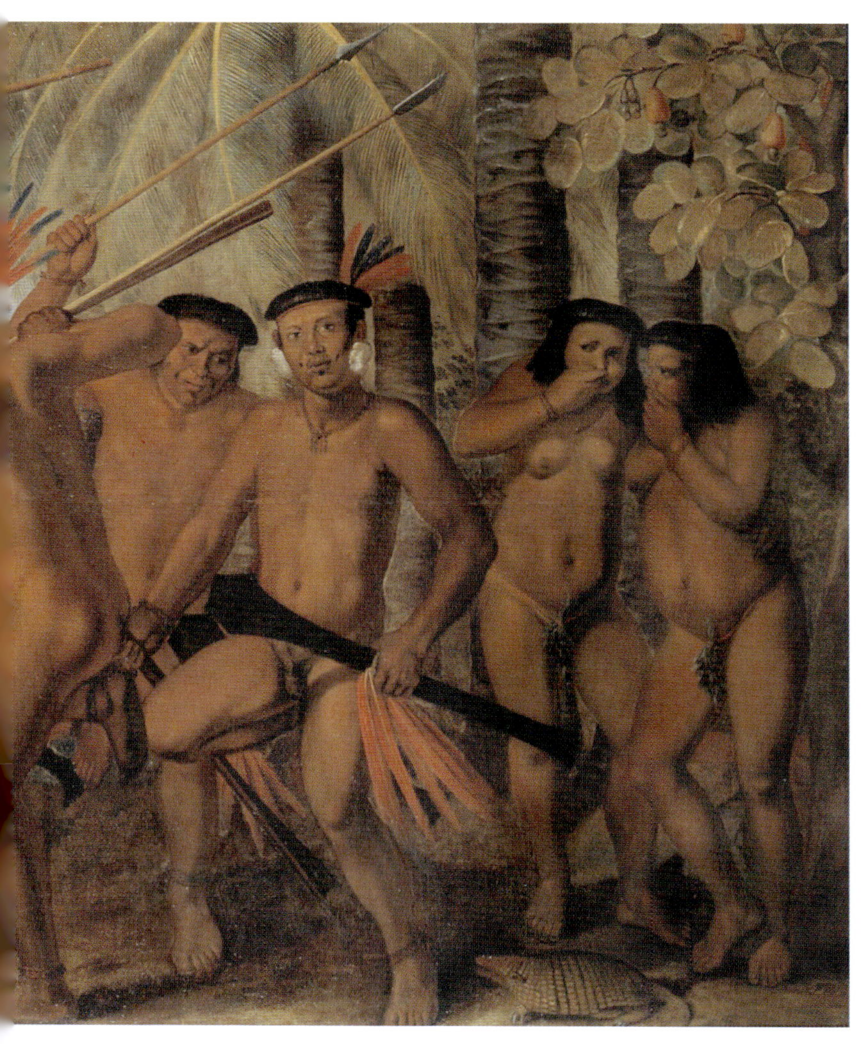

Maurits's capital, Recife. The old city of bridges and canals, though much destroyed by the same twentieth-century concrete that wrecked so many cities across the world, still feels different from other big cities in Brazil, and still cultivates its own separate identity—its distinct musical traditions; its own instantly recognizable dialect; its poets and writers—and its own history, based on the achievements of the Dutch.

Two major museums opened in 2002. Kahal zur Israel, the first synagogue in the New World, built under Dutch rule in 1637, has been renovated as a Jewish cultural center. And the Instituto Ricardo Brennand, a sprawling and rather tasteless bunker built by a Pernambuco magnate to display his collections, has as its centerpiece artworks and books relating to Netherlands Brazil. It also holds the world's largest private collection of the paintings of Eckhout's fellow traveler Frans Post, who painted the first Brazilian landscapes and whose works are, like Eckhout's, widely admired in Brazil. Post, from Haarlem, introduced that city's venerable landscape tradition into Brazil, and showed how effectively its principles could travel abroad.

There is a more poignant reason for the paintings' popularity among the masses of Brazilians: a sense that something went wrong in a country that seemed to have been so naturally blessed. In 1941, shortly before killing himself in the Brazilian resort town of Petrópolis, Stefan Zweig could still call Brazil the "Country of the Future." In *Tropical Truth*, published in 1997, the singer Caetano Veloso described his country as "a failed nation ashamed of having once been called 'the country of the future.'" Whenever Brazilians are asked what went wrong, *"colonização portuguesa"* will immediately be mentioned. If only we had been sired by an industrious, modern, tolerant people—people like the Dutch—rather than by the lazy, bumbling Portuguese, with their Inquisition and their exploitative economy, we would have stood a better chance.

The argument is more than a little nonsensical. The Dutch were certainly more tolerant of the Jews than the Portuguese. (Not all wanted to be; Holland had so many different sects that even those who dreamed of religious uniformity were forced to compromise.) But they were just as dependent on African slavery, the extractive monoculture that it sus-

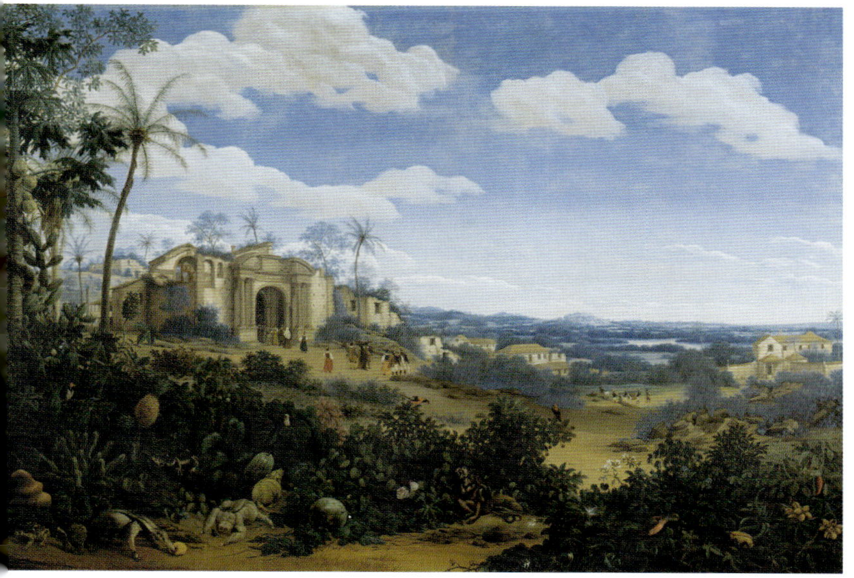

Frans Post exported the techniques of the Haarlem still-life to Brazil, and populated his scenes with anteaters and palms.

tained, and the generally dictatorial government that kept the system in place. Even Johan Maurits, whose artists and scientists contributed so much to Brazilian memory, spent most of the rest of his life as stadtholder of Cleves, today just across the border in Germany—a dogged defender of princely absolutism.

But none of this really matters to Albert Eckhout's work. The reason his paintings are so much admired in the land that inspired them is the undeniable impression he gives: of seeing the world for the very first time, a world complete, before the fall and the flood.

PART IV

MAYFLOWER AND MAY FLOWERS

IN A PICTURESQUE CORNER of Rotterdam is an all-but-unvisited church. "Picturesque" is rarely a word applied to Rotterdam. Its center, which resembled Amsterdam's, was destroyed by German bombs in 1940, and the city's postwar embrace of architecture expressing modern progress in different garish ways makes it unlike any other city in the country. Everywhere else, a Baroque or medieval core allows you to forget, and sometimes even forgive, the concrete that creeps every year further across the flat landscape. In Rotterdam, only the waterways remind you that you are in an old Dutch city. Everywhere else, the twentieth century is impossible to escape.

Almost everywhere. One such waterway, the Aelbrechtskolk, Aelbrecht's Deep, is the only place I know in Rotterdam that allows you to imagine this place as the village of its origins. Lined with boats, it is located in a neighborhood called Delfshaven,

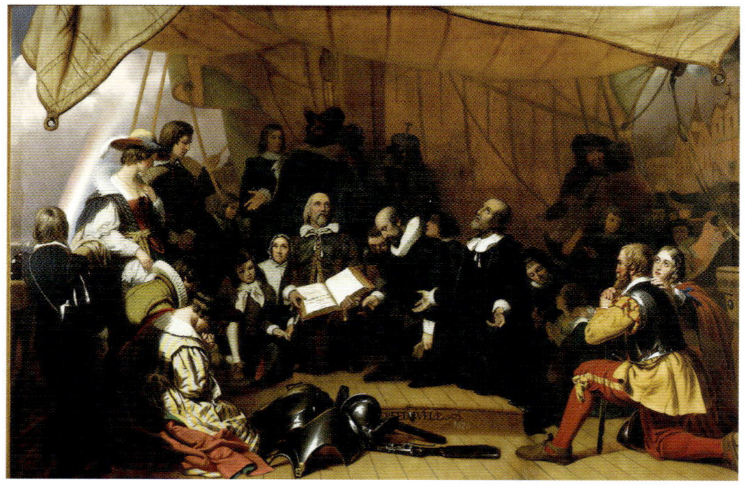

In the Rotunda of the Capitol, Robert Weir's Embarkation of the Pilgrims *shows the quay of Delftshaven, at right.*

which means the port of Delft. The name reminds us how small this country is: though in the center of Rotterdam, the area is connected by water to the center of Delft, a couple of miles away. And Delft, for all intents and purposes, is a suburb of The Hague, whose suburbs blend into those of Leiden, which is quite close to Haarlem—a city that, by train, is around fifteen minutes from Central Station in Amsterdam.

In another Dutch city, this canal would not attract much attention. In Rotterdam, it comes as a relief. It has galleries and cafés and that human scale that makes the cities of Holland so pleasant. And on the quayside is a church with a brown brick façade, indistinguishable from thousands of others in this country. This is the Pelgrimvaderskerk, a word that, like many composite Dutch words, initially daunts the foreign eye, but in which, broken into its three parts, the English speaker can distinguish the words for Pilgrim Fathers' Church. Besides this name and a cartouche in one of the stained-glass windows, nothing suggests the drama that this church witnessed four centuries ago: the departure of the Pilgrims for the New World on July 22, 1620.

Standing on the quay in front of the church on a blustery, dark day, looking down the canal that leads to the river and then to the sea, one can easily imagine the courage of these people boarding their leaky ship and heading to an unknown continent. This is how William Bradford described the scene in *Of Plymouth Plantation*, his record of the establishment of Massachusetts:

And yᵉ time being come that they must departe, they were accompanied with most of their brethren out of yᵉ citie, unto a towne sundrie miles of called Delfes-Haven, wher the ship lay ready to receive them. So they lefte yᵗ goodly & pleasante citie, which had been ther resting place near 12. years; but they knew they were pilgrimes, & looked not much on those things, but lift up their eyes to yᵉ heavens, their dearest cuntrie, and quieted their spirits. When they came to yᵉ place they found yᵉ ship and all things ready; and shuch of their freinds as could not come with them followed after them, and sundrie also came from Amsterdame to see them shipte and to take their leave of them. That night was spent with litle sleepe by yᵉ most, but with freindly entertainmente & christian discourse and other reall expressions of true christian love. The next day, the wind being faire, they wente aborde, and their freinds with them, where truly dolfull was yᵉ sight of that sade and mournfull parting; to see what sighs and sobbs and praires did sound amongst them, what tears did gush from every eye, & pithy speeches peirst each harte; that sundry of yᵉ Dutch strangers yᵗ stood on yᵉ key as spectators, could not refraine from tears. Yet comfortable & sweete it was to see shuch lively and true expressions of clear & unfained love. But the tide (which stays for no man) caling them away yᵗ were thus loath to departe, their Revẽᵈ: pastor falling downe on his knees, (and they all with him,) with watrie cheeks commẽended them with most fervente praiers to the Lord and his blessing. And then with mutuall imbrases and many tears, they tooke their leaves one of an other; which proved to be yᵉ last leave to many of them.

They boarded the *Speedwell* and went first to England, where they met another ship, the *Mayflower*, at Southampton. Soon after departing for America, the *Speedwell* proved unseaworthy, and the party returned to England. The ship was repaired and set out again; *Mayflower* and *Speedwell* returned, one more time, to England, where the group decided to abandon the *Speedwell* and crowd onto the *Mayflower*. The party's history was summed up by a nineteenth-century senator who greeted Bradford's manuscript, looted during the Revolutionary War, upon its return to Massachusetts.

There is nothing like it in human annals since the story of Bethlehem. These Englishmen and English women going out from their homes in beautiful Lincoln and York, wife separated from husband and mother from child in that hurried embarkation for Holland, pursued to the beach by English horsemen; the thirteen years of exile; the life at Amsterdam "in alley foul and lane obscure;" the dwelling at Leyden; the embarkation at Delfthaven; the farewell of Robinson; the terrible voyage across the Atlantic; the compact in the harbor; the landing on the rock; the dreadful first winter; the death roll of more than half the number; the days of suffering and of famine; the wakeful night, listening for the yell of wild beast and the war-whoop of the savage; the building of the State on those sure foundations which no wave or tempest has ever shaken; the breaking of the new light; the dawning of the new day; the beginning of the new life; the enjoyment of peace with liberty,—of all these things this is the original record by the hand of our beloved father and founder.

This story is little known today. The places associated with it are not much visited by Americans: in all my years in the

Netherlands, no American friend has ever expressed any interest in seeing the church, or—unless I mention it—known it was there. The same goes for the other American monuments in Holland, particularly the Pieterskerk in Leiden, where the Pilgrims worshipped and where John Robinson, their pastor, lies buried. Beyond elementary school Thanksgivings, the story of the Pilgrims has vanished from popular memory; but to read Bradford is to be filled with wonder at the daring, the determination, the idealism of these founders. It is to realize, no matter whether we ourselves descend from the *Mayflower* party, that all Americans inhabit the world they created. For the American writer, it is to see a story and an author that are hopelessly intimidating. The senator who believed the story to be the greatest since Bethlehem was not far off: what more consequential event has there been in modern history than the English colonization of North America, and the establishment of the government that descends from the Mayflower Compact? The Pilgrims reached Cape Cod four years after the death of Shakespeare: what modern writer can equal the grandeur of Bradford's language?

Of Plymouth Plantation is the first immigrant memoir, and all subsequent tellers of such tales struck the same notes. From that first group came the idea of the immigrant as pilgrim. The person who came to America was going somewhere else and, over the course of that journey, becoming someone else, seeking, in Roger Williams's words, "to take off that bond and yoke of soul oppression."

TODAY, to an eye used to Dutch cities, the buildings in Delfshaven do not look especially old. By Italian standards, they would be almost modern. But so much had happened since the *Speedwell* that it did not bear thinking about. Like standing in one of Brazil's gigantic cities and imagining it as a tropical forest dotted with isolated plantations and inhabited by mamelukes and

Tapuyas, standing in Delfshaven and trying to imagine the world the Pilgrims came from, trying to imagine the world they went to—trying to imagine how entirely the world had been turned upside down since—is nearly impossible. You walk on the stones they walked on, pray in the church they prayed in; but too much has happened since.

It did not bear thinking about how distant the Pilgrims' destination would have been, how dangerous their journey, how final their farewells. I felt a bit ashamed that so little was asked of me. A few hours reading or napping or watching a movie and I was back in the old New World. The only peril was jet lag. I often thought about the Pilgrims whenever I felt annoyed that my bags were delayed, or that there was a line for a taxi at Kennedy Airport. It was so easy; I could live on one continent, and work on another. Yet over the years I spent in the Netherlands, America, which was so close by, kept moving further out of reach. The ease of travel and communication masked this, to a certain extent; but the country I grew up in had changed, and it was hard to feel good about these changes. Some, however depressing, seemed reversible. Others did not. Still, time passes, and one might feel lucky to have lived at a time of expansion and prosperity—a time when things seemed to be improving.

And: the close of one age is the opening of another. By the end of the seventeenth century, Holland seemed finished. In a way it was; in a way it wasn't. The art that had marked its Golden Age would transform into something else, and its great tradition would perdure because of the commitment of certain people— often isolated and eccentric people—to their own cultural tradition, to a vision of what it had been at its best, and not at its worst. When I was depressed about how things were going in my country, I thought of two painters who carried their tradition into a new century in an apparently unlikely way.

One painted fruit. The other painted flowers.

16

RACHEL RUYSCH

My Manly Art Heroine

I N ST. PETERSBURG, in a toothpaste-green palace along the Neva, is one of the spookiest relics of the Dutch Golden Age. It was not intended to be weird. When acquired by Peter the Great in 1717 for thirty thousand guilders, the collection that would form the heart of Russia's first museum, the Kunstkamera, was the *dernier* scientific *cri*—a symbol of the ambition of the new, Dutch-inspired capital that Peter had founded fourteen years before.

The tsar visited Holland twice. On his first visit, in 1697, he knocked on the door of a little wooden house in Zaandam. He told the man who opened it that his name was Peter Mikhailov, and that he was seeking work as a shipbuilder. But in that small town a handsome, moustachioed, six-foot-eight Russian had trouble remaining inconspicuous, and after only eight days in the house he retreated to Amsterdam.

He stayed four months, acquiring the knowledge he needed to build a new navy. He also acquired a model for St. Petersburg, a city of canals in a swampy northern delta that he was planning as part of his forced modernization of Russia. While in Amsterdam, he took a keen interest in public executions—he would later order his own son tortured and killed for attempting to defect—and, in his off-hours, toured the local tourist attractions.

One was the Museum Ruyschiana. Located in the Ruysch family's house on the Bloemgracht—if they know where to look, the house can be seen by visitors waiting to tour the Anne Frank House—Frederik Ruysch's collections attracted tourists from across the continent. Europe boasted many private collections that were open to the public. What was exceptional about Dr. Ruysch's was the subject of its collections: dead bodies.

Dr. Ruysch had many claims to scientific fame. One of the most energetic personalities of the age—at ninety he was still rushing to finish volume twelve of his *Thesaurus anatomicus*—he was renowned for discovering how to make corpses look as if, rather than dead, they were quietly sleeping. His skill astounded visitors. According to legend, the tsar was so moved by one embalmed infant that he kissed it.

Dr. Ruysch's tools were a special syringe and a secret formula that included talc and black pepper. He preserved some bodies in liquid; but

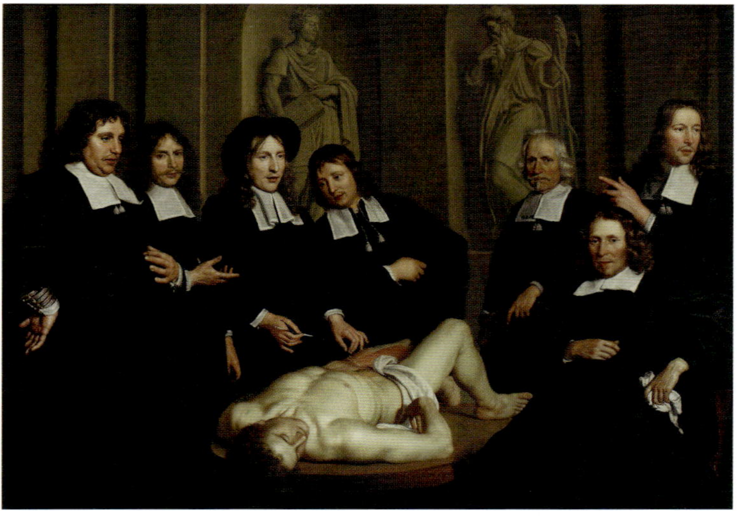

Compare Adriaen Backer's Anatomy Lesson of Frederick Ruysch *(third from left) to Rembrandt's wrenching pictures of the same subject: Ruysch was famous for his ability to make the dead look alive.*

such was the excellence of his method that he could leave some, like the baby the tsar kissed, out in the clammy Amsterdam air. And rather than displaying these bodies as anatomical examples—among his other positions, he was the city anatomist—he displayed them as works of art.

Today, when we have circumscribed the display of human remains with complex ethical considerations, it is hard to know how to respond to Dr. Ruysch's intricate displays. Did these people, for example, consent to being displayed in such a way? Surely not: in old age, Dr. Ruysch confessed that, when he was a beginning anatomist, he asked gravediggers to assist his studies by providing him with fresh corpses.

———

BUT THOSE ETHICAL CONSIDERATIONS, which postdate Dr. Ruysch by a couple of centuries, weren't what I was thinking about when I walked through the Kunstkamera, where so many of Dr. Ruysch's specimens still float in formaldehyde. I wasn't, in fact, thinking. I was feeling: queasiness, revulsion—the same feeling I get even from reading descriptions of his anatomical displays. For example:

> a group of three four-month-old aborted fetal skeletons placed upon a pyramidal mountain of biological material including: canine teeth, molars, kidney and gallstones, an embalmed human bladder, tarsals and metatarsals from a woman's foot, embalmed blood vessels which resemble trees, and a stuffed bird. The skeleton on the right is in a pose of mourning, wiping its blank eye-socket with a piece of embalmed lung-tissue which looks like a handkerchief.

Maybe—not maybe—I have a weak stomach. I should be able to look at these bodies without disgust. They don't look alive after three hundred years. It's not a freak show. Although anatomical oddballs are on display in the Petersburg museum, they come from other collections, not Dr. Ruysch's. Whatever these people suffered is long over. And, I tell myself, it's magical to see people who might have seen Rembrandt.

If Dr. Ruysch's specimens attract and repel, that is because anatomy itself attracts and repels. We all have felt the fascination of seeing—preferably in others—the tissue and nerves of which we are made. We badly want to see inside ourselves. We want, even more badly, to forget that what we see there is all we really are.

There was something else that made it hard to know how to look at these specimens. The hardest thing was seeing them as things of beauty, as works of art, the way they were seen in Dr. Ruysch's time. His elaborate still-lifes—never did the term for this art in the Latin languages, "dead nature," seem so apt—placed him somewhere between science and art. It was easy to see him as a scientist. But it was hard, at least for me, to see him as an artist.

Yet what is art except the meaning we append to that assemblage of veins and hairs that we call ourselves, our lives? We know not whence we come nor why; why we go, nor where. Only art gives the illusion that we are more than animal. Ruysch's aestheticization of the stuff we are made of—a bit of lung made into a fancy kerchief—is too explicit, too confrontational. It shows us how absurd art is. And it shows us why we need it.

SHORTLY BEFORE HER DEATH, Dr. Ruysch's daughter Rachel gave an interview to an artist named Jan van Gool, who was compiling an encyclopedia of the artists of the first part of the eighteenth century. Rachel Ruysch was—barely—a rare survivor of the Golden Age that is commonly reckoned to have ended in the disastrous year of 1672. She was born in 1664, five years before Rembrandt's death, and died in 1750, the year of the publication of Van Gool's book, which she presumably never saw.

Van Gool fell for Rachel. She showed him a painting done when she was eighty, and a gift of silverware that she had received from the Elector Palatine. He, in turn, gave her an extraordinary amount of space, exhausting his supply of adjectives. She was "our *Amsterdam* PALLAS," "the immortal Minerva," "the Flower-goddess," "one of the

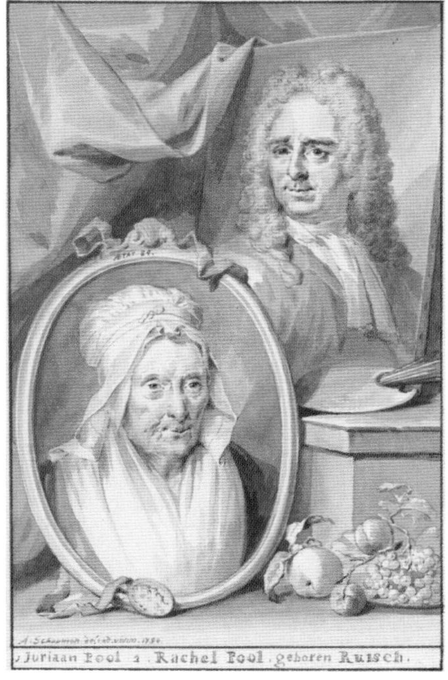

Rachel Ruysch at eighty-four, alongside her husband Juriaan Pool: they had ten children, and she was most productive in her fertile years.

greatest Artists of the known world"—and—a high compliment—"my manly Art Heroine."

Her life had been extraordinary. Her father was one of the most eminent scientists in Europe. Her mother's family, too, was illustrious: Rachel's grandfather, Pieter Post, built many of the greatest buildings of the Golden Age, from splendid palaces—Huis ten Bosch, the current residence of the king; Noordeinde, the royal "work palace"—to the most superlative and emblematic building of the age, the Amsterdam City Hall.

Pieter seems to have journeyed to Dutch Recife around 1640, where he reputedly built Vrijburg Palace for the governor, Johan Maurits van Nassau-Siegen, who also brought Albert Eckhout to Brazil, and for whom he later built the Mauritshuis. Though Pieter apparently did not stay long, his brother Frans spent seven years in Brazil and became

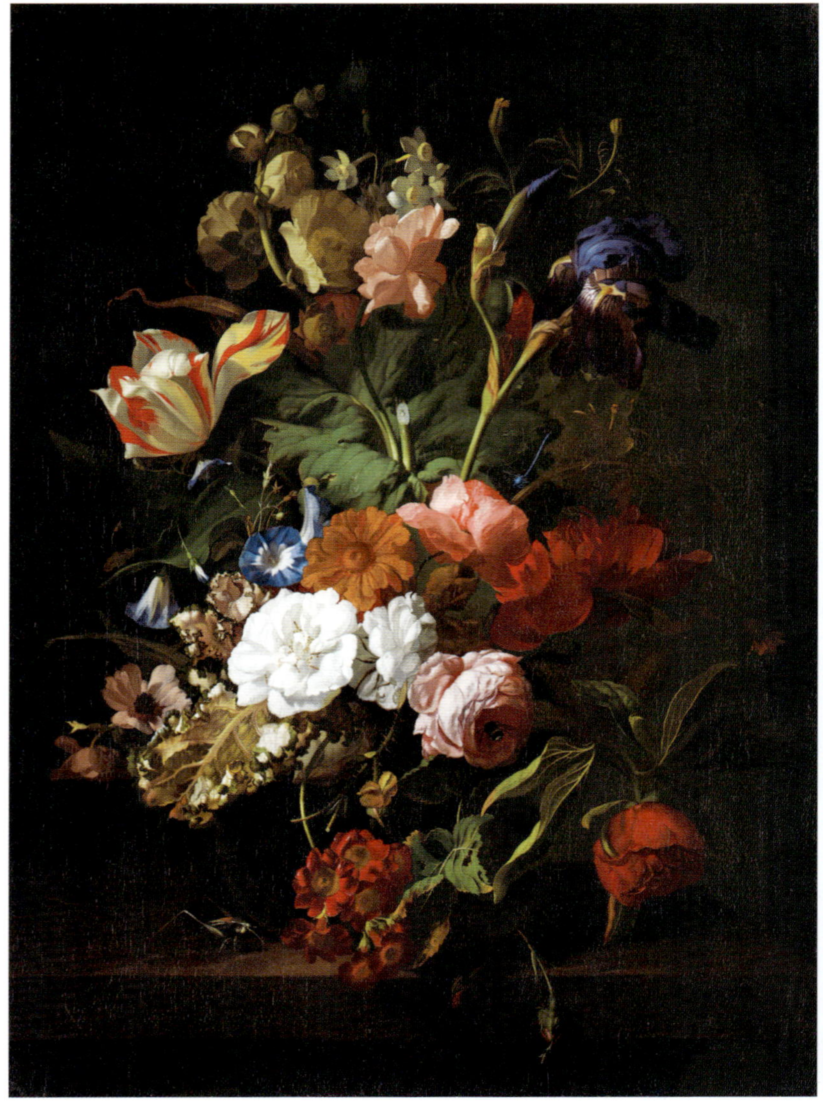

Flowers can be combined in infinite ways, but danger lurks, for the painter, if certain rules are disregarded.

renowned for paintings that incorporated his meticulous observation of that new world. Like Dr. Ruysch, Frans and Pieter Post were part-artist, part-scientist.

This was the heritage Rachel brought to her own specialty, as a painter of flowers. She grew up in the house on the Bloemgracht, where she likely helped her father make his displays. Both an amateur painter as well as the director of the city's botanical garden, her father offered an example of how a painter might extend the same immortality to flowers that he gave to bodies—of how art could bring the dead back to life.

Rachel revealed an aptitude for drawing. Her father understood that "if this natural Art-Fire were stoked by skilled means, and the noble tendance of Nature through wise lessons and rules led and directed, that something great might ensue for his Daughter." He hired Willem van Aelst, who, though louche and prone to drunken braggadocio, was cosmopolitan—he had lived in France and Italy—and a sophisticated painter.

A LOT CAN GO WRONG in an apparently genteel flower painting. The textures of different flowers must be distinguished. Petals must look transparent, and fruit must look fleshy, rather than glassy. Leaves can't be too solid; stone has to be solid enough. Your arrangement, which has nothing natural about it, must at least appear plausible— and not, as sometimes cringingly occurs, on the verge of crashing to the ground.

Likewise, the objects inside the painting must relate. They shouldn't fly off arbitrarily, but neither should they be so close together that they look cluttered. Flowers and leaves should hang, not float, and you can't put the flowers just anywhere, since some colors sharpen their neighbors, and some tone them down. Yellow and red are strong; blue and purple are weak; these harmonies and dissonance make or break your piece.

There are lots of different kinds of flower pieces, too, which are separate from other kinds of still-life, such as *vanitas*, tobacco, hunting, banquet, kitchen, and breakfast pieces. Each has its own difficulties: nature pieces, bouquets, nosegays, fruit pieces, posies, festoons (also known as clusters or bunches), garlands, wreaths, swags, and "pronk" pieces (large, and filled with costly objects like crystal or gold- and silverware).

A certain arrangement of flowers could call forth a wealth of associations. The oldest use of flowers in painting was as religious symbols—a white lily standing for the purity of the Virgin—but by Ruysch's time, flowers were pressed into service to make other suggestions. They might evoke a season, for example, or a certain region, or gather flowers that had a certain perfume, or that, slightly faded, might evoke the passage of time.

There was also a kind of flower painting that evoked danger. In these paintings, small animals are shown eating each other, or about to: a lurking snake snatching an unwitting butterfly. These can be genuinely creepy in a way that straightforward depictions of violence are not, or not quite, since you don't know what you're getting: expecting a lovely bouquet, you find yourself in the middle of a slaughter.

This was the art Rachel was sent to learn. Neither in Van Gool's account nor in anyone else's is the slightest suggestion that her sex was an obstacle. Though flower painting might seem to be a feminine art— "Women certainly delight in flowers beyond the habit of the average male," wrote a Colonel M. H. Grant in an admiring monograph published in 1956—it was, like all the other fine arts at the time, mainly practiced by men.

THERE HAD BEEN Dutch women painters before Ruysch. Some, like Gesina ter Borch, remained amateurs. The Haarlem painter Judith Leyster, a professional, gave up art in her midtwenties when she married a less talented man, Jan Miense Molenaer. Maria van Oosterwijck remained single and childless and rejected a marriage proposal from Ruysch's teacher, Willem van Aelst, in order to focus on her work.

But no Dutch woman ever had Ruysch's glorious career. To read

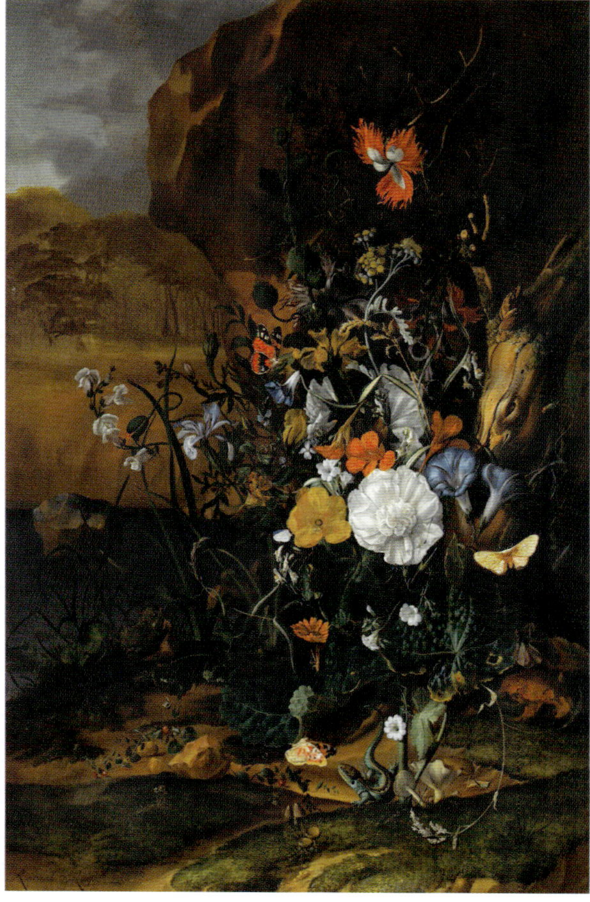

*An early Ruysch "forest floor": flowers shown outside,
in a natural setting, and attended by toads and insects.*

about her in the light of feminist criticism is to feel almost dishonest. Where was the sacrifice, the critical incomprehension, the obscure death, that was the lot of so many creative women: Germaine Greer's obstacle race, Tillie Olsen's forced silence, or the suicide that, Virginia Woolf imagined, awaited a theoretical Judith Shakespeare?

"Why have there been no great women artists?" the art historian Linda Nochlin asked in 1971. In an attempt to answer this question, she and her successors adumbrated the cultural and institutional barriers. The first, and most insuperable, was educational: girls were not encouraged to pursue the same kinds of studies that boys were, and could not count on the same family support that any beginning artist needs.

Another was marriage. Many successful women artists remained single, like Van Oosterwijck, either because they were lesbians ("The chief obstacle to a woman's success is that she can never have a wife," said the American painter Anna Lea Merritt) or because they chose work over family. In 1962, Olsen noted that "in our century as in the last, almost all distinguished achievement has come from childless women."

There were other burdens, too, including the depression that came with stifled creativity. Many, including the fictional Judith Shakespeare and the real Virginia Woolf, opted for suicide; and when the idea that a woman could "have it all"—marriage, family, career—appeared in the last generation, it was often mocked by women who felt that, despite remarkable recent victories, it held out an impossible ideal.

Yet we vainly comb Rachel Ruysch's life for any such obstacles. She was born to rich and cultured parents who offered her every opportunity and encouragement. Rather than staying single, she married a fellow painter, and lived with him for fifty-two happy years. Rather than eschewing motherhood, she had *ten children*—and produced more paintings during her fertile years, 1693 to 1711, than at any other time in her career.

Rather than being ignored, as so many women were, she enjoyed universal critical respect. Her pictures sold for high prices, and she was guaranteed an annual salary of a few thousand guilders by the prince who appointed her a court painter, and whose gift of silver she showed Van Gool at the end of her life. She inherited a fortune. And then, to top it off, she won the lottery: seventy-five thousand guilders, for a ticket that cost her ten.

ONE OF THE MOST spectacular sights in the Netherlands is one that few visitors, Dutch or international, ever see. It is called RoyalFlora Holland, and is located in the colorless suburb of Aalsmeer, right next to Schiphol Airport. At nearly ten million square feet, RoyalFlora is one of the largest buildings in the world. Schiphol is seven million square feet; the colossal Pentagon, by Washington, a mere six and a half million.

This is the flower auction, a legacy of the age when Dutch ships ranged from Australia to Japan, and from Pernambuco to Novaya Zemlya. This is where you come early in the morning—the sales begin at an ungodly hour—to buy ten thousand peonies in a specific light-pink shade that arrived from Addis Ababa an hour before, and that, by nightfall, will be decorating the tables of restaurants in Buenos Aires.

The method of selling at RoyalFlora is called a "Dutch auction." Unlike auctions that begin with a minimum price and climb, Dutch auctions begin high. The first bid is immediately the last, which speeds things along; and as the clocks tick, tick, tick, sales add up to billions. To get to Aalsmeer when things rev up is to become aware of the world-spanning industry behind something as seemingly innocuous as flowers.

This stunning piece of infrastructure has made it hard to imagine how rare and fabulous flowers once were. To us, who have abolished seasons and geography, flower paintings from Ruysch's age look luxurious and beautiful, but they don't look anywhere nearly as exotic, as miraculous, as they would have in her day. The bouquets we see are attractive. But they don't look like emissaries from a distant galaxy.

Yet the great flower paintings are the fruits of the age of Enlightenment that people like Dr. Ruysch incarnated. You might not immediately see the connection between Rachel Ruysch's flower paintings and the dead babies that her father preserved in jars, but both derived from the same source: the study of a natural world that in their time was being revealed by science, by far-flung explorations—and by art.

Her father's position as the director of the Hortus, one of Holland's great attractions—in 1727, Montesquieu said it was "the most beautiful garden I have ever seen"—gave Rachel access to a collection founded when botany, pharmacy, and medicine were not yet separate. It was a collection, the scholar Marianne Berardi has written, that shaped world history. In 1709, for example, under Dr. Ruysch's direction,

> the first batch of coffee plants arrived in the Amsterdam Hortus from Batavia (now Jakarta). It was a plant which was first seen growing wild in the mountains of Ethiopia, and had become known to Arabs in the Middle East, but was unknown to Europeans. The Dutch took to the stimulating drink, and soon coffee houses were springing up all over Amsterdam. In 1714 Mayor Pancras made a visit to Louis XIV and brought coffee plants to him as a royal gift. These were cultivated in the royal gardens of Paris and within ten years Paris had over 400 coffee houses, even more than in Amsterdam. Cuttings from the plants which were the Dutch gift to Louis XIV were later shipped to the governor of French Guiana in South America. His wife, in turn, made a gift of small plants grown in Guiana to an estate in Brazil. Thus was Brazil first introduced to coffee and coffee to Brazil, now the world's leading coffee-producing country.

One purpose of this institution, which still exists, was to produce botanical illustrations, an activity to which women made notable contributions. The best known of these artists was Maria Sibylla Merian, born in Germany, who met Dr. Ruysch when she moved to Amsterdam in 1691. With his help, she got money to travel to the Dutch colony of Suriname, where she and her daughter journeyed "without a man's protection."

Though malaria forced her to return to Europe earlier than planned, she nonetheless came back, like Pieter Saenredam from Utrecht, with enough material to keep her busy for the rest of her life. In her work, botanical illustration reached a zenith. Her books, which recall the work of John James Audubon more than a century later, are among the most

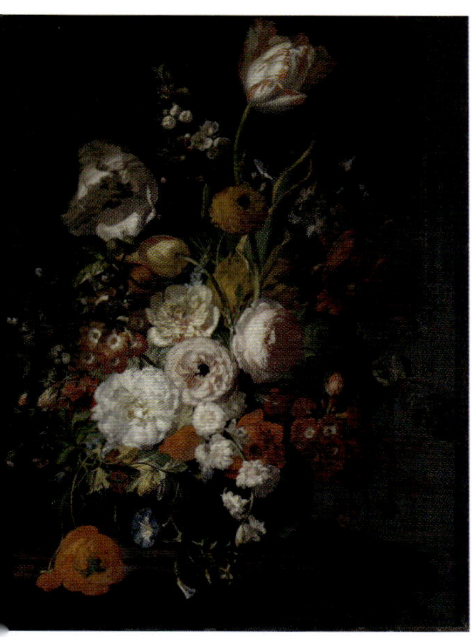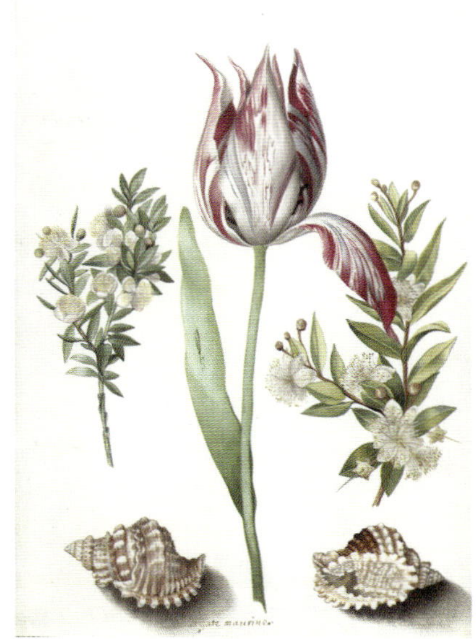

*In the works of Maria Sybilla Merian and Rachel Ruysch, a similar
red-and-white tulip takes on a very different meaning.*

magnificent ever published in Amsterdam, and showed plants as well
as insects.

Insects had fascinated Merian since childhood. In her works, she
took each through its metamorphoses and showed them alongside their
natural predators: "Every one of her paintings depicts a drama in min-
iature," wrote the nineteenth-century French naturalist Louis Figuier.
"Next to the frightened and suspicious insect one can see an avid lizard
waiting patiently, or a ferocious spider weaving its sinister snare."

Yet as gorgeous (and theatrical) as Merian's works are, they are fundamentally different from the works of the younger Ruysch. Merian
belongs recognizably to the tradition of scientific illustration; Ruysch, to
the tradition of fine art. Ruysch drew on the tradition in which her father

and Merian worked, but her works, rather than designed to be consulted in a book, were painted on canvas, and meant to be hung on walls.

Paintings like hers derived from scientific research. They were extracted from illustrations like Merian's, or from botanical collections like Dr. Ruysch's. "Atlases" collected, described, and cataloged flowers, antique inscriptions, shells. And in these books—some of which survive—we see an optimistic moment, when scientists and artists were democratizing the knowledge that had previously belonged to a tiny elite.

RACHEL RUYSCH'S ACHIEVEMENT was to turn science into art. In an age when flowers are flown in by the hundreds of thousands, we no longer see how rare the blooms were, and—as we no longer see the art in her father's anatomical preparations—no longer see the science behind her art. Her work seems beautiful; his seems bizarre; and hers lives because beauty, and not formaldehyde, gives dead things immortality.

In her works, whose quality is remarkably consistent throughout her long life, there are almost no references to science, or to anything else. She never went in for the lugubrious "symbolism" to which so many other painters succumbed. This makes her paintings more intimate than they would be if, in order to understand them now, we had to struggle through explanatory footnotes. The pleasure of her paintings is the pleasure of looking.

The pleasure she transmits to us must be the pleasure that she had in making these paintings. I wondered what kept her going; it is hard for any artist to maintain a career for *seventy years*. Even deep into old age, she remained faithful to the theme, flowers, that had inspired her to pick up a pencil when she was a girl. And she remained faithful to a way of looking that asks us to look at a thing—and see no more than that thing.

How did she keep her eye fresh? How does anyone, for that matter, keep up their enthusiasm? Even as I type it, I know this is the wrong question. I have interviewed hundreds of old people, and I've discovered that it's not the person that keeps up the enthusiasm but the enthusiasm that keeps up the person: the eighty-year-old who loves painting also loved it when she was thirty or fifty or seventy.

Van Gool, in one of the first interviews with a Dutch artist that has come down to us, found a personality I recognize. "She is, as I write, a Woman of 84 years, possessing her mind and eyesight, for a Woman of that great age"—an age that was much more extraordinary then than it would be now—"still wondrously well." She showed him "six Pieces from her best period," and something she painted when she was eighty.

"She also showed me a small Piece from the year 1747," he wrote, "that was just begun, and which she still intended to complete, yet, as it then seemed to me, if this appeared less skillful than the previous ones, that's no surprise! since there's not one in a thousand, who having reached this great age, can carry out even common tasks, and much less create such elevated Art." He concluded with a poem in her praise.

———

IN LONDON'S NATIONAL GALLERY is a perspective box painted by Rembrandt's pupil Samuel van Hoogstraten. It is the kind of invention that Fabritius might have made. When viewed through a peephole, the scene becomes a perfectly three-dimensional view of a Dutch house, a mix of science and art so incredible that you might overlook the Latin inscription on the outside. "Amoris Causa," "Lucri Causa," "Gloriae Causa." These are the artist's motivations: love, money, glory.

The art historian Elizabeth Alice Honig has written that "it is almost a standard line" that artistic women did not have the same motives for making art as men: "Women paint from a pure love of art." If this was often a way of dismissing women as amateurs, this motive, "Amoris Causa," is also what one feels in the presence of the professional Rachel Ruysch, and why her paintings still look fresh today.

Cyril Connolly asked how one could write a book that would last ten years. A decade is more than enough time to consign most books to oblivion. And the evolution of language means that even those that do last eventually become hard for modern speakers to read. In English and French, which are conservative in matters of spelling and lexicon, it seems to take around two and a half centuries. In Portuguese, for example, books more than 150 years old are rarely read.

In Dutch, for a variety of reasons, including an accumulation of spelling reforms, and because of an educational system that has traditionally placed more emphasis on teaching foreign languages than on cultivating the national language, literature ages even more quickly. I have heard that even books from before the Second World War can't be assigned, since students can't be presumed to understand the language easily.

The cutoff feels about right. The Dutch are not nearly as familiar with their own literary tradition as educated speakers of English or French are. The reason seems wrong, though: like every other language, Dutch has changed in the last hundred years, but nineteenth-century Dutch is hardly more unreadable than nineteenth-century English. Still, everywhere, literature eventually passes into the realm of the specialist.

Painting lasts longer. A flower from five hundred years ago doesn't look much different from a flower today. A scene from biblical history that may once have been widely understood will not be so widely understood now. But if it is beautifully painted we don't really care that we don't understand it, just as we don't really care that we don't understand much about the art we enjoy from cultures or epochs distant from our own.

If we understand a flower painting, and if visual arts last longer than language, we know, nonetheless, that not all paintings last, and that pictures of flowers last less than most. There are too many of them, and too many are ugly or—putting it generously—decorative. Because of their quantity—because of the sheer numbers of people who try their hands at them—these paintings face tougher odds than most.

This is because flower paintings show a quality more clearly, perhaps, than other paintings. We might need an artist to show us the banquet of Esther and Ahasuerus. But we don't need an artist to show us flowers: unlike languages, they haven't changed much, and because they are so much more widely available than they were in Ruysch's time, we've probably seen all the flowers she included in her work.

So why look at her paintings? There is a misunderstanding about photography (and, for that matter, about biography) that I have often had occasion to observe. In photography, people often believe that they are seeing a subject. Yet if you look at a photograph of the same person by Annie Leibovitz, Henri Cartier-Bresson, and Richard Avedon, you instantly notice that the sitter is almost irrelevant. What you see is the photographer.

When you look at a vase of flowers painted by Picasso, or Van Gogh, or Manet, you are not seeing the flowers; you are not even interested in the flowers. You are interested in Picasso, Van Gogh, or Manet, whose personalities, no matter what the subject, come through so clearly. If a flower painting is to last, the flowers must be incidental. You must feel—as in Rachel Ruysch's paintings—the hand, the soul, that painted them.

17

ADRIAEN COORTE

Art Is

WHEN I WAS SIXTEEN and attending an American school in France, an artist led our class into a musty basement several times a week to teach us art history. The teacher, Jean-Philippe Lemée, deployed images—of Duchamp's urinals, for example—bound to excite teenagers, though he was at his best when revealing the mysteries lurking behind works that would not have immediately attracted our inexperienced eyes. I remember his exposé of a picture, *The Ray*, by the eighteenth-century painter Jean-Siméon Chardin. An attacking cat, its back arched, its tail raised, intruded on a ledge bearing some usual implements of the still-life: a jug, a protruding knife, a few oysters. Above the whole, impaled on a hook, a grimacing ray fish's side was ripped open to reveal its hemorrhaging organs.

The right half of the picture was homey; the left half shockingly violent. The border between the two passed neatly down the middle of the martyred fish. The image was so powerful that it demanded some kind of explanation. Jean-Philippe, after minutely leading us through its possible symbolic content, offered one. He returned to the painting's title, *La Raie*.

La raie? he asked. Or—a dramatic pause—*L'art est?*

AT THE BEGINNING OF his career, Chardin's decision to devote his visibly great ability to an inferior genre was considered exasperating. "Though they are very good, and promise even better," one critic impatiently allowed, "if the author made them his occupation, the public would despair at seeing him abandon, and even neglect, an original talent and an inventive brush to devote himself out of complacency to a genre that has become too vulgar."

The suggestion of the painter's indolence and the genre's tackiness indicates that still-life, even deep into the eighteenth century, was for the unambitious or the semitalented, appealing to the kind of unadventurous people who would buy pictures to match their sofas. After all, one needed no advanced religious or classical education, no particular erudition, to appreciate a spray of flowers or a plateful of fruit. And the rather common things still-life portrayed, even when splendid, tended to mean that the wrong people liked it.

In 1779, the year Chardin died, Goethe's friend Johann Heinrich Merck rallied to the genre in terms that left the underlying assumption intact:

> People so often laugh at the taste of our German collectors, when they, as is said, are enthralled by lowly objects, staring in wonder at a crab, a Roemer glass, a well-painted napkin, a bunch of grapes or a peach. Yet those good people are quite right. They are delighted by what they understand. They can judge the form of a glass, and nothing escapes them about the shape of the peach, if it is wrong in any particular.

Merck's suggestion that the appeal of still-life lies in its sheer unintimidating ordinariness, in its perfect suitability to the discriminating eye of "our German collectors," does little to elevate the poor still-life painter. Comfortable, bourgeois, boring: Merck might just as well have been writing about the pictures that a later day's comfortable, boring bourgeoisie admired, the Monets and the Renoirs that, where I came from, defined no-risk good taste.

Of course, Merck was partly right. Sometimes a cigar is just a cigar. Sometimes the value of a still-life may reside in nothing more than sheer mechanical skill. But standing before *La Raie*, we immediately know that there is something else, even if we can't quite say what, beyond the artist's obvious technical mastery, or even its strange violence, so apparently out of place in a still-life: something jarring that cannot be accounted for by its individual parts.

DESPITE DEFENSES LIKE Merck's, and despite the evident popularity of their works, even the most eminent still-life painters had to wait a remarkably long time for serious critical recognition. It was not until around 1930, at the same time that Clara Welcker was excavating Hendrick Avercamp from the Kampen archives, that the genre began to be looked at as something more than decoration. This belated attention was largely due to a few freelancers, one of whom, Laurens-Jan Bol, a schoolteacher in Middelburg, a little town near the Dutch border with Belgium, threw himself passionately into the study of the art of his native province of Zeeland.

In his writings, Bol comes across as a tireless enthusiast. His articles and books bubble with missionary zeal, and indeed it is thanks to him that many artists who now sit securely at the center of the Dutch canon got there in the first place. Unlike Merck, Bol and others like him no longer saw still-life as an amusement but as a worthy branch of art in its own right.

Perhaps his proudest discovery was of Adriaen Coorte, an artist obscure even by the standards of the still-life painters of hoary Zeeland. Bol came to think of Coorte as his "foster son"—an emotional attachment all the stronger because Bol's struggle on his behalf was so protracted. He rummaged the Netherlands in search of Coorte's work, poring over almost two centuries' worth of Middelburg sales catalogs and turning up a solitary shred of documentary evidence of the

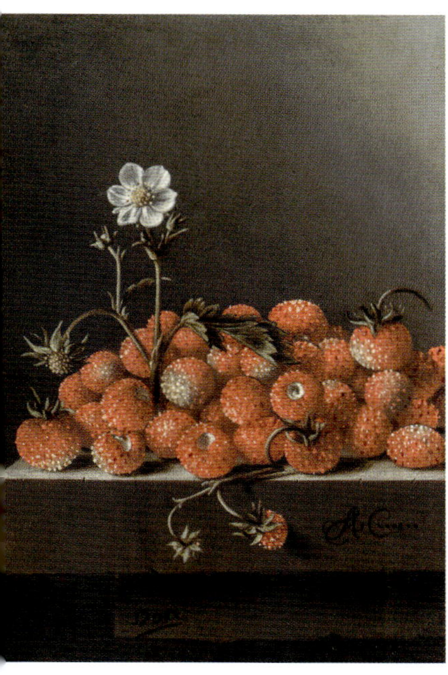

Forgotten or dismissed as folk art, Coorte's tiny still-lifes would later inspire passions.

painter's life at the end of the seventeenth century, twenty-one ambiguous words in the records of the St. Luke's Guild of Middelburg.

Bol's preliminary study was complete by 1949. But when he tried to publish the fruit of his labors in the august *Netherlands Art History Yearbook*, it was rejected: a member of the editorial staff objected to a piece about a "dilettante." Three years later, the article finally appeared; and in 1958, Bol, who had left Middelburg to direct a museum in Dordrecht, had the satisfaction of putting together the first exhibition dedicated to Coorte.

In his book on the artist, Bol, like a loving parent, traces the higher prices (in the nineteenth century, Coorte's paintings could be had for fifty or seventy-five cents); the inclusion in international exhibitions ("2 out of a total of 127 still lifes from diverse centuries and countries" in the Paris still-life show of 1952 were by Coorte, Bol raved: "That was more than acknowledgment, it was acclamation"); and the consecration by great museums (he entered the Museum Boymans in Rotterdam in 1960, the Louvre in 1969) that his dogged efforts had brought his foster son.

In 2008, Adriaen Coorte received the highest honor the Dutch museum world can bestow: a monographic exhibition in the Mauritshuis. Laurens-Jan Bol, who died in 1994 at the age of ninety-six, did not live to see it.

THE STORY OF Adriaen Coorte since his rediscovery has not been an undiluted triumph. In 1960, for example, only two years after Bol's show in Dordrecht, the Hague Gemeentemuseum unburdened itself of a piece bequeathed twenty-eight years before, a little bowl of strawberries that was said to reek of folk art. But it is safe to assume that much of Coorte's halting, ambiguous reception has to do less with the quality of his work than with the doubts surrounding the genre he chose to work in.

From 1747, when a critic accused Chardin of laziness, to 1909— when the Netherlands Archaeological Society noted that "even many members of art clubs think very little of still-lifes"— the genre always seemed a bit prosaic. Its primary appeal, after all, was not to the mind but to the eye. Clever and refined allusion to older stories always ranked higher in the hierarchy of painting. Part of this was due, of course, to snobbery. People who might not grasp complex religious or classical allusions—"our German collectors"—could surely understand a beautifully rendered breakfast table.

Still-life just seemed too obvious, too easy. Few weekend watercolorists try their hand at the rape of Europa, or have a go at the Annunciation. But anyone can plunk some daffodils into a vase, and everyone has a vegetable lying around the kitchen. The copying of everyday objects seems like a logical starting point, a practice run, before an artist works himself up to weightier subjects.

Though perfectly fine for beginners—or for women like Rachel Ruysch—these subjects were hardly adequate for a promising young man. This is what the critic prodding the young Chardin to get on with it already was saying: devoting oneself to still-life was to "abandon, and even neglect, an original talent."

Yet this is a compliment in disguise. By Chardin's day, still-life had flourished to the point that it could be spoken of as an inevitability. It was easy to forget that only a couple of centuries before, the genre, and the new and difficult conception of art that it heralded, had been unimaginable.

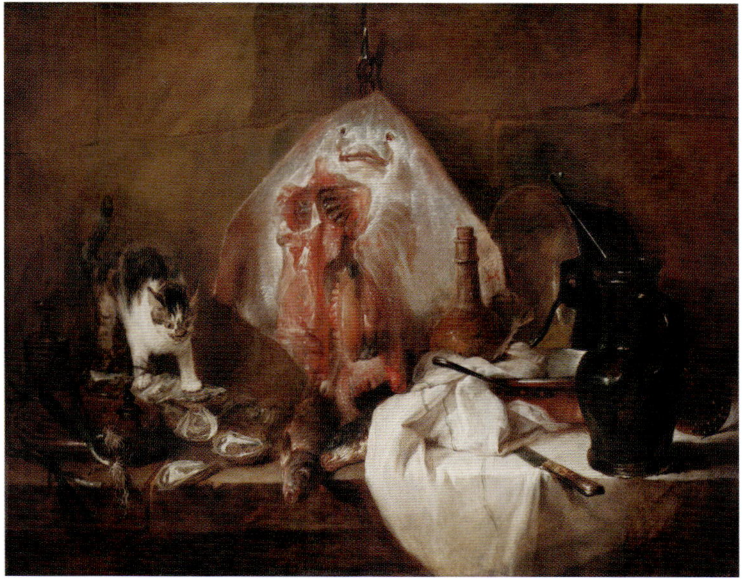

In The Ray, *Chardin revealed the full monumental potential of the
still-life—alongside its underlying creepiness.*

FOR ALMOST A THOUSAND YEARS, three genres practiced in
antiquity—landscape, portraiture, and still-life—disappeared, along
with so much of what the Romans would have recognized as civilization. By the ninth century, cows were grazing in the Roman Forum, and
the demise of the old Roman arts was so complete that the very notion
of portraiture had vanished. No portrait we would recognize as such—a
roughly accurate impression of either physiognomy or personality—
exists even of a person as famous as Charlemagne.

The rebirth of the Roman genres would have to await the reap-
pearance of the Western cities. Shortly before 1350, the first known
independent painted portrait, an anonymous panel showing "Jehan roy
de France," was created, perhaps in Paris. Hundreds of miles away, at

Siena, Ambrogio Lorenzetti revived landscape. Miraculously enough, after the interval of a millennium, his gigantic (forty-six-foot-long) picture of *The Well-Governed City* appeared almost the same year as the portrait of the king, around 1340.

Completing the trio, in yet another place—but, again, at almost exactly the same time—still-life was reborn when Giotto's pupil Taddeo Gaddi, in 1337 or 1338, painted a niche with bread, a plate, a jug, and a couple of vases on a wall of the Church of Santa Croce in Florence. Nowhere is the notion of "Renaissance" more immediately visible. Standing before these works, we can see, ever so tentatively, the rebirth of the old civilization.

Yet these beginnings were fragile, and for a long while these forms struggled to establish themselves. Illusionistic trompe l'œils like Taddeo's notwithstanding, most of what we recognize as the ancestors of the still-life do not really show objects for their own sake but objects that represent something outside themselves. When the Bruges artist Hans Memling painted a vase of lilies on the back of a portrait in the early 1480s, he was showing a famous symbol of the Virgin.

But objects were starting to emerge as a worthy genre in their own right. In the sixteenth century, the Netherlandish painter Pieter Aertsen, for example, still included a tiny token *Flight into Egypt* in a picture of a butcher's stall. But the religious scene is a wobbly little excuse for the glorious still-life. Soon after, in Aertsen's Netherlands, still-life finally shook off the religious picture and became a full-fledged category of its own. The capital of the new art was Antwerp.

———

THE DUTCH REVOLT, which began in 1566, was not kind to Antwerp. The city, the most important in the Netherlands, fell into Spanish hands in 1585. In 1648, a major condition of the peace that ended the Eighty Years' War—decided at the conference that Gerard ter Borch painted—was the continued blockade of the River Scheldt. Closing Antwerp's port was as effective as sowing salt in the fields of Carthage. The population was more than halved. Most of its refugees, like Frans Hals and his family, headed north.

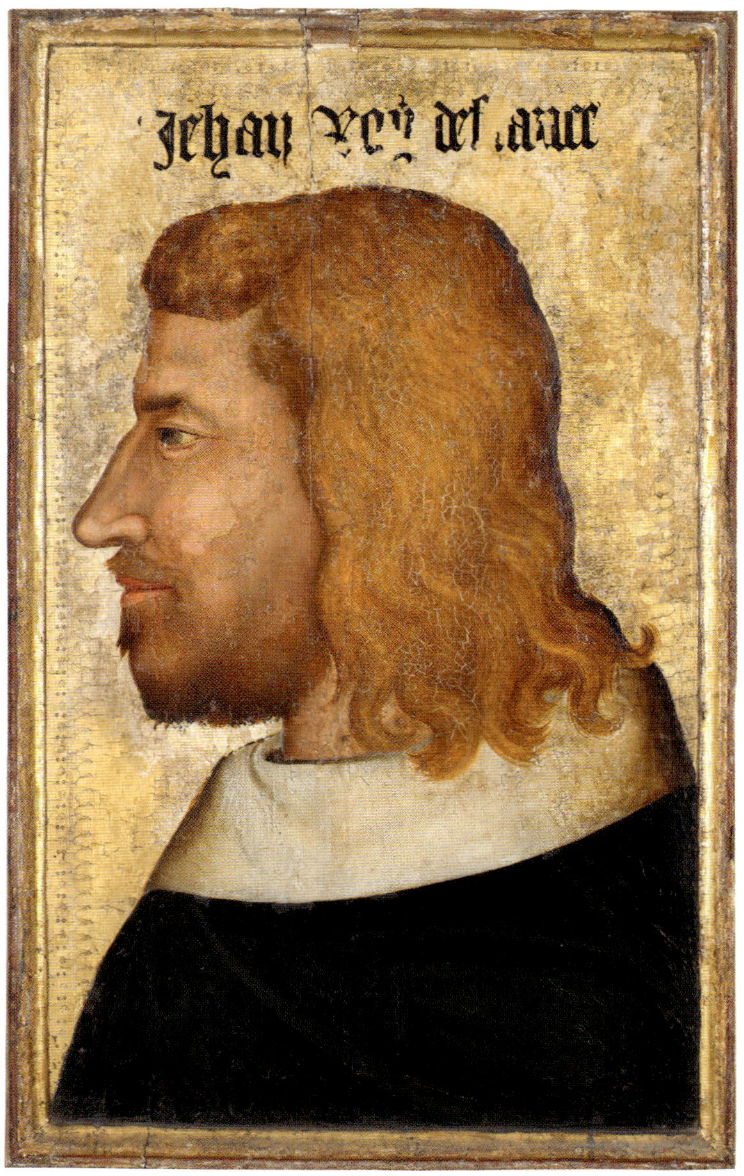

Painted in the middle of the fourteenth century, this picture of the King of France was the first portrait created in a thousand years, made in Paris at almost exactly the same time as the ancient arts of landscape and still-life were being revived in Italy.

With the influx from Flanders, hitherto middling cities—Haarlem, Leiden, and especially Amsterdam—became proud capitals. One town, Middelburg, was especially well placed to profit from the closure of the Scheldt. In the middle of the island of Walcheren, which commands the river's mouth, Middelburg, capital of the province of Zeeland, is less than an hour's drive west of Antwerp.

Its zenith came with the blockade of Antwerp. The hardy Zeelanders, whose navigational daring had done so much to win the war against Spain, left their mark across the globe. The Roosevelt family of New York came from Zeeland; the islands of New Zealand, almost twenty thousand kilometers away, were named for the once humble province. For a while, Middelburg, after Amsterdam, was the second port of the Dutch Republic.

These days, you don't hear much about Middelburg, even in the Netherlands. It has the slightly musty appeal of places where time has stood still. Fields can be seen from the park that replaced its old walls, and you can walk around the city's circumference in a leisurely half hour. In this languid place, the mind turns, like Laurens-Jan Bol's, to the contrast between its present slumber and the dozen towers shimmering atop its massive central abbey.

"Behold the memorable grave of the Spanish people," shout the great jeweled tapestries preserved in Middelburg Abbey; but even by Adriaen Coorte's day the heroic days of Middelburg, and of the Dutch Republic, were in the past.

⸺

ALMOST NOTHING IS known about Coorte's life.

(That phrase again!)

He was born in IJzendijke, in the southern part of Zeeland, now within walking distance of the Belgian border, between 1659 and 1664, when the painters associated with the Dutch Golden Age, like the Golden Age itself, were dying: Hals in 1666, Rembrandt in 1669, Vermeer in 1675. He inherited some land. His signed works are dated from 1683 to 1707. Around 1680, Coorte seems to have studied with the painter Melchior d'Hondecoeter in Amsterdam.

His parents were well off. The country, however, was not. In 1673, following the Year of Disasters of 1672, when the Dutch Republic was invaded by four enemy powers, one Amsterdam art dealer, declaring bankruptcy, noted that prices of everything, "especially paintings and such rarities have greatly declined and slumped in value, as a result of these disastrous times and the miserable state of our beloved Fatherland."

When Vermeer died two years later, his widow testified that "her husband during the war with the king of France and the next years, had been able to earn very little, or almost nothing, so that the works of art" he left behind had to be sold off to feed their children. The country would never again be a first-rank power; and by the time Coorte

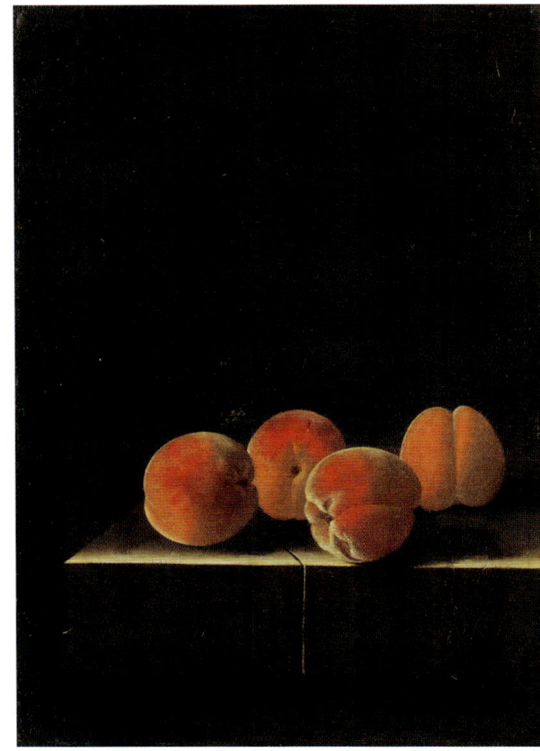

Coorte infused fruit and vegetables with the mystic emotions that explicitly religious paintings often failed to evoke.

headed to Amsterdam, he would have been aware that the prospects for a young painter were not nearly as bright as for a man of his talents a generation before.

Hondecoeter, Coorte's presumed teacher, was a bird painter, but when Coorte's earliest pictures are placed beside the work of the master that inspired them, one personal tendency—toward simplification—is immediately obvious. Hondecoeter's busy canvases groan under a mind-boggling quantity of poultry. In a picture of a *Pelican and Ducks in a Mountain Landscape*, probably painted in Amsterdam and closely mod-eled on a painting by his teacher, Coorte omitted at least half of the birds Hondecoeter had included, creating a far less busy composition.

When he returned to Middelburg, Coorte did not enroll in the local painter's guild, which we know from the single surviving piece of docu-mentary evidence of his life that Laurens-Jan Bol discovered: a fine of one Flemish pound paid in 1695–1696 for selling "a number of paintings on the market, not being licensed to do so." Perhaps, having had a bit of money of his own, he didn't feel the need to set up as a professional painter. Or maybe, taking stock of the possibilities in a depressed econ-omy, he had chosen a more secure profession, pursuing in private his idiosyncratic vision: still-lifes, often no larger than a postcard, showing simple objects—berries, asparagus, nuts, shells—arranged on a cracked stone table, against a boundless black background.

BACK IN ZEELAND, Coorte continued to sharpen his focus, tinkering with his still-lifes with a concentration that borders on the obsessive. He fiddled with what looks like the same bunch of asparagus—zooming in and out, toying with the lighting, adding, and then removing, a few cur-rants; now trying them out in combination with an artichoke, now with a bowl of strawberries—for no less than eighteen years.

Coorte was not, at least in Middelburg, authorized to sell his paint-ings. Did he mind? We sense, especially when seeing a large collection of his work together, that a viewer, and a market, were secondary consid-erations, if indeed the artist considered them at all. His intense focus on the bunch of asparagus suggests that his paintings were primarily private attempts to solve aesthetic problems. It is telling that, most unusually for a seventeenth-century artist, Coorte often painted on paper. A modern restorer discovered that one still-life is painted on the back of a receipt from a merchant in Danzig. Other evidence suggests that these paintings on paper were only affixed to canvas or panel many years after they were made.

It seems that when he had a new idea he sketched it out on whatever was nearest to hand; and then, if he liked the results, worked it up into a completed painting, directly atop his original sketch. When seen on their own, his experiments are not always felicitous. At one point, for example, Coorte is exploring the placement of a single butterfly in the air above the objects he has arrayed on his cracked table. He struggles. The butterfly looks inert, immobile, as if tacked onto a taxidermist's board; and then, in another picture, gaining momentum, it seems dangerously near to careening into a bowl of strawberries.

But then Coorte solves the problem with a delicacy that justifies the inclusion of his paintings alongside the works of the great masters of his age. In a picture from a Dutch private collection, the butterfly hovers above three medlars, a rare fruit the color and size of an onion. The arrangement is so flawless that we can only second Laurens-Jan Bol's appraisal: "the Mona Lisa of the late seventeenth century Dutch still-life art."

It is hard to say exactly what makes this painting so perfect. A centimeter higher and the butterfly would seem detached from the rest of the scene, unrelated to the medlars, floating past them irrelevantly. Half an inch lower, it would be crashing in to them. As Coorte has placed it, the butterfly is wafting gently toward the fruit, enhancing, not disturbing, the tranquillity of the scene.

But if the faultless balance of the painting can be suggested, the actual object is so refined that describing it inevitably involves something as ethereal as the quiet air that holds the butterfly. Taste, the practiced and sophisticated eye, is the heart of still-life painting; and as its greatest practitioners have understood, as we see when watching Coorte's painstaking struggle to get his pictures exactly right, the subtle transformation of everyday objects into vehicles for wordless emotional reflection is this art's glory, as well as its most maddening difficulty.

COORTE PAINTED HIS *Still Life with Three Medlars and a Butterfly* between 1693 and 1695, as the poet Bashō lay dying in Osaka. For Bashō, as for any oriental poet or painter, depictions of nature and natural phenomena occupied the same lofty place as scenes from religion and history did in the West.

The artists of the European Middle Ages placed their holy figures against a gold background that eliminated any hint of the mortal, earthly plane; but in Japan, and in particular in those Japanese arts inspired by Zen Buddhism, the sacred world is within—and never above or without—the earthly world. When approached in the correct spirit, the placement of a rock in a garden, or the serving of a cup of tea, transcends aesthetics, and touches upon the divine.

It is hard to imagine that Bashō's poetry could even have been recognized as such in seventeenth-century Europe. Even today, without extensive study, it is hard for a Western mind, taught to admire the intricate and difficult, to fathom. His most famous masterpiece, for example, described as a "revolutionary alarm" ("So many people in the past have commented upon this poem," writes one critic, "that it seems to me that its poetic resources have been well-nigh exhausted") is nothing more than this:

The old pond, ah!
A frog jumps in:
The water's sound!

Concreteness and simplicity, rather than intricacy and elaboration, were the highest values of this culture; and watching Adriaen Coorte's struggle with his butterflies and asparagus, seeing his vision evolve through his life, is like reading the works of Bashō in the order that they were composed. A simplicity of this kind is as difficult to achieve as building a great cathedral, and all the more elegant for its apparent denial of its own difficulty. Coorte's long movement toward the achievement of a few perfect paintings brings to mind a saying of Clarice Lispector's: "Art is not purity: it is purification. Art is not liberty: it is liberation."

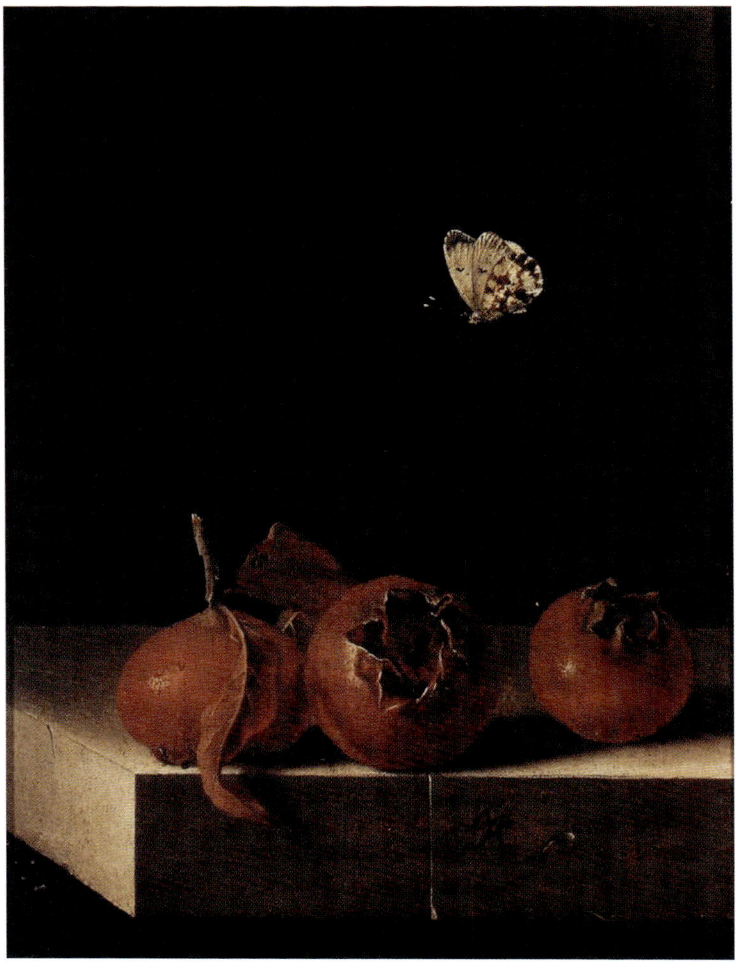

"The Mona Lisa of the late seventeenth century Dutch still-life,"
according to Coorte's rediscoverer.

IN A DEVASTATING *MOT* on the emotionalism of the German Romantics, Max Friedländer wrote: "Looking at their works, people could think thoughts." How far Coorte's medlars are from making people "think thoughts" can be seen by comparing them with a work another Middelburg painter produced almost two centuries earlier.

Jan Gossaert's *Carondelet Diptych* originated in 1517, when a mighty official, Jean Carondelet, was called to accompany the Emperor Charles V to Spain. Carondelet probably meant to commend himself to God as he embarked on the hazardous journey. The inside shows the prayerful magnate facing the Virgin and Child. Closed, the front shows his coat of arms, and the back—mocking this pride in ancestry—a skull with a grotesquely dislocated jaw.

Still-life is peculiarly well suited to remind us of death. If, historically, the genre is intimately connected with cultural rebirth, its most resonant connections are with death. In all the Romance languages, death is in its very name: in French, *nature morte*, "dead nature." In the countless *vanitas* still-lifes produced in the seventeenth century, death looms in all those snuffed-out candles, watches, skulls, and hourglasses.

Contemplating these paintings after a day at the emperor's fabulous court, Carondelet would have been inspired to reflection on the passing things of this world: a powerful man—himself—on the one side; the skull underneath his attractive face. If the object is costly and magnificent, its primary value would have been to recall the fleeting nature of even the greatest material things.

It is not to accuse Jan Gossaert of vulgarity, however, to see that when placed alongside Adriaen Coorte's medlars, the skull seems far too blatant an encouragement to "think thoughts." No matter how beautifully painted, this kind of symbol, like a vase of lilies beside a radiant Virgin, refers a bit too insistently, a bit too pedagogically, to something outside itself.

Coorte's object of contemplation is infinitely subtler. Capturing the slightest flicker of passing time in the butterfly's suspended flight, his painting achieves the quality of symbolism without the least pretention to being symbolic. Like wordless music, it stimulates feeling without directing it, shutting off the intellect and appealing directly to the senses.

In the hands of a great master, the most seemingly obvious of genres becomes the richest and most paradoxical. It is one thing to show mortality upon the face of a twisted and crucified Savior. "Art" is showing it on a gooseberry, a bunch of asparagus, a frog. Adriaen Coorte, like Bashō, sought "a vision of eternity in the things that are, by their own very nature, destined to perish." Passing time, and therefore death, is the still-life painter's real subject.

AFTERWORD

Going Back Home

J UST BEFORE THE PANDEMIC, I was back in Houston, the city where I was born. Jet lag roused me early, and I left the hotel to take a walk through my old neighborhood. The oaks spread against the sky like wooden veins, forming long green tunnels over the streets. Their acorns crunched beneath my feet, and their roots lifted and cracked the slabs of the sidewalk. It was beautiful—even, unexpectedly, romantic. It was a lovely place to grow up.

When I was a child, these streets looked normal to me. They certainly didn't look like relics from an ancient civilization. The city would soon be celebrating its bicentennial, but it had always been a place that lived from its future rather than, like so many European places, from its past. That was why I was astonished to look at these streets and be reminded of the Amsterdam canals built three hundred years before.

Here they were, attended by bushy pink azaleas and flanked by shadowy lawns, these monuments to the proud bourgeoisie of a great empire. There were so many of these houses, hundreds, thousands, just here, on these few streets; and they stretched out, block after block, neighborhood after neighborhood, in dozens of cities across this immense country: a dream of American wealth, of American ease.

They were mementoes of a golden age, and like all golden ages, this one seemed to be in the past. My own past, but also—I hoped that this was not the voice of middle age—a collective past. The impulse that built these streets had waned as it had not when I was young. Something had shifted. I was sure that I belonged to the last generation to grow up with the confident assumptions that built them.

Was I seeing it this way only because I had left? I didn't think so. Americans, in America, spoke of our country so much more pessimistically than they had when I was young. The unbearable politicians, the shot-up kindergartens, had changed the way we saw ourselves. Before, even the most skeptical had borrowed a bit of their self-confidence from their awareness of belonging to a great nation. Did they still?

That self-confidence had built this place; and though some houses had been torn down, the place, physically speaking, was the same. It hadn't been torched by invaders; it hadn't been abandoned to the jungle. I knew places like that, Greek emporia that had been sacked by the Persians, Colorado boomtowns whose silver had ran out.

That hadn't happened here. Yet a mentality had shifted, and the results were as palpable as a physical calamity. Here, there was no lost battle, no exploding volcano, no stock market crash; future historians wouldn't be able to point to a single event from which they could date a broader decline, as they had located the end of the Dutch Golden Age with the invasion of the Netherlands in 1672.

But sometime after I left this neighborhood, our golden age had ended. Something about this neighborhood had started looking like something from another civilization. How had it happened? As we get fat, one bite at a time; as the body ages, one gray hair at a time. It was an old story; it was a long story, a story for another place; and it was a story that, when I took the longer view, might not really matter.

Events pass. Nations carry on. The Dutch did. Some of their greatest achievements would come in the century after their Golden Age. Despite many disasters and reversals—and what land can avoid them?—the country remained what it is today, one of the happiest, most successful societies in the world. The canals laid down in the Amsterdam of Rembrandt's day were still there—a kind of consolation.

AS I WALKED DOWN streets built not a hundred years before, I was enjoying this new feeling: of thinking of myself as belonging to an ancient civilization. This was not how Americans thought of ourselves, but at the same time I knew what Gertrude Stein meant when she said that the United States was the oldest country in the world—"the right age to have been born in and the wrong age to live in."

America had started to feel old. It seemed to change less than Europe did. It had invented the modern world—that is why Gertrude Stein thought it was so old—but at a certain point other places had passed it by. Nothing ever improved, not that I could see; but I had been gone so long that I wondered what I was seeing, or if I could see it at all.

Was there a right way to look at this old place? I saw it differently now because it was a place I knew from childhood—and because I could also now see it through foreign eyes. I knew how Europeans would see these streets. They would see something out of a movie, for example, since the only thing an American neighborhood shares with Paris or Venice is that it looks exactly the way it does in the movies.

Europeans would notice—they always noticed!—the squirrels. They would see how titanic, by European standards, the houses were. They would notice the empty sidewalks—and marvel, condescendingly, that people drove everywhere. Through the filters that any culture applies when looking at another, they would see a place that nobody from inside that culture ever sees—until you leave.

I was from inside that culture. And what I could see of America was: everything. I understood how things worked. I knew, at a glance, who was who. I could look at a house and tell you who lived there; I could look at a car and tell you who drove it. I understood every word of the language, and when I spoke, it would never occur to anybody to compliment me on my accent, or ask how long I'd been here.

To those who never left home, that way of seeing and speaking was so automatic, so natural, that it could never seem the way it seemed to me. To me, after so long away, it felt like a superpower. It was like recovering the use of both eyes after having grown used to blindness. It was like having normal internet service restored after weeks of waiting, byte by agonizing byte, for pages to load.

To those who don't know what it is to live in someone else's country, in someone else's language, by someone else's unconscious rules, it is hard to explain the physical relief of being back among your own people. For years, I had wondered why, though I had friends all over the world, I gravitated to English speakers, particularly to Americans—even to Americans that, I realized, I didn't especially like.

During my first years abroad, some of these relationships felt like those I formed during the first months of college, before I found enduring friends. Away from home, thrown together with strangers, I spent time with people with whom I had little in common. I needed time to discover the real friends among the new faces. As an adult, making friends got harder—and it was even harder in a foreign country.

As I tried, I discovered that even though I didn't have that much in common with certain people, a language and a culture were often enough. English was a relief. The ultimate prize was an American with similar interests, from a similar background—*someone I would actually hang out with at home.* Even after twenty years, such discoveries were rare, and our encounters could have a nearly illicit thrill.

Now, here, I was in a whole country—street after street, city after city, state after state—of people who spoke my language. It was so easy to be here. Why had I ever left? Why would I—why would anyone— leave the place, the culture, for which they had been made? For the first half of my life, America was the only place that had been entirely real to me. In many ways, it still was.

I felt it every time I came back. Europe vanished. You stepped off a KLM plane and poof! went the Dutch language, never to be heard from again. And not only Dutch. I was amazed, when I was here, at how European languages, such a fundamental tool of my daily life, seemed like cute hobbies, decorative flourishes, like the faux French signs ("café," "boulangerie") in a pretentious American bakery.

When I checked the Dutch newspapers, I was struck by how naïve, how wrong, much Dutch reporting on the United States sounded. Reading the things the Dutch wrote about us was like watching someone gaze upon a distant planet. Television, music, and instant communication didn't bring us closer, as they seemed to. Instead, perversely, they ended up emphasizing how far away we really were.

Likewise the Dutch knowledge, almost always embarrassingly superficial, of our language. I called it Dutch English—Dutch, expressed in English words. You could replace the Latin letters on this page with Cyrillic but the language would be the same. And you could switch Dutch words with English, but they would nevertheless express what, to me, were foreign ideas, foreign thoughts, foreign minds.

I knew how this felt because I knew that my own mind was fundamentally inalterable. To spend many years abroad was to realize that what I thought of as my personality was, increasingly, fungible. My uniqueness—which is to say: whatever it was that made me different from other people—paled in the face of what made me the same as other people, especially those who came from my own country.

In the same way that I slipped into different clothes depending on the weather and the occasion and the time of day, I had seen my personality change as languages and countries and situations changed. And I had seen that what didn't change was the stratum laid down when I was a child, on these streets, speaking this language. "4" would always be "four" to me. It could never be *vier* or *quatre* or *četiri*.

⸻

AS DUTCH ENGLISH WAS Dutch, the America I found in Holland was Dutch, too. It had its own independent life. For a long time, I was struck that the Dutch would instruct me, correct me, on whatever American matters were in the news: racism, guns, the Electoral College. I thought that if there was anything I knew about, it was my own country and language—and so I instructed, corrected, right back.

For example: the phrase "happy end." I would explain that you were supposed to say "happy ending," that nobody said happy end, that it sounded stupid, that it was weird—and would see Dutch people look confused, and keep saying it anyway. The mistake was mine. Though the words were of English origin, the phrase wasn't English. It was Dutch, and they used it according to their own rules.

I was like a Frenchman who, arriving in Houston, set himself to boring everyone with lectures about the word "entrée," explaining that it meant appetizer, not main course. This, though it is an unchangeable fact that it does mean main course in America, and a foreigner who started insisting we were wrong would merely annoy people. In France, he'd be right. In America, he'd be an asshole.

And so I saw that their America and ours were like two individuals with the same name. Countries produce images of others according to their own history, their own traditions; and in the modern world the United States has been produced in this way more than any other country, in as many different versions as there are nations. Amerika and America referred to the same land. But the similarities stopped there.

In order to understand what the Dutch thought about America, Americans were, in a way, irrelevant. What was relevant was what earlier Dutch writers and thinkers had said about America. The country those writers described was the one that lived in the Dutch mind, and though it was not my America, that did not make it fake or artificial. It was another image, and had the reality that images have.

It was, in fact, like a painting. Just as Potter's bull had never—could never—have existed, the Holland that I had learned to see through the prism of the Golden Age artists was a country that had never really quite existed. Yet it had a reality that was far more convincing than whatever other reality skulked behind those images. That reality, lost with the passing of the centuries, no longer mattered, or not exactly.

It was also, for me, far more romantic than the reality of daily life. As the Dutch had their America, so did we have our Europe. To the average tourist, Europe would always mean palaces and cathedrals, antiquity and culture, Eiffel Tower and Leaning Tower: some other way of living, some connection to the past that, in some unbridgeable way, was unavailable to us back home.

Was this Europe? It was our Europe. Europeans seldom recognized it, any more than we recognized their America. But I always thought that it helps to be from Texas in order to appreciate a Gothic church, and that if you grew up in Paris or Rome, it becomes hard to see Paris or Rome. Overfamiliarity—seeing something every day—makes it hard to summon the wonder that comes naturally to the foreigner.

This was part of what I was trying to hold on to when I was writing about the Dutch painters. When you see a place every day, its bright colors fade, and its edges are smoothed over; and the longer you stay, the more it is stripped of its initial magic. The past fades. The present is more urgent, more important. And the future never stops flinging itself in your face.

As much as I could, I avoided the present. I lived in my own foreigner's Europe. I ignored politics, depressing in every country. I ignored news, idem. I wriggled through prehistoric caves; I read old poems; I haunted ruins. I went to museums, where I found a reality as real as any other. At least sometimes, at least for a few minutes, I could choose which reality to inhabit.

———

NOW I WAS TRYING to look at my own place, or what had once been my own place, half a life after I left it. Until adolescence, I had been a tourist everywhere else. Could I look at it with a gaze that combined the freshness of the foreigner with the intimacy of the native? Could I see the world as Jan van Eyck had, with microscope and with telescope simultaneously? It was a challenge thrown down by the old painters. I squinted; I opened my eyes.

But all those years had changed nothing. To come back to the United States was to realize that nothing had changed. I hadn't either—not really. Was the country different? When viewed from abroad, across the internet, through the prism of the breaking-news alerts that were forever yelling from my phone, the country was convulsing, melting down. Viewed from this street, it was exactly the same.

So were the people. They weren't necessarily the same individuals.

Over the years, I knew fewer and fewer people in a place where, I once imagined, I knew "everyone." New people had been born, moved in, moved on; many I knew had moved away, or died. Yet I still knew these people. They had a quality of Americanness that made them so familiar that they were, in some way, interchangeable.

Everywhere, always, I could recognize my own people. I was never sure exactly how, never sure what exactly I was seeing. Americans do not all look the same. And over the years, the differences had narrowed in clothing, for example, that used to be a sure way to separate Americans from other people. But they didn't need to wear anything—or do any-thing, or say anything—in order to be recognizable.

If you knew how to recognize Americanness, it was impossible to mistake or confuse, like a facial tattoo that no makeup could cover. We all had it, and it was something of a mystery to me as to how, or when, we acquired it. My sister's children, by the time they were three years old, already looked and acted differently from children born in other countries. One glance at them—and you could tell.

Could you lose that quality? I hadn't. All I had to do was get off the plane—and *voilà*. It was a thrill, physical and emotional, to be a native speaker once again. I savored it. But the funny thing was that nobody noticed. They didn't know how long I'd been gone—had no idea that anything about me had changed. In so many ways, nothing had; I could no longer change my nationality than I could the color of my skin or my eyes.

Yet when I got off the plane, this overwhelming fact of my life became invisible. You don't notice that something everyone shares; it lives only in contrast. Outside my country, forced to feel the difference between me and those around me, I became aware of how much of me was the culture I came from. I tried to think about what that culture was, and what would be left when that culture was taken away.

At home, it was nothing. Abroad, it was everything. How easy life would be in a place where you could read all the signs, I would think after a long day of struggling to make myself seen or understood. I reflected that such a place existed, a few hours away. There, I could become the person I was engineered to be. I would fly back and wonder why I had ever left. These trips were like visits to a friend from childhood.

I would check up on the old friend. *That's* what you've been up to, I'd say. That's the person you married; that's where you're living; that's where you ended up working. I'd say it was nice to meet his partner, see his apartment. The conversation would flow in that awkward, wistful way of an encounter with someone you once were close to, and know you won't see many times again before you die.

In a way, I would envy his life. *He* would always know what was going on. He could be seen and judged on his own terms—on terms he understood. He wouldn't be invisible, as I had so often felt. How easy his life would have been, I would think—knowing that nobody's life is easy, and knowing, too, that he wasn't someone else: he was another version of me, and nothing was stopping me from coming back.

IT RARELY TOOK more than a couple of days for me to remember why I left. Americans often imagined reasons why it would be a relief to leave. Another horrible president, another appalling war, another story about someone bankrupted by a routine treatment for a minor medical condition. It was undeniable that the United States that I had left, just before 9/11, had become much darker.

But people who live abroad know that getting on a plane doesn't scatter the darkness. It doesn't scatter anything. *Au contraire*: you find that you care even more. If the only country you see is the one you find on an internet that feeds off calamity, you don't see other realities: your friends, your streets, your language. Unanchored by the comforts of everyday life, you feel the disasters even more keenly.

Anyway, I wasn't fleeing. There are so many refugees in the world, so many people who couldn't get on the planes I could get on—the Pilgrims would not have been able to imagine that 253 flights departed Schiphol for the United States every week—in order to return to far worse countries than mine. My reasons changed. I had left to be with someone I wanted to be with, and I still wanted to be with him.

And: I liked being abroad. I was the same kid who loved *National Geographic* and felt a thrill in the face of a thousand-year-old building. Whenever I went back to the United States, I realized that, as much as I missed being a native, I missed being a foreigner, too. I liked the challenge of it, the unexpectedness: I liked the same things that were frustrating, and kept it from being easy.

It was true that I could feel invisible. But in my own country, in a different way, I was invisible, too. Because so much about me was superficially visible—everything that foreigners couldn't see—much else was hidden, including that secret feeling of not belonging that had always been with me. Any American would see all the ways in which I did belong. They might not see all the ways in which I didn't.

Becoming a foreigner meant assigning one's own inner oddity a name, issuing it a passport. At home, I wore a certain costume. When I took it off, I could be something besides what my culture expected of me. Nobody expected anything of me. Nobody, in any country, cares about foreigners. They are extraneous. Nobody pretends to understand them, and this allows them to float in a vast zone of privacy.

I understood people who had moved abroad only to find themselves alienated from the only world that was real to them. I knew the feeling: the land in which I grew up was the only country that could ever really matter to me. Anywhere else, I was on the periphery. But there are certain people who like being on the periphery. I was one of them. For some, it was alienation; for me, it was liberation.

———

BUT IT WAS HARD to keep the foreigner's eye. After twenty years, Dutch life feels—has long felt—utterly normal. Normality can, often enough, snowball into tedium; but any writer knows that the way to keep something interesting is to write about it. So I wrote about it. At first, I was writing as an attempt to understand a strange new place; then I was writing as an attempt to make a normal place strange.

That is how I have been writing this book for twenty years. It is the product of many different phases of my life. Any coherence it has is the result of a middle-aged person's vigorous effort to scrub the evidence of his younger self. Though I have always made it a rule not to despise my younger self, my younger self, often inadvertently hilarious, sometimes made it hard to stick to this rule.

The delete key has excised my pretentious predecessor's mention of a "rather cramped" Rembrandt and "the dark palette of the early works." You won't see his suggestion that the reader "may recall Alois Riegl's remark" about something or other, or his references to "a lucid catalog essay," or to "a canvas in the Salzburg Residenzgalerie," or to "visual experiments of astonishing range and virtuosity."

Yet I understand how these phrases got there. And I feel some tenderness toward them, and toward the kid who wrote them. He had published nothing. And though he lacked self-confidence in many areas, he had nonetheless found the courage to move abroad and try to start writing. If they bear the marks of striving, of trying too hard, that is because their author was, in fact, striving and trying too hard.

I always thought it was better to strive than not to. But at a certain point, things—not everything, but a lot of things—become easier. If you manage to reach middle age more or less in one piece, you know how to do things, and not having to try so hard is the great pleasure of middle age: because you know how things work, because life seems less fraught than when you were embarking on adulthood.

But—as a singer from my homeland wrote—"The gold-plated watches have taken their toll." Stay anywhere long enough and foreignness fades into ease, which fades into ennui; you lose the edge, the sharpness, of the novice. Stay in Rome or Paris long enough, and you find yourself brushing past the Colosseum or the Eiffel Tower on your way to pick up a bottle of toilet cleaner.

I tried not to become jaded. Still, I eventually stopped being the clueless foreigner. I no longer cared about the odd grammatical mistake. I didn't mind that I was missing a lot; I knew that the foreigner often misses less than the native, and that the person who has to make an effort—to learn the language, to understand the culture—sees many things that the native would never consider.

Through writing about art, I was trying to write my way into a new culture. Eventually, I devoted a lot more time to Fabritius or Metsu than almost anyone in the Netherlands, for whom these were the names of streets. I don't know why this surprised me. Few Americans know about Whistler, say, or John Singer Sargent. Was my surprise an insecurity, a colonial suspicion that Europeans are cleverer than we are?

I ended up knowing more about this side of Dutch culture than most people I met. It was lopsided. I knew more about the old artists. But I knew less about politics, sports, music, the culture of the present that was more relevant to most people. Four centuries had rolled over Holland since Rembrandt. I liked the museum more than the freeway or the mall. But the culture I was trying to write myself into was long dead.

———

LOOKING BACK, I realize now that I was trying to write myself into a different culture—a different present, and one that, I hoped, would lead to a different future. When I came here, I left the tiny, fragile position I had found in the cultural world of New York—a city with thousands of people like me, and the only place I ever felt entirely at home. That, I knew, was why I would have to leave.

I suspected that whatever I wanted to write could not be written in a place that was constantly prodding me into the social life that (I had to admit) I loved. To be around too many people like yourself is to lose your sense of yourself; and in order to hold on to your sense of yourself, you can become a loud caricature of yourself: the streets of New York were littered with these corpses. I needed to be quiet, isolated, in order to become what I wanted to be, and I wasn't going to become anything in New York: I was going to keep on being what I already was.

But as soon as I left, I feared disappearing to that world—and so, when I started writing about Dutch art for American publications, I wanted to show that I had done the reading. I was desperate to find the kind of language that would make me sound smart, authoritative, Not From Texas: to make the adults who gave me my first chances to be published take me seriously, and think of me as an adult.

I see my rush to become an adult in the language that I hope I have cut. (Some must linger somewhere.) When I look back at it now, I see a bar mitzvah boy standing uncomfortably in his first suit. I see a teenage girl awkwardly applying her mother's makeup. I see myself trying to speak in a way that wouldn't betray my insecurity. To my astonishment, it worked: I soon found myself with a career.

As soon as I did, another fear loomed. When I look back at the first chapters I wrote, I see another reason that I was in a rush: a fear of being stopped before my time. I'm not sure that I realized how haunted I was by stories of artists who had died young. But the fear of early death—of being cut off before one has done what one needs to do—comes through so often in this book that I can't deny I felt it.

I do remember the feeling from writing other books. What a shame, I would think, to die with this book only 60 percent finished. I would try to reckon when I could safely expire. Seventy percent wasn't enough. If you had a good editor, 80 percent might be closer. But I let myself stop worrying only once the bound galleys arrived. Even if it never got further, it would exist, in a few copies, in a booklike form.

When was this book finished? It wasn't; it's not. It's not a complete record of my own encounters with the Dutch painters, and it's certainly not a complete record of the Dutch painters: Arnold Houbraken wrote about 1190 of them in the three volumes of his work—but Houbraken also died after the publication of the second volume. Though I see the omissions, completeness was never my goal.

My goal was a record of my encounter with this culture, of how its great figures helped me explore my own questions: about love and death and art and money, about how to see and how to be. Contact with the foreign always stimulated me. The stimulus I got from *this* culture—one that I easily could have overlooked if I had not happened to meet a Dutchman when I was twenty-three—is here on every page.

———

IT WAS GETTING HOT. I always forgot how hot it was here, my God, how early in the morning the heat started, how deep into the fall it lasted. I walked down Banks Street, where my grandparents lived after getting married. I turned right on Yoakum, where my parents lived after they got married. Then I took a left on Bissonnet, a wide, tree-covered street. I was born just a few blocks away, a stone's throw from the museum.

As I walked through the tunnels of oaks, I felt the exile's fantasy of lineage, of rootedness, of living out my life in the land where my fathers died. I recalled the trepidation I'd felt when I decided to strip off everything assigned to me at birth and make a new life abroad. I'd needed to find a life of my own, though I wasn't sure why, or what that meant. I was more prepared for it to go wrong than for it to go right.

What if I had stayed? Spinoza wrote that there was no what if; there was only what is. My life could not have happened in any other way than in the way it had happened, and the proof was that that was how it had happened. The glimpse of another life, of a road not taken, had something poignant, even something poetic about it, but it was not a real possibility. For some reason, I was meant to go to Holland.

Now, when I looked back at the half a life I had lived in someone else's country, I saw how good that life had been. It hadn't been perfect and it hadn't always been easy. But when I looked back from the vantage of middle age, I could see that it had been far more perfect than most lives get to be. And for that life, I was grateful to my friends among the Dutch: the ones in this book, and the one for whom I left in the first place.

I was proud of a life that wasn't inherited. I was glad I had traded my ancient civilization for a new world, one in which I could take nothing for granted and in which I had sought friendship, guidance, from the artists of the past. Would I have found them if I had stayed at home? There were no what ifs. And now they were as much a part of me, of my past, as these steamy streets. I headed into the museum lobby, gratefully savoring the air-conditioning—and then walked upstairs, into the Dutch galleries.

ACKNOWLEDGMENTS

MY FIRST DEBT IS to the late Robert Silvers and Barbara Epstein, who gave a young man his first chance to write about art. For the opportunity to publish early versions of some of these chapters, I am grateful to Roger Hodge and Jennifer Szalai at *Harper's Magazine*, Don Guttenplan at *The Nation*, and Leon Wieseltier and Celeste Marcus at *Liberties*. For years of conversations, Quentin Buvelot, Mia You, and Hugo van der Velden, and for help finding the books I needed, the Utrecht booksellers Paul van den Hoven and Jan van Hassel. For years of support, my literary agents, Bill Clegg, Marion Duvert, and Matthew Hamilton. For putting this book into the world, my excellent editor, Robert Weil, and his tireless deputy, Haley Bracken. At Liveright, I would also like to thank Peter Miller, Clio Hamilton, Bill Rusin, Anne Somlyo, and David Achar. In the United Kingdom, Maria Bedford and Corina Romonti; and in the Netherlands, Paulien Loerts, Elik Lettinga, and Esther Hendriks. For the beautiful cover, Paul Sahre. For help with images, Maaike Koeten at the Frans Hals Museum; Joyce Edwards at the Amsterdam Museum; Mariska de Jonge and Cécilie Tainturier from the Fondation Custodia; Sean Livingstone at the North Carolina Museum of Art; Caroline van Cauwenberge from the Leiden Collection; Luisa Berretti of the Museo Nationale di Palazzo Mansi; and Mark Tansey and Putri Tan from Gagosian; Neel

Wijshake from the Stadsarchief Kampen; Susan Anderson from the Harvard Art Museums; Natalie Dubois and Frederik Markusse from the Centraal Museum, Utrecht; Robert Wenley and Helen Cobby from the Barber Institute of Fine Art, Birmingham, UK; Katja Kleinert and Lea Hagedorn from the Gemäldegalerie, Berlin.

Finally, to my Dutch family, Arthur, Lex, Basso—and to Joop and Janine, who, for all these years, have made me feel at home in Holland.

NOTES ON SOURCES

PART I

John Lothrop Motley's *The Rise of the Dutch Republic* (1856) and *The History of the United Netherlands* (1860–1867) remain a valuable, and exciting, introduction to the story of this period.

1. REMBRANDT

The bibliography surrounding Rembrandt is measureless, technical, and often repetitive: I limit myself to the works cited here. More on the wartime protection of the national art collections is in Henk Baard "Nachtwacht uitgerold: Meesterwerk terug in het Rijks," *NOS Journaal*, https://nos.nl/75jaarbevrijding/bericht/2339808 -nachtwacht-uitgerold-meesterwerk-terug-in-het-rijks; and Peter Hecht, "Als de kunst weg is, blijkt pas wat zij betekent," in the magazine of the Vereniging Rembrandt, https://www.verenigingrembrandt.nl/nl/doe-mee/word-lid/bulletin/als-de-kunst -weg-is-blijkt-pas-wat-zij-betekent. Hitler's description of Rembrandt comes from John Toland, *Adolf Hitler: The Definitive Biography* (New York: Anchor, 1992). The great Max Friedländer's *Landscape, Portrait, Still-Life: Their Origin and Development*, (The Hague: Stols, 1947, p. 180) is, despite its dry title, one of the most brilliant and perceptive books ever written about the emergence of these genres. The negative view of Rembrandt's character is taken from Gary Schwartz's "Whitewashing Rembrandt, Part 2" (March 1, 2020), http://www.garyschwartzarthistorian.nl/380 -whitewashing-rembrandt-part-2/. Jean Genet's short *Rembrandt* (Paris: Gallimard, 2016), is a view of one subversive artist by another. And Junichirō Tanizaki's *In Praise of Shadows* (1933; repr., London: Vintage, 2006), fascinating in itself, raises the question of what Tanizaki would have written if he had considered Rembrandt (and Caravaggio). "A good painting, like a good fiddle" comes from Sheldon Keck, "Some Picture-Cleaning Controversies," *Journal of the American Institute for Conservation* 23, no. 2, https://www.jstor.org/stable/3179471.

2. JAN LIEVENS

Erin Thompson's quote about the different neurological reactions to paintings that are or aren't by Rembrandt comes from "Foulest, Vilest, Obscenest," in the *London Review of Books* 44, no. 2, https://www.lrb.co.uk/the-paper/v44/n02/erin-thompson/foulest-vilest-obscenest. This chapter is greatly indebted to *Jan Lievens: A Dutch Master Rediscovered* (New Haven: Yale University Press, 2008), a catalog edited by Arthur K. Wheelock Jr. The speculation about Lievens's mental state comes from Ken Johnson, "A Forgotten Baroque Painter, Shown Free of Rembrandt's Shadow," *The New York Times*, October 31, 2008. Caravaggio had seen works by artists including Marinus van Reymerswaele and Jan van Hemessen and employed some of their compositional devices. See Albert Blankert, "Caravaggio en Noord-Nederland," in *Nieuw Licht op de Gouden Eeuw: Hendrick ter Brugghen en tijdgenoten*, edited by Albert Blankert and Leonard J. Slatkes (Utrecht and Braunschweig: Centraal Museum and Herzog Anton Ulrich-Museum, 1987), p. 17. Another good source for this debate is Duncan Bull et al., *Rembrandt–Caravaggio* (Zwolle and Amsterdam: Waanders and Rijksmuseum, 2006), p. 16. Gerard de Lairesse's famous denunciation of Rembrandt's paint as looking "like crap" comes from Blankert, "Caravaggio en Noord-Nederland," p. 40. The German painter Joaquim von Sandrart, who himself studied in Utrecht, attributed, in his *Teutsche Academie* of 1675, Rembrandt's taste for unattractive reality to his humble origins, including his presumed illiteracy. The quote from V. S. Naipaul is from *The Enigma of Arrival* (New York: Knopf, 1988).

3. FERDINAND BOL AND GOVERT FLINCK

This chapter relies on two major publications, Norbert Middelkoop's *Ferdinand Bol and Govert Flinck: Rembrandt's Master Pupils* (Zwolle: W Books, 2018) and Stephanie S. Dickey, ed., *Ferdinand Bol and Govert Flinck: New Research* (Zwolle: W Books, 2018). Bredius's evaluation of Bol comes from *New Research*, p. 102, and the quotations "even those who . . ." and "A talent without creativity . . ." come from ibid., p. 228. Houbraken is quoted there as well, p. 45. "Here is the stock exchange . . ." is from *Rembrandt's Master Pupils*, p. 105, and "ecstasy and chaos . . ." comes from ibid., p. 32. Louis Viardot's appraisal is from *New Research*, p. 227, and "following nature" is from ibid., p. 224.

4. CAREL FABRITIUS

This chapter relies on *Carel Fabritius 1622–1654* by Frederik J. Duparc, with contributions by Gero Seelig and Ariane van Suchteren (Zwolle: Waanders, 2005).

5. JOHANNES VERMEER

There are many sources for the few facts about the life of Johannes Vermeer, including John Michael Montias, *Vermeer and His Milieu: A Web of Social History* (Princeton, N.J.: Princeton University Press, 1991); Anthony Bailey's *Vermeer: A View of Delft* (New York: Holt, 2002); and Karl Schütz's *Vermeer: The Complete Works* (Cologne: Taschen, 2020). The discussion of the Cupid relies on Stephan Koja, Uta Neidhardt, and Arthur K. Wheelock Jr., *Vermeer: On Reflection* (Dresden: Staatliche Kunstsammlungen, 2021).

6. GERARD TER BORCH

The description of the discovery of the Ter Borch archive comes from the two fascinating volumes of Alison McNeil Kettering's *Drawings from the Ter Borch Studio Estate in the Rijksmuseum* (Amsterdam: Staatsuitgeverij, 1988). Zbigniew Herbert's essay on Ter Borch is in *Still-Life with a Bridle: Essays and Apocryphas* (New York: Ecco, 1993). For a good overview of Gerard ter Borch Junior's work, see Arthur K. Wheelock Jr., with contributions by Alison McNeil Kettering, Arie Wallert, and Marjorie E. Wieseman, *Gerard ter Borch* (New Haven: Yale University Press, 2004).

7. PIETER DE HOOCH

Peter Sutton's two books on De Hooch, *Pieter de Hooch: Complete Edition with a Catalogue Raisonné* (Ithaca, N.Y.: Cornell University Press, 1980) and the catalog to the exhibition I saw, *Pieter de Hooch 1629–1684* (New Haven: Yale University Press, 1998), remain the standard works on this painter. The descriptions of the early artists come from Christopher S. Wood, *A History of Art History* (Princeton, N.J.: Princeton University Press, 2019); and the characterization of all Europe as Bosnia comes from Lawrence Wechsler, *Vermeer in Bosnia: Cultural Comedies and Political Tragedies* (New York: Pantheon, 2004).

8. GABRIËL METSU

The two catalogs I discuss in this chapter are Adriaan Waiboer, ed., *Gabriel Metsu* (New Haven: Yale University Press, 2010); and Jeroen Giltaij et al., *Senses and Sins: Dutch Painters of Daily Life in the Seventeenth Century* (Ostfildern: Hatje Cantz, 2005).

9. JAN STEEN

Much of this chapter relies on Perry Chapman et al., *Jan Steen: Painter and Storyteller* (Washington, D.C.: National Gallery of Art, 1996); and Ariane van Suchtelen et al., *Jan Steen's Histories* (Zwolle: Waanders, 2018). Susan Sontag's "Notes on 'Camp'" is in *Against Interpretation* (New York: Farrar, Straus & Giroux, 1966). The prints described are in the collection of the Rijksmuseum.

10. HENDRICK AVERCAMP

Clara J. Welcker's monograph, *Hendrick Avercamp 1585–1634, bijgenaamd "De stomme van Campen," en Barent Avercamp 1612–1679 "Schilders tot Campen,"* was originally published in Zwolle in 1933 (Erven J. J. Tijl), and then reprinted, under a slightly different title, by Davaco Publishers, Doornspijk, in 1979. Thea Beckman's children's novel *De Stomme van Kampen* was published by Lemniscaat in Rotterdam in 1992. Ariane van Suchtelen, *Winters van weleer: Het Hollandse winterlandschap in de Gouden Eeuw* (Zwolle: Waanders, 2002), offers a general overview of the genre of the winter landscape. J. ten Hove's recollection of Clara Welcker is taken from *Overijsselse biografieën*, available at https://www.wieiswieinoverijssel.nl/zoekresultaten/p2/96 -clara-johanna-welcker.

11. FRANS HALS

Seymour Slive, *Frans Hals* (London: Royal Academy, 1989) was a valuable source for this chapter. The description of Whistler's final journey to Haarlem comes from Elizabeth Robins Pennell and Joseph Pennell, *The Life of James McNeill Whistler* (Philadelphia: Lippincott, 1908). Vincent's description of Hals's twenty-seven blacks is from a letter to Theo van Gogh, October 20, 1885, https://vangoghletters.org/vg/letters/let536/letter.html. Edward Said's *On Late Style: Music and Literature Against the Grain* (New York: Pantheon, 2006) and Theodor Adorno's *Beethoven: The Philosophy of Music* (New York: Polity, 2002) also inform this chapter.

12. PIETER SAENREDAM

My discussion of Saenredam's months in Utrecht is based on Liesbeth M. Helmus et al., *Pieter Saenredam: The Utrecht Work* (Los Angeles: Getty Publications, 2002). Further biographical details come from Gary Schwartz and Marten Jan Bok, *Pieter Saenredam: The Painter and His Time* (New York: Abbeville, 1990). Discussion of perspective also comes from Erwin Panofsky, *Perspective as Symbolic Form* (New York: Zone Books, 1991).

13. PAULUS POTTER

Amy Walsh, Edwin Buijsen, and Ben Broos, *Paulus Potter: Paintings, Drawings, and Etchings* (Zwolle: Waanders, 1994) offers an overview of Potter's work. Tobias van Westrheene, *Paulus Potter: Sa vie et ses œuvres* (The Hague: Martinus Nijhoff, 1867) is a fascinating example of an early artistic monograph. Antoine Sergent was the deputy who praised the Romans for conserving Greek monuments—see https://www.vivantdenon.fr/l-oeuvre-museale/les-prelevements-napoleoniens/.

14. JACOB VAN RUISDAEL

Seymour Slive's *Jacob van Ruisdael: Master of Landscape* (London: Royal Academy, 2005) is still the standard introduction, and Slive's *Jacob van Ruisdael: A Complete Catalogue of His Paintings, Drawings, and Etchings* (New Haven: Yale University Press, 2001) is a more complete version. For the story of Ruisdael and Berchem's journey to Germany, I am indebted to Quentin Buvelot, *Jacob van Ruisdael Paints Bentheim* (Zwolle: W Books, 2010).

15. ALBERT ECKHOUT

The best and most complete introduction to the Dutch artists in Brazil remains Ernst van den Boogaart, ed., *Johan Maurits van Nassau-Siegen 1604–1679: A Humanist Prince in Europe and Brazil* (The Hague: Johan Maurits van Nassau Stichting, 1979). For an overview of the period, see Charles R. Boxer, *The Dutch in Brazil, 1624–1654* (Oxford: Clarendon Press, 1957). Quentin Buvelot's *Albert Eckhout: A Dutch Artist in Brazil* (Zwolle: Waanders, 2005) gives an excellent overview of the artist's achievement. For a more recent view of Eckhout, including new attributions of certain paintings that were previously given to him, see Katie Heyning, *Terug naar Zeeland: Topstukken uit de 16e en 17e eeuw* (Middelburg: Zeeuws Museum, 2008). For a Brazilian view of Eckhout in a wider context, see Adriano Pedrosa et al., *Histórias Afroatlânticas: Antologia* (São Paulo: Museu de Arte de São Paulo, 2022). For the history of negative views of America, see Philippe Roger, *L'ennemi américain: Généalogie de l'antiaméricanisme français* (Paris: Seuil, 2002), pp. 28–29; and Henry Steele Commager and Elmo Giordanetti, *Was America a Mistake?* (New York: Harper and Row, 1967). For a good history of Dutch colonization across Latin America, see Eleazar Córdova-Bello, *Compañias holandesas de navegación, agentes de la colonización neerlandesa* (Seville: Escuela de Estudios Hispano-Americanos, 1964).

16. RACHEL RUYSCH

Much of this discussion relies on Marianne Berardi's excellent dissertation "Science into Art: Rachel Ruysch's Early Development as a Still-Life Painter" (University of Pittsburgh, 1999). Colonel M. H. Grant's *Rachel Ruysch, 1664–1750* (Leigh-on-Sea, Eng.: F. Lewis, 1956) gives a shorter overview, and Julie V. Hansen's "Resurrecting Death: Anatomical Art in the Cabinet of Dr. Frederik Ruysch," *Art Bulletin* 78 (December 1996), no. 4, gives a description of Dr. Ruysch's views of art and science. I have also relied on *In Full Bloom* by Ariane van Suchtelen et al (Waanders, 2022). For a general view of women's artistic achievement, including Ruysch's, see Eleanor Tufts, *Our Hidden Heritage: Five Centuries of Women Artists* (London: Paddington Press, 1974); and Linda Nochlin, *Why Have There Been No Great Women Artists?* (1971; repr., London: Thames and Hudson, 2021). See also Tyler Cowen, "Why Women Succeed, and Fail, in the Arts," *Journal of Cultural Economics* 20 (1996): 93–113; and Elizabeth Alice Honig, "The Art of Being 'Artistic,'" *Woman's Art Journal*, Fall 2001/Winter 2002.

17. ADRIAEN COORTE

This chapter draws on Quentin Buvelot, *The Still-Lifes of Adriaen Coorte* (Zwolle: W Books, 2009), as well as on Laurens-Jan Bol, *Adriaen Coorte: A Unique Late Seventeenth-Century Dutch Still-Life Painter* (Assen: Van Gorcum, 1977). For Coorte's early life in Zeeuws-Vlaanderen, see the recent discoveries of Ton de Jong and Huib Plankeel, *Adriaen Coorte uit IJzendijke: Een eenzame stillevenschilder* (2015). For other views of the origins of still-life, see Wolfgang Müller, *Der Maler Georg Flegel und die Anfänge des Stillebens* (Frankfurt: Waldemar Kramer, 1956) and Charles Sterling, *La nature morte: De l'antiquité à nos jours* (Paris: Pierre Tisné, 1952).

ILLUSTRATION CREDITS

38   Private collection, United Kingdom / Image courtesy of Lullo
      Pampoulides

39   Jan Lievens, The Penitent Magdalene, around 1631, oil on canvas.
      Agnes Etherington Art Centre, Queen's University, Kingston. Gift of
      Dr. and Mrs. Alfred Bader, 1975 (18–126)

41   Jan Lievens, Forest Interior with Draftsman, Maida and George
      Abrams Collection, Boston, Long Term Loan, Photo President and
      Fellows of Harvard College, 1.2018.260

44   incamerastock / Alamy Stock Photo

45   Printed with permission of the Ministry of Culture, Regional
      Directorate of Museums of Tuscany, Florence

46   Rijksmuseum

48   On loan from the City of Amsterdam, Rijksmuseum

49   Jonkheer J. S. H. van de Poll Bequest, Amsterdam, Rijksmuseum

50   Museum Catharijneconvent, Utrecht / photo: Ruben de Heer

54   Bibliothèque nationale de France

62   Rijksmuseum

65   Courtesy of The Leiden Collection

67   Collection Museum Boijmans Van Beuningen, Rotterdam / photo:
      Studio Tromp

68   Purchased with the support of the Vereniging Rembrandt,
      Rijksmuseum

70–71 Photographed by the author in National Gallery, London

74   Mauritshuis, The Hague

81   © Gemäldegalerie Alte Meister, Staatliche Kunstsammlungen
      Dresden. Photo: Elke Estel/Hans-Peter Klut

84   Rijksmuseum

86   Städel Museum, Frankfurt am Main

87   (Left) Photographed by the author in National Gallery, London;
      (Right) Photographed by the author in Kunsthistorisches Museum
      Vienna

88   Widener Collection, National Gallery of Art, Washington, D. C.

90   © Gemäldegalerie Alte Meister, Staatliche Kunstsammlungen Dresden
      / photo: Wolfgang Kreische

91   © Gemäldegalerie Alte Meister, Staatliche Kunstsammlungen Dresden
      / photo: Wolfgang Kreische

93   Mauritshuis, The Hague

98   Collection Museum Boijmans Van Beuningen, Rotterdam / photo:
      Studio Tromp

105   The Picture Art Collection / Alamy Stock Photo

108–9   Collection Museum Boijmans Van Beuningen, Rotterdam / photo: Studio Tromp

110   On loan from the National Gallery, London. Presented by Sir Richard Wallace, 1871, Rijksmuseum

113   Andrew W. Mellon Collection, The National Gallery of Art

115   De Bruijn-van der Leeuw Bequest, Muri, Switzerland, Rijksmuseum

116   Rijksmuseum

118   (Left, Right) Robert Lehman Collection, 1975, The Metropolitan Museum of Art

119   Purchased with the support of the Rijksmuseum-Stichting, Rijksmuseum

122   Rijksmuseum

124   On loan from the City of Amsterdam (A. van der Hoop Bequest), Rijksmuseum

125   Robert Lehman Collection, 1975, The Metropolitan Museum of Art

129   Photographed by author in National Gallery, London

130   H. O. Havemeyer Collection, Bequest of Mrs. H. O. Havemeyer, 1929, The Metropolitan Museum of Art

132   Diego Delso, delso.photo, License CC-BY-SA

134   Pieter de Hooch: Woman weighing Gold, around 1664; Photo credits: Staatliche Museen zu Berlin, Gemäldegalerie / Property of Kaiser Friedrich Museumsverein / Jörg P. Anders; Public Domain Mark 1.0

144   Courtesy of The Leiden Collection

145   © Gemäldegalerie Alte Meister, Staatliche Kunstsammlungen Dresden. Photo: Hans-Peter Klut

148   Image, National Gallery of Ireland

149   Image, National Gallery of Ireland

152   Gabriel Metsu: The Sick Woman, 1657–1659; Photo credits: Staatliche Museen zu Berlin, Gemäldegalerie / Jörg P. Anders; Public Domain Mark 1.0

154   Yogi Black / Alamy Stock Photo

158   Rijksmuseum

160   Rijksmuseum

164   Mauritshuis, The Hague

167   classicpaintings / Alamy Stock Photo

170   The Henry Barber Trust, The Barber Institute of Fine Arts, University of Birmingham

172   Mauritshuis, The Hague